MODERN BRITISH POTTERS AND THEIR STUDIOS

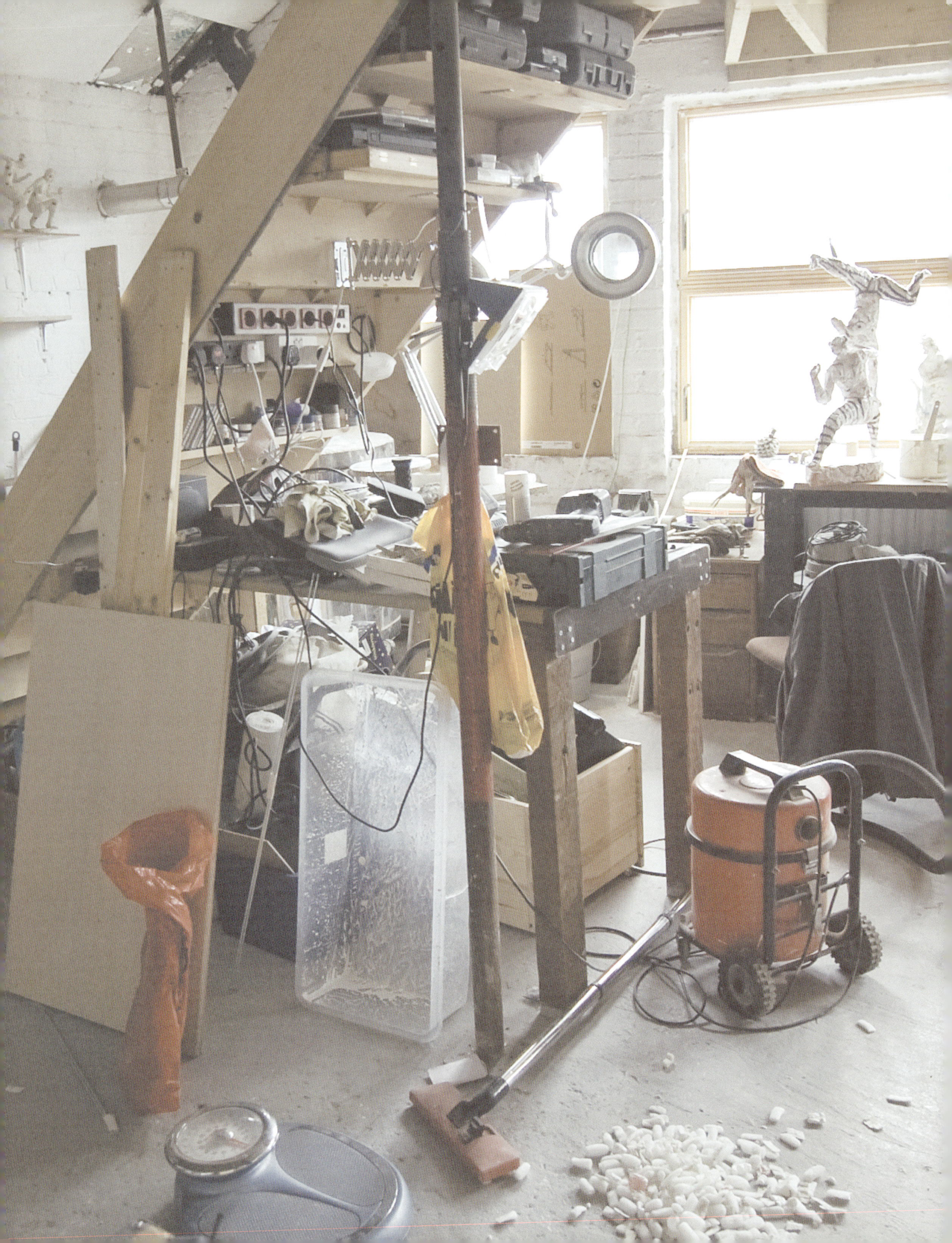

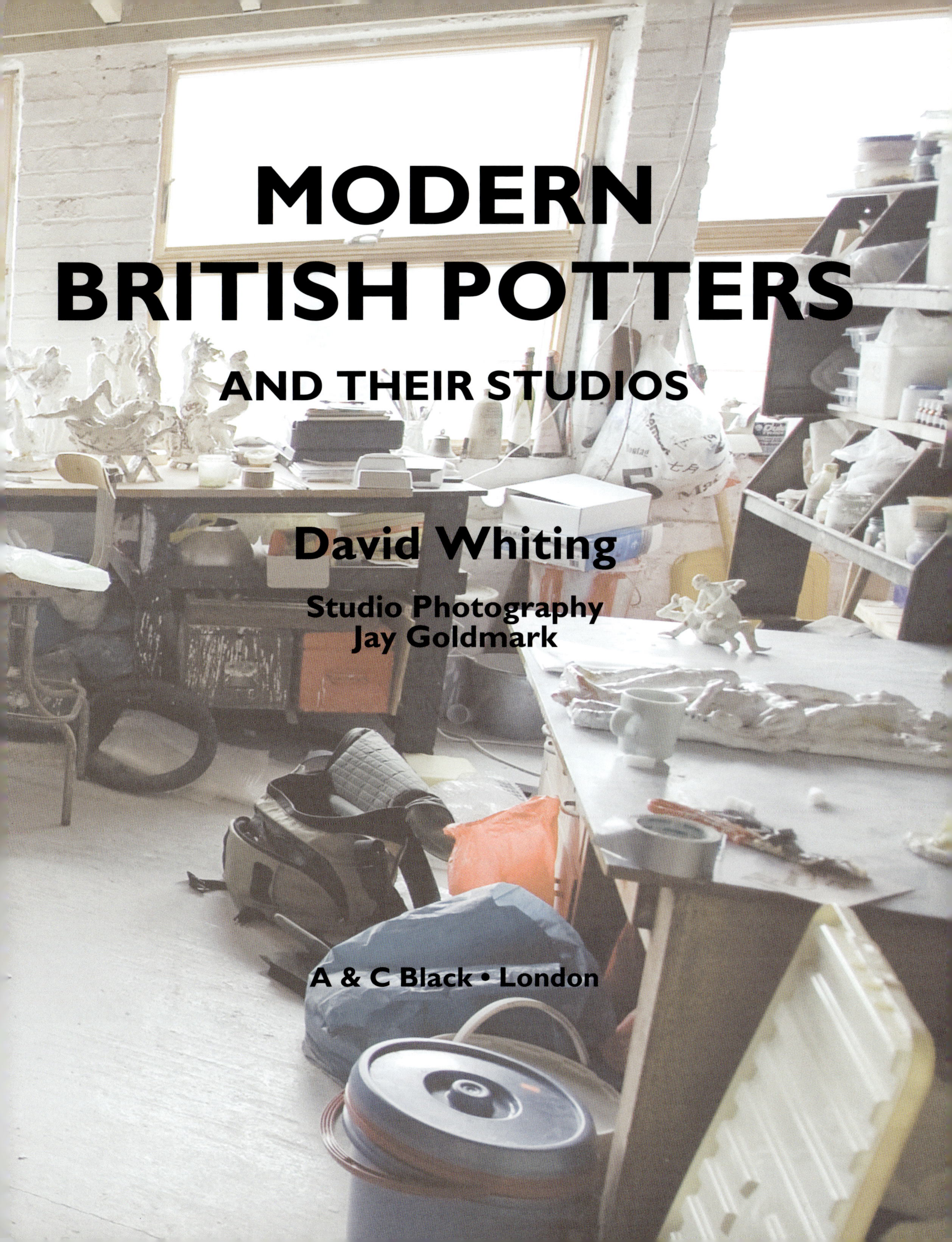

MODERN BRITISH POTTERS

AND THEIR STUDIOS

David Whiting

Studio Photography
Jay Goldmark

A & C Black • London

First published in Great Britain in 2009
A & C Black Publishers Limited
38 Soho Square
London W1D 3HB
www.acblack.com

ISBN 13: 978-0-7136-8732-3

CIP Catalogue records for this book are available from the British Library.

Book design by Penny & Tony Mills
Cover design by Sutchinda Rangsi Thompson

Cover photo (front): Detail of Jennifer Lee's studio.
Cover photo (back): (Left), Detail of Geoffrey Fuller's studio. (Right, top to bottom), Emma Rodgers, Jim Malone, Carina Ciscato, Geoffrey Fuller, Sara Radstone.
Title page photo: Part of Michael Flynn's studio in Cardiff.
Dedication and contents page photo: Walter Keeler throwing in his studio.
Photos by Jay Goldmark, courtesy of Goldmark Gallery.

Printed and bound in Singapore.

This book is produced using paper that is made from wood grown in managed, sustainable forests. It is natural, renewable and recyclable. The logging and manufacturing processes conform to the environmental regulations of the country of origin.

Acknowledgements

I PARTICULARLY WISH TO THANK Jay Goldmark, Alison Stace, Linda Lambert and Diana Phillips. I feel so fortunate to have collaborated with Jay, whose beautiful and sensitive studio photographs make this publication what it is. His intuition and perception gave me just the images I wanted. Without his energy and passion this book could never have happened. Alison Stace at A&C Black has been enthusiastic about this project from the outset and offered much valuable advice and guidance along the way. I am especially grateful to Alison for her patience, and that of her colleague Linda Lambert, who has been trying to get a book out of me for longer than I care to recall. Diana Phillips has steadfastly helped put my manuscript into a more presentable and coherent form, and always with understanding and good humour.

Anita Besson of Galerie Besson, Ken Stradling and the late Jill Day-Lewis have all been particularly generous with support for my research. My deep gratitude goes to all three. I am also most grateful to Mike Goldmark and the staff of Goldmark Gallery, to Juliana Barrett and Tatjana Marsden at Barrett Marsden Gallery, and Louisa Anderson and Matthew Hall at Galerie Besson. Initial help was given by Carol McNicoll, Phil Rogers, Anthony Shaw, Mike Abrahams and Tina Vlassopulos. I also received assistance from Philip Eglin, Amanda Fielding and Jack Doherty, and special thanks are due to Matthew Greenhalf for his constant encouragement. Three of the essays here – those on Annie Turner, Neil Brownsword and Jane Hamlyn – are revised and reworked versions of articles I originally wrote for, respectively, the RBSA Gallery in Birmingham, *Kunsthandverk* magazine in Norway and *Ceramics – Art & Perception* in Australia, all of whom I warmly acknowledge. My gratitude also goes to Penny Mills, for her hard work on the imaginative design, and the copy editor Julian Beecroft.

Last but not least, I offer my thanks to all the artists featured here. Their cooperation and enthusiasm has been invaluable, and helped to make the work on this book such a pleasure for Jay and myself.

David Whiting, December 2008

For three friends and teachers:

Geoffrey Whiting 1919–88
Joanna Constantinidis 1927–2000
Ewen Henderson 1934–2000

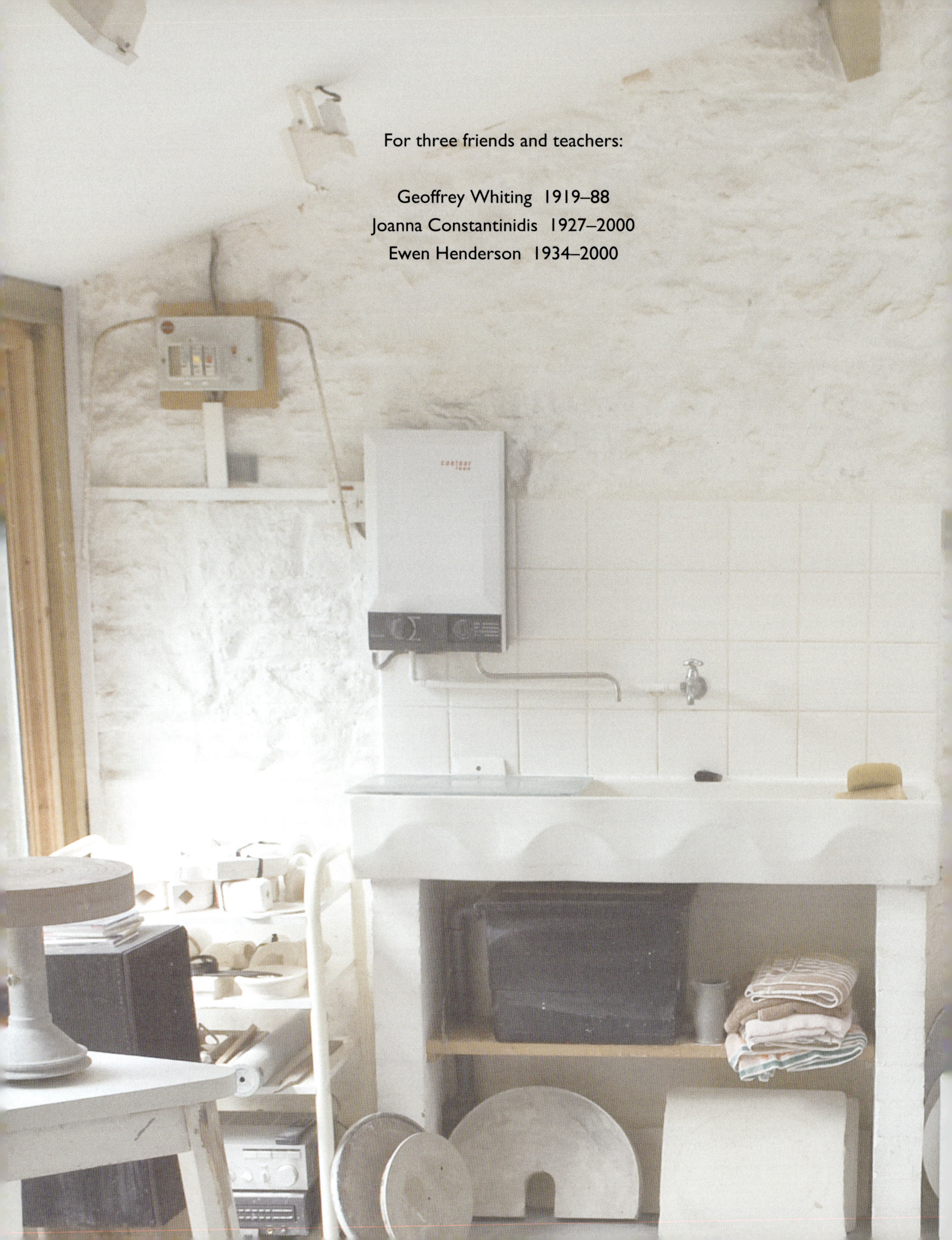

Contents

Acknowledgements 5
Dedication 6
Preface 8
Introduction 11

Part One:
The Art of Function 16
Clive Bowen 18
Carol McNicoll 24
Daniel Smith 30
Jim Malone 34
Sandy Brown 40
Jane Hamlyn 46
Phil Rogers 52
Walter Keeler 56

Part Two:
The Sculptural Vessel 62
Gordon Baldwin 64
James Robson 70
Carina Ciscato 74
Jennifer Lee 78
Dan Kelly 84
Daniel Fisher 90
Tina Vlassopulos 96
Ken Eastman 102

Part Three:
The Figure and the Object 108
Michael Flynn 110
Annie Turner 116
Claire Curneen 122
Neil Brownsword 128
Emma Rodgers 134
Philip Eglin 140
Sara Radstone 146
Geoffrey Fuller 152

Select Bibliography 158

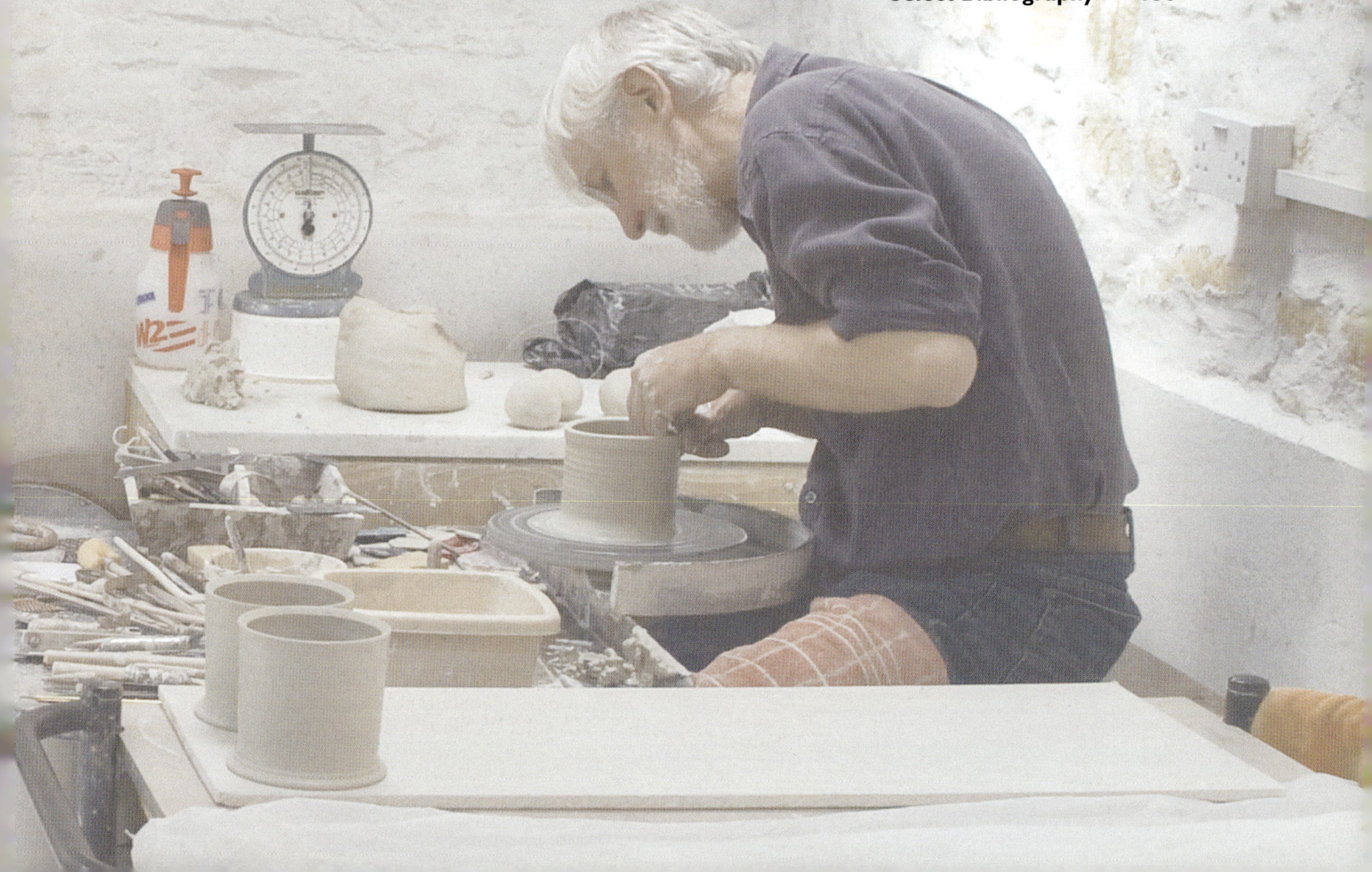

Preface

THIS IS A BOOK ABOUT British artists who work in clay. It is also about where they make – the spaces these people occupy, whether that be a studio in central London or a workshop in deepest Devon. The intention is to introduce a personal selection of 24 potters and ceramists whose work shows the exceptional stylistic, philosophical and technical range of British ceramic art in the first decade of the 21st century – from pots made for everyday use in the house to more sculptural expressions in clay.

The book is essentially a series of photographic essays. The text provides an overview of each artist's activity, accompanied by Jay Goldmark's photographs of them at home and in the studio, along with images of their ceramics. I wanted to give a strong sense of visual context – the *genius loci* – of these places, their character and texture. It is, if you like, a voyeur's handbook – one that also gives, I hope, some insights into the creative imagination. What it is *not* is a book about method and process – the photographs often show potters deeply involved in making, but the approach is impressionistic, not technical.

The book is divided into three sections: The Art of Function; The Sculptural Vessel; The Figure and the Object. Like most divisions, these are of a somewhat arbitrary nature, designed for convenience and structure but not always wholly accurate. Not all the ceramists here fit so easily into these categories, such is their ability to move freely from one area to another, making work that embraces several aesthetic and philosophical outlooks. For example, Philip Eglin and Geoffrey Fuller are primarily known for their figures, but they also make pots. More recently, Sandy Brown has begun to make large-scale sculptures alongside the pots discussed here, and Jane Hamlyn, famous for her tableware, is now producing one-off vessel forms with her domestic pieces. Sara Radstone, considered here as an artist of sculptural 'objects', has an aesthetic rooted in the vessels she began to make in the early 1980s. For several potters there is a fine line to be drawn between one field of enquiry and another – for example, explorations of function that can develop into more consciously 'sculptural' pieces. The ceramics of Jane Hamlyn, Carina Ciscato and Carol McNicoll inhabit this realm. All of this notwithstanding, I hope that on balance my simplistic classification best reflects the work as a whole of all the artists featured.

If there is an occasional imbalance of choice – for example, more makers of 'figures' than 'objects' in the third section – then this is more to do with my well-weathered opinion of the current strengths and weaknesses of the ceramics scene than simple miscalculation. Nor do I pretend, despite the variety, to cover every aspect of current practice. Conceptual, installation and architectural projects are excluded, not only for reasons of space, but because I wanted to focus on work that makes its impact in the form of individual pieces, first and foremost. Nevertheless, I am acutely aware of many important ceramists who I am unable – again for reasons of space – to include. They could fill another volume. It is a matter of particular regret that I could not feature the work of the late Ewen Henderson, or the late Joanna Constantinidis, with both of whom, many years ago, I discussed the idea of this book. Moreover, Gillian Lowndes, another obvious choice and as pure a sculptor in clay as you will find, had sadly stopped working, due to ill health, when this was being written. Nevertheless their presence, as important artists and teachers, is certainly felt in much of the work that follows.

right: Part of Walter Keeler's studio at Penallt.

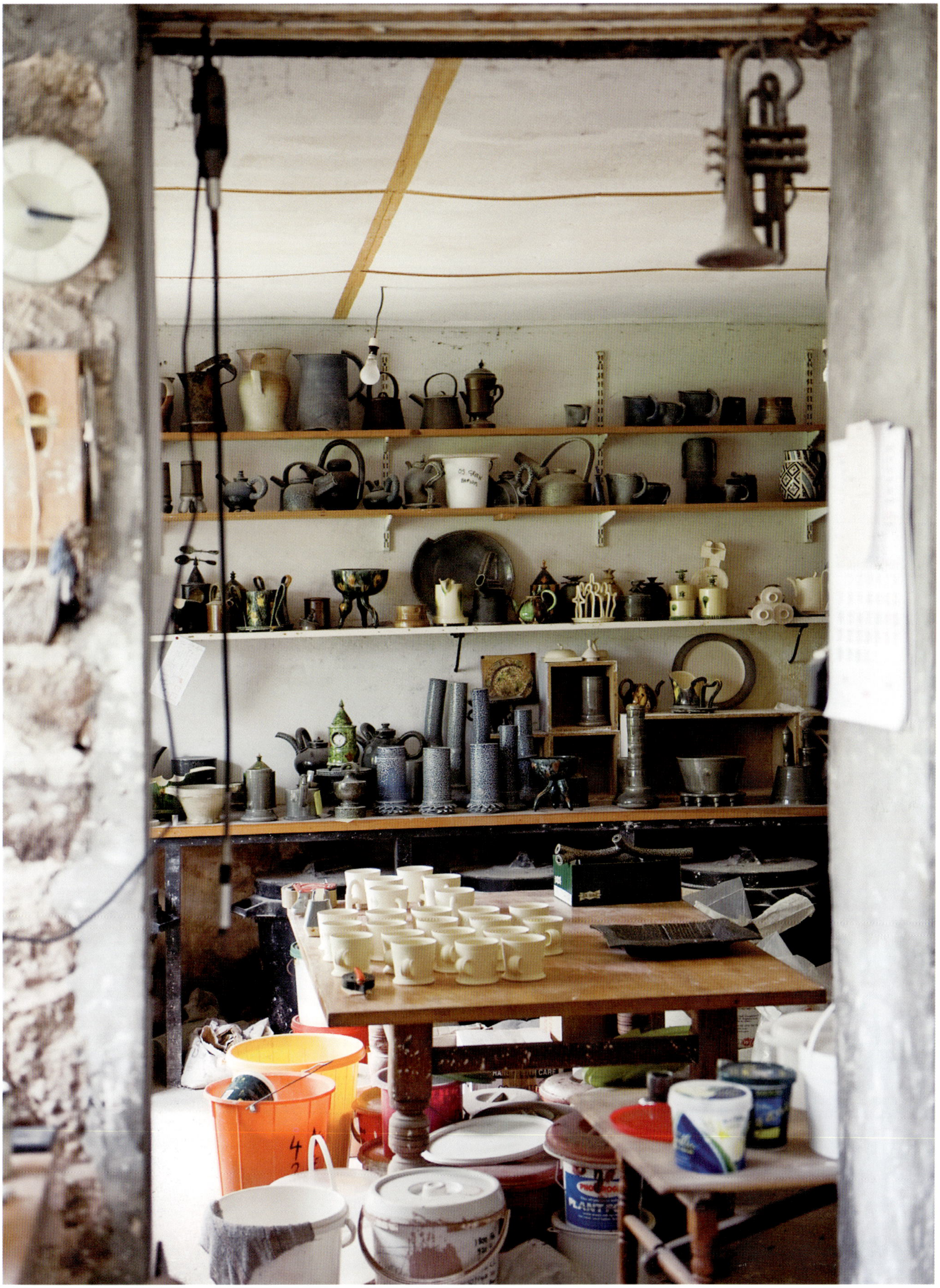

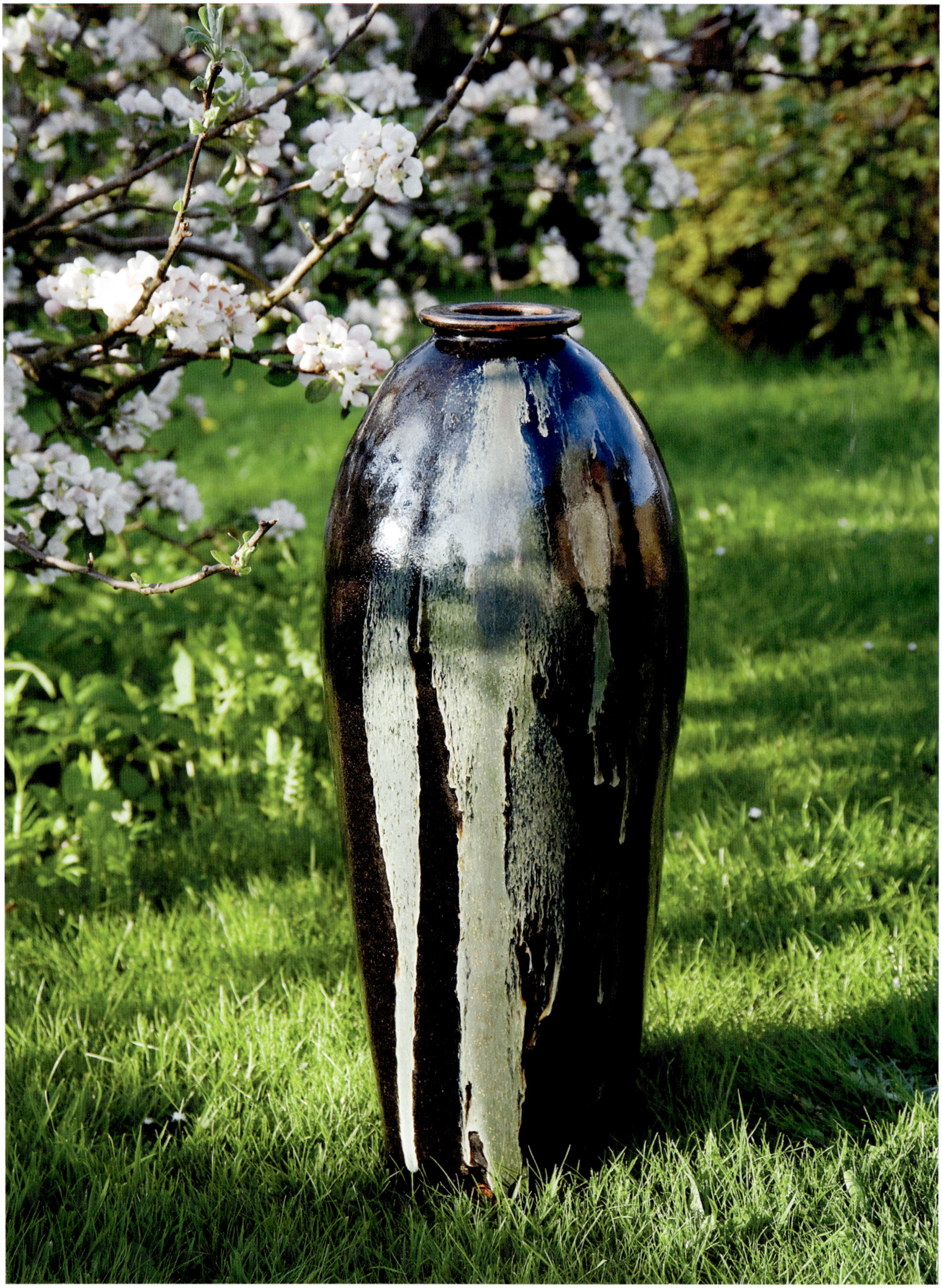

Introduction

WHILE THIS BOOK ATTEMPTS to show some of the range of current British studio practice, much of course is excluded. It is such a diverse and complex field. From the wheel-thrown to the handbuilt, from the conceptual to the figurative, from large-scale installation work to more intimate decorative pieces, it is impossible, more than ever, to generalise about clay – a far cry from the traditional notion of 'pottery', pure and simple. Familiar as a craft medium, in the last 50 years clay has been very much reclaimed as an art medium too (a role it has had in fact for thousands of years), a vehicle as much for personal credo and expression as for the functional values with which it has long been associated.

After the Second World War only a comparative handful of studio potters were established, and Bernard Leach remained the most influential, both in terms of style and ethos. The infrastructure was pretty basic: there were only a few shops and galleries specialising in this work, and supportive institutions were few and far between. Exceptions included the Crafts Centre of Great Britain, established in 1948, and promotional organisations such as the Red Rose Guild in Manchester and the Rural Industries Bureau, both founded in 1921. There was no Craftsman Potters Association until 1958 and no Crafts Council until 1972.

Art colleges, on the other hand, were beginning to establish ceramics courses, following the lead of fledgling pre-war departments at the Royal College of Art and the Central School, pioneered respectively by potters William Staite Murray and Dora Billington. A burgeoning apprenticeship system at potteries like St Ives and Winchcombe was also beginning to produce potters. Many among this new generation became influential teachers in their turn, setting up their own potteries or new college departments. In their workshop in London's West End émigrés Hans Coper and Lucie Rie were producing consciously European and modernist work, in contrast with the orientally influenced pots of Leach and Murray and the indigenous slipware revival of Michael Cardew. Important progressive centres for teaching were to be found at the Institute of Education and a reinvigorated Central School. These and other London art colleges fostered more personal experimentation, both technical and aesthetic. International influences, from the Continent to the USA, as well as Japan, were also being felt. The literature began to grow, magazines were now being published and ceramics looked increasingly beyond clay – to painting, sculpture and other influences – for ideas and inspiration.

Though functional ware remained an important mainstay of studio work through the 1950s and 60s, bolstered by throwing courses such as that devised at Harrow School of Art in 1963, there was an emerging body of sculptural work, both thrown and handbuilt. Some of it had figurative connotations, though the ideas were often organic and abstracted in form (it was not until the 1980s that a more direct figuration emerged as an important subject in its own right). Some artists who had experimented with more expressive vessel work in the 1960s had moved away entirely from recognisable 'pots' by the beginning of the next decade, laying the ground for ceramists concerned with various forms of abstraction.

The sculptural vessel became an even more important

opposite: Tall Bottle, *Jim Malone, 2008, stoneware. Height: 59cm (23 in). Photo: Jay Goldmark, courtesy of Goldmark Gallery*

aspect of studio practice, reinforced by a new generation of potters emerging from art schools such as the Royal College of Art and Camberwell School of Art in the 1970s and 80s. Throwing was still undergoing changes. Alongside the survival of more traditional work, there were potters who sought to reinterpret familiar table shapes through technical and structural innovation. For many, greater freedom of form and decoration was the principal aim. Far from being prescriptive and tyrannous, the functional aspects of ceramics could be a springboard for personal experiment and reinvention.

Today, some artists have moved away from purist notions about clay. It is often just one in a string of materials they employ in addressing wider sculptural concerns. By the 1990s there was a growing interest in conceptual installation work. This has broadened the environment for ceramics, requiring us to think beyond more conventional contexts and presentation. British studio work, along with the rest of the clay world, has grown into an intricate web of values and value systems, reflecting not only wider artistic aspirations, but also the cultural flux and change we now take for granted. Yet it is clay's domestic intimacy, as well as its larger-scale expressive power, that makes it a continually effective tool for all kinds of narrative and expression. Tactile and sensual, it is often brought into our homes in a way other art forms are not. It can sit confidently in our museums but still has a special place in the everyday consciousness of the spaces where we live.

Boundaries, for better or worse, have become increasingly blurred. Yet, despite the philosophical and stylistic proliferation in ceramics, despite the strength and variety of work in these pages, there is much cause for concern. Few of those excellent ceramics courses have survived intact. Over the past 15 years there have been many closures. Most of those lucky enough to survive at all have been absorbed into broader 3D art and design degrees, a process of dilution accompanied by a significant fall in student numbers – the result, in part, of a worrying evaporation of ceramics teaching at school and foundation level. Despite the sterling efforts of certain individuals, there are few workshop apprenticeship schemes available to more functional makers. With less and less interest and support from the state in visual arts education, organisations like the Crafts Council, now a client of the Arts Council, have shed many of their responsibilities in subsidy and education in favour of institutionalised marketing. A faltering and shrinking infrastructure is now largely dictated to by myopic management-speak.

On the other hand, there is enough evidence in these pages and elsewhere of a basis for future growth. Strength of individual vision remains, with every area of ceramics full of invention and possibility. Some aspects of the ceramics world are still thriving: we continue to see a good range of individual and group exhibitions, for instance, as well as regular ceramics fairs and potters' festivals, and a healthy round of conferences and seminars. Annual surveys of graduate talent like *New Designers*, at the Business Design Centre in London, give evidence of ceramics of continuing strength, from thrown and cast pieces for the table to pieces of sculpture, mirroring our cultural and stylistic pluralism. It is clear that clay remains a great technical and imaginative challenge, the most extraordinarily versatile material we have.

Imagination's chamber

As Alice Bellony-Rewald and Michael Peppiatt wrote in their book *Imagination's Chamber: Artists and their Studios*, '… art history can be told through the studio. The shape, the light, the location, the look and the "feel" of a studio constantly shape the images conceived and produced there. What the space contains may exert an even greater influence. The works on the wall (whether the artist's own or by others whom he admires), the engravings or photographs he refers to, the books read and the objects collected ... form the constant background to the artist's activity and frequently plays a specific role in what he creates.'

This is as true, of course, of those who work in clay, but the terminology used to describe their place of work is rather more complex, reflecting a discipline that draws its roots not only from craft and applied art, but from fine art as well. Whether those who make ceramics talk of their 'studio', their 'workshop' or simply their 'pottery' can be as revealing of their intentions as the name they give themselves, be that 'potter', 'ceramist', 'artist in clay' and so on. These descriptions of activity, these statements of belief, have become something of a linguistic minefield. For example, those who make wheel-thrown functional work can be distinctly proprietorial about the word 'potter' when they hear it used by those in other areas of ceramics activity. Yet 'potter' and 'pottery' have for centuries been generic terms for those involved in a wide variety of clay work – not just the makers of everyday pots and vessels.

Terms like 'studio' and 'workshop' are just as loaded, suggestive not only of location but of the kind of work created. Such vocabulary mirrors the changing status of handmade ceramics in the 20th century, from the 'craft' object conceived in the communal workshop to the 'art' object made in the more private and personal studio – the transition from the vernacular, artisanal pottery of local town and country workshops to that of artist-potters making consciously, intellectually willed individual ceramics. The definition of craft has changed with it, the lines of demarcation now more difficult to discern. While we may often read too much into the preferred terminology, it still traces, to a considerable extent, the social and cultural changes in what, it is worth noting, we now call 'studio' ceramics. These transitions loosely echo those that happened, over a far longer period, in the world of painting and sculpture, from the communal artists' workshops of the Middle Ages and the Renaissance to the ivory towers of the 20th century.

Despite the egalitarian aims of potters like Bernard Leach, certain subtle distinctions have to be made. It was Leach, after all, who differentiated between his workshop standard ware, introduced at the end of the 1930s, and the more individual work he and others produced at St Ives. The Leach Pottery was essentially a place of small-scale craft production, involving assistants and apprentices, but Leach's personal space, where he produced his own pots, has often been referred to as his 'studio', a term that confers a particular status. Production potteries that followed the St Ives model through the 1930s, 40s and early 50s, such as Winchcombe, Crowan, Shinners Bridge and Avoncroft, also put primary emphasis on their everyday tableware, continuing the tradition of the old, more anonymous country workshops.

Leach's background – the Slade School and the London School of Art – was that of a fine artist, but the St Ives enterprise followed the kind of Arts and Crafts ethic espoused by William Morris and C.R. Ashbee, which in turn was inspired by the workshop collectives of the Middle Ages. Leach's standard ware, attempting to make good handmade pottery widely accessible (and a necessary means by which Leach could stabilise his business) was really a formalised modern version of those town and country wares long produced to meet local needs. However, two of Leach's pioneering contemporaries, William Staite Murray and Charles Vyse, were more conscious of their artist and 'studio' status, producing expensive work almost exclusively for leading London galleries.

As the art colleges began to include ceramics in their visual arts syllabuses, particularly in the 1950s and 60s, and the discipline increasingly embraced more individual and sculptural work – reflecting the concerns of fine art – so the studio became philosophically as well as physically central to ceramic endeavour. But it is easy to oversimplify matters. The word 'studio' carries connotations of silence and separation, but such qualities are as true of functional makers like Phil Rogers or Clive Bowen, whose workplaces may match our visual notions of the country pottery, but are also strikingly remote. These potters in their own way feed off a kind of creative isolation. For makers of this kind, people who derive much from their locality in terms of locally sourced materials, the creative place takes on other important implications. The landscape is sublimated, directly and metaphorically, into their work. Meanwhile, the sculptural potter Gordon Baldwin's favourite locations – the sites that sustain much of his art – are some distance from his studio in Shropshire. He cannot see them through his subterranean window, but they are there nonetheless, both in his mind's eye and in the photographs and drawings pinned to the walls.

Other potters can seem almost oblivious to their surroundings. Devon-based David Leach, for example, was able to operate in a decidedly basic corrugated tin shed, much to the amazement of his son John, who, by contrast, needs the thick stone walls of his Somerset pottery for creative empathy. Some makers have been very dissatisfied with the available lexicon if it has fed preconceptions about their role. Joanna Constantinidis called the studio in her Essex home her 'workroom' and, at the end of her life, decided upon the term 'clay worker' to describe her activity. But even this phraseology might sound too loaded, with its distinctly utilitarian overtones. Given Constantinidis's ascetic work and lifestyle, her choice of words was more telling than she might have realised. Many other ceramists are far more relaxed about the names employed, not attaching much importance to their usage.

Why the fascination with these rooms and spaces? Several potters have considered this question in terms of their own particular visitors and what they derive from the experience. Modern studio craft has long been perceived as a more open and public activity, its makers generally accessible in a way that most painters and sculptors are not. This is particularly true of functional potters, who often sell their ceramics directly from the premises. What is the attraction? Perhaps that, when you buy a pot, you also buy vicariously into a way of life. You can get a rare insight into a particular set of values and mode of living. Of course, you may also pick up some of the thought processes of the creative mind. You find not just the work, not just the potter, but a wealth of other information, part of a very particular world.

We might expect those functional workshops to be more matter-of-fact, less revealing, but they too betray a great deal – not just the obvious aspects (the size and type of kiln, the buckets of glaze and slip, the kind of wheel used) but the images on the wall, the sketchbook drawings, the exemplar pots on a high shelf. Some workspaces are Aladdin's caves of information; others are more Spartan, even clinical, but no less indicative of artistic character and intention. Most potters find their creative den a room of refuge, even if, as many do in urban centres, they share it with others. In London and other cities, a combined studio is a practical and economic necessity, but it can also be a matter of psychological importance for many artists. Such shared spaces are another continuation of those workshops inhabited by artists and artisans for hundreds of years, only now the creativity is of a more diverse and individual nature.

Part of the allure is that, shared or not, publicly accessible or not, these places remain essentially mysterious, often hidden by an anonymous façade, be it in a London backstreet, a country barn or a suburban home. Lucie Rie's pottery (she generally called it that), which she used from 1939 until shortly before her death in 1995, was lofty and quite dark. It occupied the ground floor of her modestly sized mews house in west London, just a short distance from Marble Arch. It was a world of silence, *rus in urbe*, paradoxically within yards of the busy Bayswater and Edgware Roads. The atmosphere, despite the train of visitors she tolerated, was one of prolonged concentration. Here, famously, she rose early to work, day after day, for almost 50 years. The quiet order and dignity of her pottery said it all; somehow conversations about her pots (which she resisted, saying, 'I am just a potter') became superfluous. She was, in this sense, the urban equivalent of silent country craftsmen like Richard Batterham in Dorset, a distinguished functional potter who has always discouraged theory, preferring to let the work speak for itself. Examining Rie's wheel and kiln, her various glaze tests and larger pots covering shelves and benches, the imprint of her artistic mind became obvious. Albion Mews was a rare time capsule, virtually unchanged since her arrival from Vienna before the Second World War, when she had asked her friend, the architect Ernst Freud, to convert the property.

Meanwhile, the Camden Town studio of the sculptural potter Ewen Henderson (a pupil of Rie's) could not have been more different. It was approached through his garden, a winding path punctuated on each side by various ceramic forms combining with the plants and undergrowth, clay structures reverting, it seemed, to nature. The studio was just as full of Henderson's two-dimensional activity – his drawings, watercolours and collages – as his work in clay. Cluttered and a little chaotic, the space seemingly reflected the complexity and restlessness of his creative mind. It had an air of impatience which was quite distinct from Rie's organisation and calm. One sensed an artist beginning new ideas before he completed old ones, someone who really preferred questions to answers. If Rie's workshop reflected her self-containment, Henderson's studio welcomed debate and conversation from his friends and visitors. The various projects in progress gave clues about an artist who spoke publicly and vehemently about the possibilities of clay, of wanting to expand its language. These two studios told us so much about their potters' respective artistic credos, and offered real insights into what exactly made them tick. It is to be hoped that what follows will be equally illuminating.

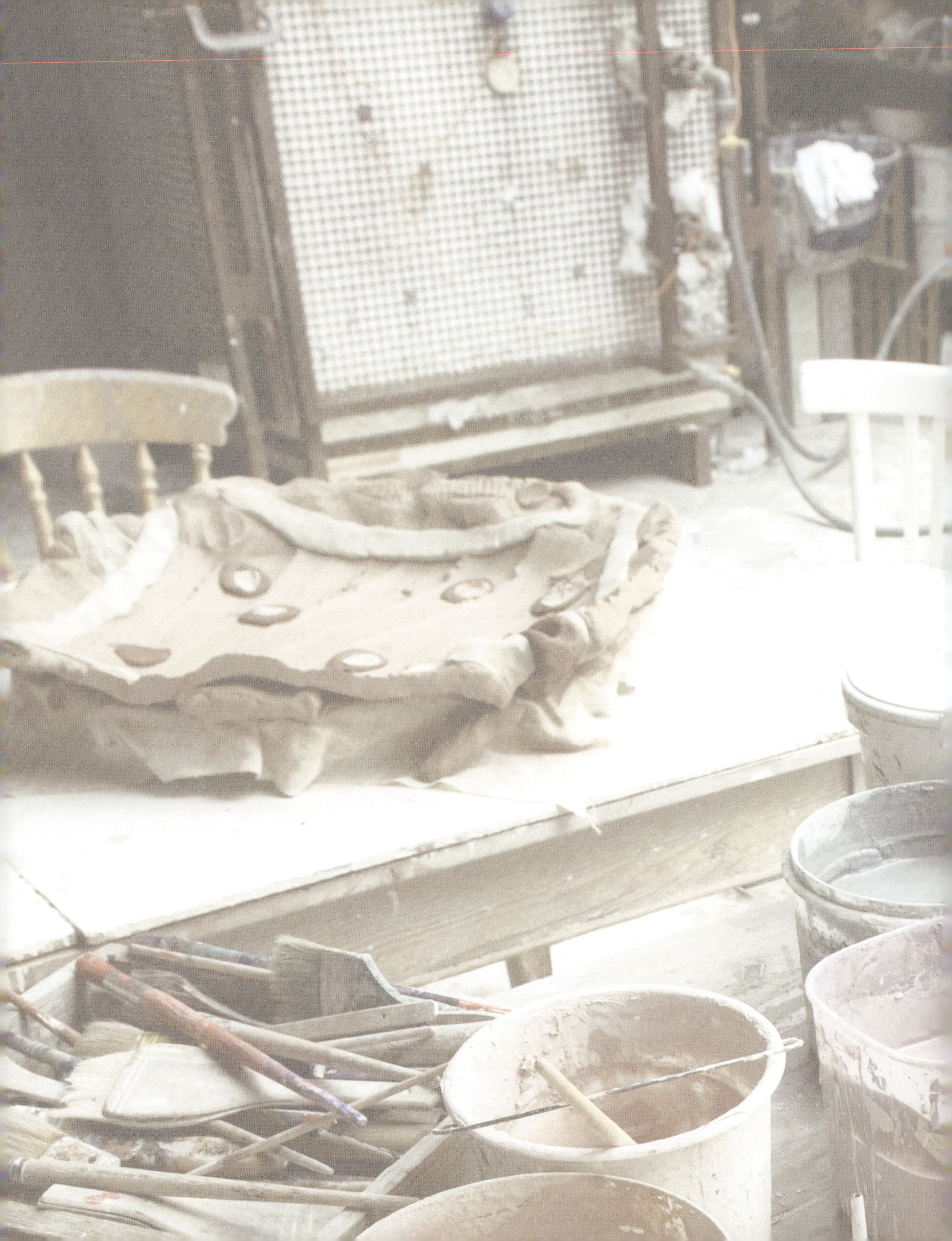

Part One: The Art of Function

POTTERS LIKE Jim Malone, Phil Rogers and Clive Bowen are often described as 'traditional', as they owe a primary debt to a range of pre-industrial ceramics, including those of medieval Britain and various oriental kilns. They have added their own individuality to the rich synthesis of these influences expressed in the work of Bernard Leach, Michael Cardew and other members of the 'Leach School'. Yet *all* the potters in this section operate within parallel traditions, in and outside ceramics, often making eclectic use of what they have found to arrive at their own variations on the functional.

Walter Keeler and Jane Hamlyn have re-evaluated the riches of European salt glaze in their commitment to tableware, virtually reinventing familiar shapes and forms to do this. Carol McNicoll draws on a variety of materials, from fabrics and wallpapers to household ornaments, her work a surreal continuation of the more bizarre ceramic conceits of the 18th and 19th century factories. If Sandy Brown's work is about a very modern liberation of throwing and colour, it also owes much to traditional Japanese making concepts. The purity of Daniel Smith's porcelain shows how the functionality of certain factory wares, from Wedgwood to the Bauhaus, can be eloquently re-expressed in studio terms. All the potters here have remained committed to the idea that a baseline of pottery remains its everyday use, its enrichment of daily tasks and rituals.

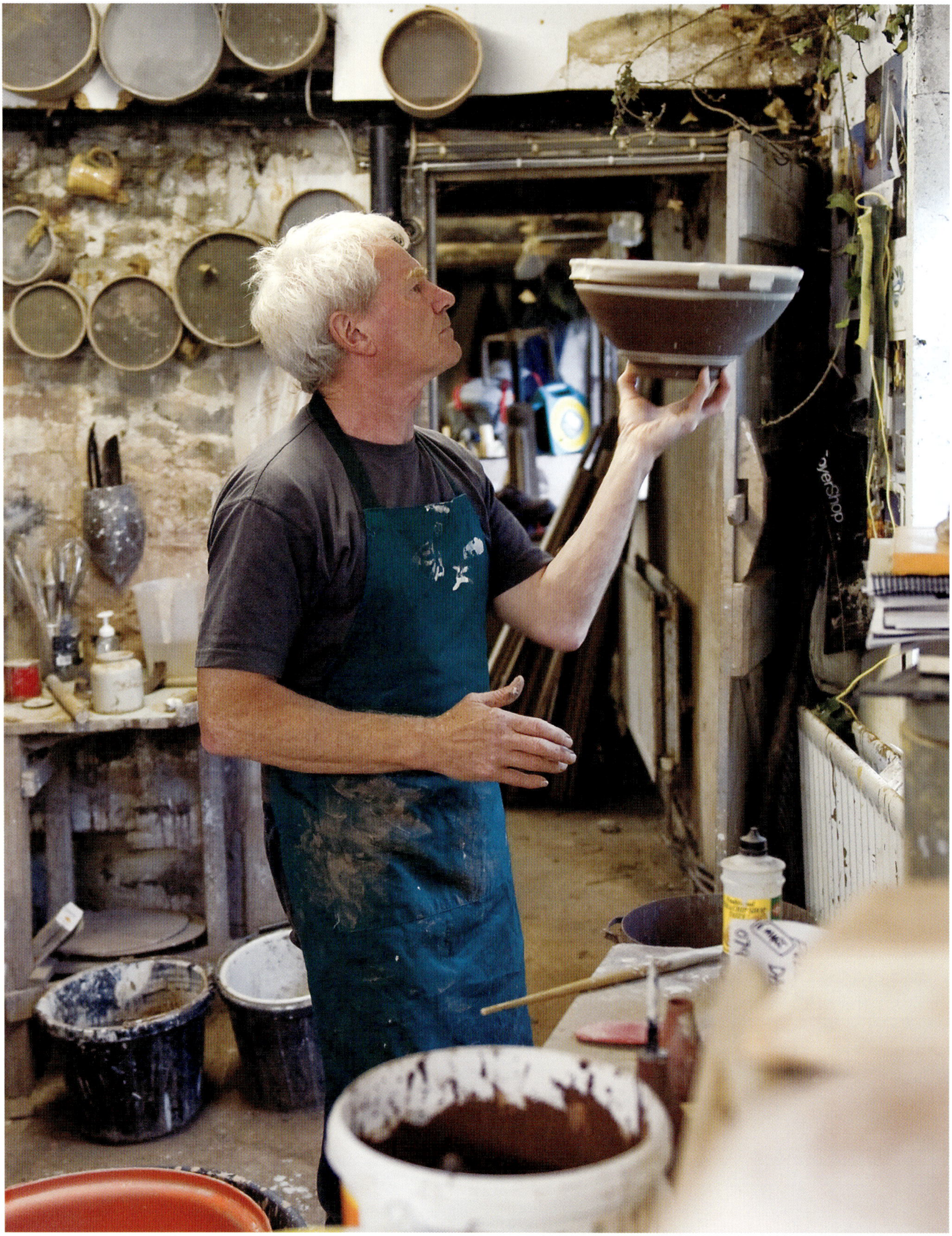

Clive Bowen

CLIVE BOWEN comes as close as anyone to our romanticised notions of the archetypal country craftsman. He is that rare species, a full-time potter, one who lives in an idyllic and secluded stretch of western England – the lush green valleys of north Devon. On the face of it, he seems a particularly English type of potter, too – a true inheritor of our rich native traditions of pre-industrial slipware. But Bowen has also, like his mentor Michael Cardew, helped to reinvent it, to transform it into a particularly robust and expressive 20th-century art form – with his bigger pieces often very sculptural in presence. While Bowen, a shy man, is not a great talker – he doesn't theorise or provide long explanations – he can speak with youthful enthusiasm about the challenge of what he does, perhaps of a new artistic discovery in Japan or a particular piece of music recently heard. Crucially, he still has that ability to be surprised, a strong sense of revelation that he brings out in the vigour of the work. His pots have a perennial strength and energy – treated with an abstract opulence of surface and colour that is quite new to slip.

Within a limited but evolving repertoire of forms – big-bellied jugs and dishes, tall bottles, lidded jars, bowls and platters of various sizes – there are always new variations of marking, surface and texture. Moreover, as Bowen gets older this relaxed and fluid integration becomes more complete, a rich synthesis that springs not only from his knowledge of good medieval and vernacular English and European pots, but a passion for Japanese ceramics and the best 20th-century abstraction. Catholic in his tastes, Bowen may live and work in the country, but his aesthetic also draws from a broader 20th-century culture. In fact born in a city (Cardiff in 1943), he began as a painter, studying at the local art college before moving to London in the early 60s. Finding the capital's art scene difficult to penetrate, he still had the good fortune to meet there his future wife, Alison Leach, daughter of Michael Leach and granddaughter of Bernard. It was at Michael's pottery at Yelland, in north Devon, that Clive rediscovered a facility for clay first experienced on his intermediate course at Cardiff. Taken on as an apprentice by his father-in-law, Bowen acquired useful experience not only at the wheel, but in all aspects of workshop activity, very much in the Leachian mould.

However, Bowen was also drawn to a wider visual world. As a painter he was very attracted to the vibrant in-vogue abstraction of the 1960s; he was keen to transfer these ideas to pottery, but at the same time he was soon being motivated by the idea of functionality – of making pots that people could eat from and use. Going on to C.H. Brannam in Barnstaple – a traditional earthenware pottery – as a production thrower not only gave him vital technical experience on much bigger pots, but instilled in Bowen a deep respect for traditional, largely anonymous, craft skill, for pure manual power in 'everyday' pottery. It related to the vitality of oriental artisan craft, eulogised in a text that was one of Bowen's key early sources of inspiration, Sōetsu Yanagi's *The Unknown Craftsman*, adapted by Bernard Leach for English publication in 1972.

Soon Bowen was working with an artistically very conscious reviver of English slipware, Michael Cardew (1901–83), helping him with the epic weekend firings at his Wenford Bridge Pottery. It led him to an appreciation not only of Cardew's pre-war Winchcombe slipware in particular, but of the north Devon tradition in general. The strength of the local earthenware – direct and individual – using the indigenous Fremington clay, provided a material and philosophical basis

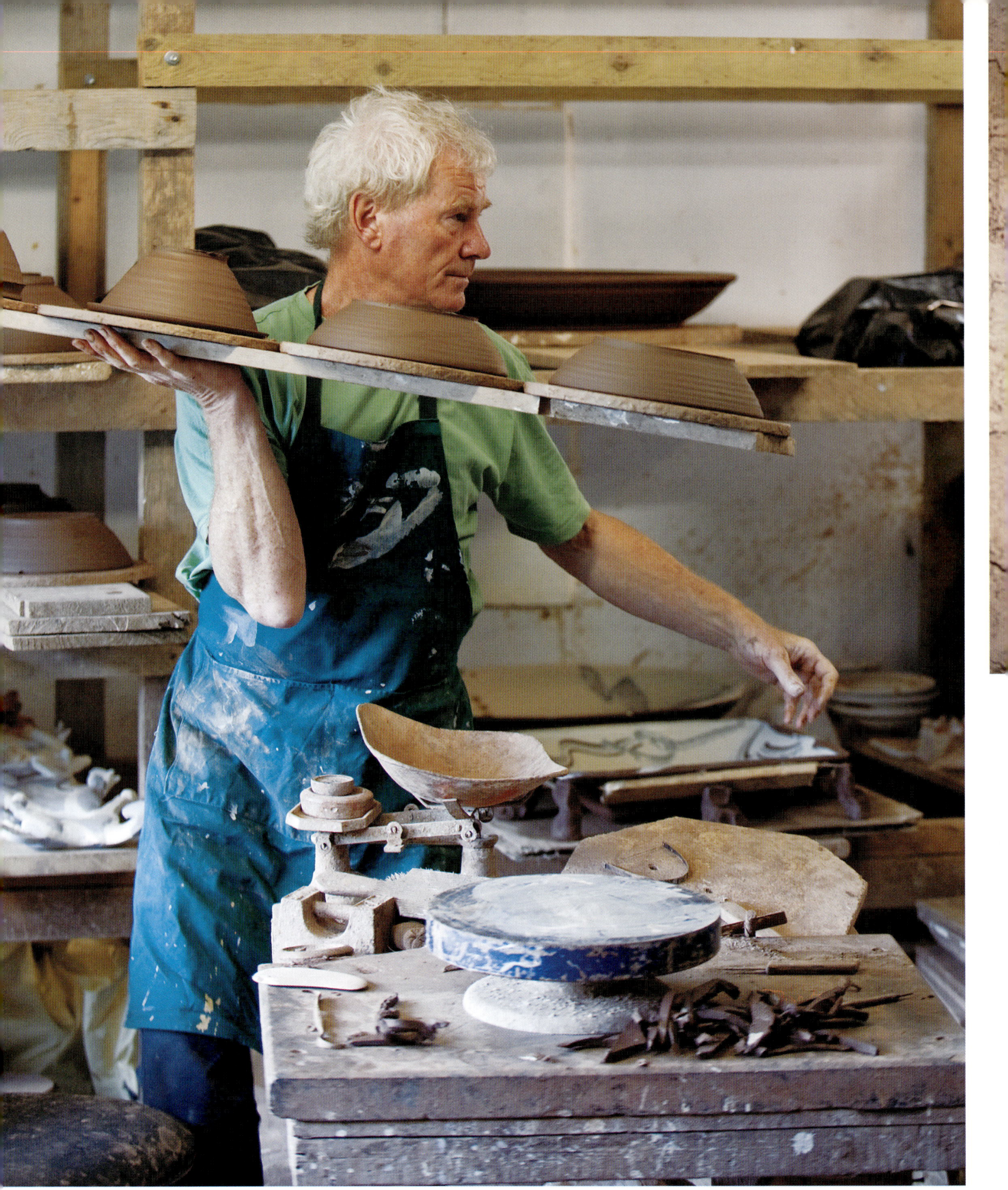

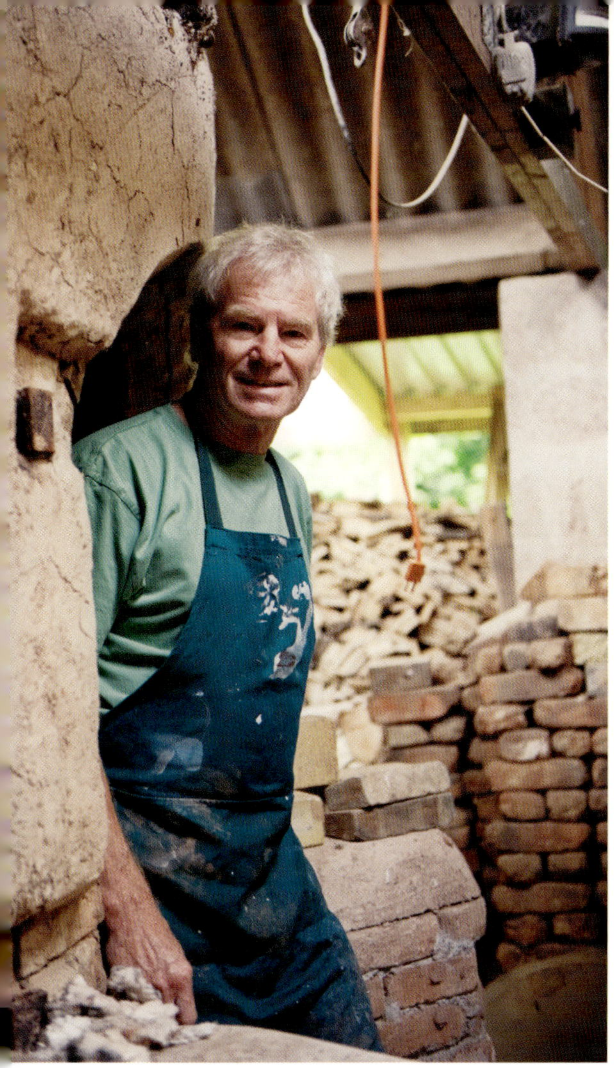

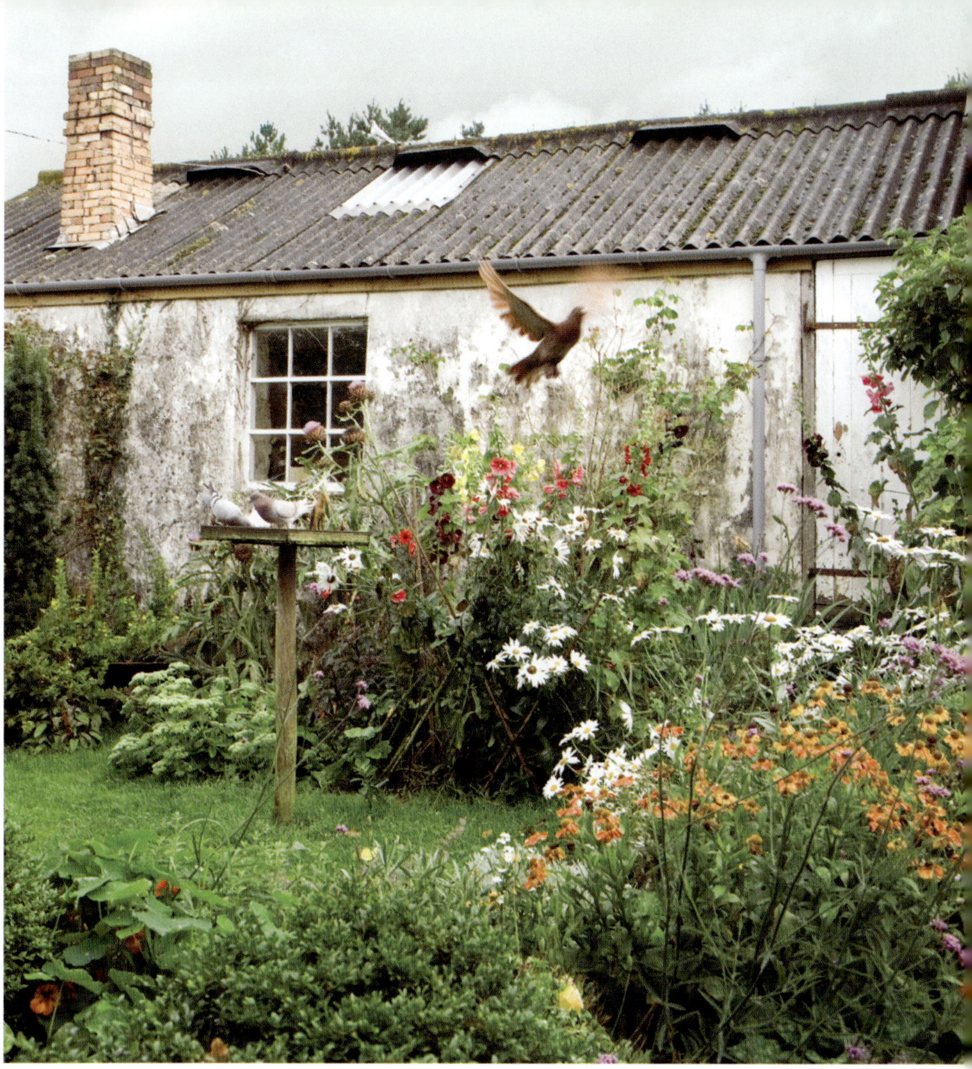

for his own work, excited as he was by the painterly aspects of slipware and the pyromania of large-scale wood-firing. Clive Bowen's purposeful life as a potter had begun.

In 1971 he found an isolated property at nearby Shebbear in beautiful hilly dairy country, where he still lives with his second wife Rosie. He converted the ample outbuildings into a spacious pottery and constructed a sizeable kiln. By the middle of that decade Bowen had got into the full swing of making, producing with the help of assistants a full range of domestic ware and big garden pots. Soon a much larger double-chambered structure was needed, the firing of which helped to establish a cyclical and seasonal pattern of making. Holding up to 1,000 pots, it is fired two or three times a year, a Herculean task that requires about 24 hours of constant watching and stoking. Doing it the hard way shows Bowen's genuine love of the whole lengthy process. Though he occasionally says, rather unconvincingly, that he dreams of being a city potter with a push-button kiln and not an animal in sight, deep down I think he knows he would hate it.

For many years now Bowen has mostly potted alone, with occasional help called upon when required. There is considerable demand for Bowen's exhibition pieces – large jugs, bottles, ceremonial dishes and ambitious storage jars – objects which make forceful statements about the continuing power of the functional. They have all the generosity of past exemplars – for example, the big expressive platters of Thomas Toft and the celebratory harvest jugs made at nearby Fremington – but are ultimately Bowen's own, very modern response. As he says, it is about 'being in a tradition without being traditional', an important distinction. It

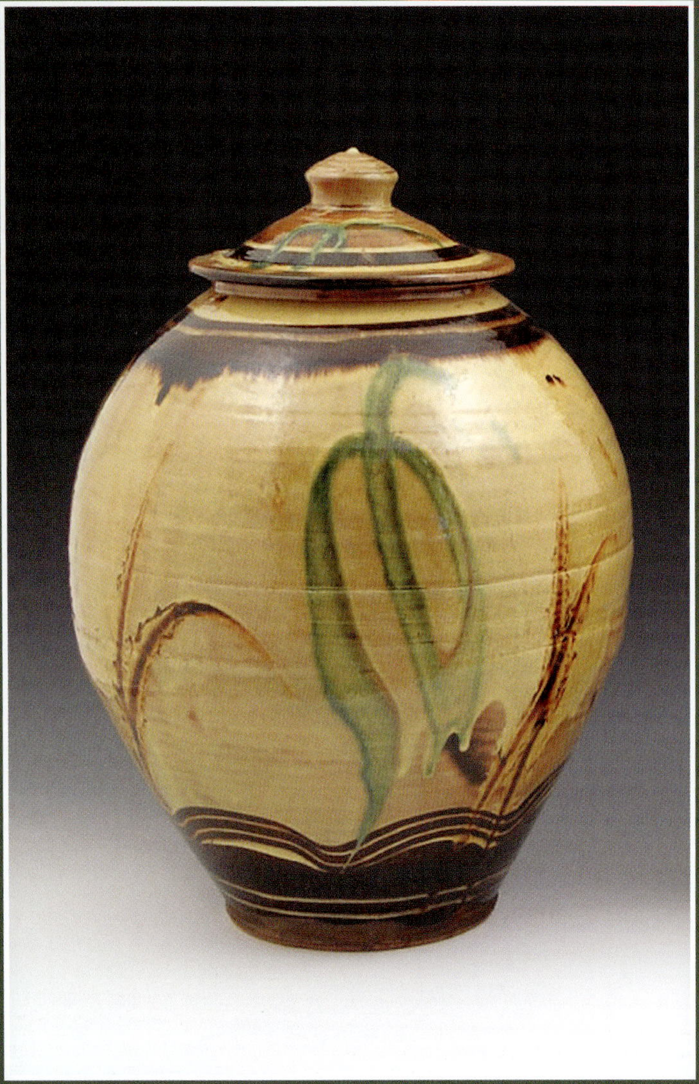

Lidded Jar, 2006, *earthenware.*
Height: 52cm (20½in.).
Photo: Jay Goldmark, courtesy of Goldmark Gallery

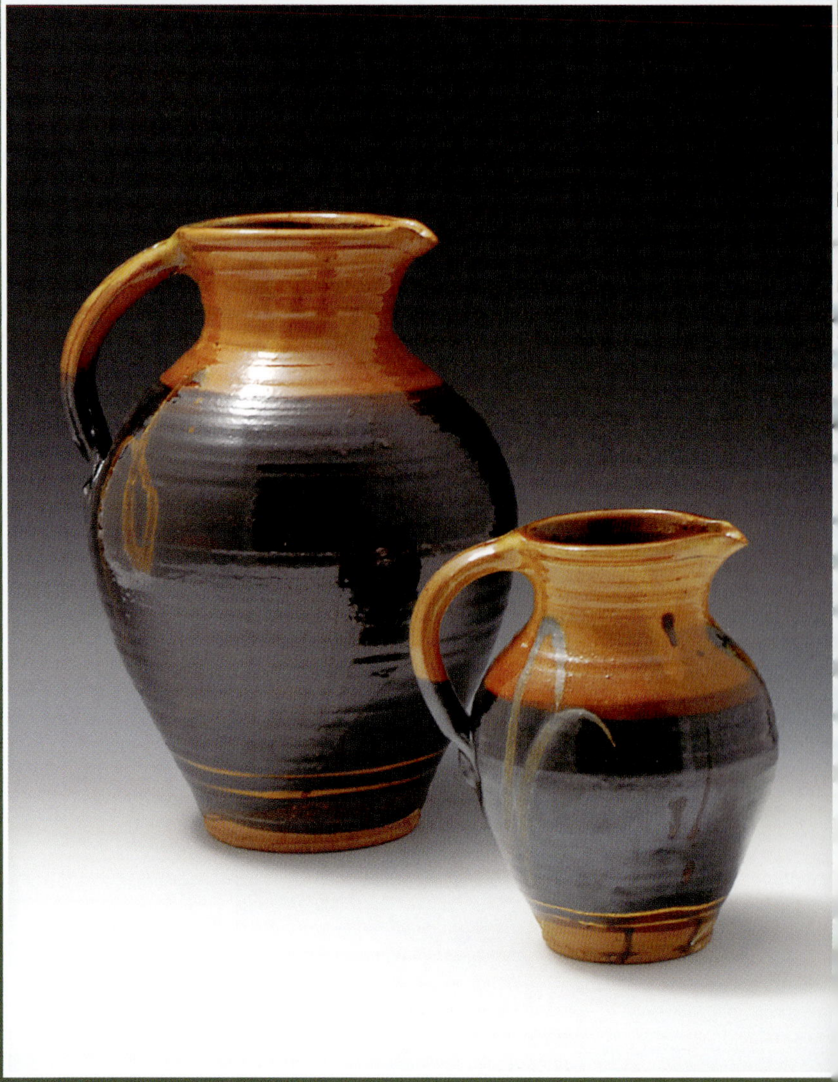

Large Jug, Medium Jug, 2006, *earthenware.*
Height: 33cm (13in.); Height: 21cm (8¼in.).
Photo: Jay Goldmark, courtesy of Goldmark Gallery

is also true to say that Bowen is not really a glazer *on* his pots; his free trails and pourings of slip extend and animate his strong sense of form, just as Hamada's glazing ignited his surfaces. This very physical method connects these potters to the abstraction of the New York School in the 1950s: the almost calligraphic paintings of Franz Kline and Robert Motherwell. Whether in painting or ceramics, artists have often used gestural spontaneity to preserve a sense of innate motion in the finished object.

The broad action of Bowen's throwing and glazing deepens with repetition. A rhythmic and dynamic flow is induced. The parameters of a limited number of forms seem only to encourage personal inventiveness – resulting in pots of increasing subtlety and boldness, expansively combining iridescent colour, contour and marking. The way he finger-swipes through a glaze, incises and adds sgraffito, or achieves those deep lustrous or matt glazes, reveals a consistent avoidance of formula. The luminosity of colour

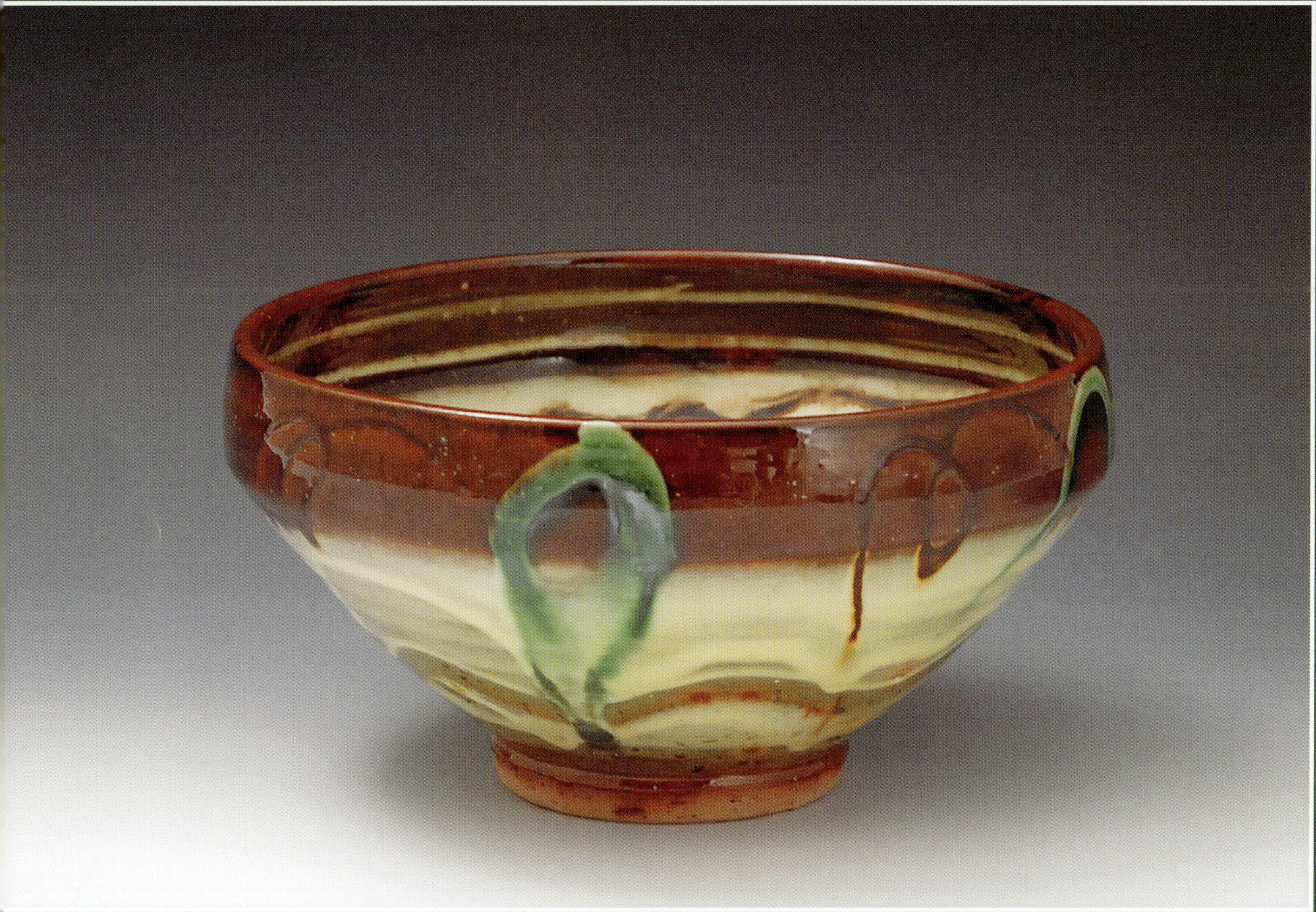

Bowl, *2006, earthenware.*
Height: 12.5cm (5in.).
Photo: Jay Goldmark, courtesy of Goldmark Gallery

over the warm Fremington clay – perhaps deepened by the flame – creates a distinctly Mediterranean and festive quality. Bowen's best pieces are simple and direct, but he is successful in attempting more complex surfaces, the kind of synthesis of dipping, pouring and incising that parallels the work of Japanese potters like Kitaoji Rosanjin and Ryoji Koie. It extends that sense of improvisation in Bowen's work – an improvisation you can also find in music, particularly in jazz of course, one of Bowen's great passions. It is Bowen's continuing ability to play, his youthful approach to clay, that makes his pots so life-enhancing. He is a member of that select band of 'potters' potters', enjoyed and respected by the broadest spectrum of fellow makers, including many who might not be particular adherents of the Leach–Cardew tradition. These are objects that belong to both city and countryside, genuinely adding something vital and fresh to a much-loved aspect of our ceramic history, pots in which we can take the greatest pleasure.

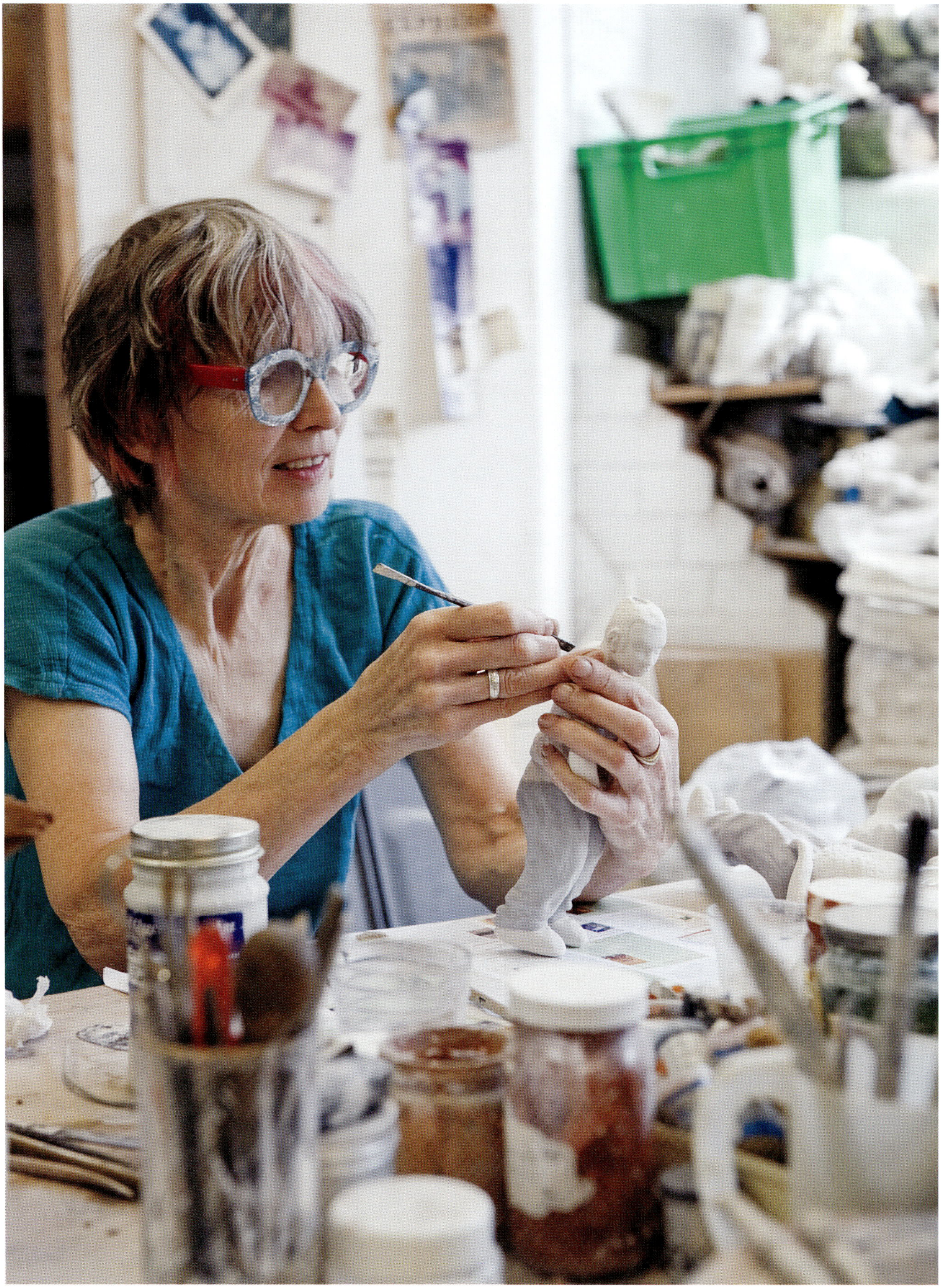

Carol McNicoll

CAROL MCNICOLL has a vivid personality, and she makes vivid pots. Part of the famous generation of women ceramists who graduated from the Royal College of Art in the early 1970s, she is the only one of that group who has remained committed to the idea of functional form, to the making of domestic tableware, albeit of a very offbeat kind. She thinks of herself as a potter, pure and simple, one whose *raison d'être* is to make objects that are a decorative embellishment of one's living space. Her vibrant, richly coloured slipcast pieces reflect the various items of exotica she finds and utilises, the bric-a-brac of London junk shops and the bazaars of foreign markets. She takes equally from the world of wallpapers and textiles and from direct observation in the street. A keen cyclist, McNicoll knows London – where she has been based since 1970 – as well as anyone. Nothing seems to escape her eye, whether it is the body language of tourists or the innate visual luxury of objects and fabrics, many mass-produced, that we might normally overlook. She celebrates the unfashionable and neglected corners of our artistic culture. The pots resulting from such a diverse curiosity have been opulent, sensual and full of humanity.

McNicoll's work is reflected in her home and studio, a converted piano factory in Camden Town with high airy rooms, where she has been living since the early 1980s. The original flat was designed for her by her friend the architect Piers Gough (in return for a McNicoll tea set). Carol now lives and works in the basement and has added her own exuberantly tiled interiors. It is a place which exemplifies McNicoll's vision of life, drawing as she does on the more eccentric and ignored aspects of our environment. It also seems appropriate that, just as McNicoll's work is such a forceful extension of her personality, her studio is such an integral part of her home. Her art and her life really do seem to merge.

McNicoll, a Midlander born in Solihull in 1943, came to ceramics via experiments in theatre design, film-making and painting, and it is this sense of visual connection and experience that she brings to the making of pots. It remains difficult to classify her. Recent solo shows and exhibitions shared with her old friend the artist Jacqueline Poncelet have shown her disdain for gallery minimalism and neutrality, her horror of the clinical white space. Her exhibition interventions have included imported furniture, *objets d'art*, and various textiles and trinkets, all making the succinct visual point that her pots primarily draw their energy from the accumulated decorative history of the home, but given, as with the work of her contemporary Richard Slee, a distinctly surreal slant.

McNicoll's art over nearly 40 years has never subscribed to the more doctrinaire aspects of the studio tradition. She is something of a maverick, intensely eclectic in her subversions of functional form, not a potter who subscribes to any particular philosophy other than the wish to enrich. Catholic by upbringing (though no longer practising), something of its ritual pervades the aesthetic of her work. She has a keen interest in the art and architecture of the 19th century, perhaps in part because it was such a strong negation of the visual Puritanism that took hold in Britain after the Reformation. Her jugs, cups and saucers, and vases, abstract or figurative and richly covered with vivid glazes and transfers, are a forceful response to the visually anti-sensual incursions of Protestantism that began with the artistic destruction and iconoclasm of the 16th century.

In the 1960s, at Leeds Polytechnic, McNicoll was already

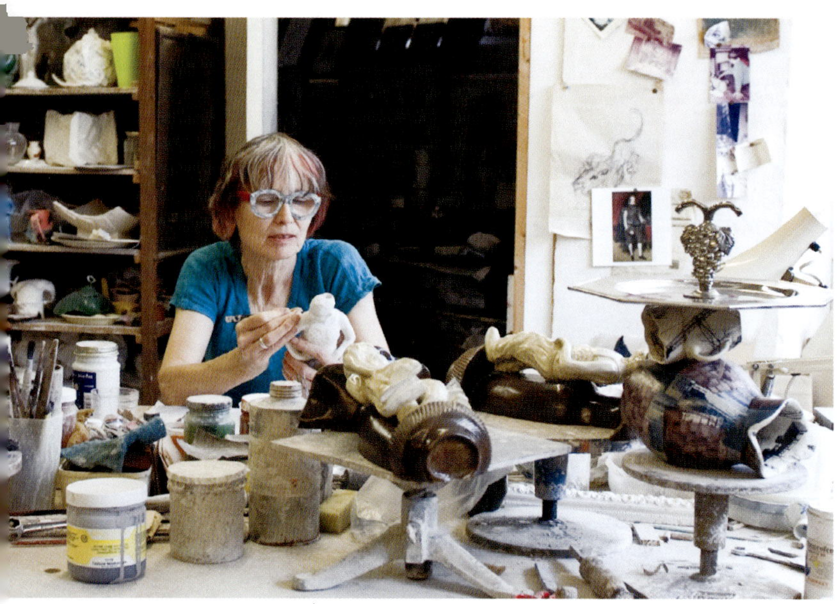

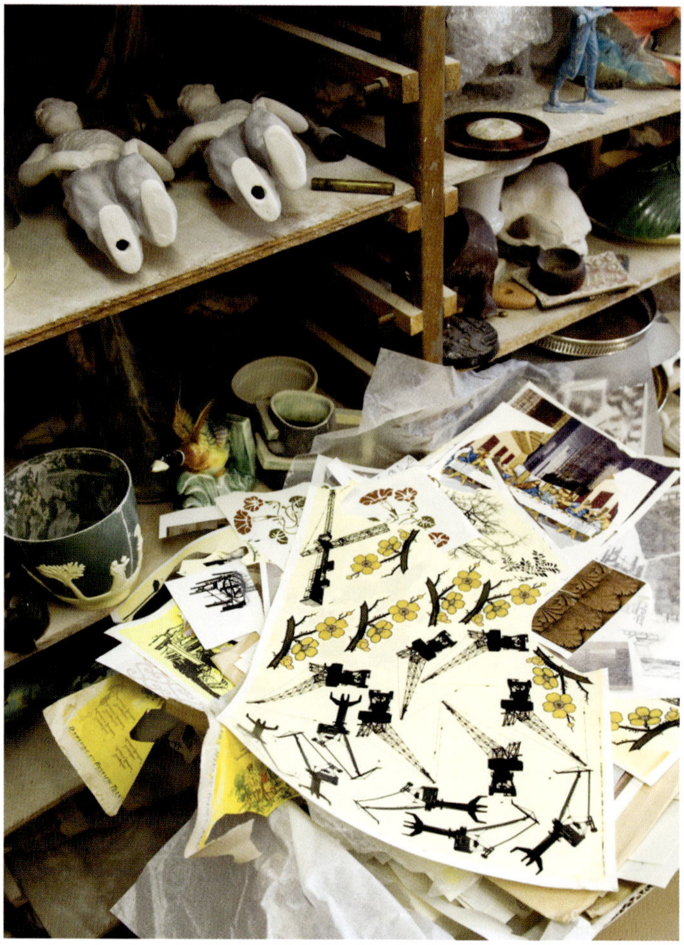

beginning to experiment in slipcasting, making 'holding' objects, the importance of containment already apparent. Her interest in colour, pattern and surface was partly triggered by memories of dressmaking projects with her mother and the lasting influence of oriental rugs. She spent several months working for Zandra Rhodes in London, helping to produce textiles, before taking up her scholarship at the Royal College of Art. Here she learnt more about mould-making, developing a keen interest in industrial techniques that reflected her enthusiasm for multiple production methods with individual finishes. She made whimsical, playfully conceived tea sets that made varied reference to ceramic history from the 18th century onwards. But she has taken virtually nothing from the modern studio tradition, finding more sustenance in Longton Hall's cabbage-leaf teapots or Wedgwood's pearlware. By the 1970s McNicoll's production tableware and more individual pieces were far more geometric, distinctly Cubist, with echoes of Russian Constructivism too.

By the early 1980s she was taking the notion of function to the edge as her work because increasingly open and sculptural. But these were still objects rooted in their domestic context and history. Like Walter Keeler, she has helped us to rethink our notions of what a teapot or a plate might look like, wrapping or cutting clay like a piece of fabric or applying lush patterns like exotic wallpaper. Today her trawls through the riches of household objects, from pieces of decorated china to the ubiquitous ornamental glass vases and bowls many of us grew up with, seem even more direct. Her use of Victoriana and Edwardiana, of 20th-century knick-knacks, for stylistic and imaginative source

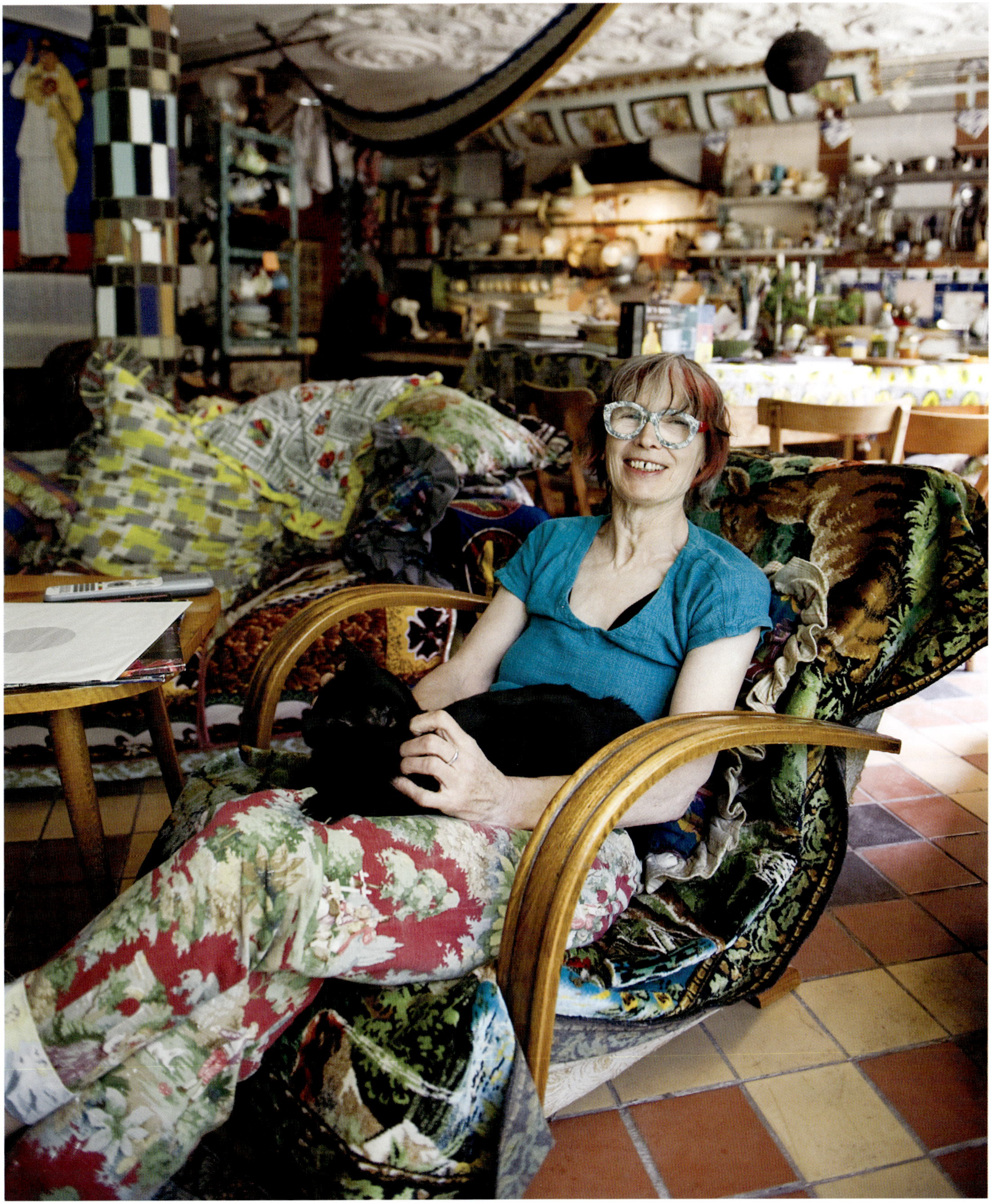

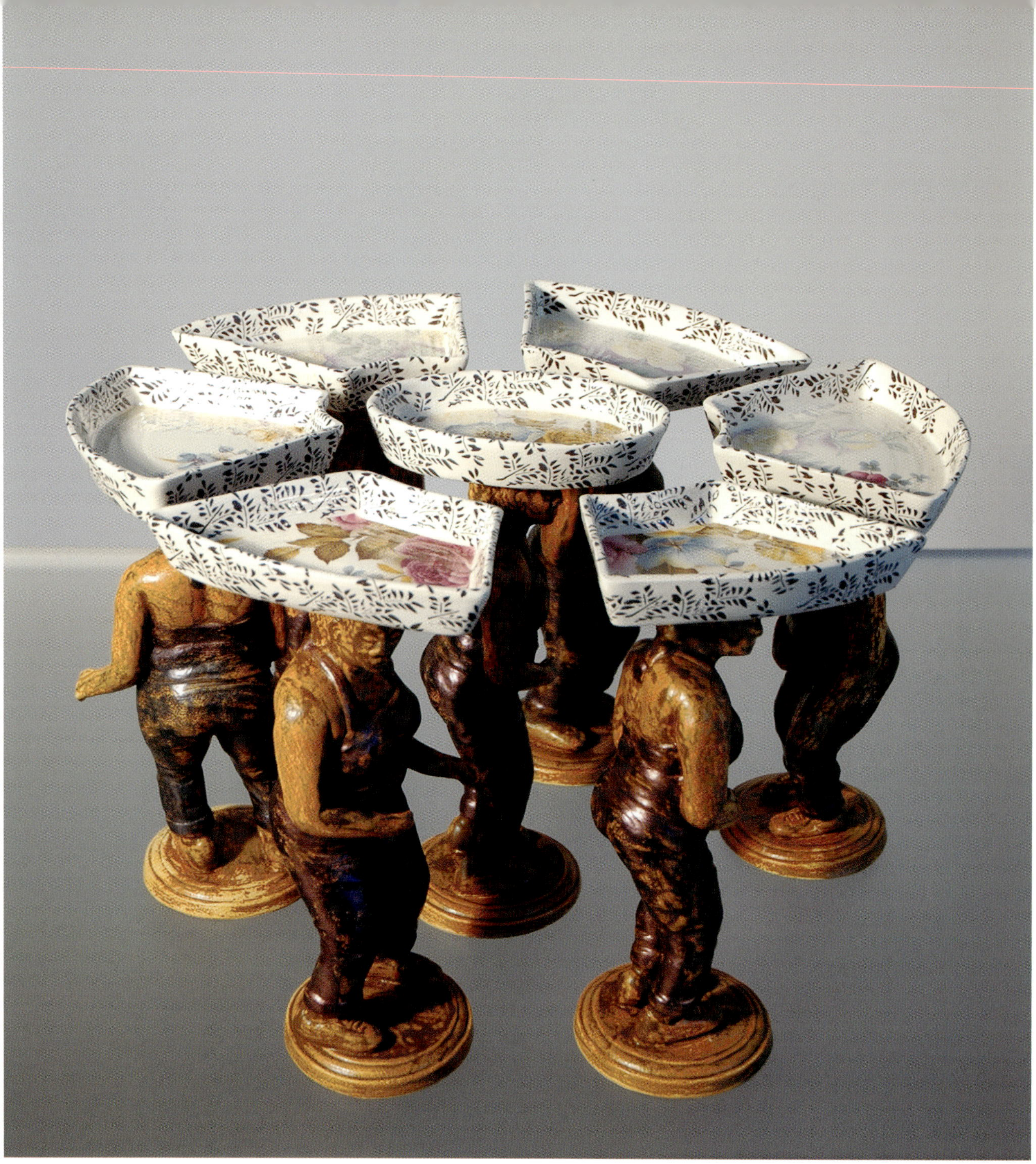

Girls' Night Out, *2006, earthenware. Height: 28cm (11in.).*
Photo: Barrett Marsden Gallery

material gives her work an intentionally popular and democratic bent. Yet her interventions and deviations in form also have a Dadaesque hybridity that subverts what seems to be familiar. Up to the mid-1990s she revelled in a syntax of opposites, not only of colour and texture, but the hard and soft qualities of ceramics. She made bizarre cups, for instance, their forms softly squeezed by the embrace of geometric handles; and then there were the rippling animated surfaces of her 'Rome' planters, made in the late 80s. Over the last decade her work has become more relaxed, even serene. It has a greater sense of baroque luxury and adornment. Her 'Giraffe' bowls and 'Bird Vase' holders are wonderful

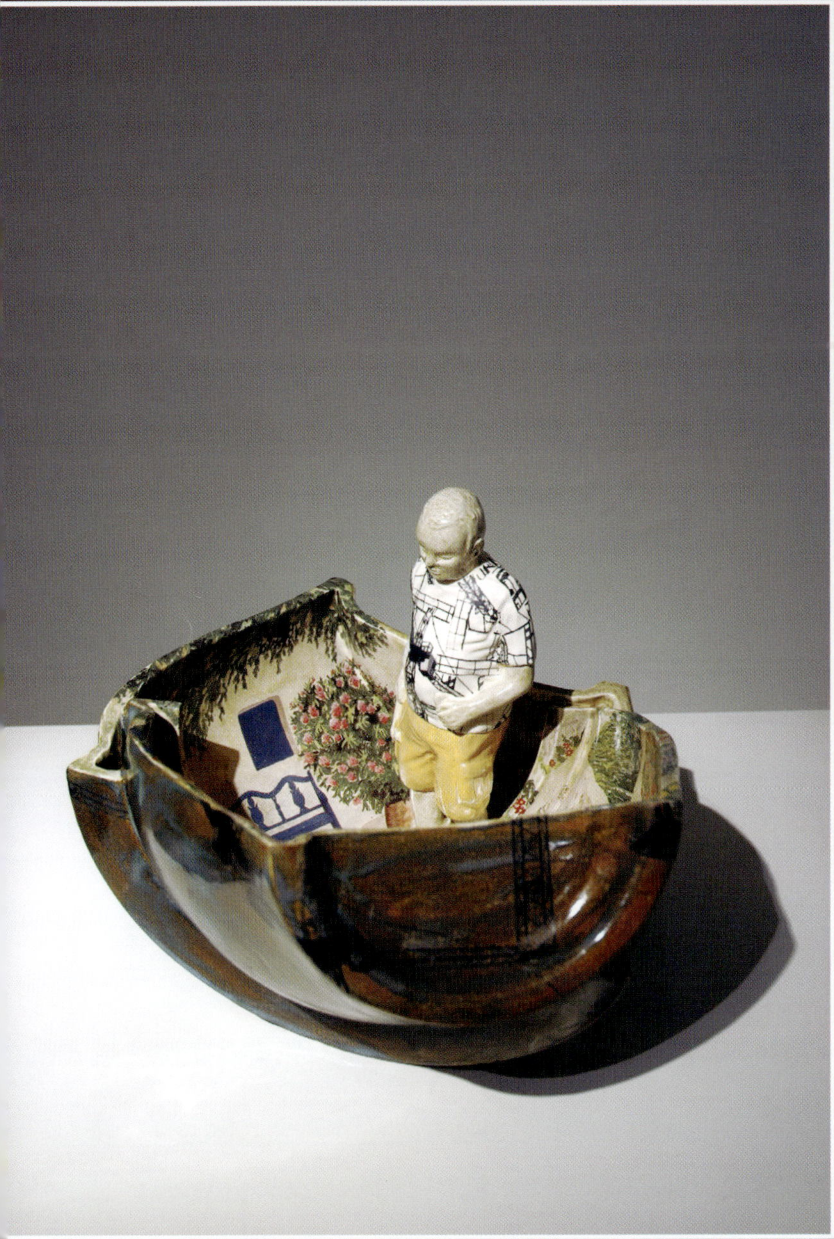

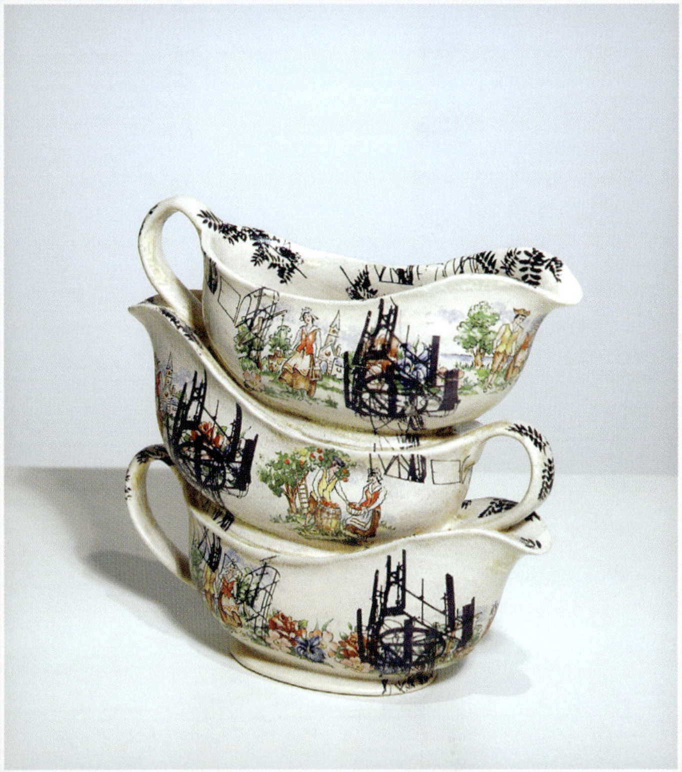

left: Urban Renewal, *2007, earthenware. Height: 32cm (12½in.).*
Photo: Barrett Marsden Gallery
above: Three Jugs, *2008, earthenware. Height: 17cm (6¾in.).*
Photo: Barrett Marsden Gallery

objects, glossy and embellished with grapevines and tropical birds, evoking a quite refreshed nostalgia and opulence.

Recent work has made reference to the social and political complexities of our post-colonial world and misguided foreign policies, to the omnipotence of our consumer culture, well expressed in her use of repeat casting and commercial transfers, combined with lively motifs derived from her own sketchbook drawings and photographs. On her travels in London and abroad her fascination in watching people – natives and visitors alike – has resulted in a series of humorous and touching tableaux. Her constant interest in far-off and exotic places, as well as what may lie on the doorstep, has resulted in an art that is essentially celebratory. Like Carol herself, it is intentionally a little decadent, but it also has a strong underlying seriousness, helping us to see the world around us with fresh eyes.

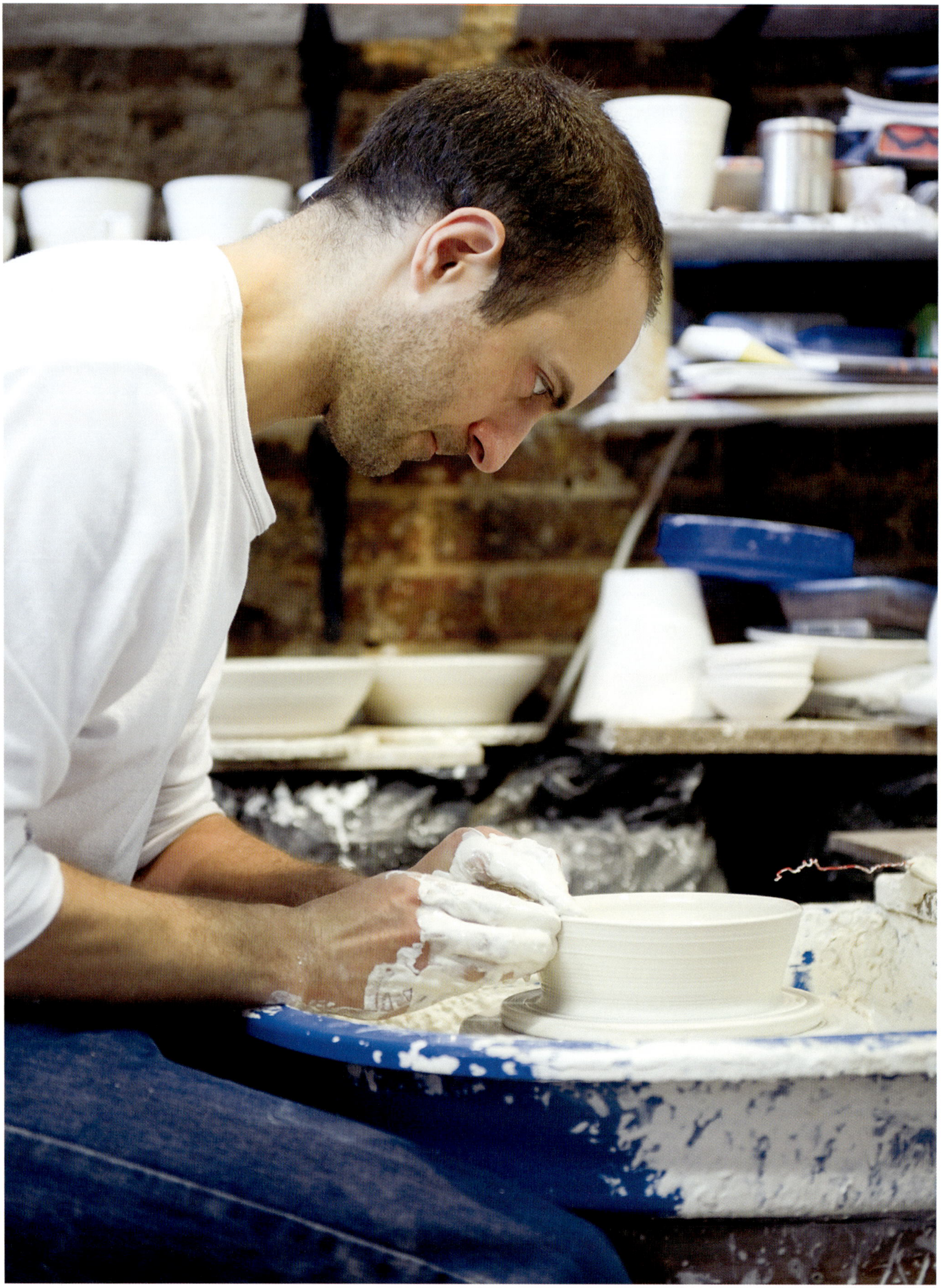

Daniel Smith

THE INTRIGUING THING about potters' studios is that they can be found in the most unlikely places, not necessarily in an 'artists' quarter' in a cultural corner of a town or city, but often more hidden away than that. Archway Ceramics, the shared workshop where Daniel Smith works (and which he helped to establish back in 1994, on graduating from art college), utilises the cavernous space under a railway arch between Bow and Limehouse in London's East End. It isn't easy for strangers to find, but once inside you discover a hive of ceramics activity. Functional, figurative and abstract work – it is all here, with makers producing a wide range of differing styles working in close proximity.

Daniel Smith is such a self-contained and focused potter, one who has been quietly pursuing his craft of elegant white porcelain tablewares for 15 years now, that a busy studio is no hindrance. Nor are there other distractions to deflect him from his course; Smith, a shy man, thinks he would make a terrible teacher and has no interest in writing or speaking at conferences. Because he is pretty averse to self-promotion, too, it is simply through the obvious quality of his ceramics that he is becoming known. A growing number of potters and collectors admire his dedication and the understated beauty of his pots.

Born in Somerset in 1971, Smith grew up with handmade functional pieces around him. His parents ran a restaurant, so Smith had, from an early age, an awareness of good food and good presentation, and the role domestic pottery can play. Enthused by architecture, he decided against it as a career, however, drawn instead to the qualities of clay when he began to make pots at school. He responded positively to the material's directness, its three-dimensional immediacy. Though the pottery department gave him some technical grounding, it was only at Harrow School of Art that Smith really developed his skills at the wheel. He was tutored by Kyra Kane and West Marshall, a distinguished thrower, and was philosophically much influenced by Victor Margrie, who had established the famous production-throwing course here with Michael Casson back in the early 60s. Margrie, committed to the continuing value of tablewares, helped give Smith his sense of creative direction.

Looking at the pots today – bowls, storage jars, oil bottles, cups and saucers, plates and jugs, all of them eminently usable – it is surprising to know that Smith initially hesitated about functional work because of the ready availability of well-conceived manufactured wares. Yet he soon realised the craft was viable, that he could offer an alternative, one with the energy and life of the individual hand as opposed to industrially produced conformity. Nevertheless, Smith has always admired the best factory work, and his clean minimal aesthetic reflects what could be described as a pragmatic modernism. While responding positively to all kinds of functional design in the 20th century, he sees a distinct and complementary place for the handmade within this equation. In this approach there is a flexibility redolent of Scandinavia, where there has never been an imposed division between hand-craft and industry, and thus each has been able to learn from the other. Indeed, if Smith lived in Scandinavia, his designs might well have been taken up for commercial production. Certainly he would never have subscribed to Bernard Leach's anti-industrial agenda, and he has never had much time for 'rustic Leach-type pottery', as he describes it. His aesthetic is consciously urban and stripped down to essentials, in a similar way to Rie and Coper's tableware back in the 1950s.

It was the work of Joanna Constantinidis that particularly

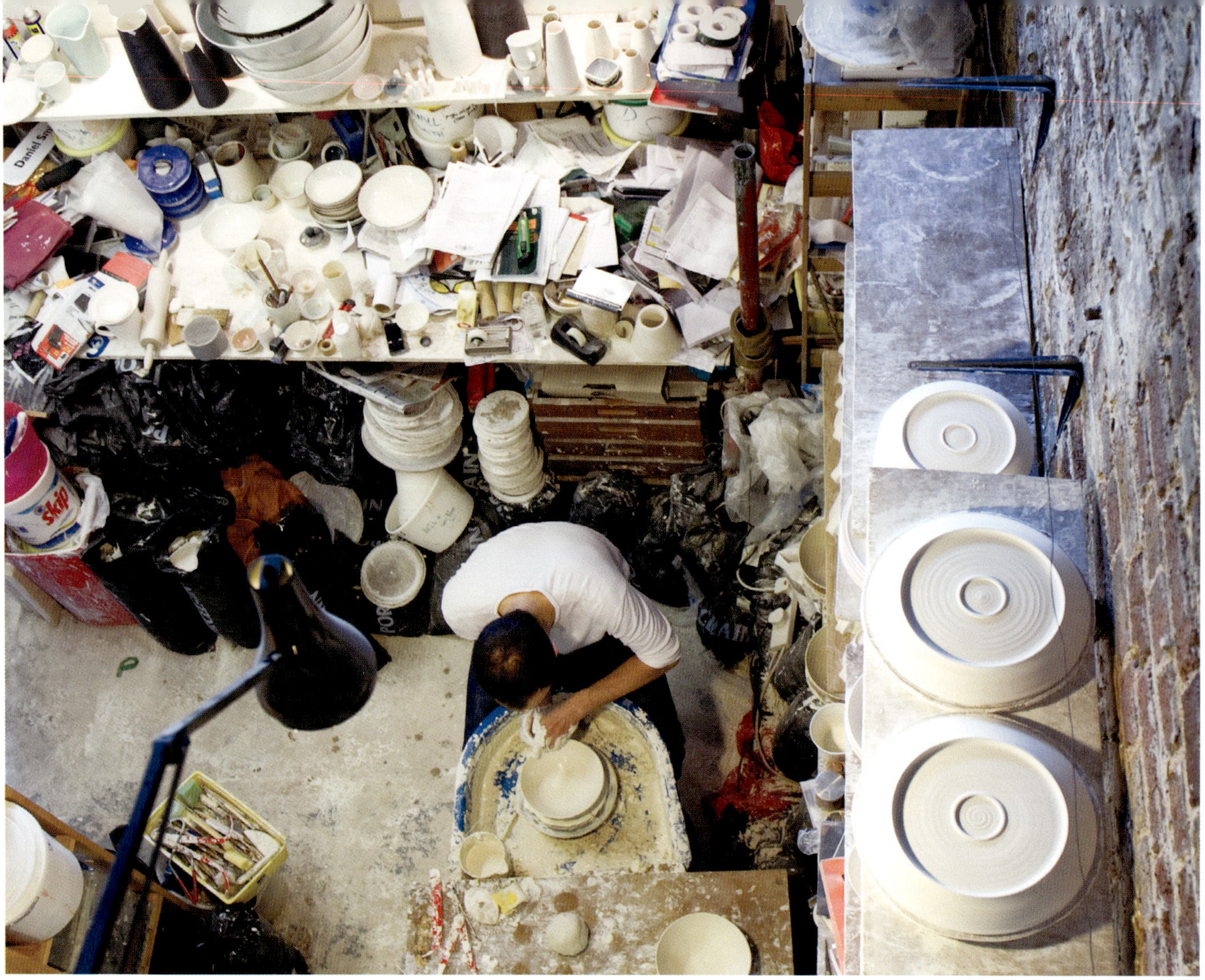

appealed when he was at Harrow; her concentrated and pure shapes in porcelain influenced his decision to adopt this material. In studio terms, her pots best reflected the broader developments in modern form and function, the famous dictum of Mies van der Rohe that 'less is more'. Constantinidis was a major forerunner of the 'New White', as it was coined in an important survey Alun Graves organised at the Victoria and Albert Museum in 1999. Along with Constantinidis and five other potters, Smith was included in the exhibition, his work characterised by good, uninterrupted design. The pots, balanced and honed down, were distinguished by their precision of throwing. With their thin walls, they had a refinement and delicacy, a natural sculptural resonance and rhythm.

There is something self-effacing about Smith and his pots. If these objects come from a 'tradition', then one must also look beyond studio wares – for example, to the purity of 18th-century Wedgwood creamware, to the forms and structures of the Bauhaus and perhaps the kind of utility objects one found in Philip Johnson's 1934 exhibition *Machine Art*. Because he thinks so much about context, the spatial values of contemporary architecture and the related objects around us, his own work has this sense of empathy with other disciplines. Plainness and simplicity are bywords for Smith, exemplified in shapes that are integrated and fluid. In an age when pots are so consciously individual and expressionistic, Smith's apparently modest vessels show how sensual the utilitarian can be. What results is a kind of sculpture of the everyday. Avoiding the creamier thickness of much of the New White, his pots are bonier, more

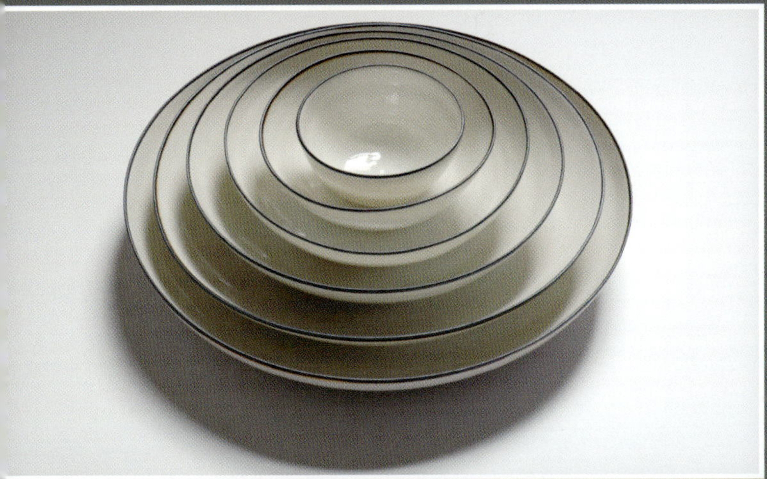

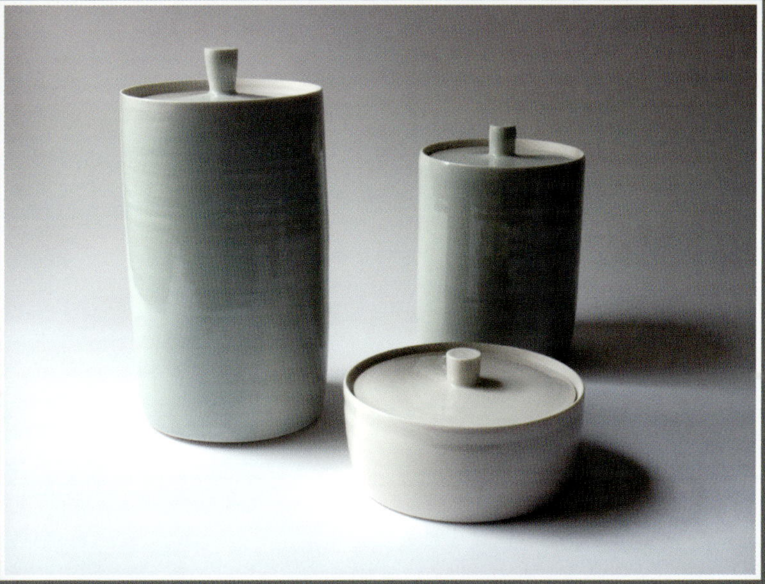

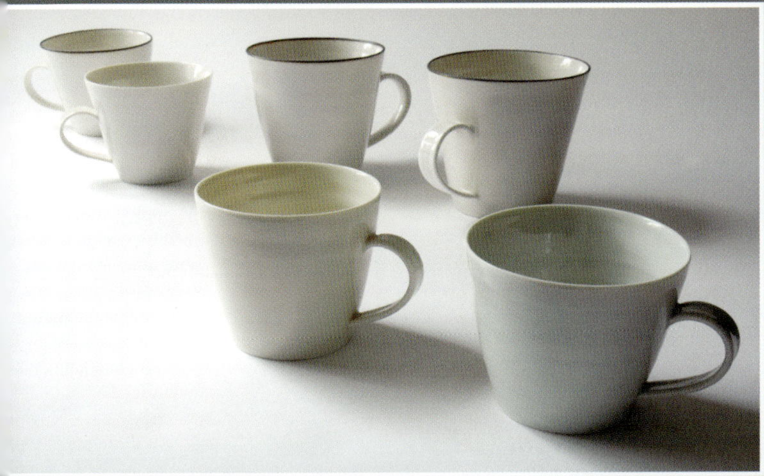

left above: Nest of Six White Bowls, *2007, porcelain.*
Height: 10cm (4in.).
left below: Large Mugs, *2007, porcelain.*
Height: 9.5cm (3¾in.).
above: Storage Jars, *2007, porcelain.*
Height:10cm (4in.); Height: 18cm (7in.); Height: 27cm (10½in.).
Photos: Courtesy of the artist

tensile. Crisp and incisive, they are concentrated into that 'abstract essence' in pottery which the critic Herbert Read wrote about in *The Meaning of Art* (1931). There is an almost industrial austerity in his succinctly conceived storage jars, the memorable nests of bowls and graceful, broadly flaring breakfast cups. But all have that indescribable tremor, the subtle vibration of individual making.

Smith will occasionally add iron oxide to complete a rim, or a deep-blue pooling glaze into some of his flat dishes, details that lend clarity and definition. But the sensory appeal of Smith's work goes beyond the visual. It is also about weight and smoothness in the hand, the particular sound of fired porcelain as you put the cup on the saucer – qualities that heighten one's pleasure when eating and drinking. And while he makes occasional one-off individual pieces, this tableware remains his baseline. This is extremely refreshing at a time when domestic production is increasingly hard to find in studio practice, due not only to the vicissitudes of market demand, but the low boredom threshold of some potters. Smith still finds repetition work creatively very satisfying, and his considerable making experience is very evident. It is not about sudden changes of direction, but about refinement and consolidation, making pots that gradually evolve over time. Rather like Richard Batterham in stoneware, Smith has that simple wish, without hyperbole, but with great self-discipline, to quietly enrich people's lives through the rhythm of the wheel. Smith may quite like the term 'metropolitan potter' to describe his activity, but these are more than metropolitan pots. They are meant for everybody.

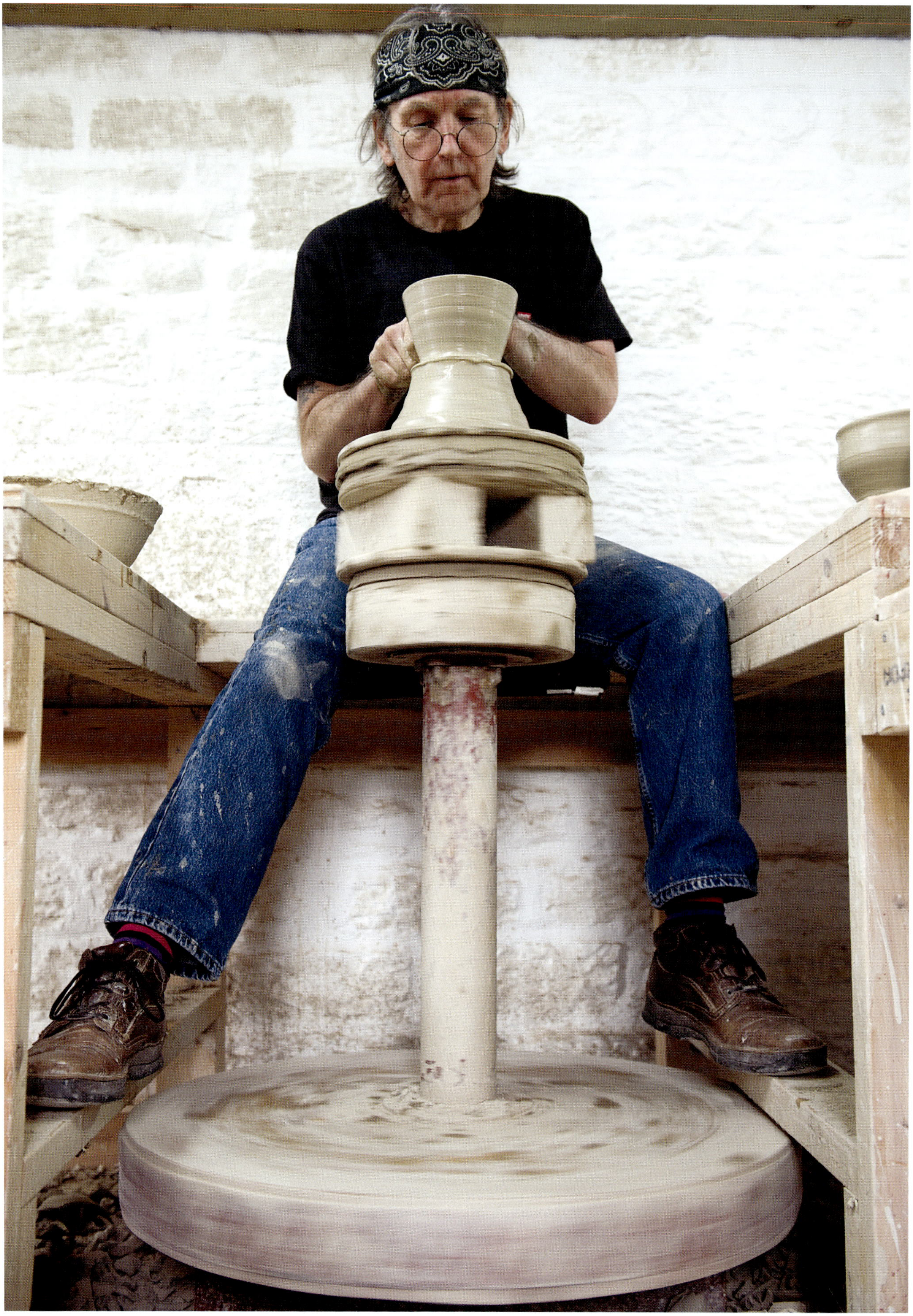

Jim Malone

JIM MALONE lives and works in a remote corner of north-west Cumbria, in the village of Lessonhall. This is a hidden workshop, where Malone pots alone. It is the antithesis of the bustle you might find in shared urban studios, with an atmosphere of quiet concentration and focus. On moving here recently Malone began by constructing his fourth kiln, a two-chambered oriental climbing design. It was a two-year project, but well worth it, because 'commercial kilns are toys ... this one has been built for the character it imparts to the pots'. Malone is in love with the drama and process of firing, and constructing one's kiln is also a way of preparing psychologically – quite literally of laying the foundations – for the work ahead.

A kiln you have built yourself is one you know better, just as you become intimate, over the years, with your wheel (in Malone's case most definitely a *manual* wheel), your tools and the materials you use. Kilns like Malone's take a few firings to settle in. The first pots to emerge are not always the best, perhaps because of teething problems, perhaps because the potter isn't back into his or her creative stride. Craftsmen in the Middle Ages made their pots day in, day out. They were not consciously 'artist' craftsmen in the modern sense, but the fluidity and invention of their vernacular idiom, engendered by repetition, had a quality that 20th-century potters like Jim Malone, and Bernard Leach before him, have greatly admired, so that they have sought to reinterpret this spirit in their own way.

Malone, a leading follower of Leach and his functional ideals, is like those medieval craftsmen a great maker of jugs and pitchers. Those made in the 14th and 15th centuries attract him because of their peculiarly English vitality and expressive nature. The jug is an archetypal functional vessel which, in the right hands, when fluently made and balanced, can have great sculptural presence. Malone's jugs have this vigour, every one individual in personality. Like all Malone's best work, they have a latent movement and a preserved plasticity, qualities strengthened by the spring of their applied handles, their free combing and faceting, the character of each lip. Completed by a range of irons and ashes, Malone uses glaze and slip as an essential extension of the clay, augmenting and emphasising its surface texture. Malone's symbiosis with his locally sourced materials – deliberately limited in number – brings out their layers of richness over many years in partnership with them.

In this respect Malone can be grouped with potters such as Ray Finch and Richard Batterham from an older generation, and, from his own, Phil Rogers, Mike Dodd and Clive Bowen. All owe a philosophical and aesthetic debt to the pots and writings of Bernard Leach and Michael Cardew, but have reached languages, syntheses, quite distinct from one another. Malone's re-evaluations of the bowl and jug, as well as jars, bottles and dishes of various shapes and sizes, reinvigorate not only the traditions of medieval English and European pottery, but the beauties of classical Chinese and Korean ceramics. For Malone, an alignment with the natural world, with the place in which he works, is integral: his pots emerge out of a daily pace of making that evolves as the seasons evolve. They reflect the face and colours of his landscape, the properties of earth and stone, the minerals from which these objects are made. It is this special connectedness which draws Malone into his workshop every day. Words like 'continuity' and 'rhythm' are important because he needs complete focus if he is to maintain the flow of his making cycle.

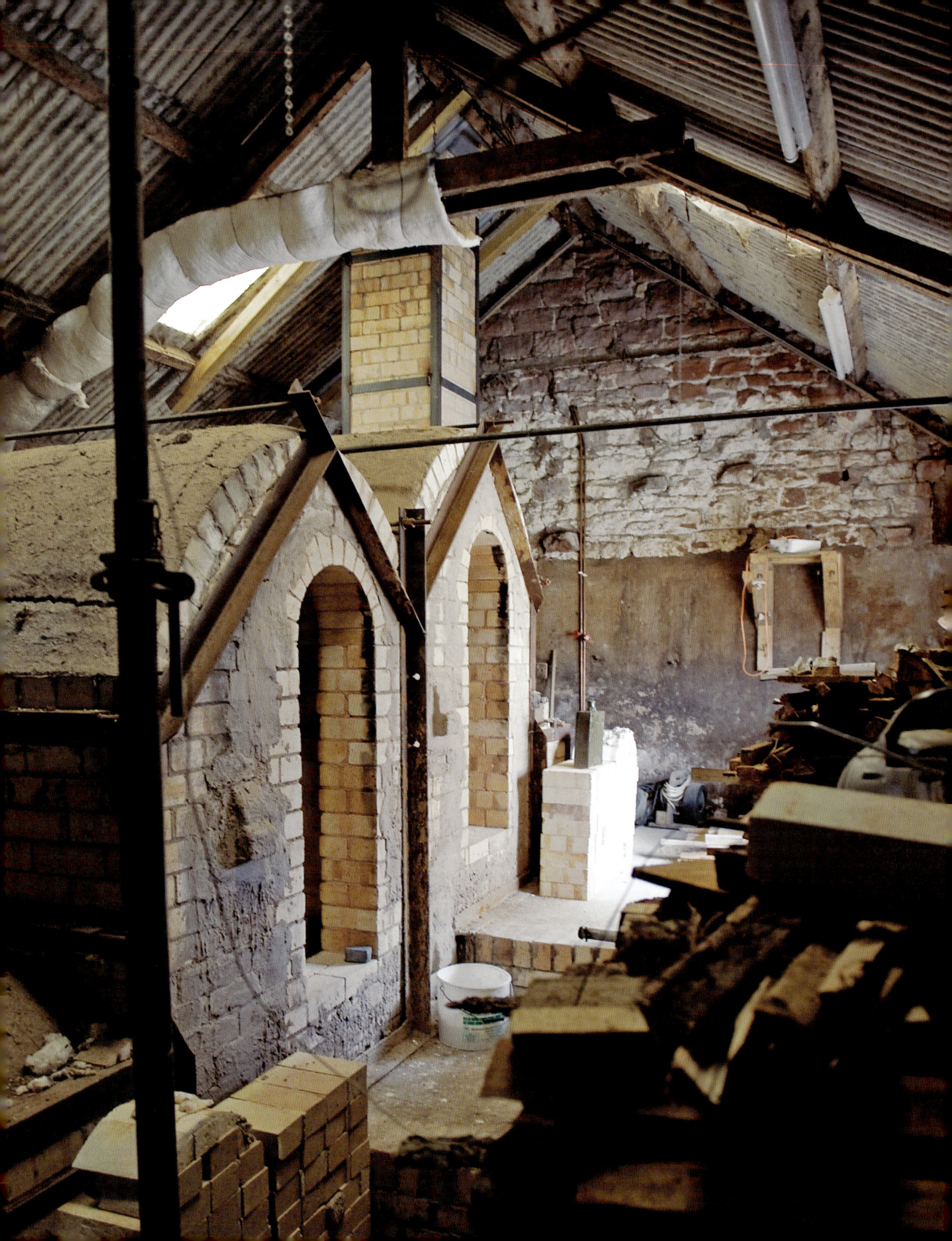

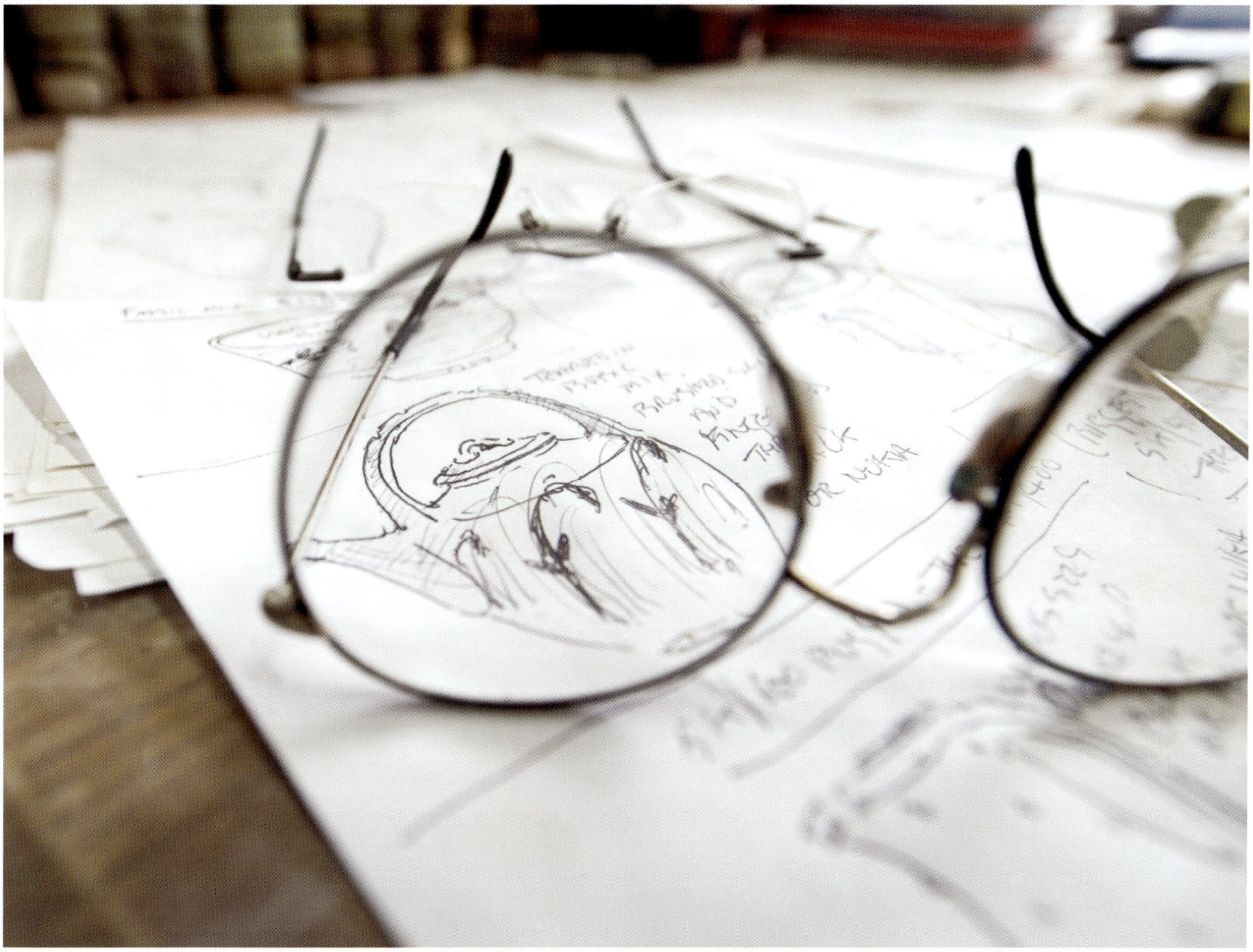

Malone is not a native of this border country. He was born in Sheffield in 1946 and in fact trained and practised as a teacher before deciding to go to art college in the early 1970s. At Camberwell School of Art he discovered clay, and was fortunate enough to have among his teachers Ian Godfrey, Ewen Henderson and Colin Pearson. Ian Godfrey was particularly important, encouraging Malone to visit London museums and see oriental and medieval European pots for himself. Henderson, another hand-builder, showed the importance of a searching and open creative mind, while Pearson's technical ability and skills as a thrower certainly left their mark. Malone was lucky that, like his contemporary Dan Kelly, he struck Camberwell during its most fertile period, a rich experience completed by a brief spell at Winchcombe Pottery. Here, under Ray Finch, Malone learnt about the communal workshop ethos – absorbing the integral nature of a craft that went beyond any notion of a 'career' and was more a committed way of living, a kind of creative marriage.

Malone established himself first in north Wales – on the Horseshoe Pass – and then, after periods of part-time teaching, to supplement his income in the 1980s he accepted a permanent post at Cumbria College of Art in Carlisle, running an exceptional vocational throwing course with his friend Mike Dodd. He moved to Ainstable in the nearby Eden Valley, and eventually returned to full-time potting and regular exhibitions. Warm and sociable he may be, but Malone has always, geographically and temperamentally, worked at the margins. His loathing of the more superficially 'innovative', conceptual and style-led aspects

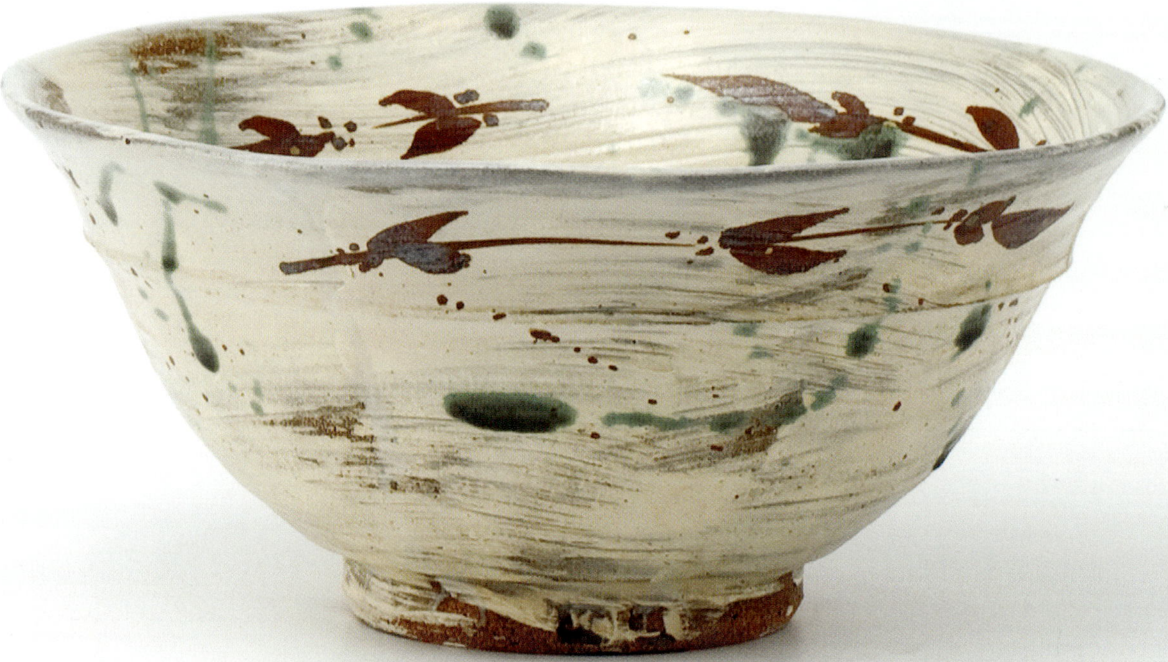

Large Bowl, *2008, stoneware.*
Height: 15cm (6in.).
Photo: Jay Goldmark, courtesy of Goldmark Gallery

of ceramics has resulted in some trenchantly expressed articles which never pull their punches. Equally, their eloquence can sum up succinctly and movingly his pursuit of 'useful beauty' and a Ruskinian truth to materials. As he stated in an article in *Pottery Quarterly* in 1986 (no. 56):

Pots such as these, no less than those historic examples we admire, are the product of an empathy with one's particular environment, where use is made, so far as is possible, of what materials are offered locally, acknowledging their virtues, accepting their shortcomings, in much the same

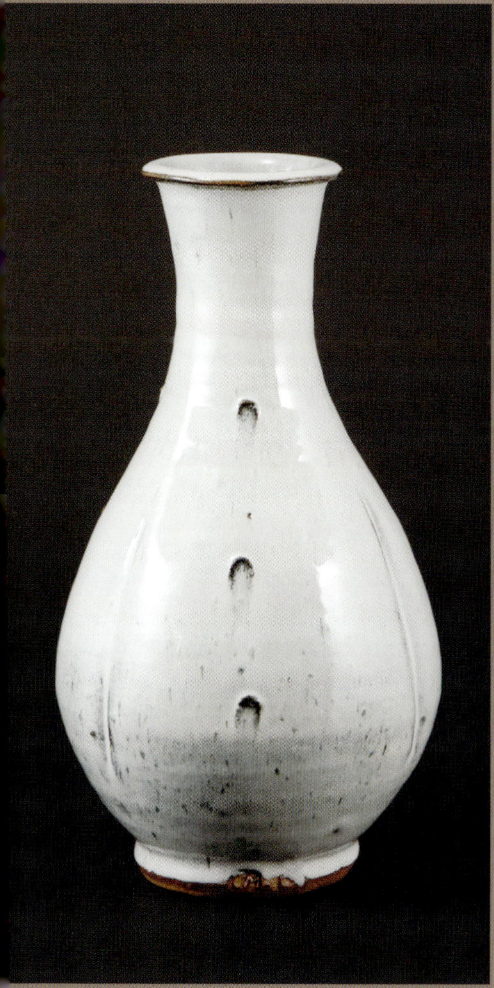

Footed Bottle, *2008, stoneware.*
Height: 32cm (12½in.).
Photo: Jay Goldmark, courtesy of Goldmark Gallery

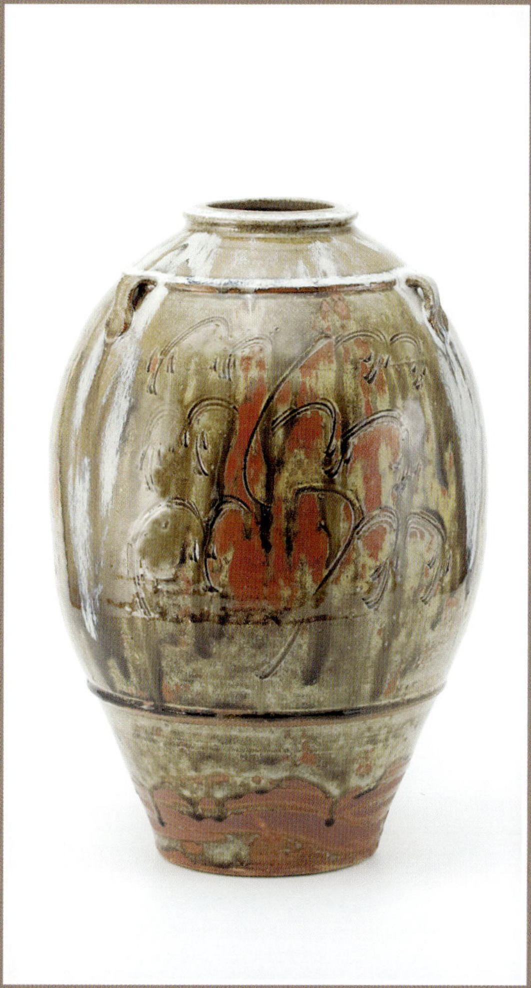

Large Globular Jar, *2008, stoneware.*
Height: 44cm (17¼in.).
Photo: Jay Goldmark, courtesy of Goldmark Gallery

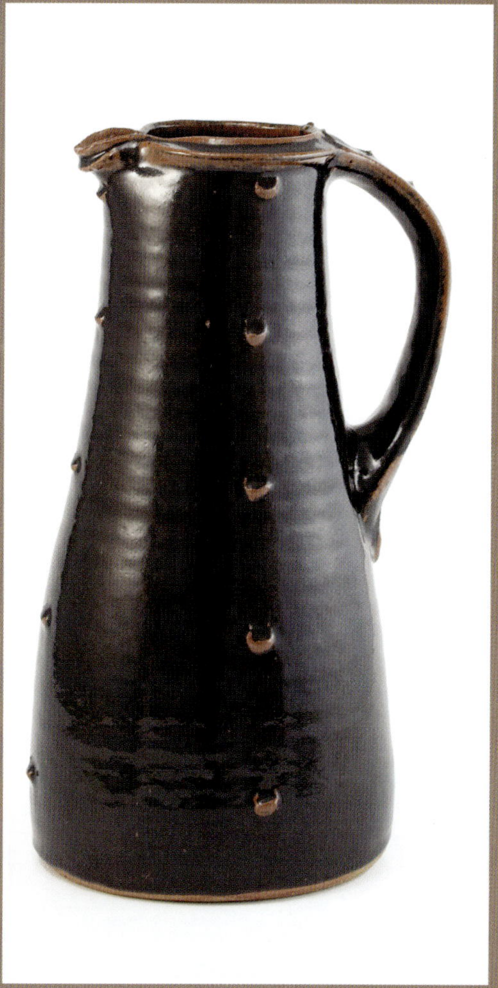

Tall Jug, *2008, stoneware.*
Height: 38cm (15in.).
Photo: Jay Goldmark, courtesy of Goldmark Gallery

way as we do with people. Such pots come to flower, as do wild flowers, in time with the natural rhythm of things, unforced.

This 'unforced' quality is one of convincing synthesis, where strong form and surface character play equal, inseparable roles. Malone's pots show a lively interaction between maker and materials, between one component and another, enhanced by his varied decoration – using incising, painting, resist, cutting, beating and so on, employing clay and slip to deepen and to unify. He brings a lyrical energy to the way he engraves foliate designs into a tall bottle, where the runs of ash or tenmoku follow and thicken the contours of a pot, emphasising its calligraphic marking, gathering in its wells and gutters. Malone's spontaneous brushwork and incising of leaping fish and grasses blowing in the wind, is full of life, emphasising the sense of lift and growth that each pot embodies. Through this mediation, Malone hopes to reveal the continually surprising properties of clay as openly and directly as he can. His integrity as a potter, his dogged belief in the core values of a particular ceramic tradition, the Leach-inspired East–West tradition, has resulted in pots that are continually fresh, and a generous antidote to the more cynical and ephemeral aspects of today's visual culture.

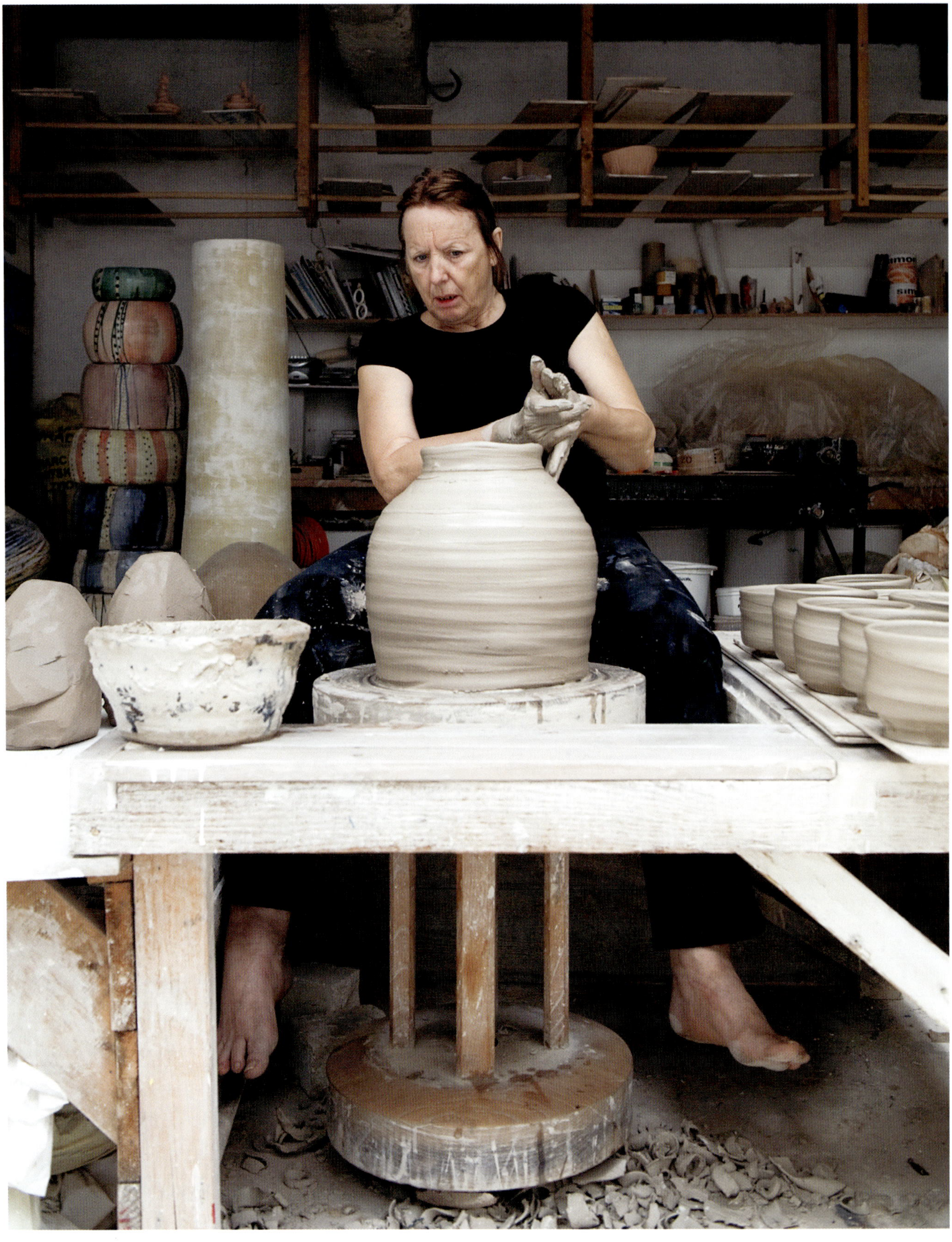

Sandy Brown

SANDY BROWN'S studio is out on a limb, located in the old fishing village of Appledore on the north Devon coast, overlooking the broad expanse of the Torridge Estuary. It occupies an old glove factory, a building where one kind of industry has been replaced by another: Sandy Brown's prodigious output as a potter. She has utilised both floors for her art, whose output encompasses not only lively colourful ceramics for the table, which remain at the core of her creativity, but her parallel work as a sculptor and painter. This workplace must be one of the most beautiful in the country – the large airy rooms and excellent light would be any artist's dream, just a few minutes' walk from Brown's Georgian house on the waterfront. It is a part of England with a strong ceramic history, for pottery has been made here since the Middle Ages, and the region is famous for the vibrant slipware produced from the 17th century onwards, some of which was exported to Ireland and North America.

This work made a great impact on Brown when she first settled in Devon. She admired the expressive invention and freedom of this vernacular tradition, particularly the harvest jugs that can still be seen in local museums. It has some of the qualities she had already experienced during her training in Japan, at the pottery town of Mashiko. Brown, who was born in 1946, could be described loosely as 'anglo-oriental', in the sense that she has taken many of her ideas from both native English and Japanese traditions. However, her work is hardly Leachian; she has never used Leach as a filter, and her style and approach emanate directly from her effervescent personality. Brown's pots are very much the woman – strong, vivid and life-enhancing. We cannot judge Sandy's personality impassively – through its very energy, it involves us. It may delight, it may irritate, but the extraordinary openness of her artistic conversation drives home. It makes us think about material expression in a quite new way.

That Brown received her training solely in Japan – indeed was *introduced* to clay in Japan, makes her virtually unique amongst English potters. 'The process of ignition', as she calls it, began when, in 1965, she left England to search for a direction and found herself in Japan three years later, a place where she would soon feel creatively and personally liberated. Brown soon discovered Mashiko, where Shoji Hamada lived and worked and, immediately enthralled by clay, was accepted as a potter at Daisei Pottery. It was a traditional workshop, where by observation rather than formal teaching, she began to feel her way into the material. What was significant was the expansive approach to all aspects of the craft: the kneading of the clay, the loose throwing, the generous quantities of glaze – liberally poured and splashed – to decorate a pot. All these years later, her work continues to be about the sheer physicality of making, for Brown an event in itself or, as Joanna Constantinidis once put it, 'a performance art without an audience'.

As with her one-time husband Takeshi Yasuda, Brown's activity as a potter springs from a keen interest in its context. Very struck by the preparation and ritual of Japanese meals, the wish to make work that enhances and underlines these occasions has been her principal motivation – encouraging us to return to daily ceremonies that have been sidelined in a rushed, frenetic 21st century. Like Yasuda, Brown makes ceramics that invite us to pause and to think, to make space in our day around pots that, in their splendour and intimacy, celebrate the art of function, the art of the meal. In this respect she has much in common with potters like Jane

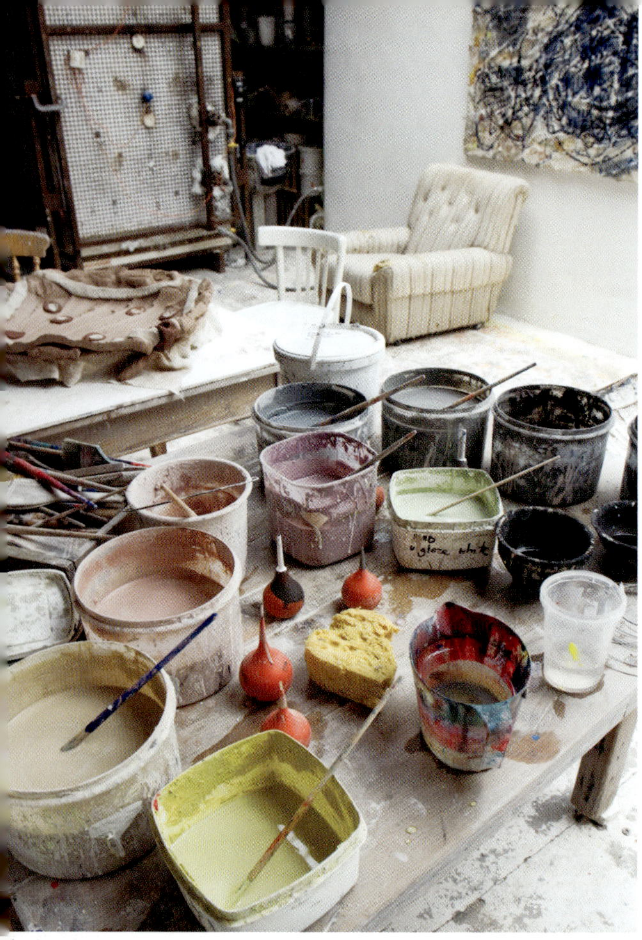

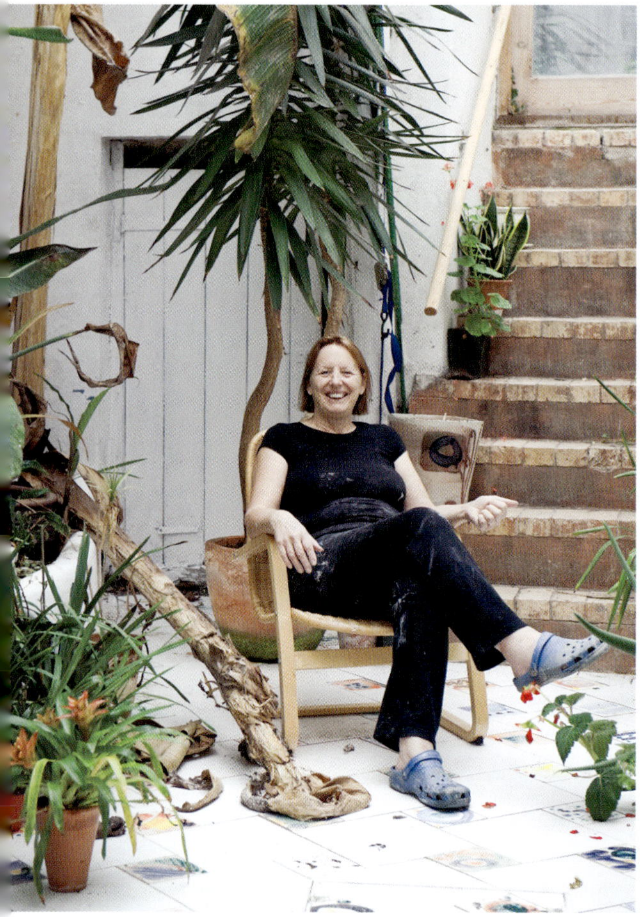

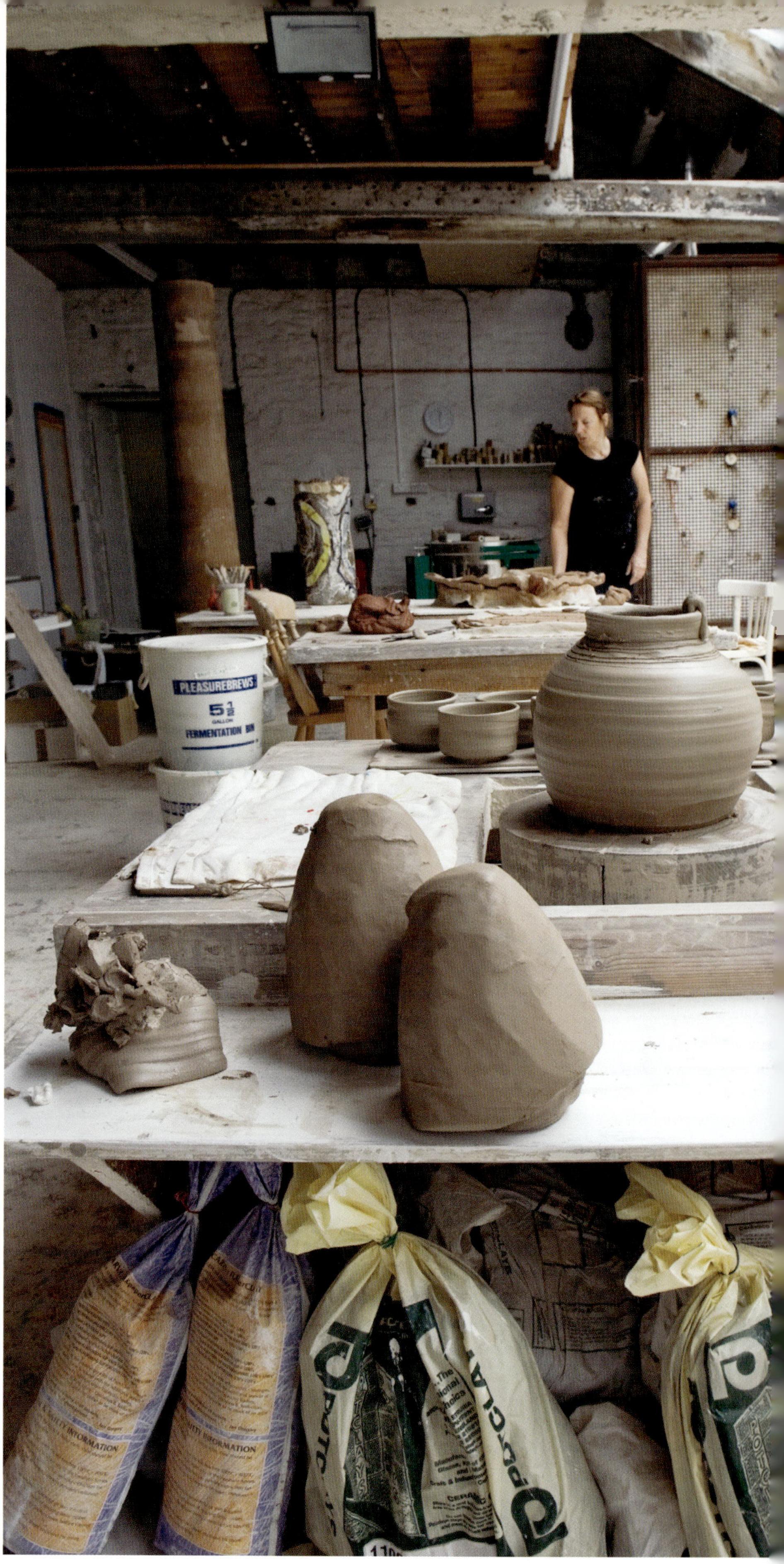
PLEASUREBREWS
FERMENTATION BIN

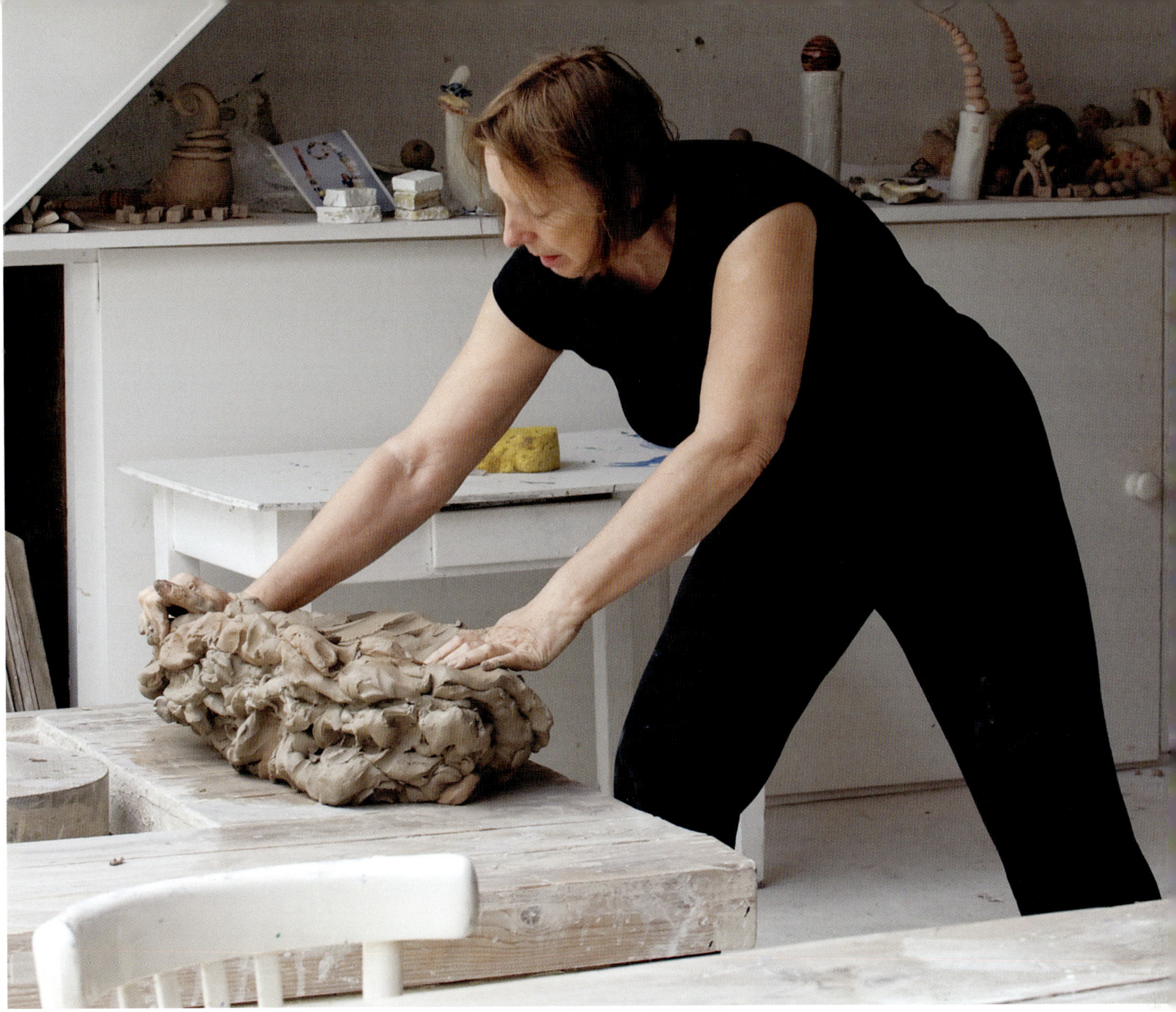

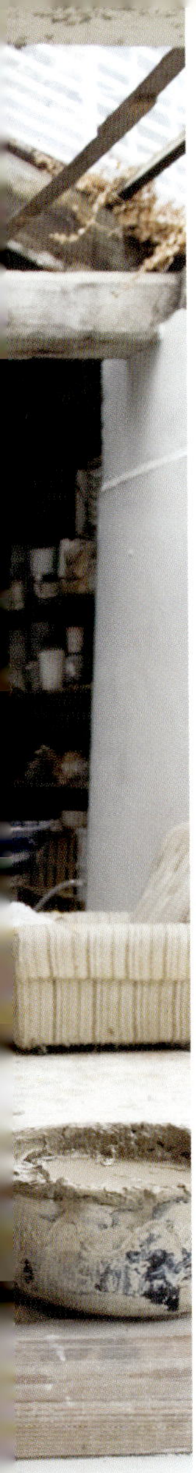

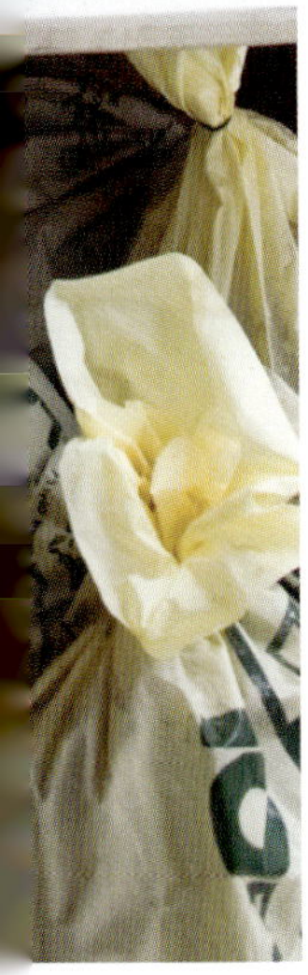

Hamlyn and Walter Keeler, makers who have thought long and hard about the hinterland of ceramics, the value and place of pots in our social lives. All three have expressed their philosophies in forceful articles, passionate manifestos for the importance of the handmade in our post-industrial age.

Brown has been significant, not only for her fresh approach to thrown form, but for the luminous colour she helped to reintroduce into English ceramics. On returning to Britain, after some experiments in wood-firing, she worked initially in slip-decorated earthenware, soon bringing some of this quality of making and decorating to stoneware – pouring swathes, drips and splashes of pigment, rather like slip, onto pots that expressed the thick sensual plasticity of the material. Superficially, it has some of the qualities of Hamada's work, but the colour became almost psychedelic, like the abstracts of Gillian Ayres or Albert Irvin. The decoration, like Brown's seemingly carefree throwing, is taken to its limits. Sandy has always resisted the temptation to impose excessive control on each stage of making, realising that some of the best forms arise when she is working quickly and at her most spontaneous. In this respect her work parallels not only some of the more lively

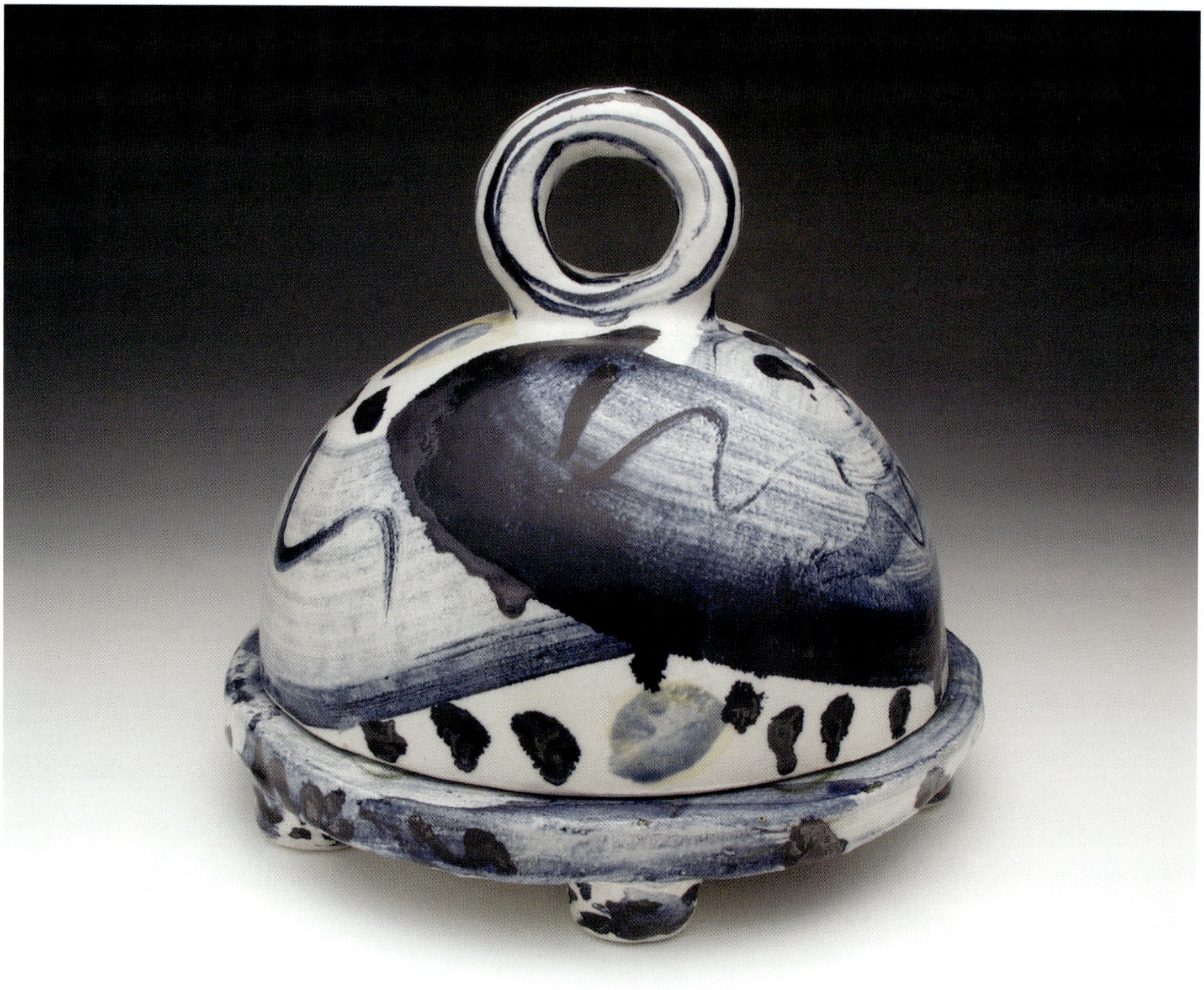

Platter with Cloche, *2001, stoneware.*
Height: 43cm (17in.).
Photo: Courtesy of the artist

aspects of British abstraction, but echoes certain artists in the New York School of the 1950s and 60s – one thinks of Jackson Pollock and Willem de Kooning.

Brown's experience and depth of practice are what allow her to take these liberties, to play what is essentially a game of chance in throwing and glazing. The resulting pots – plates, bowls, platters, jugs and so on – are undeniably fluid, indeed almost liquid, in texture and colour. Deep blues, reds, greens, yellows and pinks are used to ignite the surface and consolidate the preserved motion of the wheel. Such an approach takes courage. One can make comparisons with other types of improvisation – in music or in acting, for example – where the spontaneity of outcome may arise from a more fertile, subconscious imagination. There are potters who have followed Brown's example, though not always successfully: much of the work in this vein is reduced to static pattern-making with glaze, a kind of wallpaper, whereas Brown has always tried to extend the power of the form through a far more physical dynamic of colour.

Though this essay concerns Brown's core activity as a functional potter, one who has helped to bring a fresh spirit to tablewares, her sculptural and two-dimensional work is

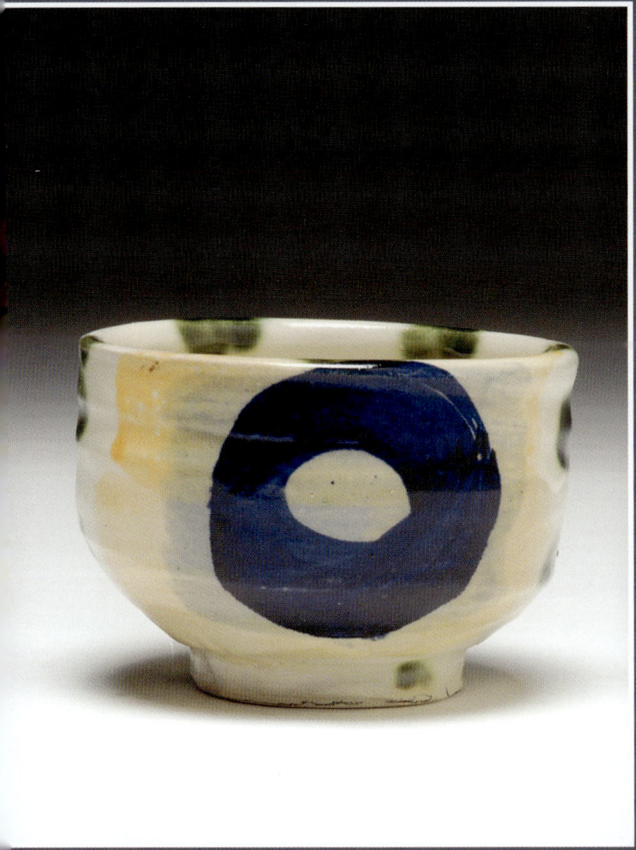

Teabowl, *2005, stoneware.*
Height: 10cm (4in.).
Photo: Courtesy of the artist

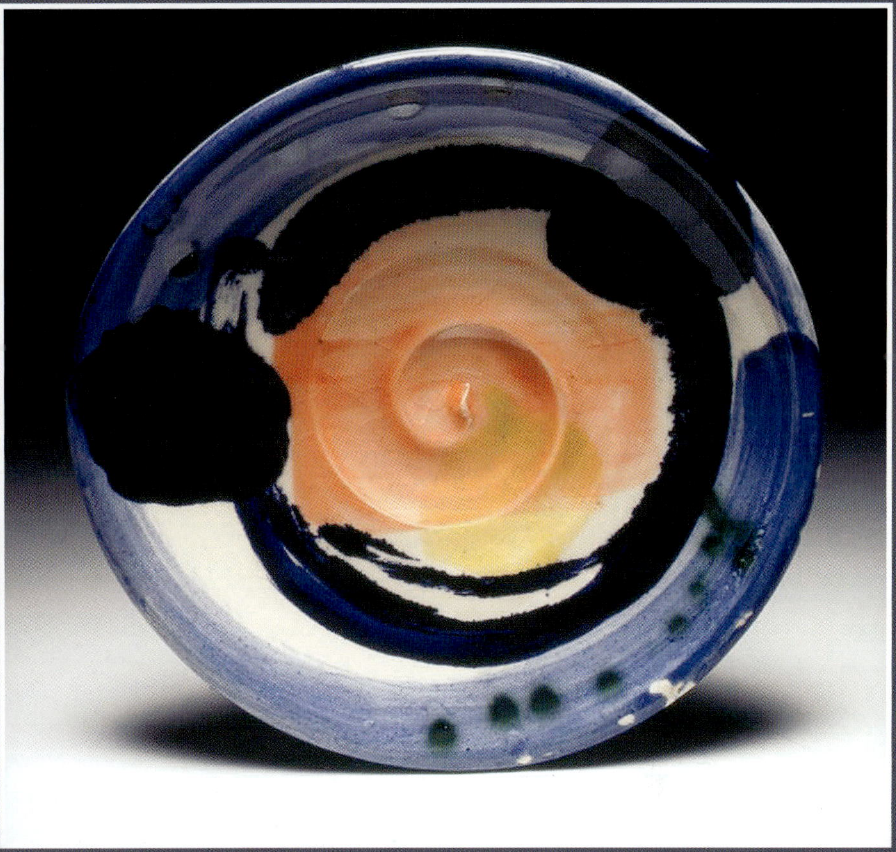

Softly Thrown Plate, *1988, porcelainous stoneware.*
Diameter: 30cm (11¾in.).
Photo: Courtesy of the artist

a closely related, if more personal attempt to express her ideas on subjects at the heart of her creativity as a whole – female sexuality, fertility and gender, released energy – all related to her own life experience. She has created a pantheon of goddess figures, bird gods and animal forms, and a rich body of abstract and figurative painting. In 2006 she completed work on a major ceramic installation *The Still Point and the Dance*, a project that brought all areas of her art – pots, pictures, sculpture and fabrics – together into one great collective statement. It investigated both the 'still point' of her activity, the calm reflection of creative preparation – represented by the silence of a recreated teahouse – and the ensuing 'dance', the artistic surge, expressed here in joyous figures and more abstract forms, symbolic of the effusion of her actual making. Completed by ethereal abstract painting on the wall, full of exuberant colour and life, this exhibition, successfully toured, represented a kind of apotheosis, not only of Brown's essential optimism, but of her vocation in ceramics, her ability to release ideas through clay and glaze. Brown has always made a virtue of 'playing' with her materials, and this childlike sense of wonder is what makes her pots so powerfully exhilarating.

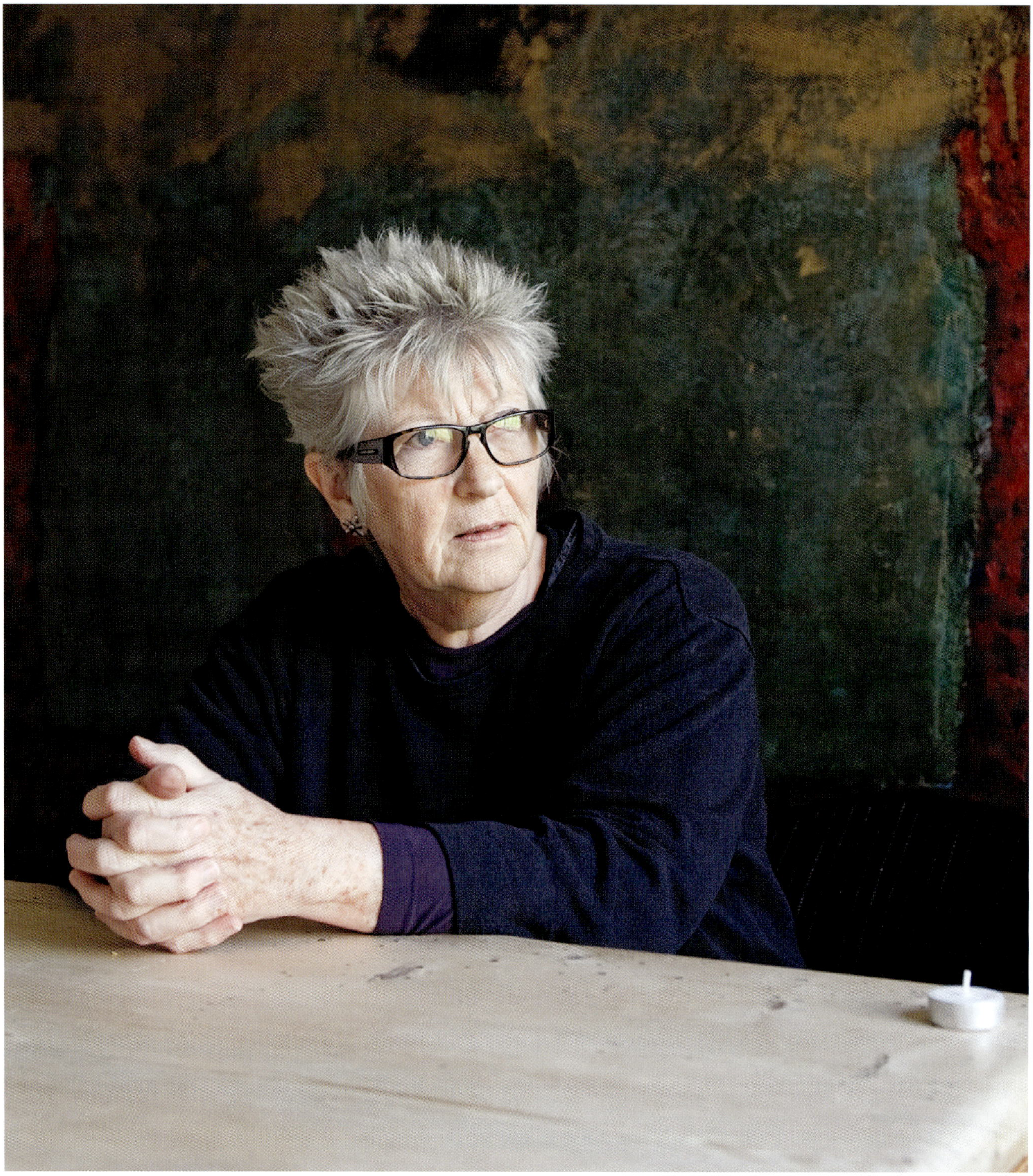

Jane Hamlyn

Jane Hamlyn is one of the most reflective of British potters, someone who, at a time when the sale of domestic pots has seen a sharp decline, has been thinking long and hard about the present and future of studio pottery and its continuing relevance to modern life. Born in 1940, she emerged as a maker in the mid-1970s, the product of an exemplary vocational throwing course at Harrow School of Art in north London, at a time when domestic pottery was undergoing a renaissance. While in the period since she has done a certain amount of teaching, Hamlyn has remained primarily at the coalface, surviving principally on her superb salt-glaze pots. She has exhibited regularly all over the world, but sells largely from the premises, mainly from the annual open-studio exhibition she shares with her husband, the painter Ted Hamlyn, Jane's technician, kiln builder and right-hand man. She is naturally interrogative and self-critical, not only about the nature of her work, but about the life it will lead beyond the pottery. She is intrigued by the various ways in which pots function at a time when the role and definition of craft has changed and expanded. With the gallery and market demand for more individual objects in ceramics, often with a basis in function, Hamlyn has responded with new developments in her pots, the result also of her natural curiosity about form, colour and space as it can be expressed in clay.

There is an enviable sense of integration about Millfield Pottery, in the small village of Everton near Doncaster, where Hamlyn and her husband have been based since 1975. They live in an attractive red-brick cottage with ample outbuildings for their studios and an imaginatively planted garden. The flower borders show an eye sensitive to form, hue and detail, which has long been a hallmark of Hamlyn's ceramics. Though Hamlyn has been much absorbed by her individual cylinders, or 'empty vessels' as she calls them, since they were first conceived at the beginning of this century, she remains loyal and dedicated to the domestic wares that made her reputation, the lively, well-designed items she has produced for the table for over 30 years. One cannot but compare her centred down-to-earth attitude with that of those who have forsaken tablewares for some 'higher' brand of ceramic art. Hamlyn makes no such judgements of value or hierarchy. Producing pots is, or should be, an egalitarian activity. She does recognise, however, that these two areas of her craft have independent roles. They are related but different.

Unlike many other pots that are essentially sculptural in character, the 'empty vessels' have their roots firmly in a functional tradition. They are the result of a particular wheel-based craft discipline. Essentially broad, leaning containers, thrown and altered to a rounded oval shape, they are robust objects, exploring the most basic and simple forms of cylinder, just as the late Michael Casson's monumental jugs proclaimed their particular essence of 'jugness'. They made a big impact when first exhibited, for here was an innovative kind of controlled throwing – voluminous structures that make one think about the face of the clay and enclosed space in quite a new way. Collectively, they give the areas in which they stand a remarkable architectural energy and rhythm. The term 'empty vessel' is multi-layered, combining superficial description with a more probing commentary on the function of these pieces, in a way that is typical of Hamlyn's enquiring pragmatism.

The vessels are superb as pieces of sculpture, satisfying in a purely aesthetic sense as one experiences these objects

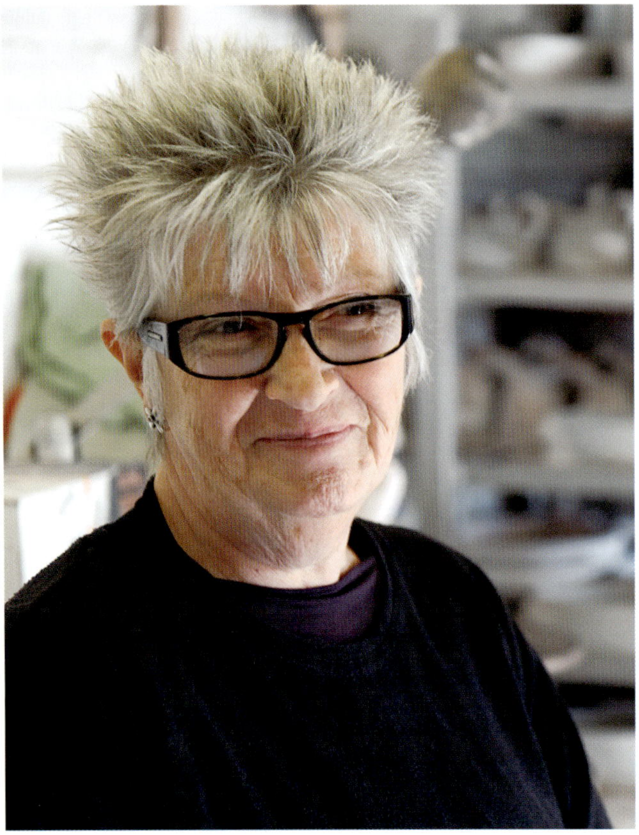

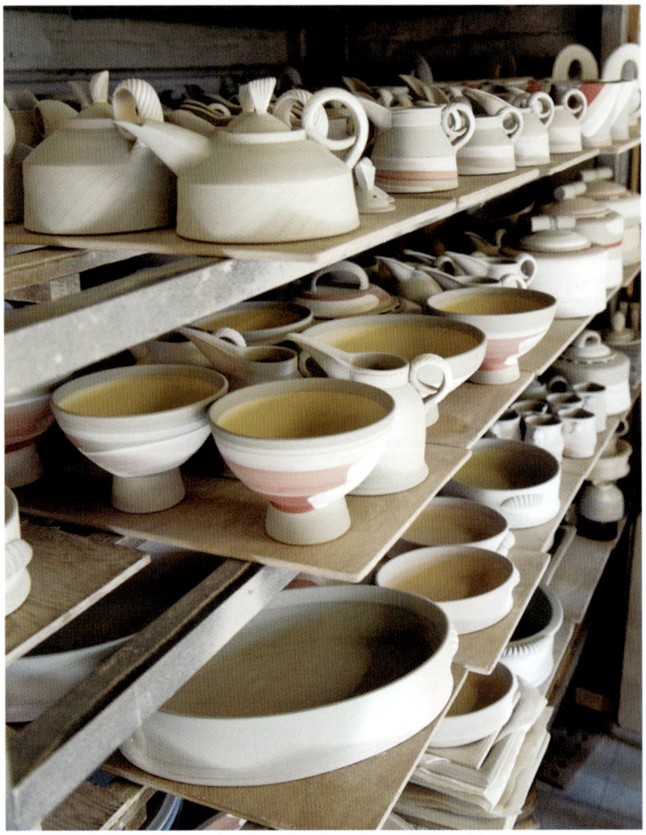

individually or in choreographed sequential groups, with their varied spatial interactions of volume, their sensitive contrasts and unities of colour. Looking at the deep oxides and slips, variously matt and lustrous, one gets a powerful sense of how the most abstract conceptions can engage the eye. However, they also have great resolution and clarity as pots, with some of the qualities of the metal sculpture of Richard Serra made domestic and tactile. A refreshing antidote to the plethora of installation porcelain popular over the last decade, which has made its impact largely through sheer weight of numbers, these 'empty vessels' are nevertheless large in scale. Their skilful leans and tensions are taxing and time-consuming to make, with the result that they are highly priced, and Hamlyn recognises that their form and expense may limit their audience. Meanwhile her recent 'closed narrative' pots, vases that narrow towards the lip, have an obvious function to which people can more easily relate. They seem to bridge the parallel aspects of her current work. Hamlyn has developed some superb new glazes – mottled greys, inky blues and green–yellows, along with vivid matt oranges, rust reds and ochres. They are a perfect foil to the increasingly pared-down austerity of her pots. Hamlyn, a pioneer of the salt-glaze revival (along with such ex-Harrow potters as Walter Keeler and Peter Starkey), recognises its continuing popularity amongst younger potters. It makes her keen to move away from the more familiar notions of the technique, to broaden her exploration and look ahead. In this spirit, she has achieved rich new surfaces and chromatics, showing just how versatile the effects of salt can be.

The Harrow ethos remains very strong in Hamlyn's work. It is there in the decorative form and texture of her plates, dishes, teapots, bowls and jugs – objects that really enhance the everyday rituals. She has developed a reputation for playful, quite baroque combinations of technique (adding modelled handles, rouletting and extruded elements),

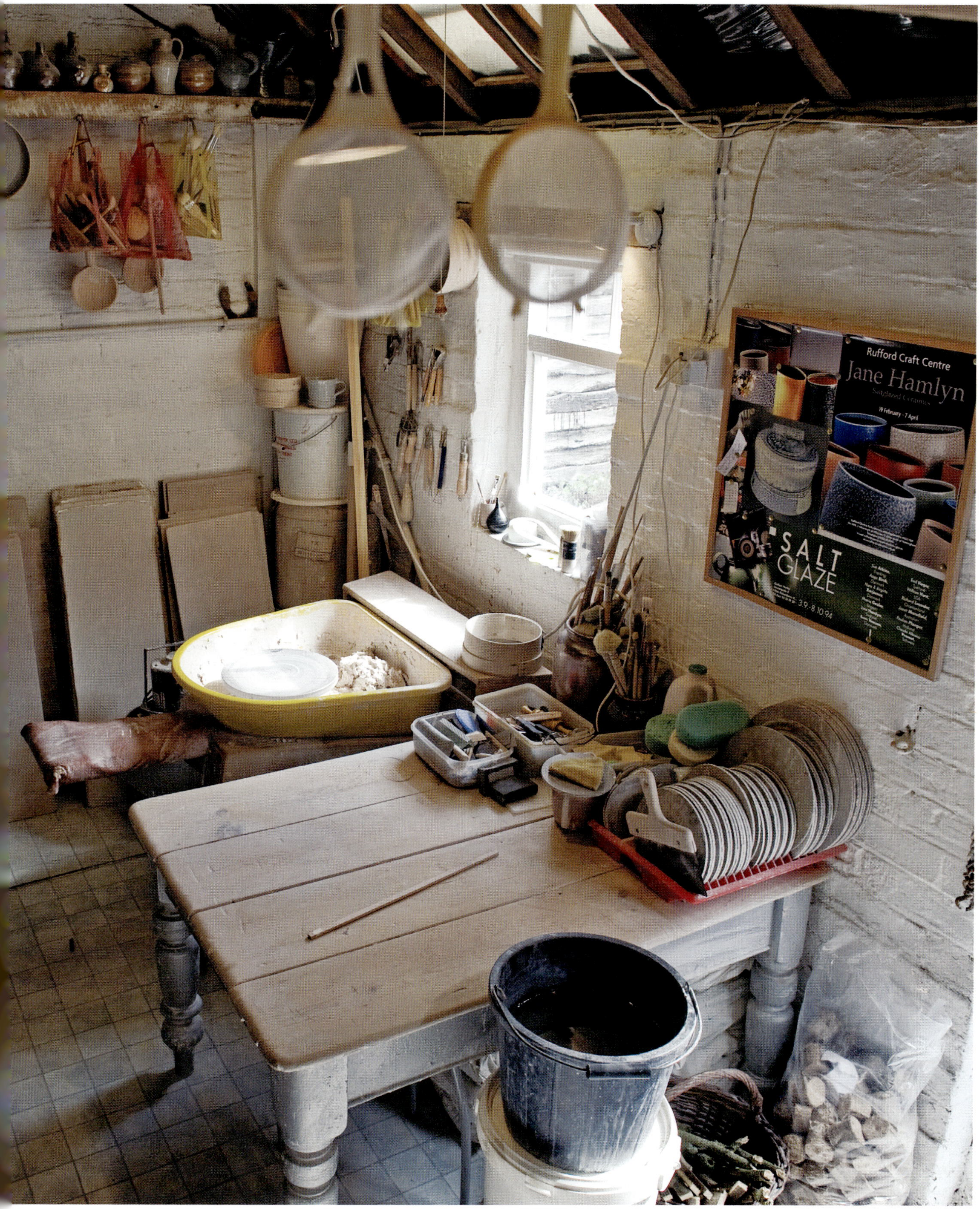
Rufford Craft Centre
Jane Hamlyn
Saltglazed Ceramics
19 February - 7 April
SALT
GLAZE
3.9.-8.10.94

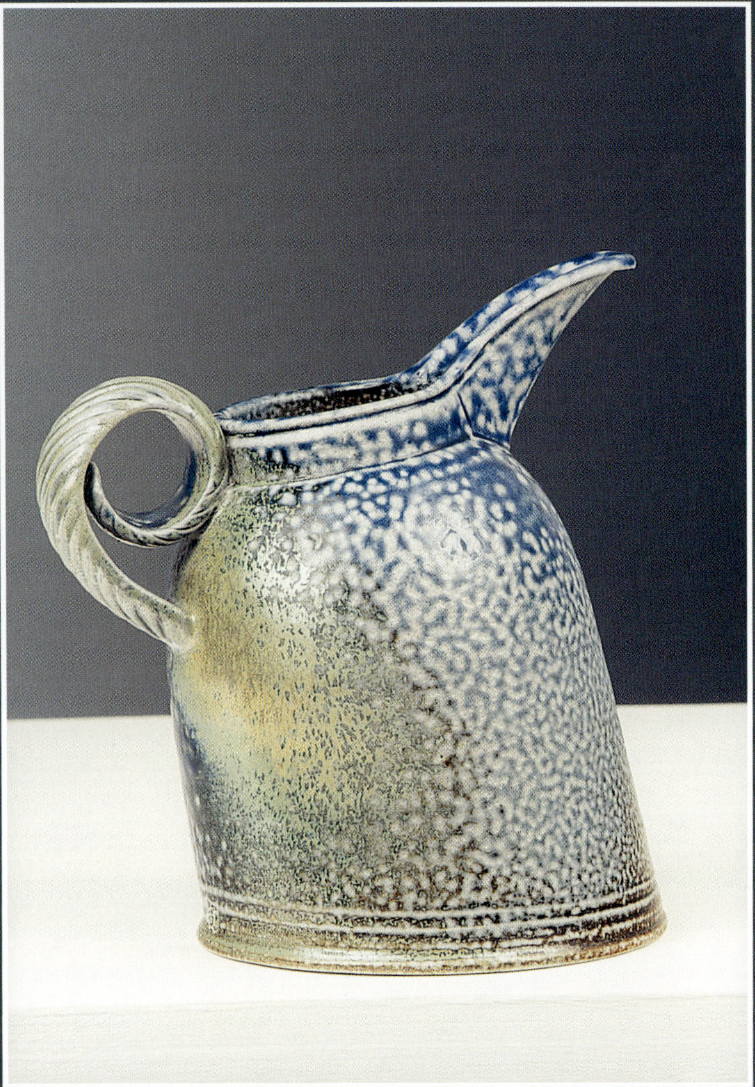

Jug, 2006, saltglazed stoneware. Height: 18cm (7in).
Photos: Courtesy of the artist

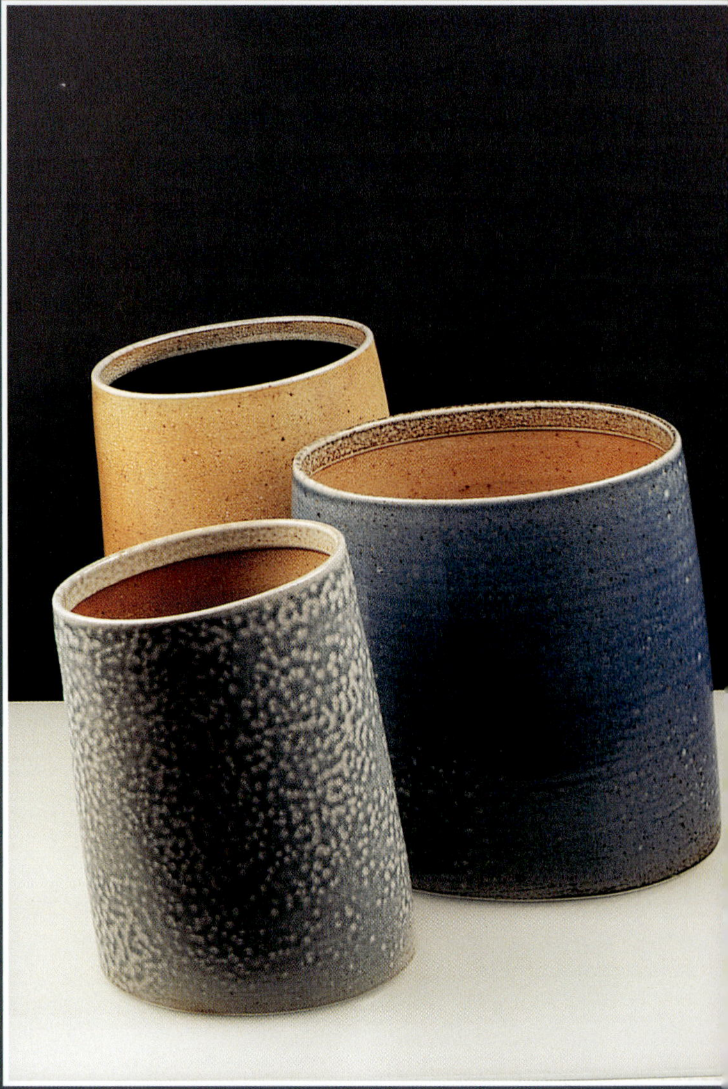

Empty Vessels, *2006, saltglazed stoneware. Height: 24, 20 and 18cm (9½, 8 and 7in).*

but the recent cylinders have introduced a greater simplicity to her work as a whole. One thinks particularly of her abstracted lidded jars with scroll handles and beaky spouts, and her generous, succinct deep dishes. She works well on a small scale, too, feeling that 'if one gets beyond a certain size the pot can lose conviction', a wise philosophy to which some other potters might do well to subscribe. It underlines her feeling for the potential intimacy of ceramics. For her the successful pot is a coveted, much-handled object, personal in its making, use and ownership. One can be very proprietorial about a favourite mug, she points out. At the same time she is the first to admit when certain items don't function as well as she would like – but Hamlyn is still keen to make them if they have good decorative qualities, which is after all another aspect of their usage.

Hamlyn is an intelligent and perceptive writer, both about her own work and about the crafts in general. She is interested in the different and shifting contexts in which

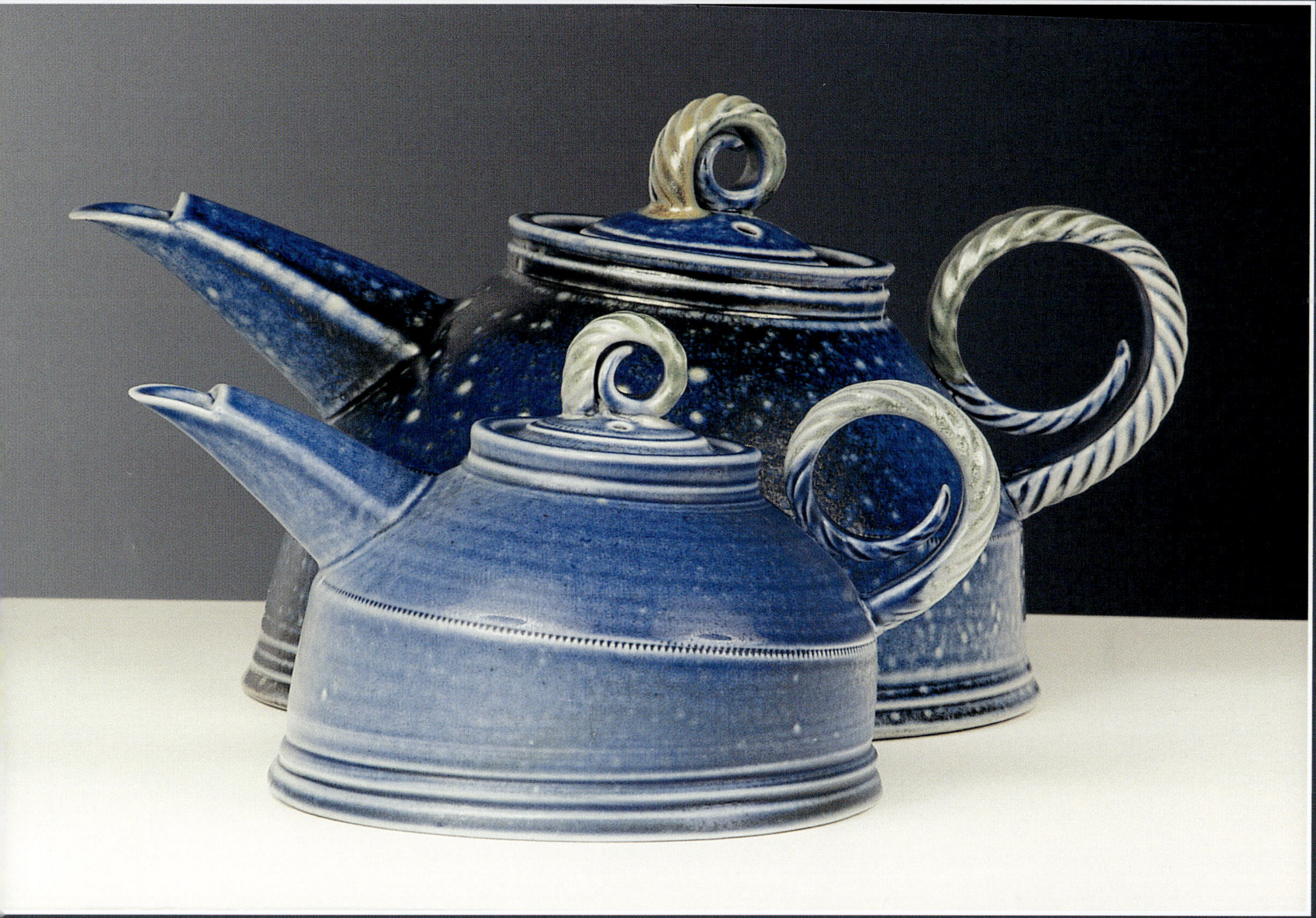

Teapots, *2006, saltglazed stoneware. Height: 13cm and 9cm (5in. and 3½in.).*
Photo: Courtesy of the artist

studio ceramics exist, in the people who sell and own them, and what they personally derive from their involvement. For some it may be a way of vicariously buying into a potter's very different mode of life; for others it may be the broader resonances that come with the pot, the chance that such objects may offer some form of consolation or release. It is because Hamlyn wants to do her job, fulfil her role, as effectively as she can, that these questions matter. She is, in essence, a humanist, one who wants to improve individual and collective experience through the pots she makes. In this age of hurry, information overload and cultural fragmentation, her work asks you to pause and digest, to make time for the important family ceremonies of eating and drinking. Hamlyn's design and making skills convey a particular sense of care, of detail and balance, an integration that instils a true respect for and appreciation of domestic life. This is what functional pottery should be about.

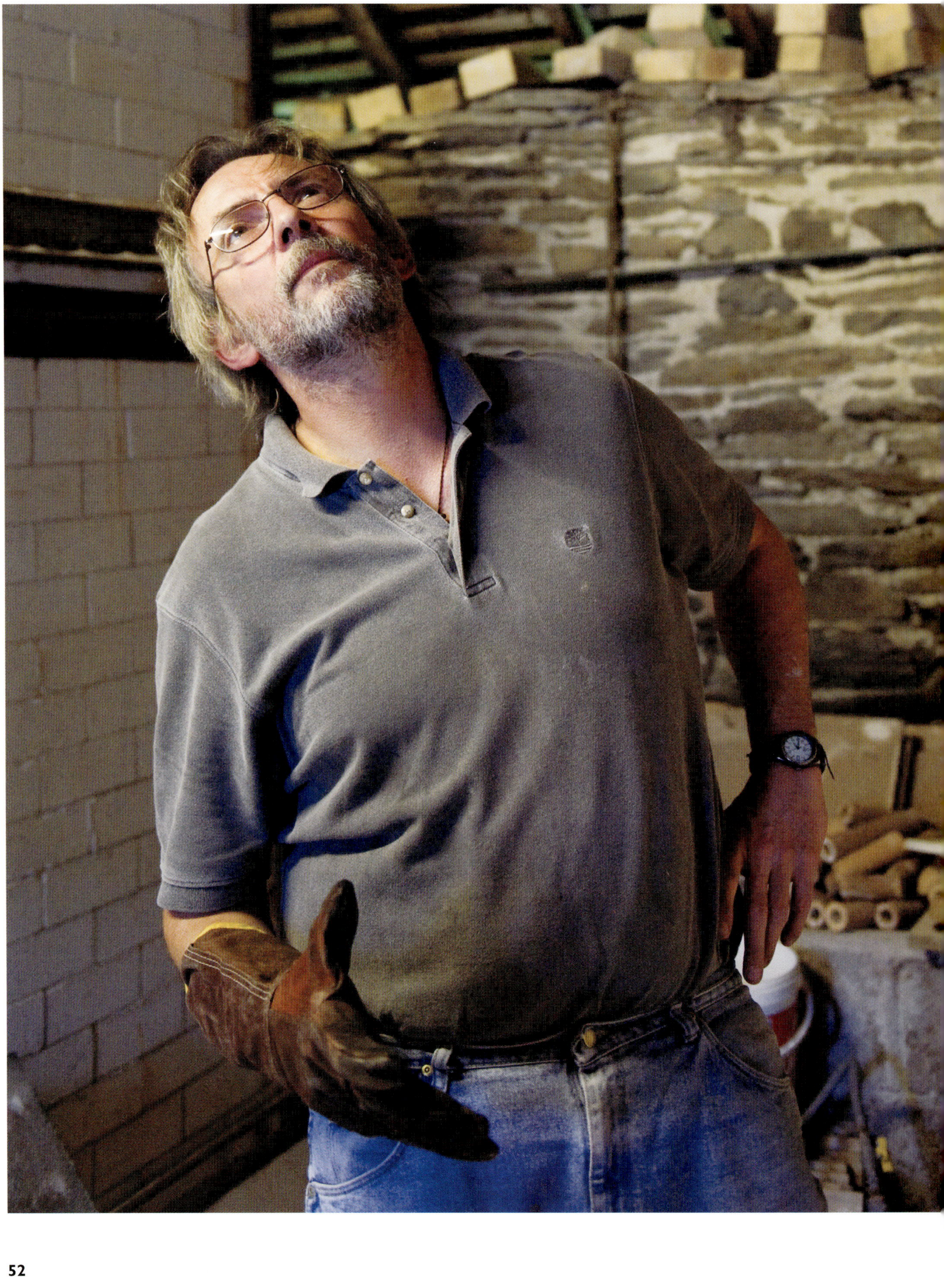

Phil Rogers

PHIL ROGERS MAKES HIS pots at Rhayader, in a beautiful stretch of mid-Wales. He has been here for over 30 years, though he settled at Cefn Faes Farm on a hill outside the town – some 1,000 feet above sea level – more recently, in 1984. Rogers is an inveterate traveller. He has exhibited and given workshops internationally, particularly in the USA, and has made extended trips to Korea and Japan, where he is also now showing his work. However, it is to this beautiful valley overlooking the River Wye that he always returns, and which gives his work such a significant sense of place, of rootedness. The farm provided ample outbuildings for conversion into a pottery, with the stone cow house ideal for the workshop and an adjacent stable converted into a kiln shed. Rogers has three kilns – one for salt, an oil-fired reduction kiln and, more recently, a wood-fired two-chambered structure – reflecting his love of the firing cycle and its integral role in his aesthetic. The abiding presence of the river and its hilly hinterland is a crucial point of reference both for his creative eye and for the essential, elemental character of his pots. With their vigorous forms and natural glazes, they echo the hues and surfaces of what the Welsh poet R.S. Thomas called the 'silence of the mountains', and the greener foothills and pastures below.

What is in a location? A great deal, where most artists are concerned. But for a potter like Phil Rogers the workplace needs to be considered in broader terms, when it provides you with so many of your raw components. In Phil's case it is a major source of his slips and glazes, the variety of tree species around the farm – including pine and beech, oak and ash – providing a good supply of wood ash. As Rogers once wrote, 'Like many other rural makers, these two aspects of my life – my work and immediate surroundings – are inexorably linked.' The significance of Rogers's kind of pottery goes well beyond the object – encapsulating geography, geology and chemistry as well as stylistic philosophy and the values of function.

Rogers was part of a small but rich flowering of Leachian potters who emerged in the 1970s – a group who resisted some of the more general trends existing at the time, which tended towards more overtly sculptural, colourful and ornamental work. Like many in the Leach School, Rogers made some domestic production alongside more individual pots, but these days, with the decline in demand for tablewares, he concentrates primarily on exhibition pieces – noble bottles, bowls, big dishes and jugs that operate primarily as objects of useful sculpture. It is precisely Rogers's strength of experience, working on repeated shapes, that gives his work, from jars and chargers to teabowls and yunomis, its inherent rhythm and balance, qualities found in the depth of the wheel and also in Rogers's respect for and knowledge of his materials and their constituent parts. If he often singles out Katharine Pleydell-Bouverie and Richard Batterham as exemplars, it is because he follows the same kind of empirical life, experimenting with different processes and finding his own unique unions of form and surface, which refresh and revitalise tradition. In Rogers's case he looks to a taproot of English medieval pots, early Chinese and Korean ceramics and the best of Japanese country pottery. He is also a keen admirer of English and Welsh slipware, and has a high regard for that of local extraction made at Buckley and Ewenny.

Born in 1951 in Newport, Rogers studied at Swansea College of Art in the early 1970s before going to Cambridgeshire to teach art and pottery. He learnt the basics of

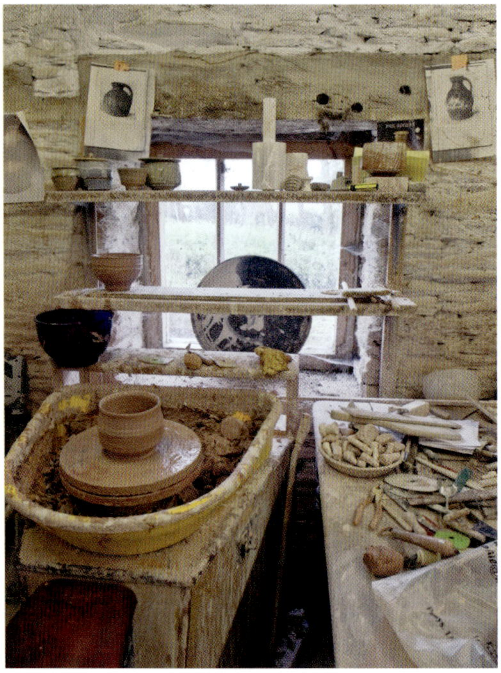

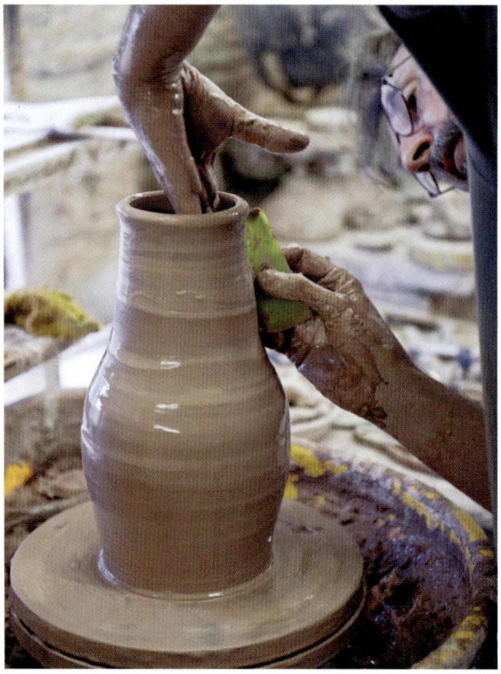

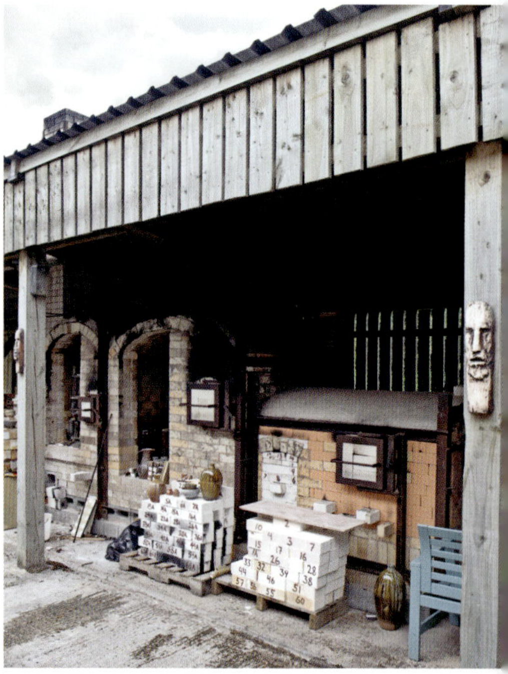

throwing and series production at Swansea, but for the rest is largely self-taught; like so many, his primary technical and philosophical guide has been Bernard Leach's *A Potter's Book*. East Anglia had its benefits (for example, discovering the wonderful collection of oriental pots in the Fitzwilliam Museum) but the day job left little time for his own work. The need to return to Wales was great. Rhayader offered not only creative solitude but the space to devote his whole life to pots. Over the years since he made that decision, his focus has deepened, the shapes and surfaces have become more fluid and relaxed, with the kind of integration and rhythmic tempo that results from a long process of editing and refinement.

Rogers's exhibitions have a remarkable unity. Glazing is rich but economic, augmented by equally succinct yet energetic marking – combing, resist, engraving and wiping being used to add waves of movement to the inner current of the form. He explores the various depths of his numerous ashes – his nukas, hakames and tenmokus – some of which he uses in combination. His salt-firing allows the warm burnt texture of the clay to speak even more directly – with areas left unglazed – forcefully expressing the passage of salt and flame. Clearly there has been a need on Rogers's part to get down to a core vocabulary that exemplifies what the critic Herbert Read called 'the essentials of this most abstract art'.

Rogers's jugs epitomise this spirit, achieving a balance and flow not easy to achieve in so complex an object. They have all 'the asymmetry of organic form', as the painter Patrick Heron described it when discussing the structural character of pottery. This is very apparent in their sense of growth, inclining and expanding into space. They explore the inherent tensions within ceramics – between the swelling and contraction of the body, and the lift and pull of the handle. Such pots become expressive without being about *self*-expression, a Leachian distinction that puts the craft before the craftsman. Rogers often adds sprigs or ridges to provide a kind of visual notation and surface activity, but without hindering the general sweep of contour or expanse of glaze. His variously sized and shaped bottles further demonstrate the infinite variation within the parameters of one type of form – pots that can be slab-built or thrown, which may be modified by faceting and ridging or by the height or thickness of a neck. His directional marking adds to that immediate sense of the potter's hand, and to the particular 'tremor' and energy of each pot.

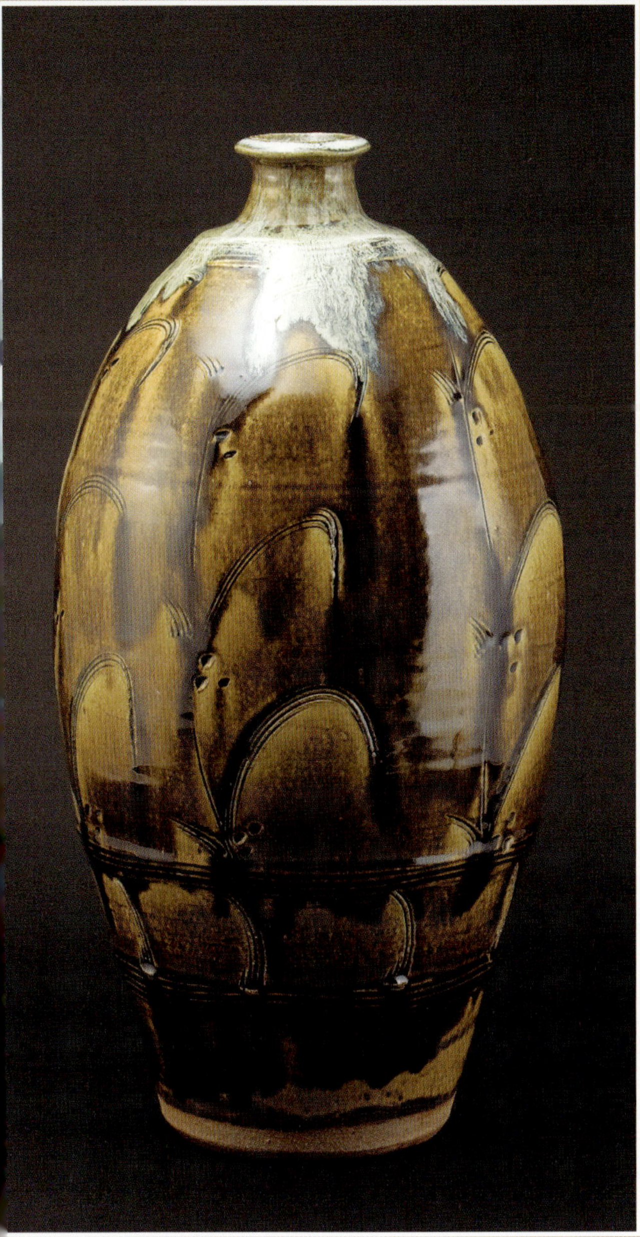

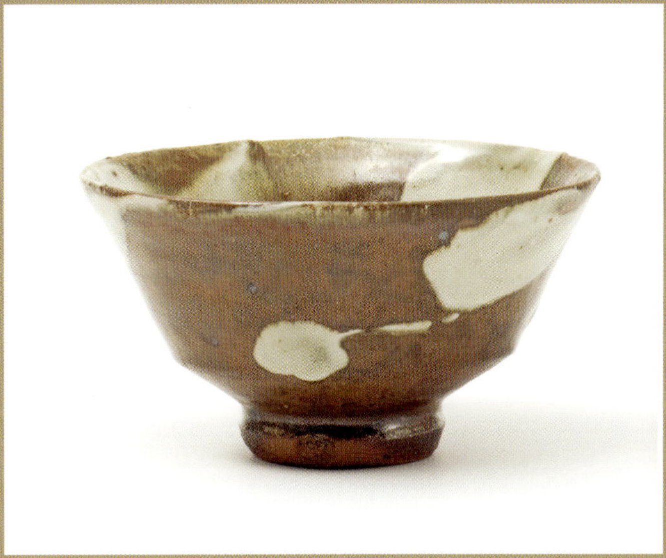

far left: Tall Bottle, *2008, stoneware. Height: 49cm (19¼in).*
left: Chawan, *2008, stoneware. Height: 9cm (3½in).*
Photos: Jay Goldmark, courtesy of Goldmark Gallery

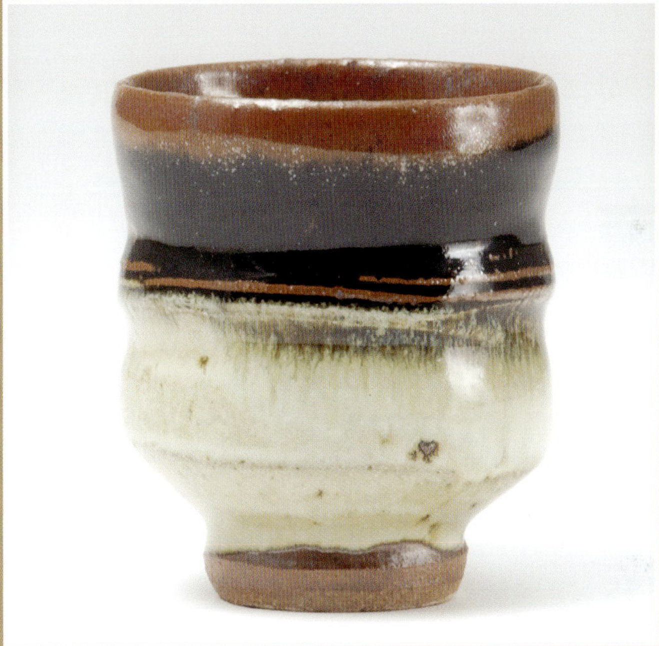

left: Yunomi, *2008, stoneware. Height: 10cm (25½in).*
Photo: Jay Goldmark, courtesy of Goldmark Gallery

Rogers shows how much can be achieved with glaze alone. His tenmokus and ashes layer and pool, they gather in the incisions made in the clay, accumulating in wells and around bases. The varying depth of a glaze, its changing nature as it travels over a surface, reveals its own surprises of colour and texture. His experimentation becomes more obvious in his teabowls and yunomis. They sum up most intimately and succinctly Rogers's sense of search, demonstrating in very personal and concentrated form his ability to play and to improvise – cut-siding, incising or impressing, applying a translucent ash or a dark iron. Small pots allow more adventure, as the risks aren't so great. As a consequence, these highly charged little bowls and cups are amongst the most rewarding objects he makes. You discover something new each time you look at and handle them: the freedom and quiet asymmetries, the tactility of their carving and cutting, the way one glaze breaks into another, spilling and trickling over the form. You begin to understand what continually draws Phil Rogers back to his workshop in search of that ever-better pot: the enduring quest for beauty in regenerated tradition.

Walter Keeler

WALTER KEELER is a north Londoner by birth who now lives in south-west Wales at Penallt, not far from Monmouth. His studio occupies one of a number of outbuildings on an extensive site in this remote and beautiful part of the borderland, where he and his wife Madoline, herself a distinguished potter, established a modest smallholding when they came here in the mid-seventies. One of the studio spaces is crowded with recently made pots and accumulated source material. Here are some of the objects from which he has derived ideas for his ceramics and which have given him creative sustenance, not only various items of historical salt glaze but also metal objects, oil cans with articulated spouts and other hardware. Keeler, for all his indebtedness to the history of ceramics – from Roman pottery to 18th-century Fulham wares – has drawn from a much broader world of architecture and industrial artefacts and archaeology for his highly original, constantly evolving, functional style, one that has helped to reinvent the vocabulary of wheel-thrown tableware.

Born in 1942, Keeler has been a pioneer, not only of new techniques, creating a new type of 'liberated' throwing through cutting and assembling, but of a spectacular new language for domestic pottery. Today Keeler has his imitators, but it is difficult for anyone else to approach his precision of craftsmanship. Yet his philosophy is down- to-earth: if his work is regarded as art, all well and good, but it is the *craft* of design and making that draws him – and in this sense he is probably as much a child of the industrial workshop (which part of his studio rather resembles) as he is of ceramic history and craft practice.

Now in his late sixties, and still youthfully passionate about what he does, Keeler sees endless possibilities for his medium. He was a student and then colleague of Michael Casson and Victor Margrie at Harrow School of Art, and his experiments on the college campus in the late 1960s, testing vapour glazes in numerous kilns he built on the site, have since entered ceramics mythology. From the outset his projects reflected not only his fascination with technology and process, but more broadly the exciting new directions ceramics was now moving in. When he set up his first pottery at Bledloe Ridge in Buckinghamshire in the mid-sixties, he made salt-glaze pots of assembled sections which were highly original and idiosyncratic, objects of joins and junctions that already betrayed his fascination with articulation. It wasn't the kind of organic throwing associated with Bernard Leach, more a sense that he was conjoining pieces from his engineer's workbench – a reconstitution of parts, of the sort of shards he collected on the Thames Estuary as a youth.

Once he had settled into a strictly functional routine after his move to Wales in 1976 (a conversation with the potter Gordon Baldwin had helped convince him that function was still a potentially exciting area), and began to make well-designed, ash-glazed stonewares, it became obvious that the need to 'break up' and reintegrate conventional ceramic form would soon re-emerge. So began the development of the famously thrown and constructed salt glaze, Keeler soon producing a range of forms that moved well away from the 'brown mug' image still hampering British domestic ware. It was also work that broke down the odd dichotomy between the Leachian model of so-called 'individual' pots and workshop standard ware for the table.

Much functional pottery suffered from the rather puritanical notion that it could not, in itself, be exploratory: a jug is a jug, a cup is a cup. Keeler's work was to be a highly expressive reassessment of what function could mean,

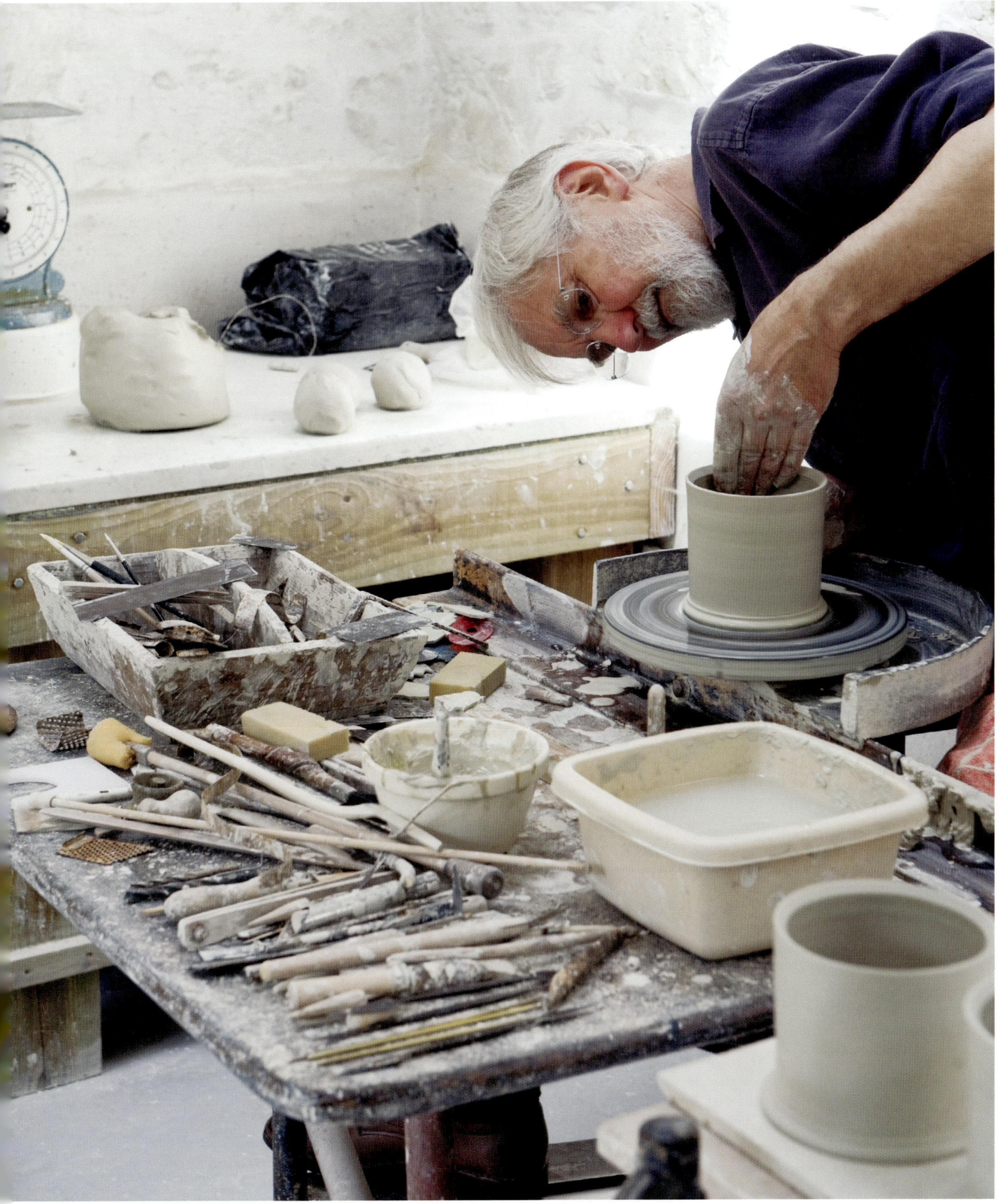

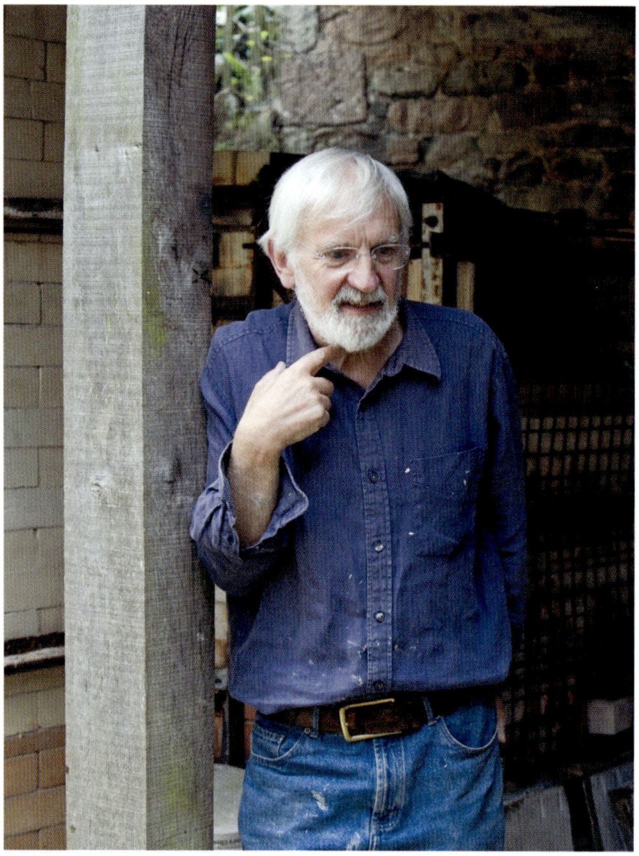

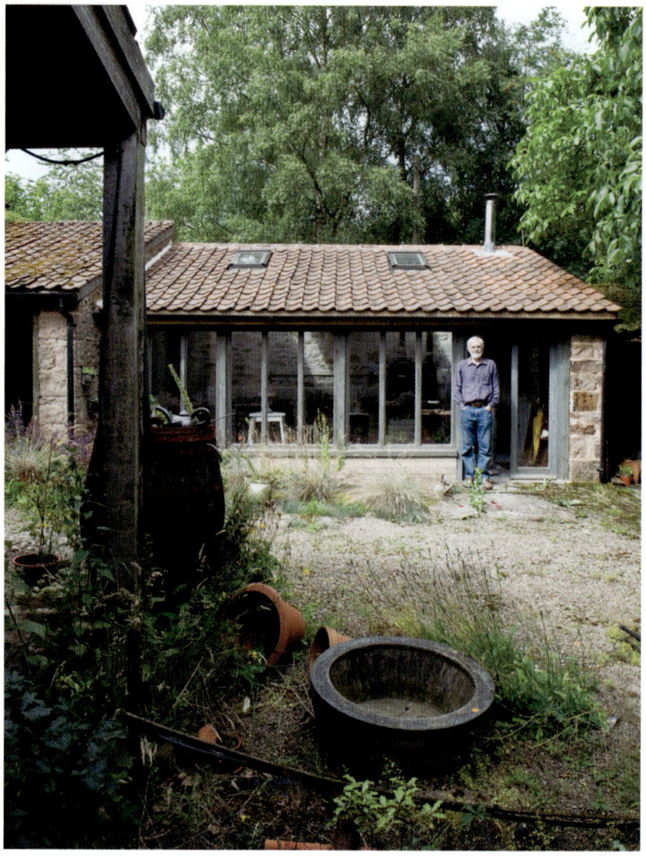

resulting in innovative teapots, jugs, dishes, lidded jars and cups in smooth and more mottled salt glaze, ranging from grey to dark blue in colour. They showed, as they developed in the 1980s, how engaging 'utility' could be. There were variously sized jugs with prominent beaky lips, and 'angular' and 'macaroni' teapots with powerful straight or curving extruded spouts. All had assertively looped balancing handles. Big dishes contrasted the centrifugal rhythms of throwing and turning with added extrusions that brought new integrations to the making process.

He derived ideas not only from Greek and Roman pots, early slipware and the clarities of salt glaze, but from other useful objects – 'from railwaymen's lamps to workhouse coffee pots with hinged lids' – as well as various glass and leather goods. While some have called this new direction, this new injection of personality, 'quirky' or 'novel', such phrases are misleading. From the outset Keeler's very serious quest has been to surprise and re-engage his audience, to make pots that are deeply conversational, involving us again in the delights not only of ceramic form and decoration but in the ceremonies of eating and drinking for which they were made.

While Keeler has never deviated from his interest in function or wheel-based construction, he is not so easy to categorise. He could easily have stayed with the now celebrated salt glaze which established his international reputation. But instead he has expanded, preferring to introduce concurrent areas of work rather than simply moving from one phase to another as, for example, the potter Takeshi Yasuda has done. In the 1990s, alongside the comparative austerity of the salt glaze, he introduced the flamboyance of his distinctly baroque Whieldon earthenware (recalling Thomas Whieldon's exotic 18th-century productions). Crabstock and Cutbranch teapots, Tripod, Hokey Cokey and Pedestal bowls, and Crown of Thorns dishes were all richly decorated in opulent peacock and tortoiseshell glazes. He

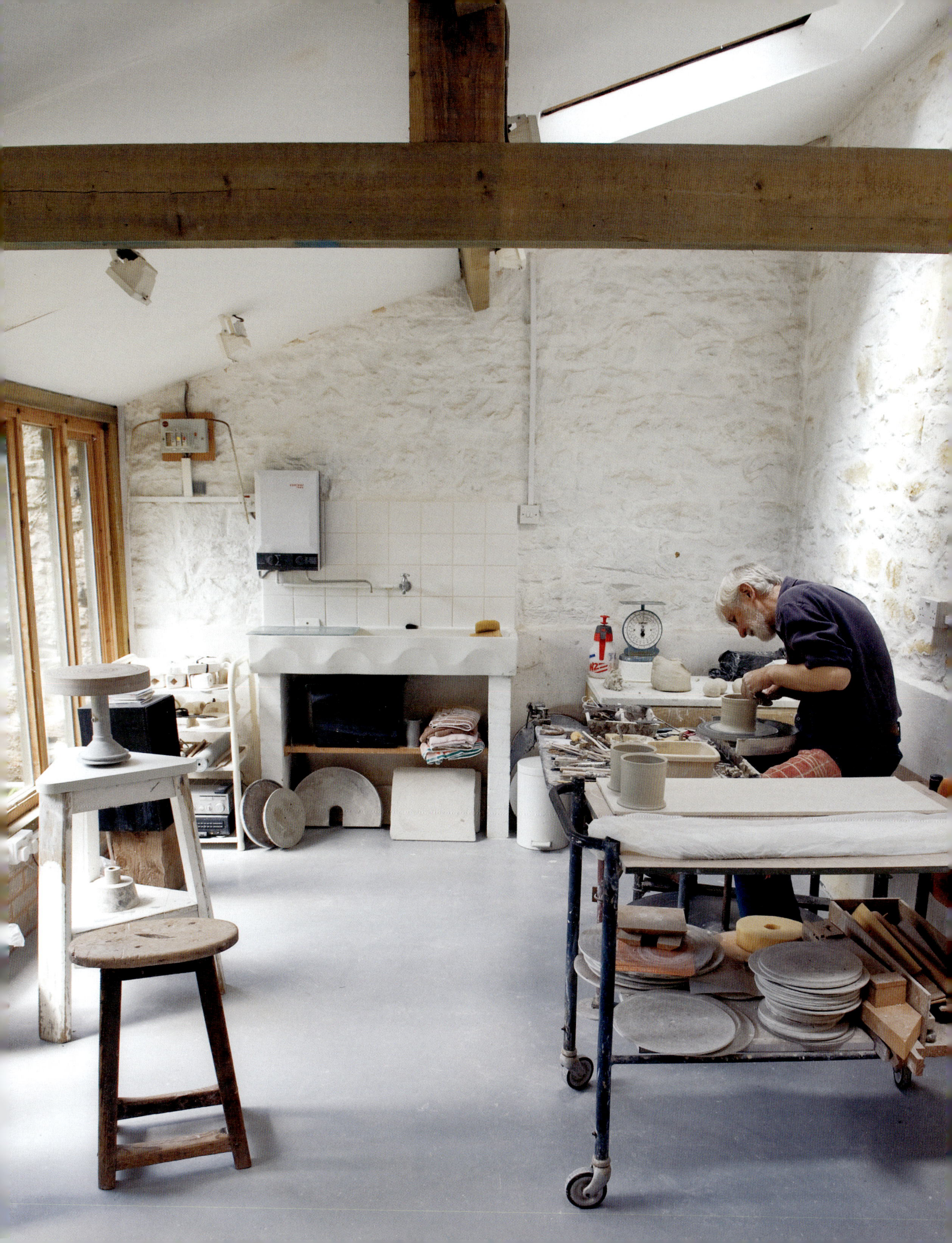

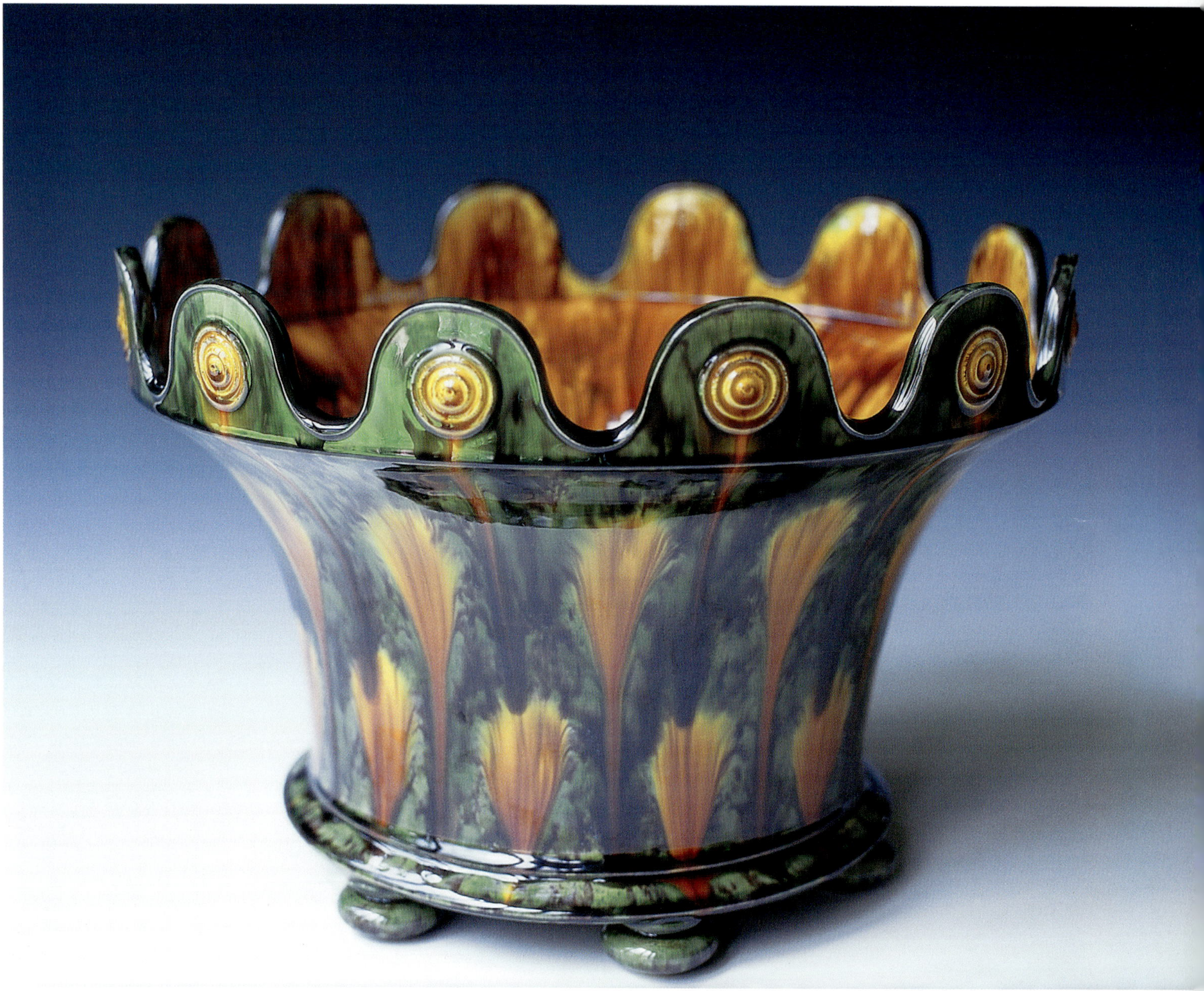

introduced broad plinth bases from which handles sprang, 'semi-detached' from the main cylinder, another example of how he dislocates and realigns the components of form. His ethereal creamwares are spare in surface but remain complex in shape, Keeler enjoying the fluidity of profile achieved in ribbon-like handles and rims that resemble the contours of Sydney Opera House.

Perhaps these more recent developments allow him a little relaxation from the long process of salt-firing, but he remains a perfectionist. There is no let-up in his consistent eye for detail, his consideration of all aspects of throwing and turning, cutting and joining, and the luxury of his glazing. His pots continually reassess the practical and sculptural possibilities of useful objects, sometimes taking his forms to the edge of function in his bid to provoke thoughtful responses. In this regard, as if needing to return to the more muted aspect of his palette, in 2003 he introduced his 'inkwash' pots, which are more closely related to the controlled surfaces of his salt glaze. Here is a new repertoire of teapots, jars and serving dishes with grey translucent glazing that concentrates the eye

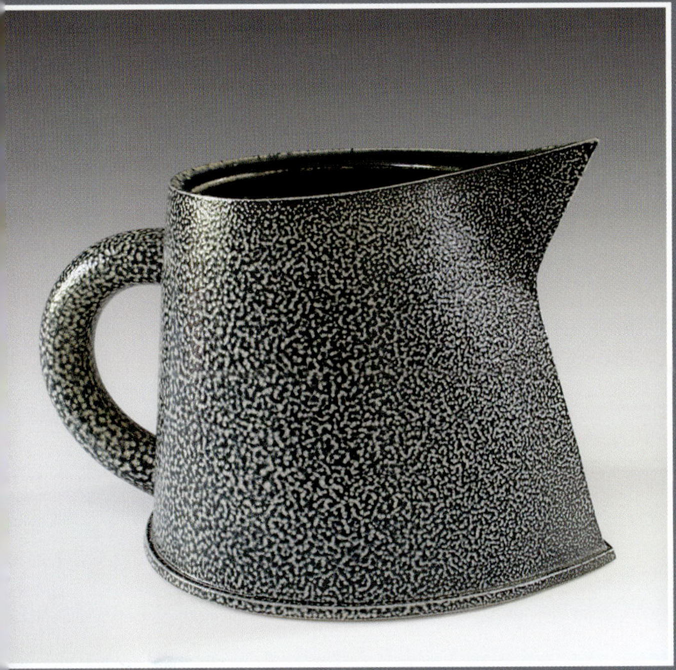

above: Beaky Jug, *2008, saltglaze stoneware.*
Height: 25cm (9¾in.).
Photo: Courtesy of the artist
right: Cutbranch Teapot, *2008, Whieldon earthenware.*
Height: 27cm (10½in.).
Photo: Courtesy of the artist
left: Montieth, *2004, Whieldon earthenware.*
Width: 36cm (14¼in.).
Photo: Dewi Tannant Lloyd

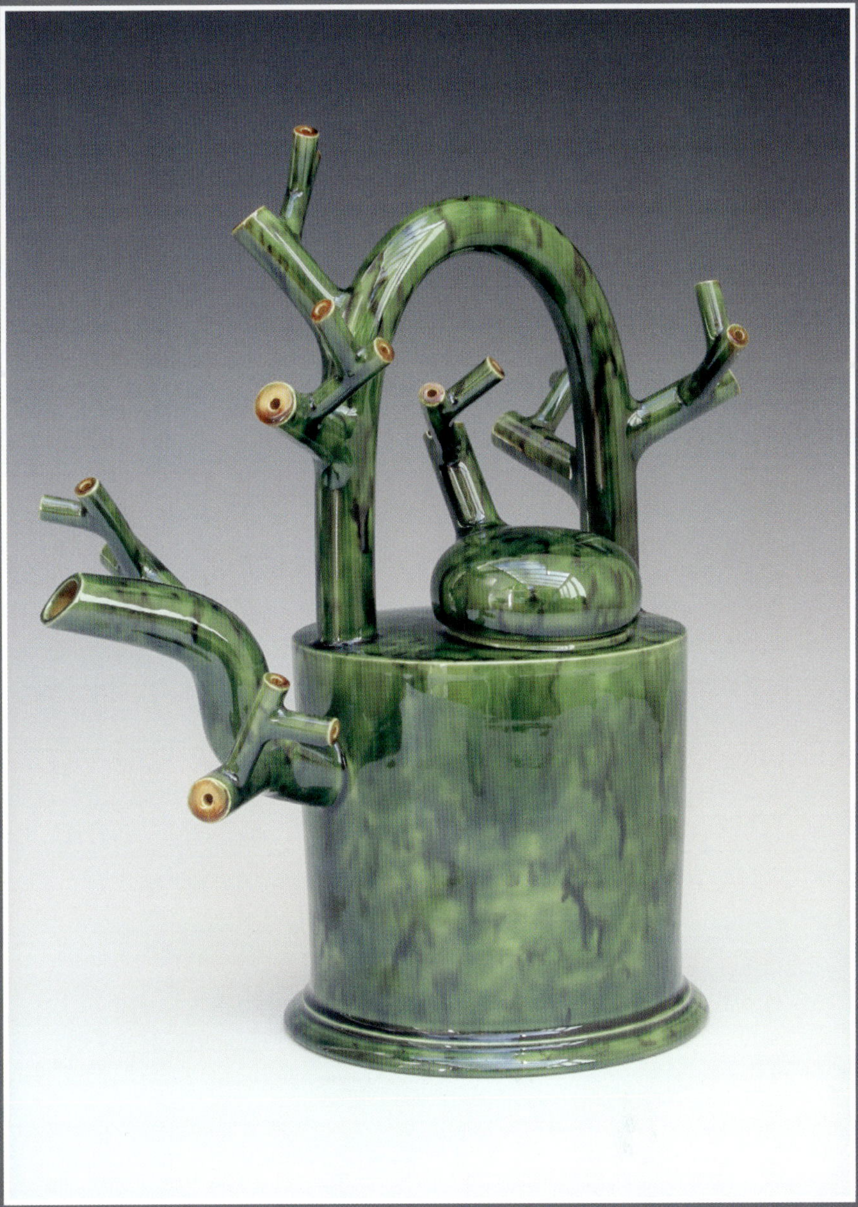

on the idiosyncrasies of form – convoluted handles and spouts, lids with unusual handles of joined sections. The salt glaze has itself become more rococo, more playful than ever.

If familiarity can occasionally breed indifference, Walter Keeler's work has, over the last four decades, striven to subvert this notion. His commitment to the domestic, both inside and outside the house (at the University of the West of England at Bristol, where he taught for over 25 years, Keeler completed a body of large pieces for the garden, planted out with flowers and grasses), has made him outspoken about the context of conventional exhibition display, in which he feels functional work often loses out because it breathes most easily in the household surroundings for which it was made. Certainly, today's curatorial climate seems unfairly biased in favour of the sculptural, with galleries often finding it difficult to display tablewares sympathetically – or confidently. Meanwhile Keeler is still extending the terms of the functional, what he has called the 'syntax' of ceramics, helping us to appreciate afresh the sensory role of useful pots in the way we live our lives.

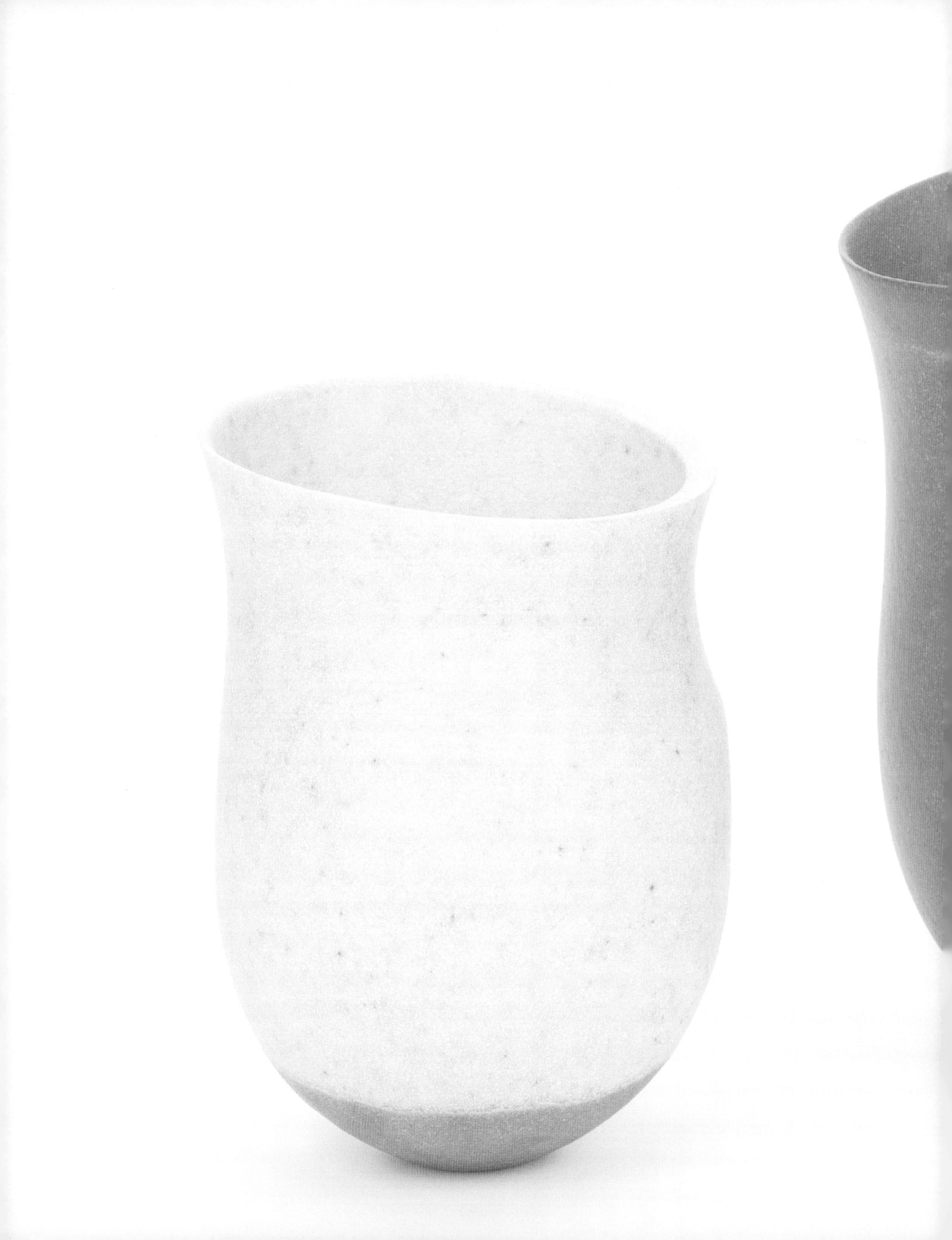

Part Two: The Sculptural Vessel

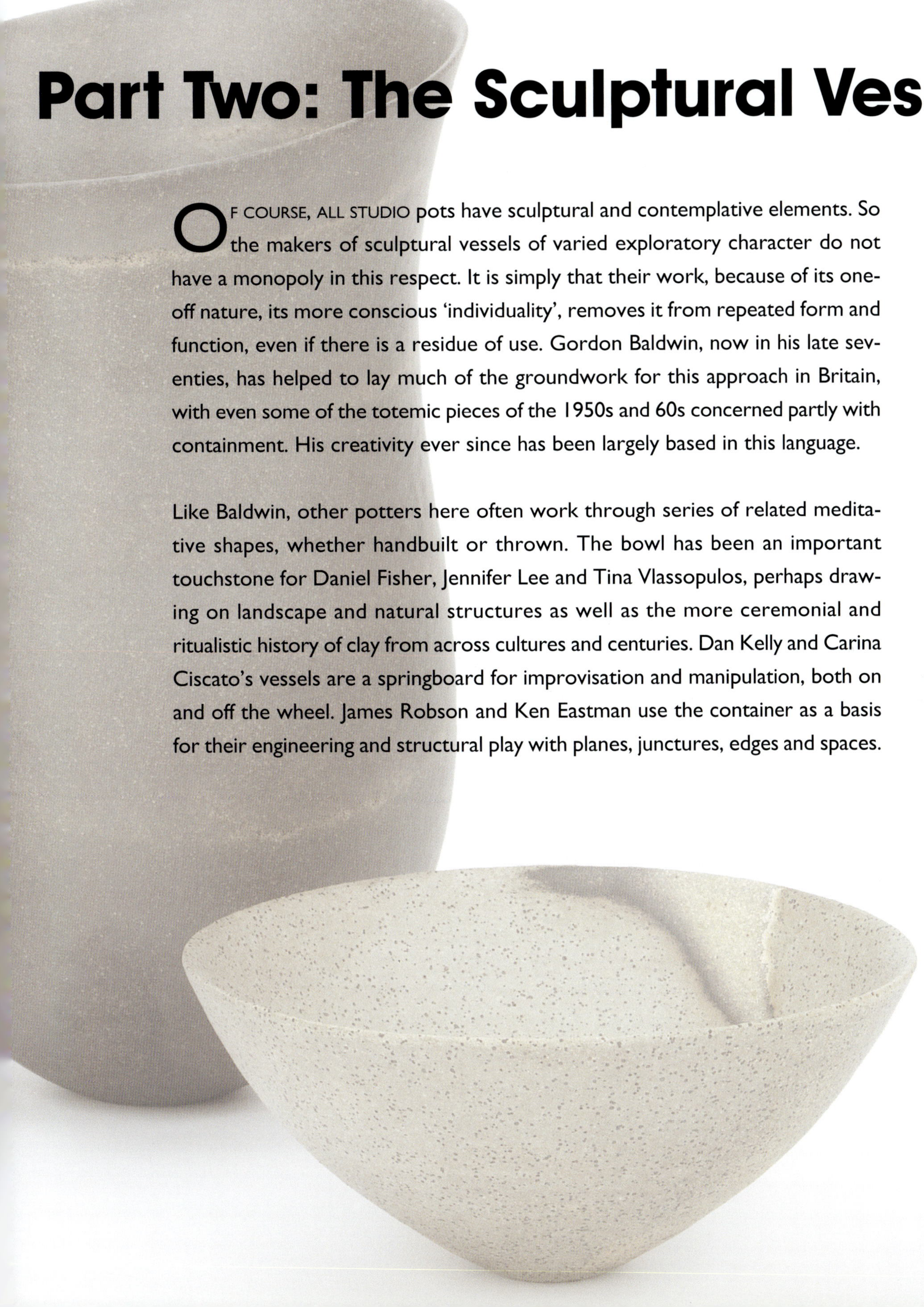

OF COURSE, ALL STUDIO pots have sculptural and contemplative elements. So the makers of sculptural vessels of varied exploratory character do not have a monopoly in this respect. It is simply that their work, because of its one-off nature, its more conscious 'individuality', removes it from repeated form and function, even if there is a residue of use. Gordon Baldwin, now in his late seventies, has helped to lay much of the groundwork for this approach in Britain, with even some of the totemic pieces of the 1950s and 60s concerned partly with containment. His creativity ever since has been largely based in this language.

Like Baldwin, other potters here often work through series of related meditative shapes, whether handbuilt or thrown. The bowl has been an important touchstone for Daniel Fisher, Jennifer Lee and Tina Vlassopulos, perhaps drawing on landscape and natural structures as well as the more ceremonial and ritualistic history of clay from across cultures and centuries. Dan Kelly and Carina Ciscato's vessels are a springboard for improvisation and manipulation, both on and off the wheel. James Robson and Ken Eastman use the container as a basis for their engineering and structural play with planes, junctures, edges and spaces.

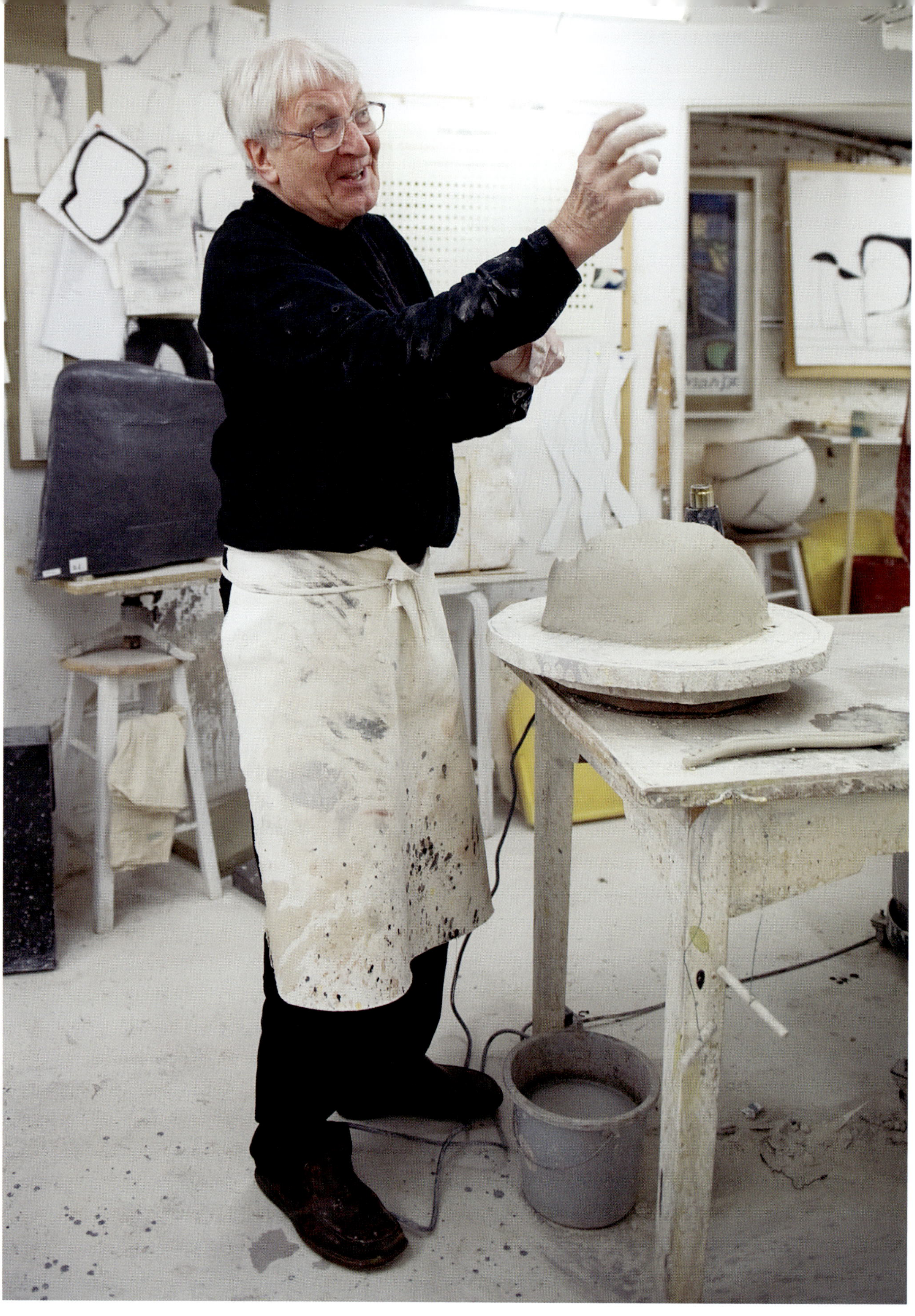

Gordon Baldwin

MUCH HAS BEEN made of the important legacy of Lucie Rie and Hans Coper in modern studio ceramics, how they helped to give throwing a different expressive voice in the 1950s, when Bernard Leach was still the predominant force in pottery. They were modernists of a different kind to Leach, whose own language, as many know, owed as much to the Far East as it did to medieval England. But there were also other throwers, builders and constructors who looked to the Continent and across the Atlantic for their ideas; some of this group were based and trained either at London's Institute of Education or, even more importantly, the Central School, two art colleges which did much to energise ceramics education after the Second World War. These teachers and students also took much inspiration from outside ceramics, from exciting contemporary developments in painting and sculpture, to find a quite different expressive voice for clay, one that grew and progressed through the fifties and sixties. Out of this particular nucleus one thinks of, among others, William Newland, James Tower, Ian Auld, Ruth Duckworth, Dan Arbeid, Gillian Lowndes, Nicholas Vergette and, of course, Gordon Baldwin.

Baldwin, born in Lincolnshire in 1932, emerged as a major talent in the mid-fifties, yet still remains at the forefront of handbuilding, with his work continuing to challenge and provoke the viewer. He began as a potter, and his early, rather menacing totemic pieces were obliquely figurative, with strong elements of surreal biomorphism, echoing some of the broader sculptural ideas of the time, seen in artists like William Turnbull and Eduardo Paolozzi, both of whom visited the Central School when Baldwin was there. However, by the 1960s, Baldwin was concentrating on quite different types of form – from open bowls and assembled structures to virtually closed pieces, some with the smallest of openings, the narrowest of slits allowing access to their dark, hidden interiors – exploring volume for both its sculptural and symbolic qualities. What has gradually emerged since has been a preoccupation with the vessel, with its different connotations and meanings.

Gordon Baldwin was brought up in a windswept landscape edged by the North Sea. He attended Lincoln School of Art before enrolling at the Central School. Baldwin, who had seafarers among his forebears, has remained an artist who explores space, sound and the elements, someone for whom particular conjunctions of land and sea have been of critical importance in his imagination. There is the coast of his childhood, but also that of Wales, most particularly the Lleyn Peninsula, where the relationship of its stony beaches to the sky and water have been a crucial trigger. More recently the Shropshire Hills have played their part. But it is also the landscape of music – and his interests here have been largely contemporary (Steve Reich, John Adams, John Cage, Karlheinz Stockhausen) – that has influenced the form and direction of his pots and vessels, their volumes and rhythms, and the complex nature of their surfaces.

Baldwin is absorbed by the primordial aspects of the visual and aural world which has drawn him to the understated and the minimal, both in nature and in music. In art this is reflected in his admiration for the archetypal sculpture of Ancient Egypt and the shifting, amorphic art of Klee, Fontana and Arp. At their most painterly his surfaces have an abstraction, a way of marking, which recalls American painters like Robert Motherwell, Richard Diebenkorn and Robert Ryman.

There is also no real distinction to be made between painting and sculpture in Baldwin's work; the two- and

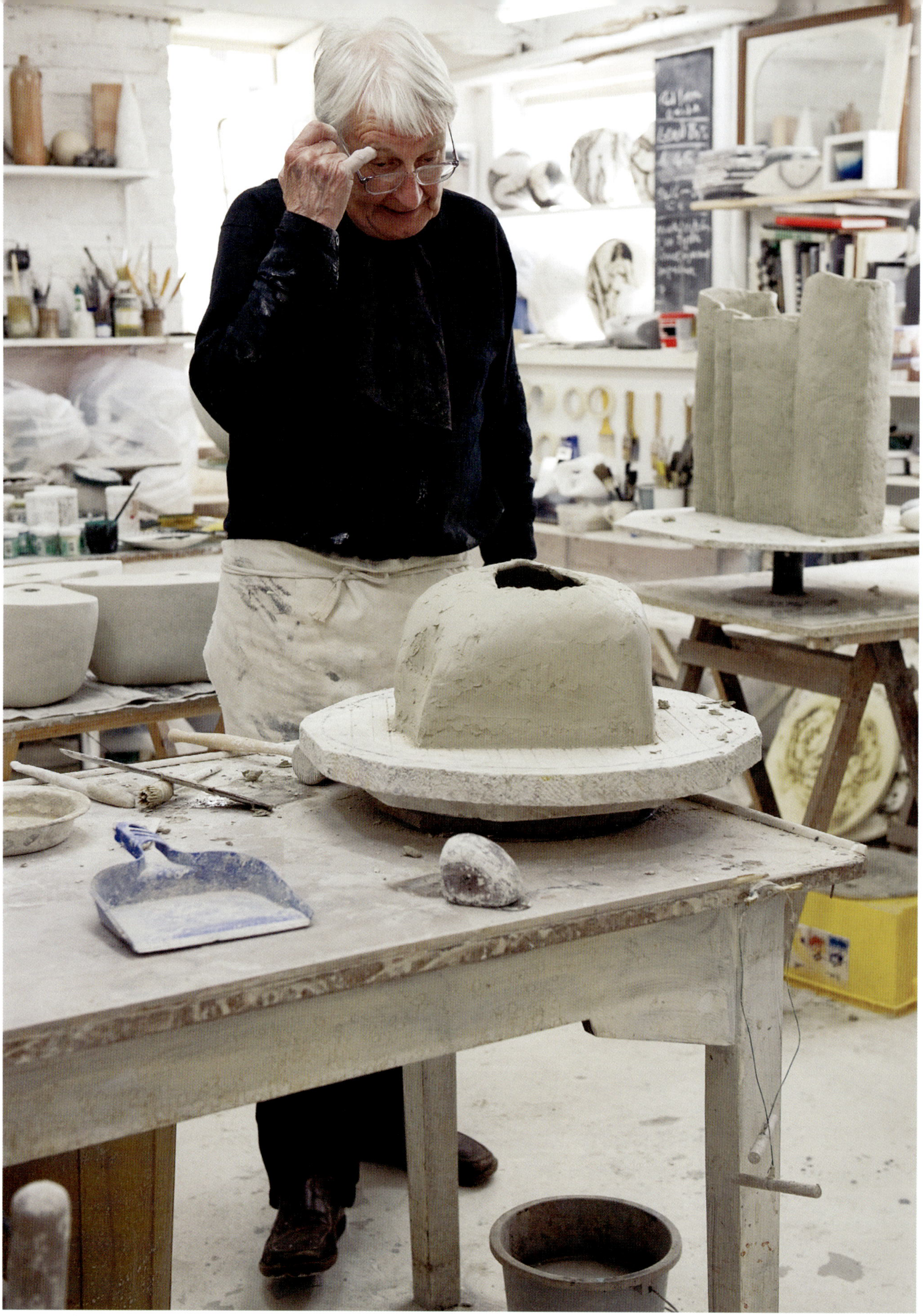

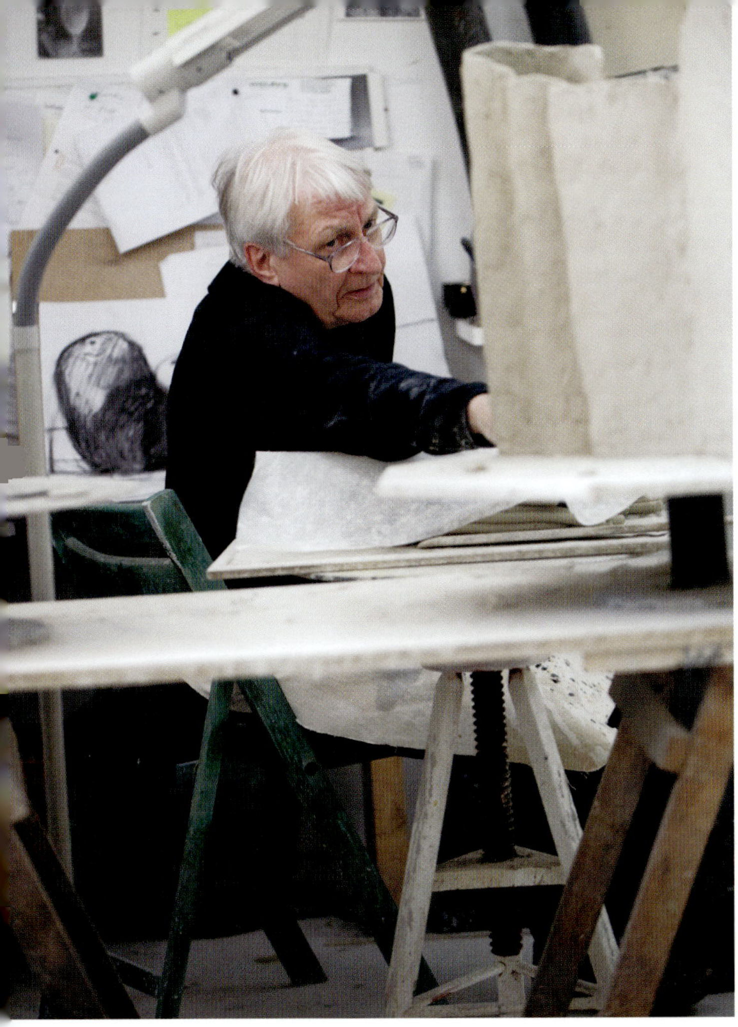

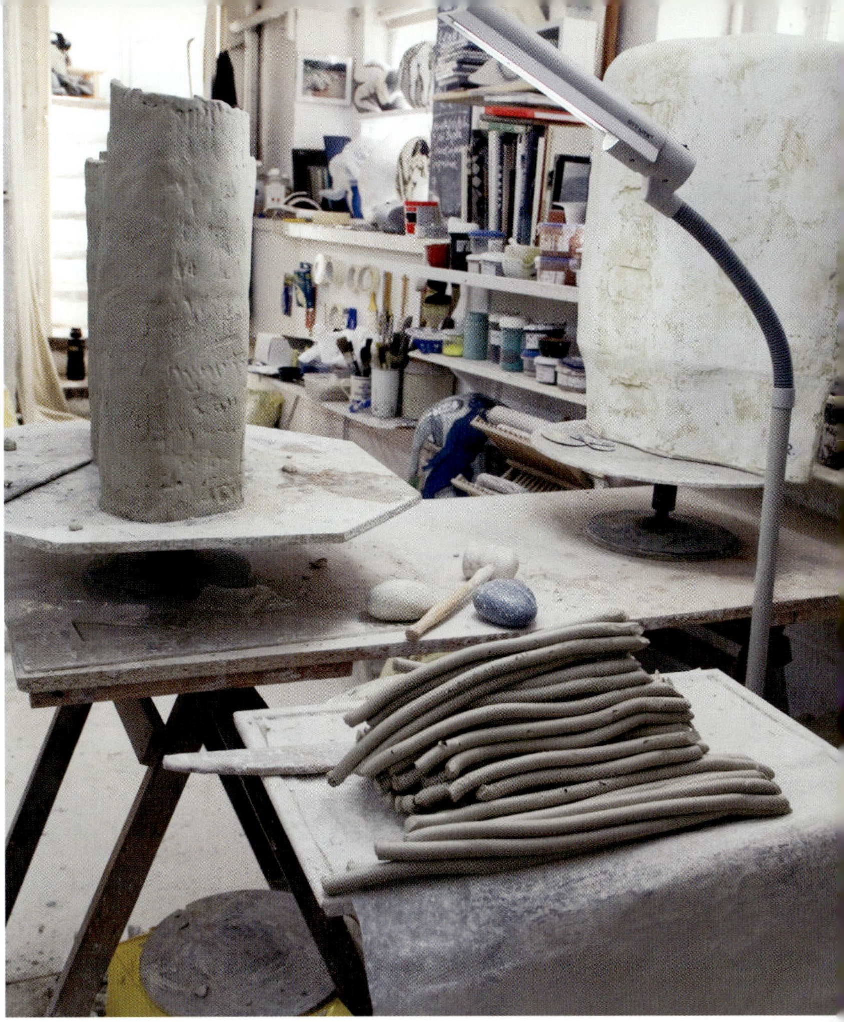

three-dimensional merge. At their quietest and most concentrated these objects are often akin to the shapes and textures of stones, washed and worn by the sea. Yet Baldwin is also capable of more dramatic gestures, sending out angular shoots and wings as he did in his various 'developed bowl' and 'developed bottle' series, or making ethereal, narrow and luminously coloured monoliths that are pointed at their summits. Baldwin has always shown that form is not necessarily about a fixed resolution or certainty, one reason why he usually works in these series, connected by a common theme or point of departure. His work continually evolves and reinvents itself.

It is no surprise to find that his subterranean, visually rich, studio – in the cellar of his 18th-century house in Market Drayton, Shropshire – not only has reproductions of particular paintings and sculptures, along with photographic details of certain landscapes, but is covered in his own drawings. They sketch out, with an emphatic sense of line, his current concerns and obsessions, his work in progress. It is here he comes early each morning, working until breakfast, and returning at intervals throughout the day. But Baldwin has not always led such an isolated existence. His interest in questions, and his deep engagement with the drama of making, has made him a great communicator and an influential teacher – principally at the Central School and at Eton College – over some 40 years. There remains a strong creative symbiosis with his wife Nancy Baldwin, a distinguished painter whose own studio is at the top of their house. Their close dialogue has recently manifested in an interesting series of energetic narrative pieces made by Gordon and painted by Nancy, her figurative linear rhythms echoing and extending each form.

It is misleading to talk too much of distinct periods in Baldwin's work. There have, of course, been a succession of changes: of black and then white phases in the late 60s and

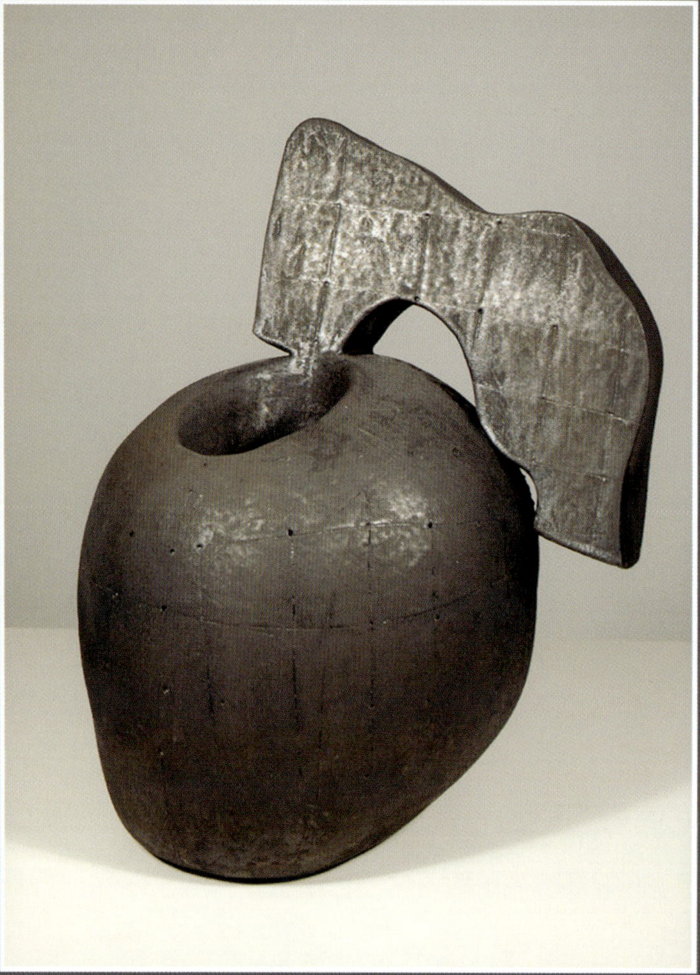

An Alchemical Vessel V, *2006, earthenware.*
Height: 62cm (24½in.). Photo: Barrett Marsden Gallery

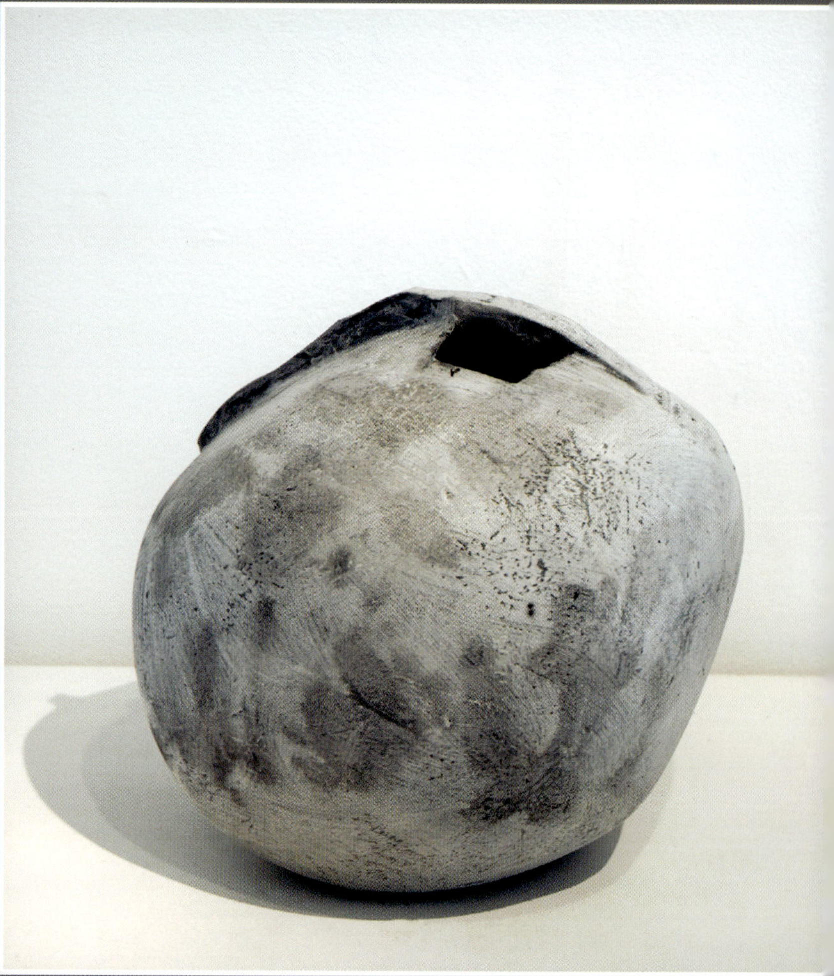

An Alchemical Vessel IV, *2006, earthenware.*
Height: 41cm (16in.). Photo: Barrett Marsden Gallery

through the 70s, followed by more articulated 'baroque' pieces in the 1980s, and then, from the mid-90s onwards, a generally quieter, more amorphic approach. Yet Baldwin really works in broken cycles, with new work often picking up (consciously or unconsciously) on earlier ideas, so there is a definite continuity – a unity – in his art. Series titles – such as Dark Vessel, Cloud, Unknown Vessel, Enigma, Ocean and so forth – are a means by which he can give his ceramics or 'events' some sort of identity. As he wrote in a recent artist's statement, 'The events that happen in the studio seem very distant at times. I coax and allow them to develop. There may be disappointments. I get very anxious. The best ones for me spread out from themselves.'

Baldwin's pots are difficult to know – as much for the artist as his audience – but they grow in power the longer one lives with them. He can never really explain or rationalise what he does. His vessels attempt to gauge those elements that obsess him – the night sky, the shape of a piece of music, a recently discovered poem or painting. His abstract marking of surface can also be read as delineations of remembered or invented landscapes. Different densities of surface and various applications of brushed-on glaze, perhaps rubbed through to reveal the layers underneath, create complex fields and depths. There are often networks of incised and painted lines, piercings and more concentrated areas of activity.

These amorphous and mysterious objects offer their

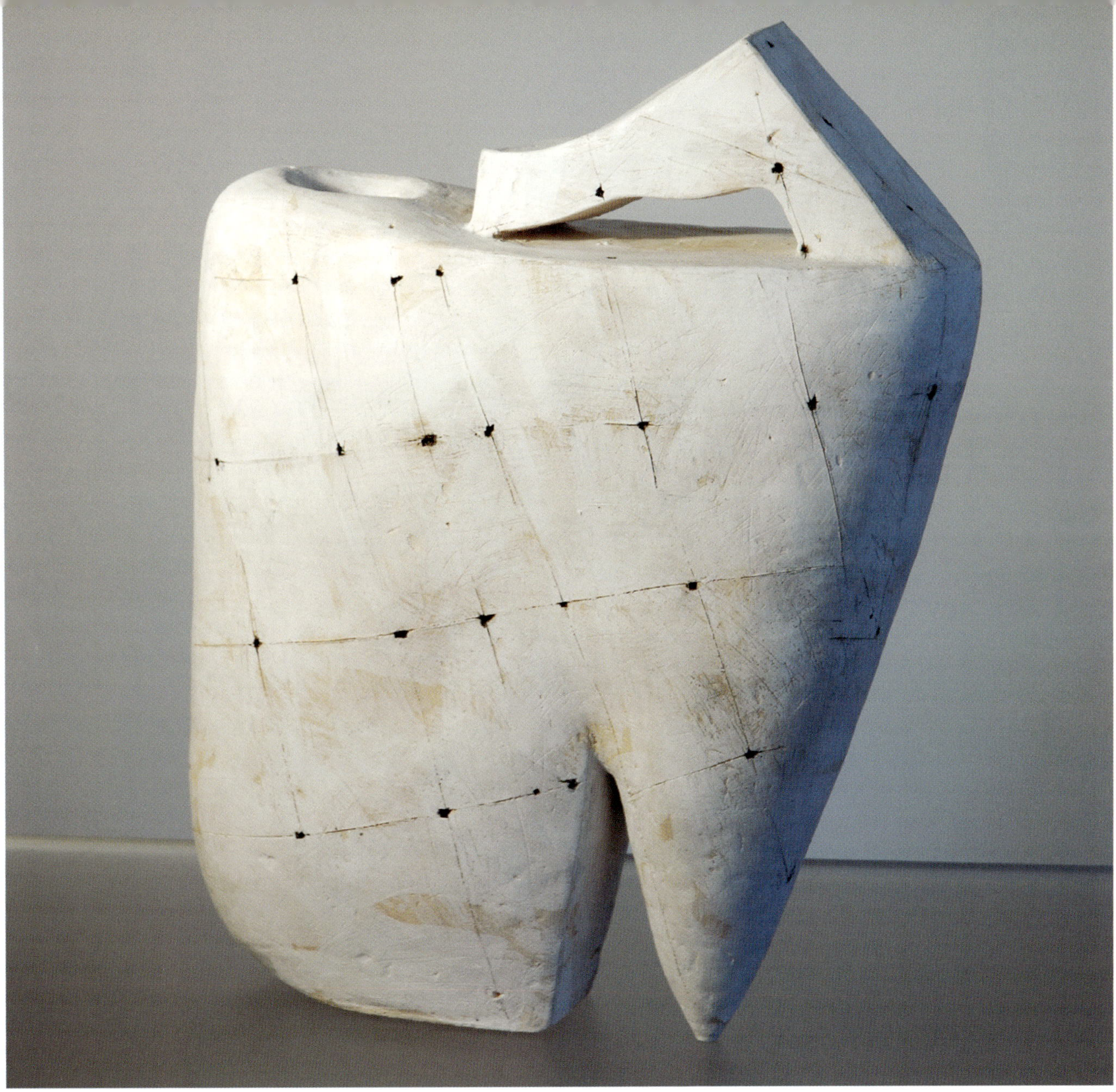

Vessel from a Pale Quartet II, *2008, earthenware.*
Height: 28cm (11in.). *Photo: Barrett Marsden Gallery*

own oblique narrative, charting their own formal and imaginative journey – a series of sculptural travel notes is how Baldwin might well describe them. Moreover, there is no object as primordial as the vessel, not only as the archetypal ceramic form, but as a seafaring maker of voyages. In this sense Baldwin is continuing, in his own way, a family tradition.

Now in his late seventies, his work is generally more understated – as if he is getting closer to some kind of quintessence. He is not a polemicist or an attendee of ceramic conferences. He does not participate in ceramics debates. Occasional exhibitions siphon off accumulated work from the previous months; he does not make work specifically *for* gallery shows, as so many potters do. His existence seems increasingly monastic, his dialogue with the vessel ever deepening. Along with artists like Ewen Henderson and Gillian Lowndes, Baldwin has helped to revolutionise ceramic sculpture in Britain – showing that clay can compete with any other creative area in power and poetry of expression.

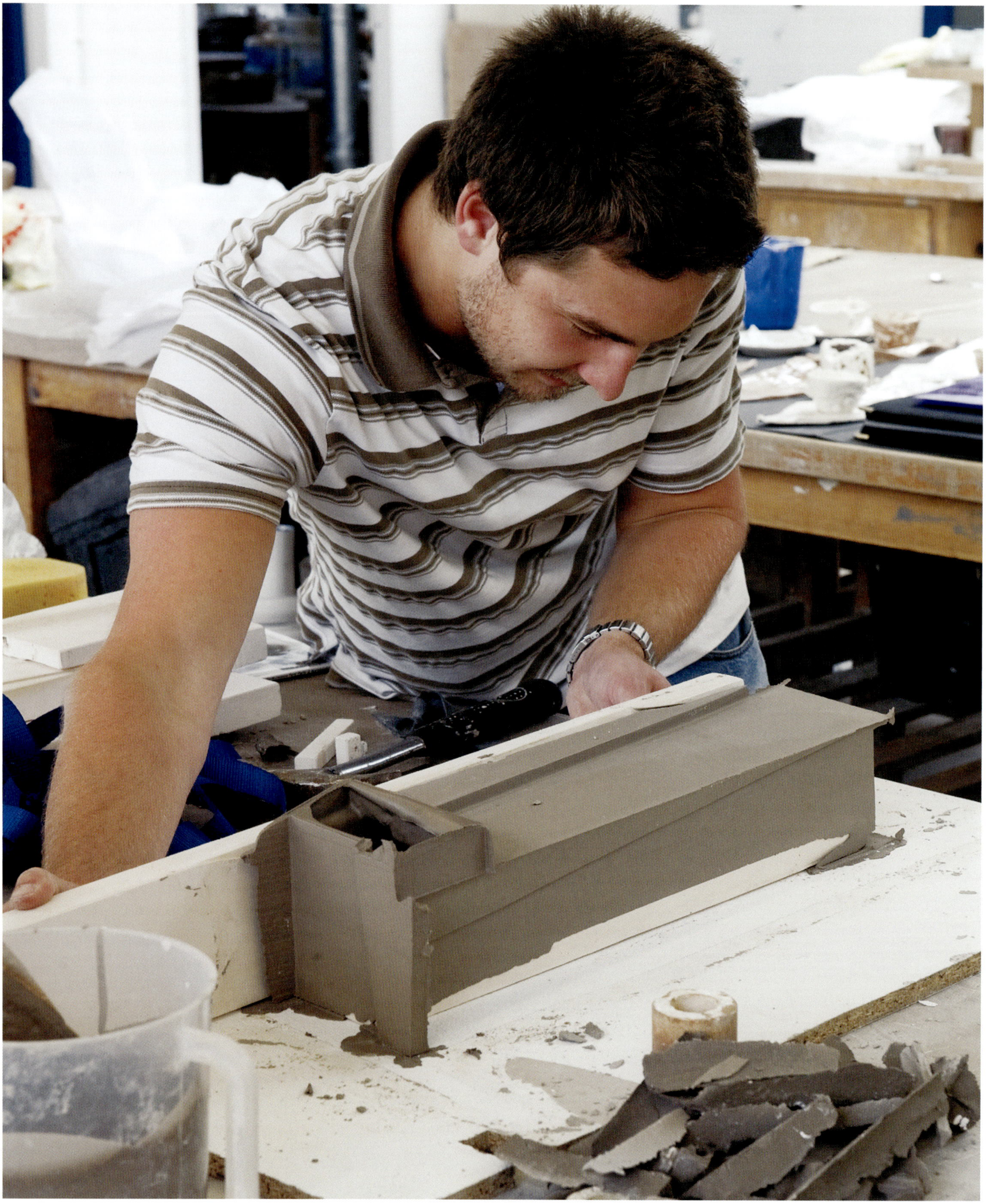

James Robson

JAMES ROBSON has been a professional ceramist for three years, having graduated from Loughborough University's School of Art and Design in 2006. He is emblematic of so many ceramics graduates past and present, having now to gear himself to pursuing clay as a career, promoting his work, getting it to galleries and hoping to find some permanent studio space so that he can continue making. Life so far hasn't been particularly straightforward. It has been a matter of working at other jobs to subsidise his ceramics activity and relying on his old college at Dewsbury for work facilities – in return for odd-jobbing, bits of teaching and technical assistance.

Potters' studios can be improvised, makeshift affairs, particularly when, like James, you are in the complex business of getting established. Yet his current position is stronger than many of his contemporaries. A large proportion of ceramics graduates vanish altogether, finding it difficult to survive unless they secure parallel teaching work or other part-time employment that balances well with their ceramics pursuits. For every successful potter there are dozens who, sadly, fall by the wayside.

So James Robson's current version of a studio – working in a communal space – is more transitory and impersonal; not that, for Robson, this is entirely a bad thing. Outgoing and sociable, he sees a shared studio in the future as preferable to creative isolation. When interviewed and photographed for this book, he had temporarily de-camped from Dewsbury to his old department at Loughborough, giving an even stronger sense of an artist in literal as well as metaphorical transit. He deserves to succeed. Self-possessed and focused as an artist, his explorations in the latter part of his time at Loughborough and in the period since have shown considerable originality. His intriguingly geometric cast vessels are not only inventive in form and conception – playing in part with structural ideas from outside the sphere of clay – but take the process of ceramic slipcasting one step further.

Robson, a Yorkshireman, was born in 1983 and lives to the east of Leeds. He had a natural ability in visual art at school, a skill which took him to foundation level at Dewsbury College of Art and Design, where under guidance from the course coordinator, Warren Dunn, he discovered an empathy for clay. He began to slab-build, became interested in the cast work of ceramist Martin Smith, and was generally being drawn to more architectural conceptions. Intrigued by surface and detail in modern buildings – their shadows, angles and edges – he photographed these features, attracted too by the colours and textures he found. At Loughborough's excellent ceramics department, where his tutors included David Scott and Jim Gladwin, he was seriously developing these themes by his second year. His interest related to other surfaces and forms too – the varied patinas of rusting metal, of discarded machinery, of other aspects of 'contemporary urban landscape', as Robson puts it.

He found further parallels in visual art. He discovered and was enthused by the steel sculpture of Richard Serra, as much for the effects of material weathering as for the shapes he made. He responded to Masamichi Yoshikawa's slab-constructed porcelain. These artists explored space, structure and enclosure in new, thought-provoking ways, whilst celebrating the varied nature of the substances they were using. Searching for a language which would encapsulate these concerns, he developed a technique by which he made up plaster slabs of varying shape and length into special, custom-built moulds. Into these a paper clay slip was then poured and a form cast.

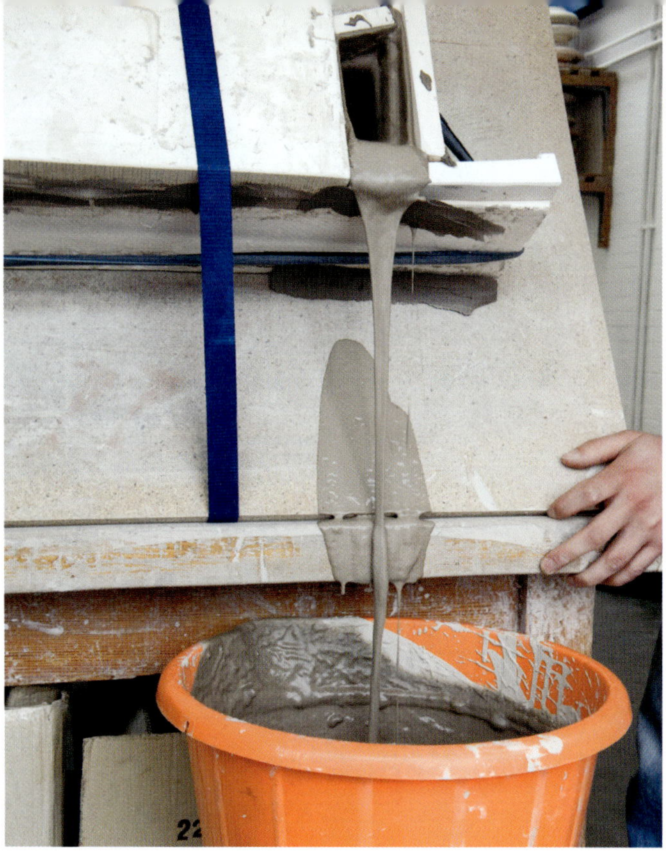

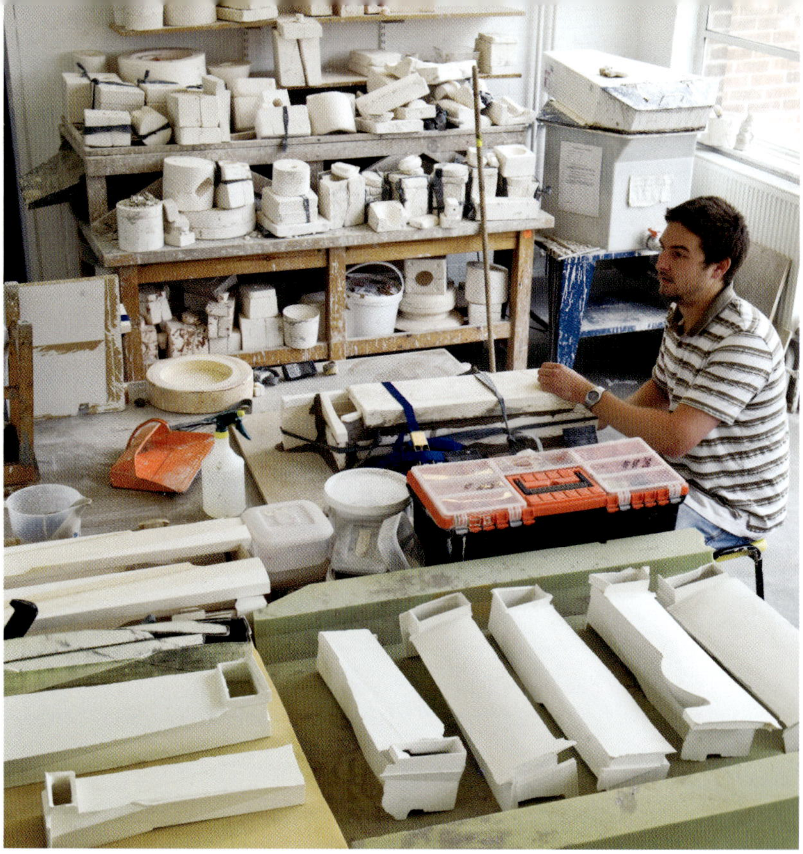

The advantage of Robson's moulds is their flexibility – they are made up in sections which can be harnessed and fixed together in different combinations, allowing him to improvise and contrive new variations of form, and new angles, edges and surface properties. As he has stressed, 'the roots of the work are firmly in the process', and he would like people to appreciate the nature of the procedures involved. The pieces made have generally been rectangular in structure, and while intimate in scale (small enough for a domestic setting), they are also suggestive of much larger objects, an impression that comes across in photographs of his work. Each is unique, too, the mould being disassembled after use and its plaster components kept for future employment. If the vessels appear constructed, this is because the first stage of their conception involves exactly this process.

The clarity of these forms – the crispness and detail of their striations, junctions and contours, reflects the precision of Robson's technique, one that looks sectional and extruded, as if made by joining parts together. The angles and serrations are softened by generous barium, nuka and salt glazes which cover and define the planes, indents and gutters – variously matt and more liquid when collecting and pooling in recesses, on ledges and at bases. The nuances of colour and surface give each piece a distinctly metallic quality. Some of the shapes are virtually closed, with single, squarish openings, while others are more perforated and open. But all are based in a residual concept of the vessel, with some semblance of function, just as these shapes are redolent of other kinds of functional apparatus. The industrial qualities they conjure up are numerous – from sections of old lathes and the rusting hulls of oil tankers to the concrete sections of brutalist architecture. The way an oxide bleeds through a barium glaze, or a mottled salt glaze thickens the face of the clay, evokes memories of corroded scrap or an architectural fabric that has seen better days.

On another level there is a playful formalism about Robson's vessels, exercises in clay that are expressive of his passion for different kinds of structural development and deviation within the confines of this technique. There is even something a touch baroque about them – reflecting the overtly

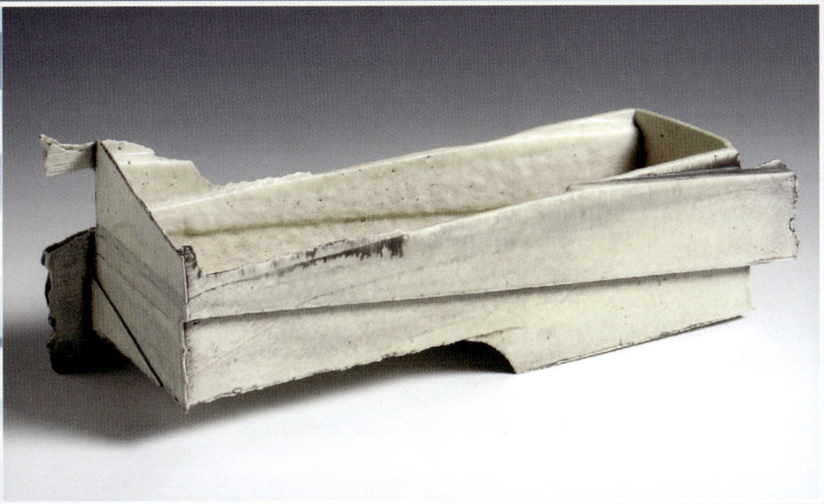

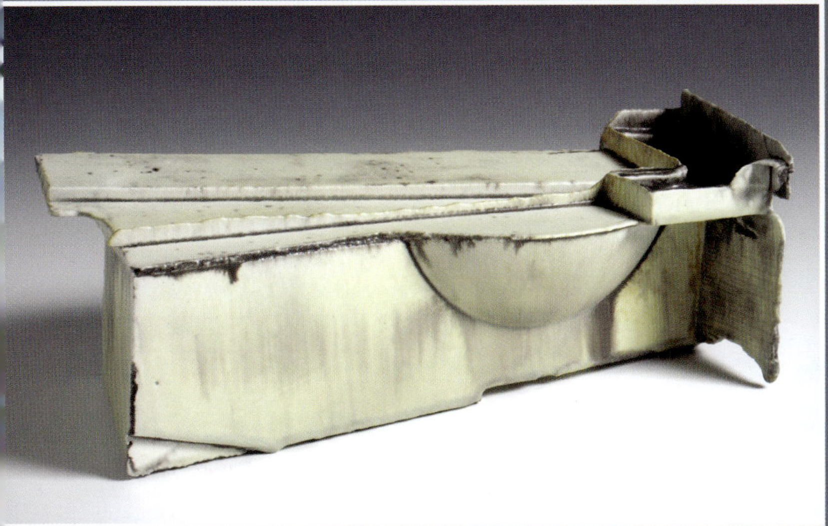

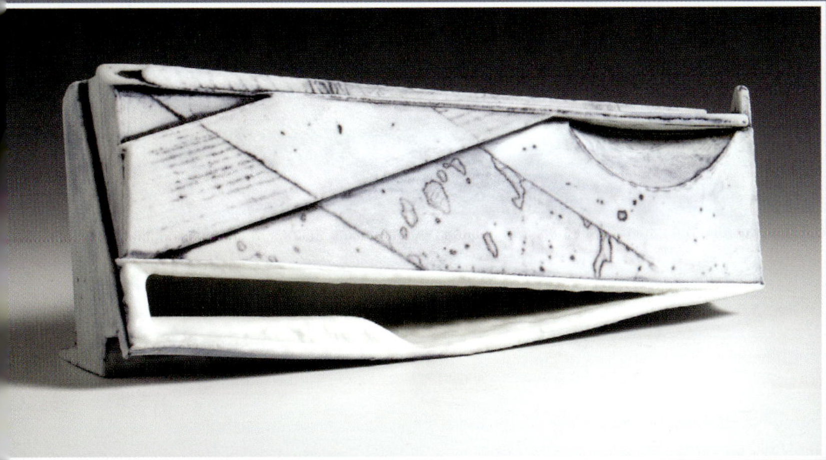

top: Vessel, *2005, slipcast paperclay.*
Length: 30cm (11¾in.).
middle: Vessel, *2006, slipcast paperclay.*
Length: 35cm (13¾in.).
bottom: Vessel, *2006, slipcast paperclay.*
Length: 30cm (11¾in.).
Photos: Courtesy of the artist

sculptural nature of many of our streetscapes or industrial yards. As an example, one could easily cite the exaggerated forms of classic American car design, the subject, it is no surprise to learn, of Robson's written dissertation at Loughborough. Robson is very much ceramist as engineer, fascinated by method and experiment and, as such, always trying to 'push the envelope'. Having already worked on more open and curvaceous forms, he would like to move further in this direction and increase his scale too. With his self-confessed low boredom threshold, once Robson has mastered one idea he is keen to move on and find another challenge. It is perhaps because he is immersed in a much broader sensory world, revelling in the ambiguities as well as the certainties of this material, pushing it into unexpected places, that his unconventional work stands out. It should take him far.

Carina Ciscato

CARINA CISCATO could be described as a maker of individual vessels based in the vocabulary of function. Her pots certainly straddle these two, very connected areas of activity. As her work progresses – fluid, thinly thrown 'wet' porcelain of great material expressiveness – her interest in pushing it to its physical limits of crisp, rippling translucency has taken the substance into a more overtly sculptural arena. Yet Ciscato – rather like a production potter – still tends to work in series, making groups and nests of bowls, 'pocket' pots, 'bags' and large, undulating folding pieces. As a result, there is a great rhythm and 'pulse' in her work.

Essentially a product of the renaissance in white porcelain that took hold in the 1990s, Ciscato's contribution to its revival has been quite distinct and individual. She has never aped the ranges of elegant tablewares on the one hand or the more conceptual installation work on the other. Instead she has managed to define – through considerable craft skill and discipline – her own area of expertise, developing intriguing new deviations of form and surface that make her a rather unconventional potter, adding something surprising to the vocabulary of the vessel, and to ceramics in general.

Ciscato currently works in a light airy space in Vanguard Court in south London which she shares with Chris Keenan, a gifted maker of tablewares. Rhythmical rows of finished pots on shelves and the spareness of interior detail gives the room a suitably functionalist air. It is all certainly a long way from her native Brazil, where she was born in 1970. She studied industrial design in her home city of São Paulo before going to Krefeld in Germany to train in furniture design, where instead she discovered ceramics and took up an apprenticeship with Marietta Cremer. She then returned to São Paulo as a student potter in the studio of Lucia Ramenzoni. Six years later, in 1999, she arrived in England, where she undertook a final apprenticeship with the potter Julian Stair, working in a studio a few steps away. The contact with Stair was significant. A leading maker of robust and inventive porcelain, he introduced her to its richness and versatility. But Ciscato took a very different route to Stair; in contrast to his 'drier', more solidly conceived, boldly turned work, she was attracted to its quality of soft creamy liquidity and also its plasticity. She loved these aspects of porcelain and began to develop her own variant of the clay.

Given her interest in some of the basic elements of ceramic structure, following a course that was more to do with the revealed tensile bone of porcelain than its 'flesh', it was inevitable that any embellishments with which Ciscato had been experimenting would soon be eliminated. She stopped painting surfaces as she got more to grips with the form itself, manipulating the clay both on and off the wheel, extemporising with different kinds of contained space and volume. Ciscato wanted to modify and intervene, to disrupt the more conventional procedures of making. She began to make bowls characterised not only by their rippled, softly swelling walls, but by their torn and serrated rims, rather reminiscent of those on Colin Pearson's pots. These rents give the work a sense of what Pearson called a 'controlled accident', a phrase descriptive of both the making process and a quality that opens up rather than closes form.

Looking at the pots she has produced since, it is clear that Ciscato has absorbed much about form and structure from outside the orbit of ceramics. Her pots are very architectural, a reflection of the modern urban landscape. They echo the precision and clarity of minimal sculpture and the contours and symmetries of 20th-century building.

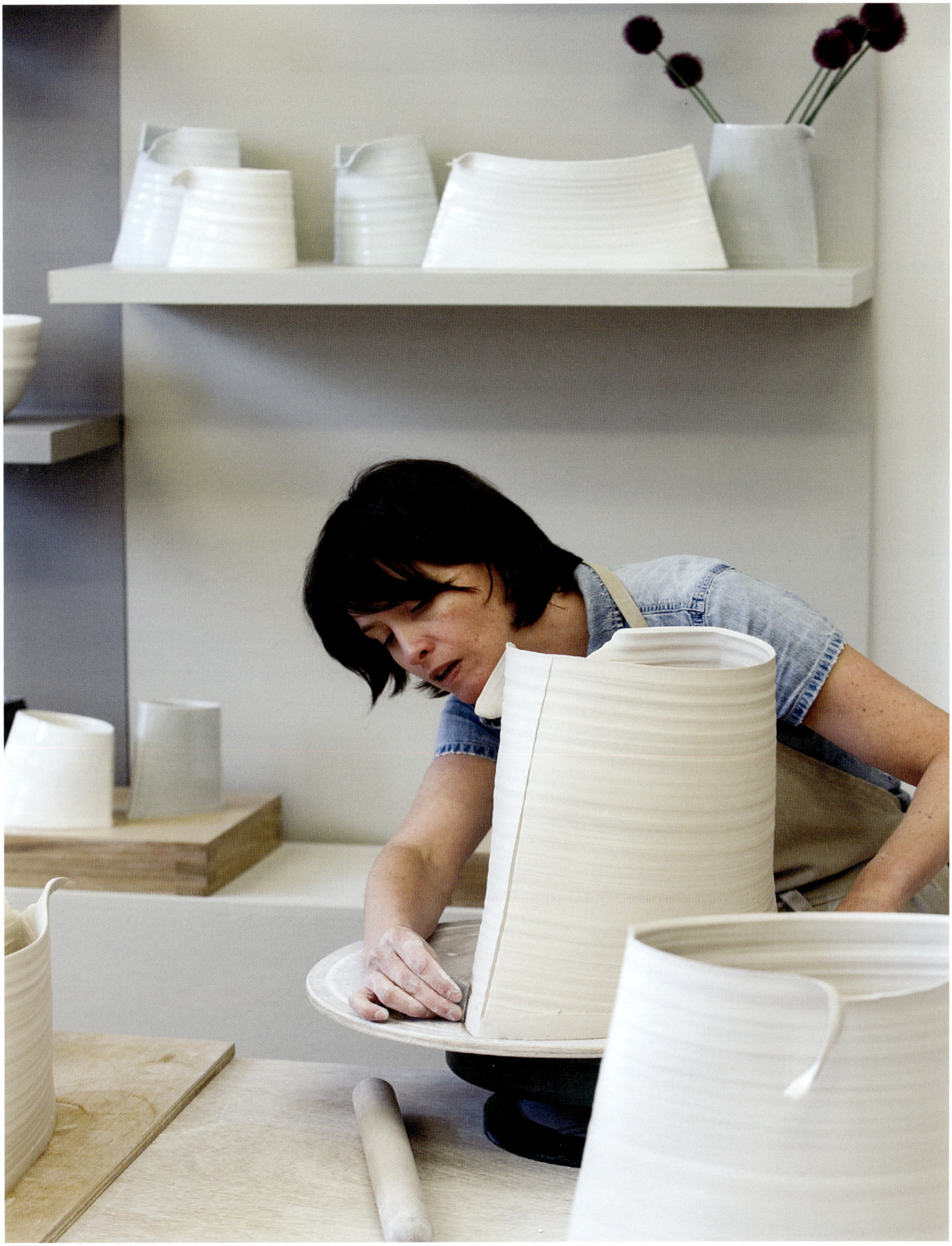

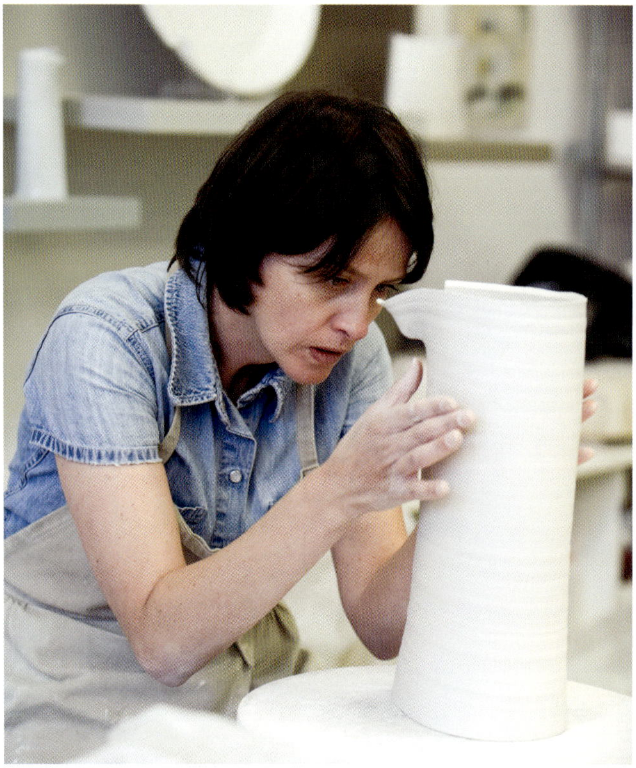

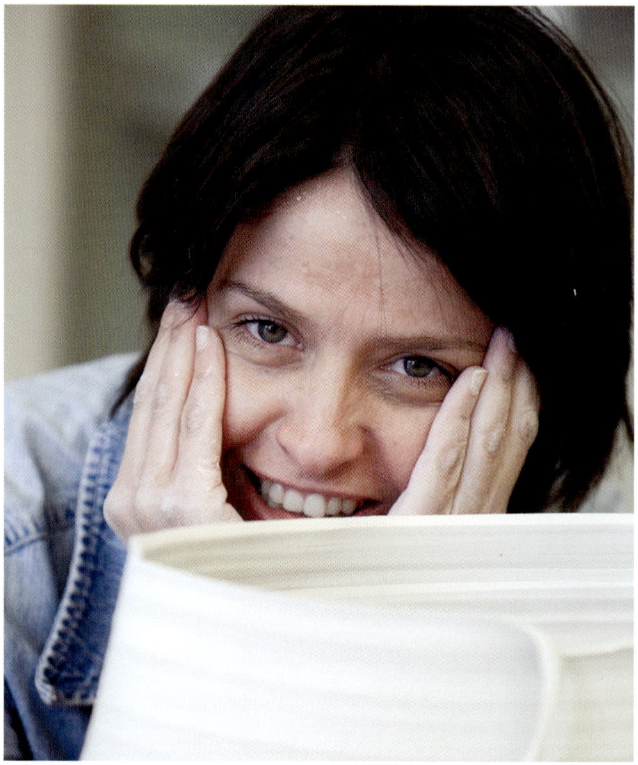

The soft corrugations of throwing, the surfaces so liquid as to appear wet from the wheel, give the work remarkable freshness. The quality is more organic than pre-drawn, a sense of growth and lift appearing to go beyond the rim. The porcelain has become, to use Ciscato's phrase, 'perfectly imperfect'. Her elongated vessels – curving, gently warped pieces with small bowls contained inside – have developed her interest in shapes that are full of latent motion, even on the edge of buckling and collapse, but with their movements fired hard by the kiln. This isn't 'safe', reassuring porcelain, but work that exploits a material capable of great elasticity and distortion, in which the structural dynamic – the interplay between tension and relaxation in the throwing – keeps on flexing. Ciscato has introduced muted colour – whites, blue-greys, celadons – wintry tones that seem to echo the hues of London's skyline. And yet these pots are far from austere; they are tactile and quite voluptuous objects, emphasising Ciscato's interest in the sensory accessibility and intimacy that is special to ceramics.

Ciscato's revisionist approach to porcelain, a material through which she can quietly subvert traditional forms, gives her work affiliations to Takeshi Yasuda's pots, and those of the late Joanna Constantinidis. She attempts to take the material to the edge, out of its safety zone. Through cutting, stretching, creasing and tearing, Ciscato has moved away from conventional potting and conventional pots to underline the fact that clay is an unfixed, ever-evolving substance of considerable range. Her long 'folded' vessels, thrown, cut and reassembled, turn porcelain into something physically akin to the flow of water or the fragility of folded and striated paper. Such objects also echo some of the adventurous experiments with this material currently being pursued in Japan and Korea.

Carina Ciscato's most recent pieces – pots with leaning walls and new variations of joinery – include billowing, pillow-like 'envelope' forms, 'bags' with single tears to the rim, the linear geometrics of her 'pocket' pots and spatially intriguing 'double-walled' vases, all shapes that extend our perception of what containment can mean. Yet while she likes to disturb accepted notions of balance and

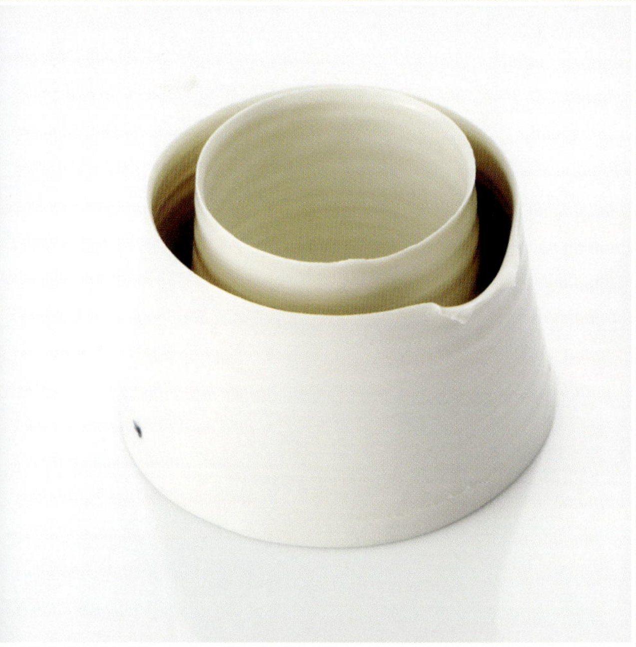

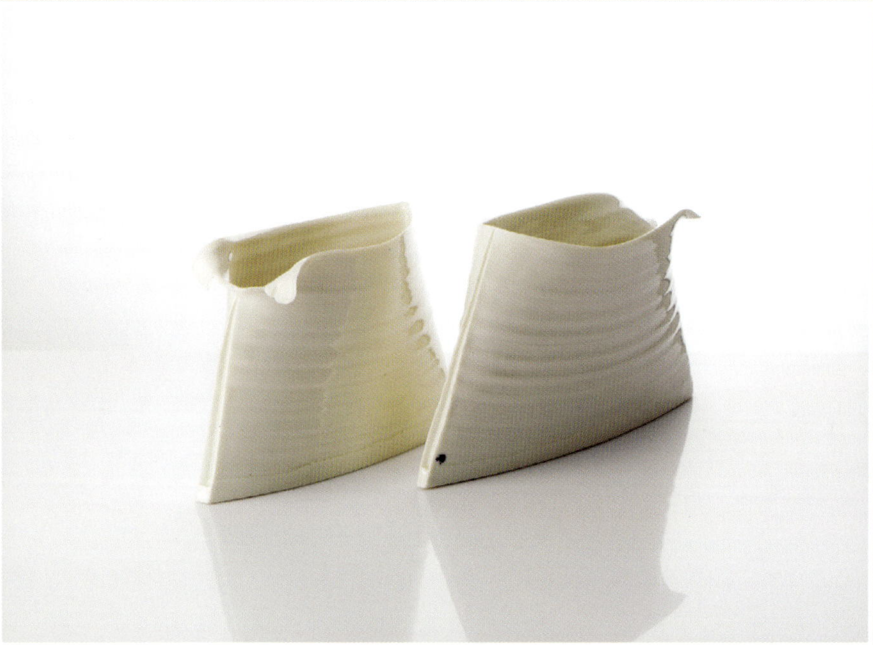

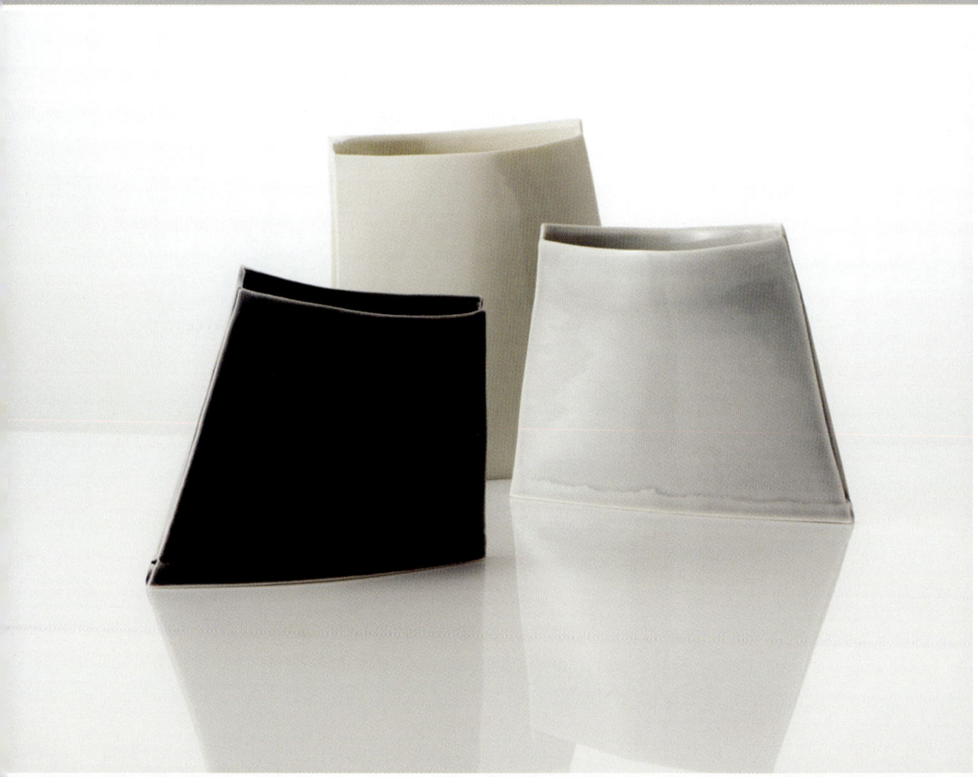

above left: Double Wall, *2007, porcelain. Height: 16cm (6¼in.).*
right: Pair of Bags with Side Tear, *2007, porcelain. Height: 20cm (8in.).*
Photos: Courtesy of the artist

Series of Pocket Pots, *2007, porcelain. Height: 24cm (9½in.).*
Photo: Courtesy of the artist

symmetry, the generic titles of these pots suggest the intimacy of domestic life and familiar things. Exuberant and passionate about the possibilities of what she does, Ciscato says she would like her pots to reanimate and refresh our modern spaces, but also to give us a visual jolt, to disturb our equilibrium a little, just as she disturbs the equilibrium of the thrown vessel. It is intriguing to imagine where she will go from here.

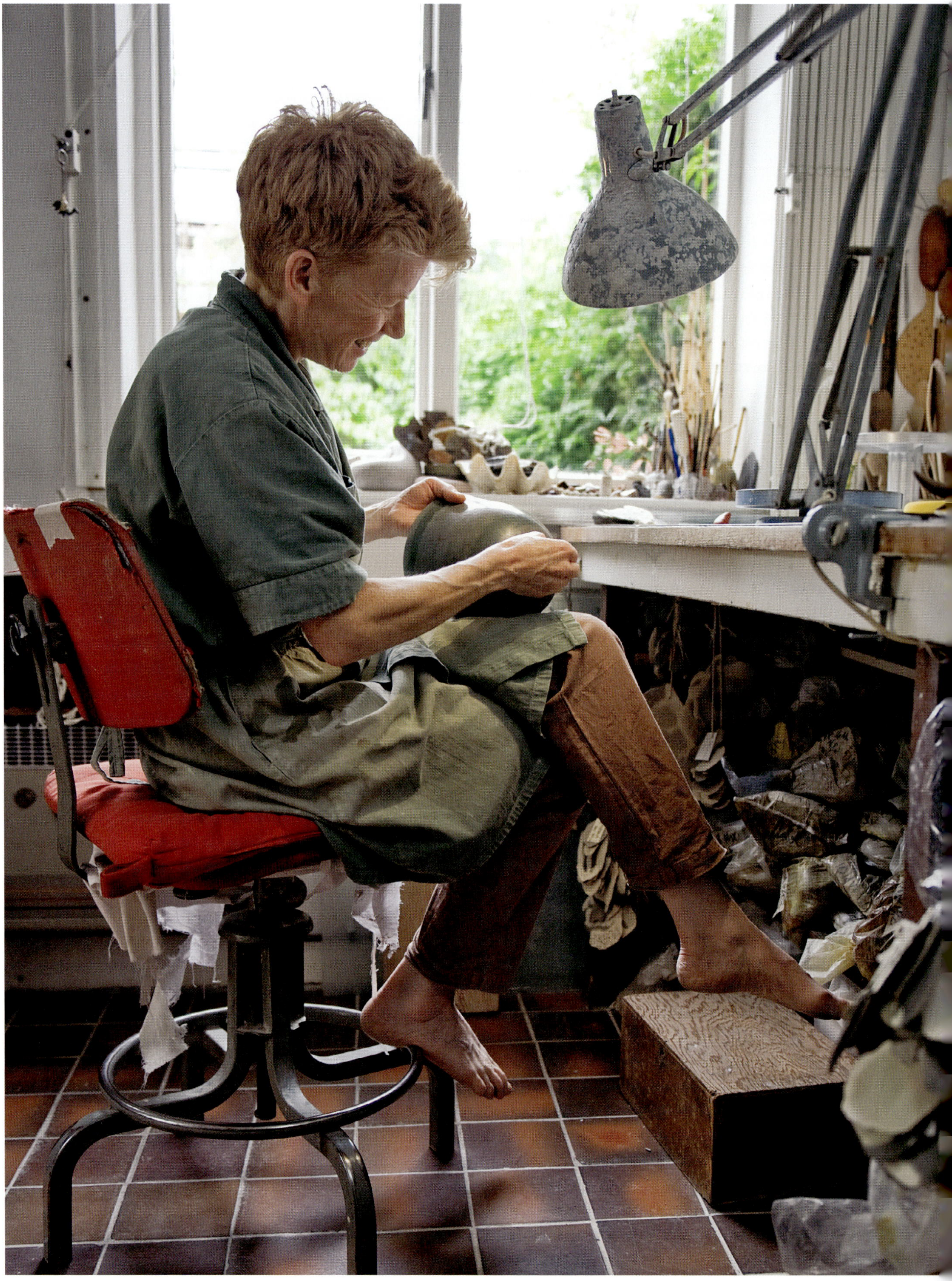

Jennifer Lee

JENNIFER LEE'S STUDIO is at the rear of her south London home, just off the Peckham Road in Camberwell. This back room faces onto her garden, but despite its close proximity to the everyday bustle of domestic family life and the busy residential street outside, this light airy space is silent and calm, as one might expect when you contemplate the self-contained equilibrium of her pots. Lee's serene, economically conceived vessels function very much on their own terms – abstractions of ceramic history from earliest times, concentrated and condensed into objects which, refreshingly in modern ceramics, are not concerned with 'commentary' or 'quotation', with irony or polemics. Instead they convey the most direct qualities of handbuilt clay, the power of the simplest containers.

It is not surprising that, considering the nature of this work, Lee prefers to distance herself from the critical forums of contemporary ceramics, from the debates that have increasingly preoccupied that world over the last 30 years. This does not mean that she is unaware of them. She goes to conferences and listens with interest, but does not write about herself, not out of stubborn resistance to creative interpretation, but because she prefers to let the work speak for itself. Her words, she feels, would be superfluous. If these pots have a function, it is in their life as objects that animate and enrich any space, that say much about the natural unglazed potency of the clay itself. Hers is an art that is painstakingly built up, walls and surfaces made and then patiently honed down, like stones on a beach washed and polished by the tide. Her pots resemble the silting layers of a riverbank or the settling tiers of earth underfoot. There is a strong, evocative sense of geology and archaeology here: her pots have resulted from years of studying not only the rhythms of different landscapes – Lee is an inveterate traveller – but also prehistoric pots and various indigenous ceramic traditions, from Ancient Egypt and America to Sub-Saharan Africa and India.

Yet Lee, who was born in 1956, is also a modernist, rooted in the developments of modern art and architecture; her pots respond to and animate the surfaces of any contemporary interior, and are seen at their best in a spacious, uncrowded setting. They reflect the language of much abstract sculpture and painting, and they also express the evolving tensions and energies built up in the rising, constructed clay, an upward motion growing out of the symmetries and asymmetries of her forms and their inner layers and strata, the way her pots grow out from their narrow bases. Lee has been measuring the seemingly endless aspects of a limited range of forms – of broad, flaring bowls and narrower, more cylindrical pots – for over 25 years, a career of continuity perhaps, but one which also (if you examine images of her ceramics from the early 80s) reveals its gradual transformations and refinements. Today's pots have a greater precision and crispness of form and surface, a deeper probing of floating structure and colour, of swelling and contracting volume – subtleties that are the result of long experience and intense observation.

Lee may now live in London but her upbringing was far from urban. She was born and brought up on her parents' remote farm in Aberdeenshire, close to the North Sea, a landscape to which she often returns. It is a country pared down to essentials, where the relationship between land, sea and sky makes one particularly aware of light, space and the elements, of the kinds of 'weather' we may also find in her pots. But Lee's ceramics are about all kinds of absorption,

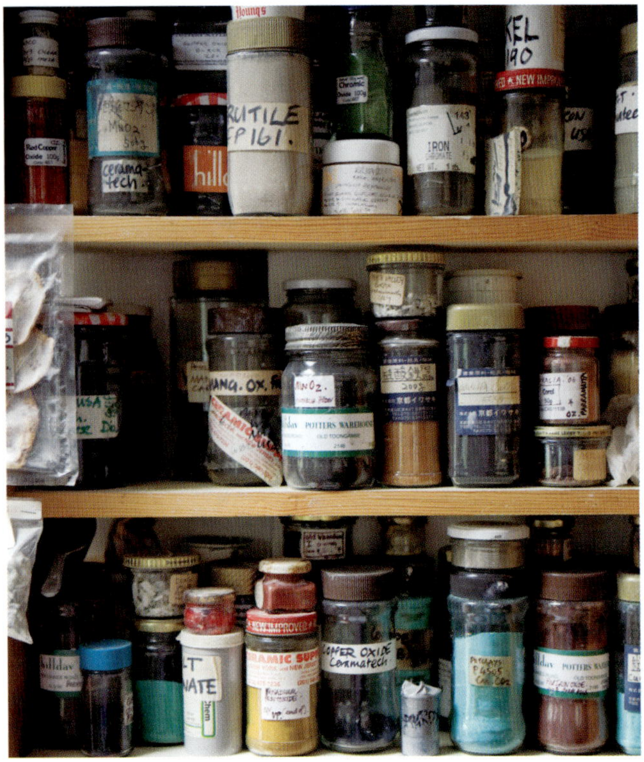

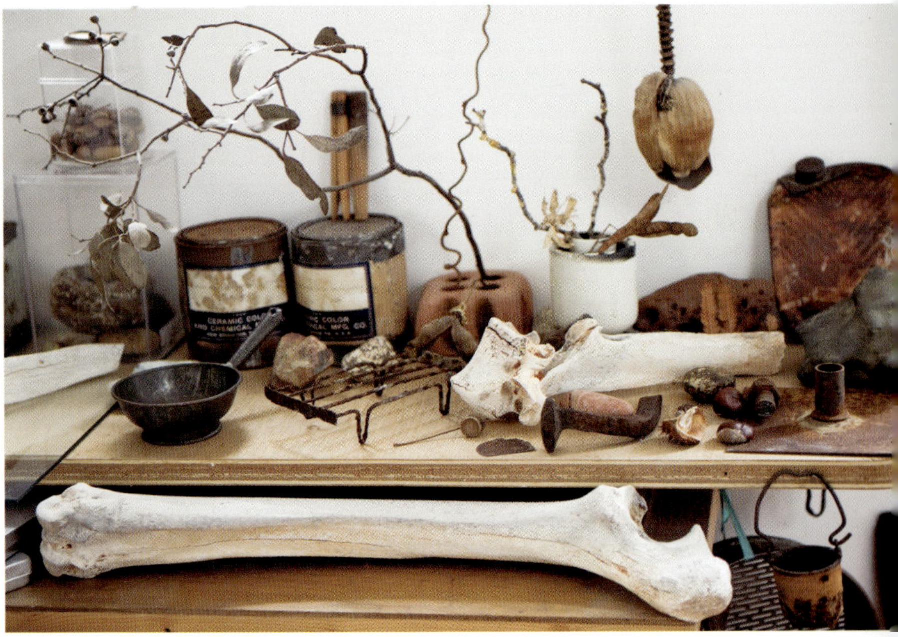

intrigued as she is by a wide range of visual and historical material. At Edinburgh College of Art in the mid-seventies, she studied tapestry alongside ceramics. She then went to the USA, visiting West Coast potters like Peter Voulkos and Paul Soldner, and researching prehistoric South-west Indian ceramics, before returning to Britain to complete her studies at the Royal College of Art in London in 1982/3. On her numerous travels since, she has collected a fascinating range of manmade and natural objects transformed by time and history. In her house you will find various delicate structures: animal bones, dried pods and flowers, numerous artefacts that have been enjoyed, handled and observed – a *musée imaginaire* of strange and wonderful things that have fed her particular sensibility and visual outlook.

Looking at the work Lee made back in the early eighties, we realise what an untypical potter she was in the context of that time. Her work did not express the prevailingly decorative glitz and baroque concerns of that era. Her allusions to natural and human archetypes, to the physical world around us, do not relate to the artistic politics or specifics of any one period. The pots of today seem more succinct, their rhythms of colour generally more understated. Some of her work grows in presence when placed with similar forms. We can fully appreciate how an idea is developed and carried through several pieces before she moves on. The pots look well in related sculptural groups, developing their own particular visual tempi.

Within her self-imposed parameters Lee's journey has, in a sense, moved inwards, gauging and re-gauging the interaction of profile and surface, interior and exterior, of spatial relationships. Right from the beginning there was the same concern with poise, balance and lift, the curvatures of her pots swelling from a minimal point of contact with the surface upon which they rest. No wonder they seem to float, adding to the natural sense of energy that abides in their stillness. It is present in their sedimentary movement, and also in her approach to contour. Rims may lean or be flattened into narrow shelves, subtly changing the nature and light of the internal space. Lips have been extended outwards and tilted. Some pieces have gently

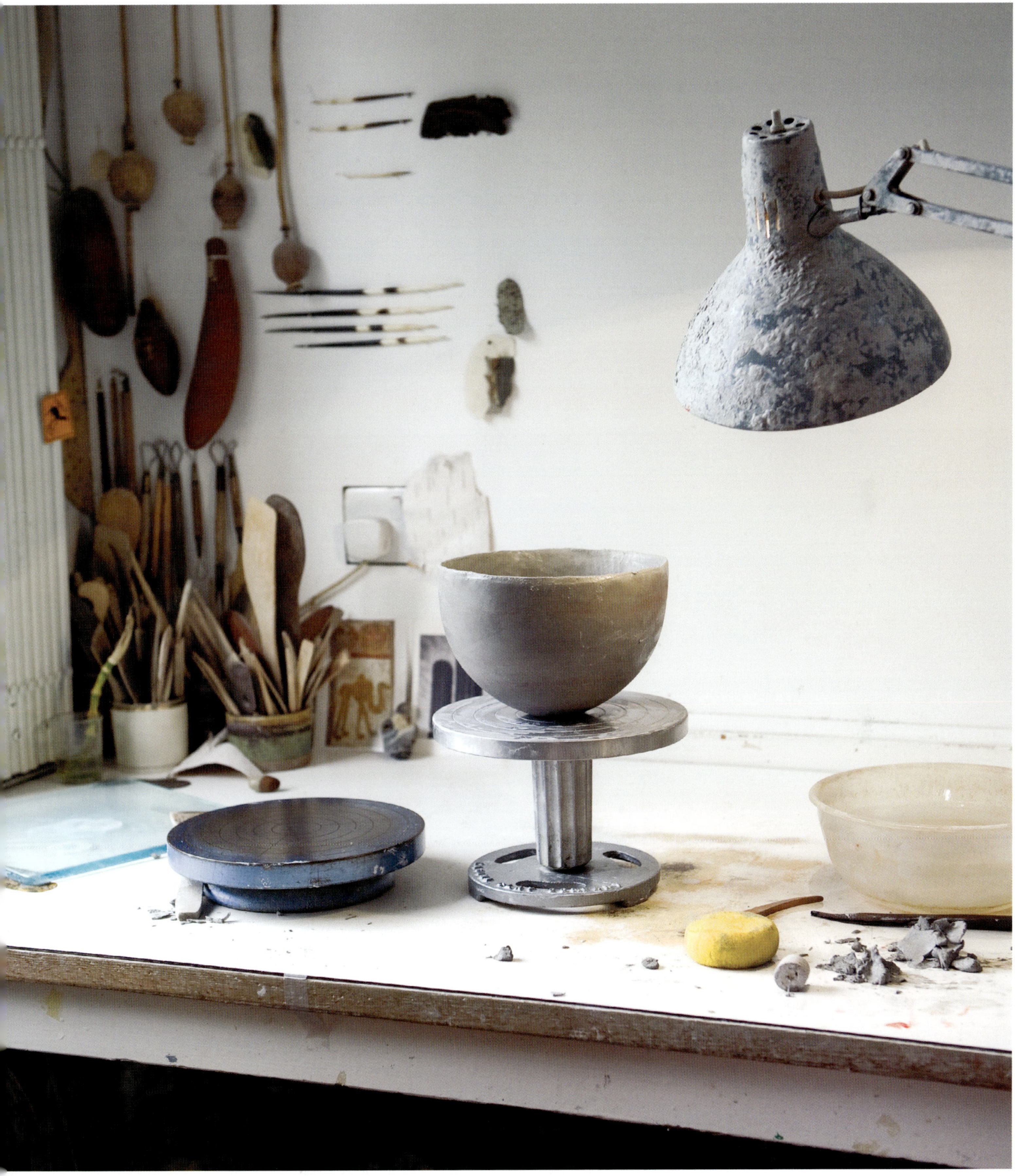

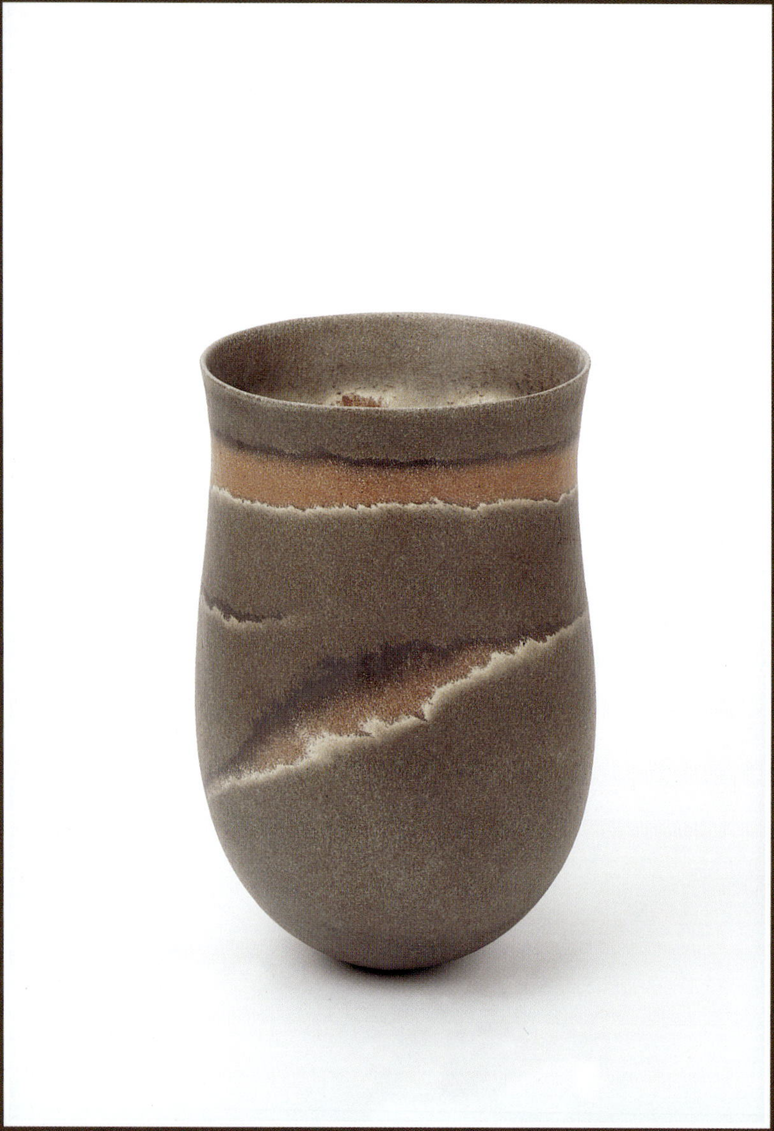

Olive, haloed umber band and traces, *2007, handbuilt coloured stoneware. Height: 28cm (11in.).*
Photo: Alan Tabor, courtesy of Galerie Besson.

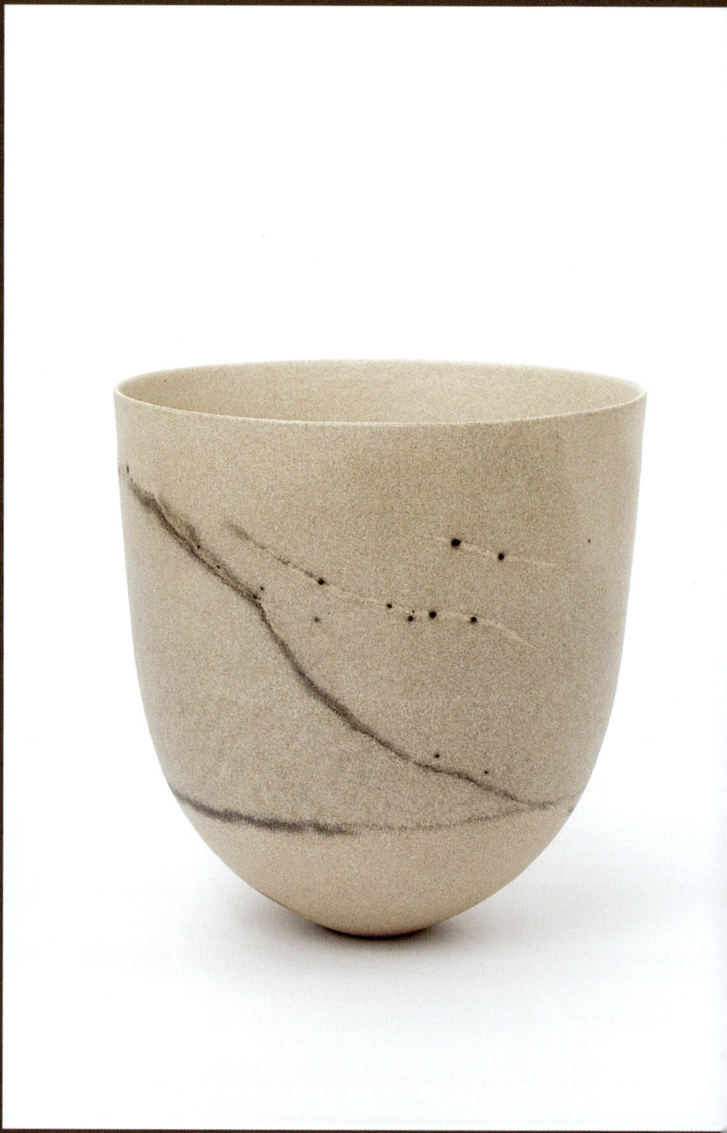

Sand-grained speckled traces, *2007, handbuilt coloured stoneware. Height: 25cm (9¾in.).*
Photo: Alan Tabor, courtesy of Galerie Besson.

emerging ridges, interventions that grow seamlessly out of the main body.

While Lee's ceramics clearly relate to some of the most archetypal pots found today at numerous grave sites, from Bronze Age bowls to the stratified coloration of Ancient Egyptian wares, they are also both technically and aesthetically very different objects. The vessels made in pre-dynastic Egypt, on the Upper Nile, certainly connect on one level with Lee's own approach. These pots, made from Red Nile silt or hard buff marl clay, are amongst the most abstract and elemental we know. Lee, too, employs ancient methods, building up her pots from coils or strips of rolled clay, but whereas the black crests that complete these Egyptian wares were made through firing, Lee's colour is

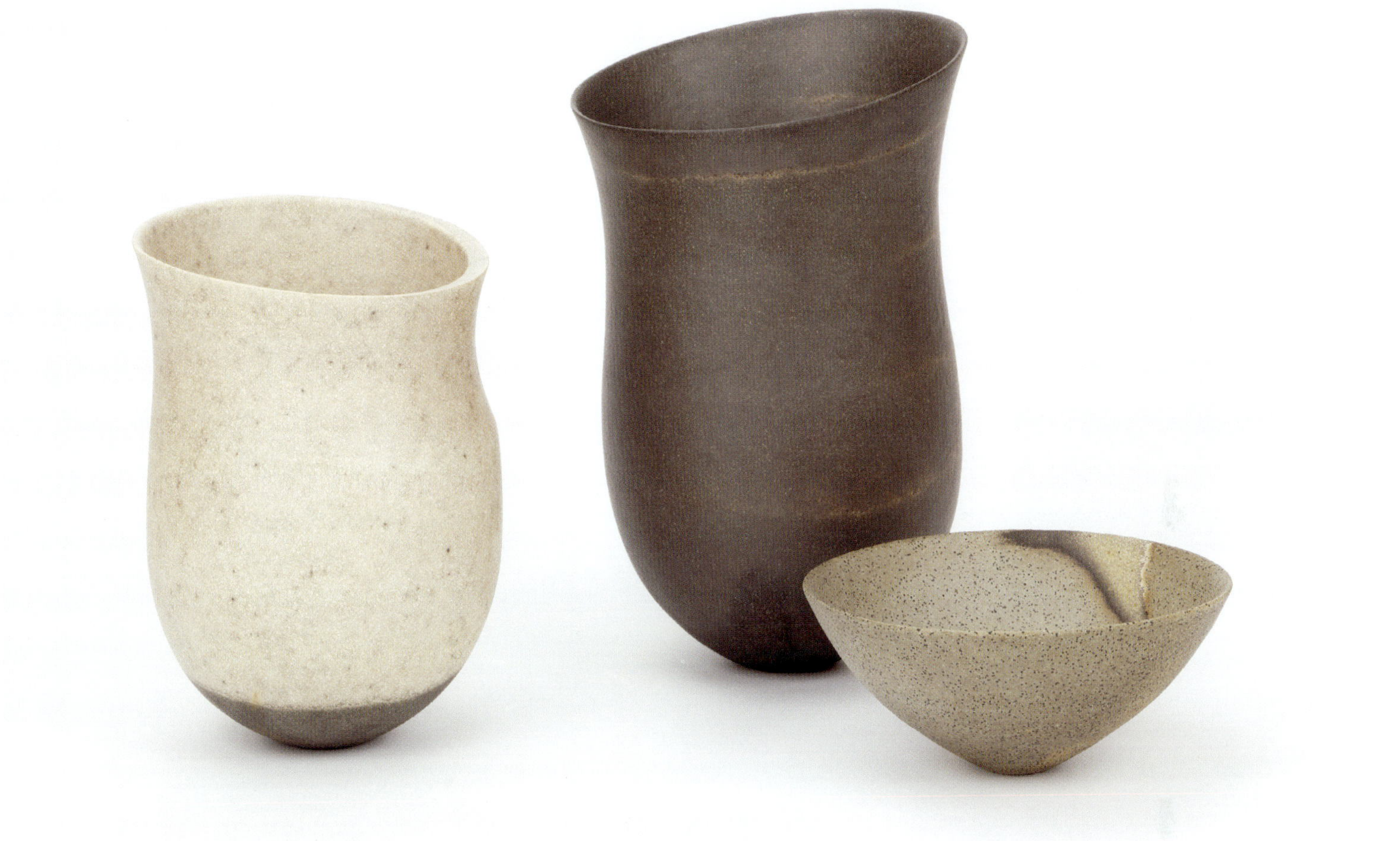

left to right: Speckled stone, graphite clusters, olive base, *2007, handbuilt coloured stoneware.*
Height: 20cm (8in.).
Photo: Alan Tabor, courtesy of Galerie Besson.

Dark metallic, vanishing traces, tilted rim, *2006, handbuilt coloured stoneware.*
Height: 26cm (10¼in.).
Photo: Alan Tabor, courtesy of Galerie Besson.

Speckled olive, haloed spiral, *2007, handbuilt coloured stoneware.*
Height: 7cm (2¾in.).
Photo: Alan Tabor, courtesy of Galerie Besson.

introduced by mixing in metallic oxides. It is a more integrated technique of colouring the clay itself, which lends a rare unity to interior and exterior. The Egyptian wares were burnished to create their iridescent surfaces, and Lee's abrading and burnishing also complete that sense of synthesis. But each Lee pot is very individual in concept, very different in feel and texture, to its historical antecedents. Her ceramics are more consciously sculptural in intention, the product of a very different kind of expressive intelligence. They are concerned with a gradually evolving meditative process, the search for an essential, fundamental language for clay.

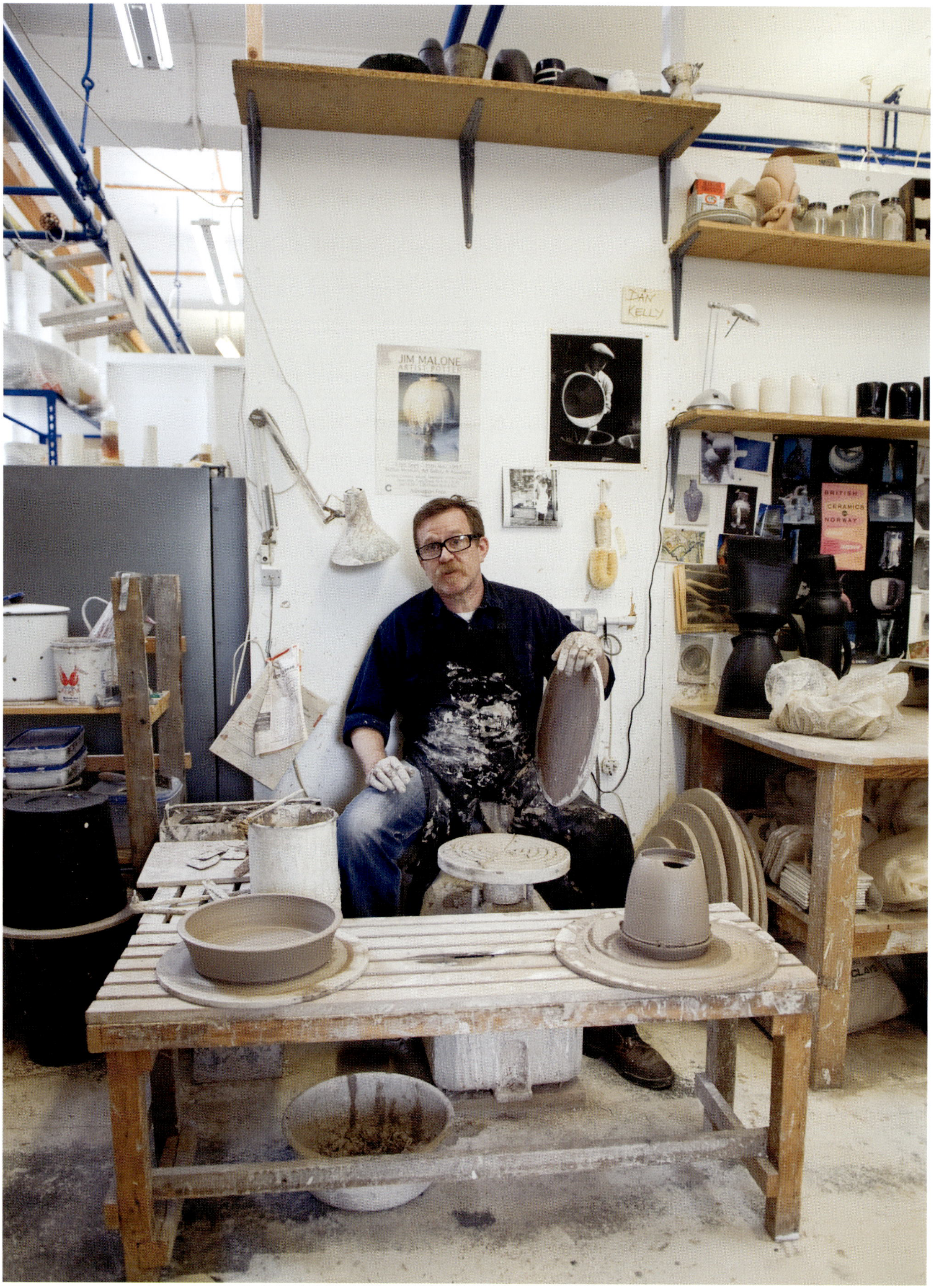
DAN KELLY
JIM MALONE
ARTIST POTTER
BRITISH
CERAMICS
NORWAY

Dan Kelly

DAN KELLY'S STUDIO is five minutes' walk from his home in Camberwell, south London, very much his 'manor', as this born-and-bred Londoner proudly and laughingly puts it. It occupies just part of a large cavernous building that was once owned early in the 20th century by the musical impressario Fred Karno. One time employer of Stan Laurel and Charlie Chaplin, he used it for rehearsals and made props and stage scenery here. The workshop is at one end of the long shared space, with conversations and banter carrying through the partitions. This all seems rather appropriate for such a sociable and down-to-earth potter, but Kelly is also deeply serious about his art and, following in the footsteps of his teacher Colin Pearson, is one of those who has shown, since the early 1980s, what a liberating tool the wheel can be, using it to create bold, freely conceived pots that, while functional in concept, are essentially sculptural objects.

Kelly's ceramics have considerable expressive strength because of their beguiling visual tactility (the potter Takeshi Yasuda once reminded us that 'form is tactile'). They are very physical pots, varied in profile and ranging in texture from the rough to the sensually smooth. With their dents, furrows and creases, they are about surface feeling as well as structure. They have subtleties which invite long consideration with the hands as well as the eyes. Whether we are looking at his straight or waisted cylinders, his monumental bowls or the more bulbous and conical pieces, Kelly's close attention to each aspect of throwing and turning his pots – to their interiors, rims and bases – concentrates our minds on the sensory complexity of fired clay. It is an approach that has also taken much from outside the specific orbit of this substance.

Attending Camberwell School of Art in the early seventies, Kelly, born in 1953, was initially interested in painting, but was converted to clay in his foundation year. He hit a golden period at Camberwell, working in a progressive department that encouraged fresh thinking and experimentation. He was lucky in his teachers, not only Pearson as a thrower but the charismatic handbuilder Ewen Henderson, who demonstrated the importance of drawing in ceramics and a freedom of approach when it came to ceramic form. Both showed persuasively that rules – once learnt – were there to be broken and re-broken. Ceramics, like any other art form, was about a continuous process of reinvention, not a slavish adherence to formulae.

Looking at Kelly's pots today, we can see that his freedom of conception, of 'attack', owes a considerable amount to the aesthetic of particular Japanese ceramic traditions – Tamba, Bizen and Oribe wares – but even as a student an inquisitive Kelly was looking beyond clay. He was drawn instinctively to the directness and invention of African tribal art and to particular contemporary painting and sculpture. When, a little later, he began to absorb the riches of Abstract Expressionism – Jackson Pollock, Willem de Kooning and Franz Kline – and then discovered the liberated throwing of Peter Voulkos, he knew he was following the right creative route. He was fascinated by various forms of visual art where pigment and glaze, surface and form, were given a free hand; where there was no real distinction, because of the physicality of the material, between two and three-dimensional abstract concerns.

Through improvisation and alteration he moved away from conventional throwing towards a more gestural examination of the substance of clay, a ceramic equivalent of the

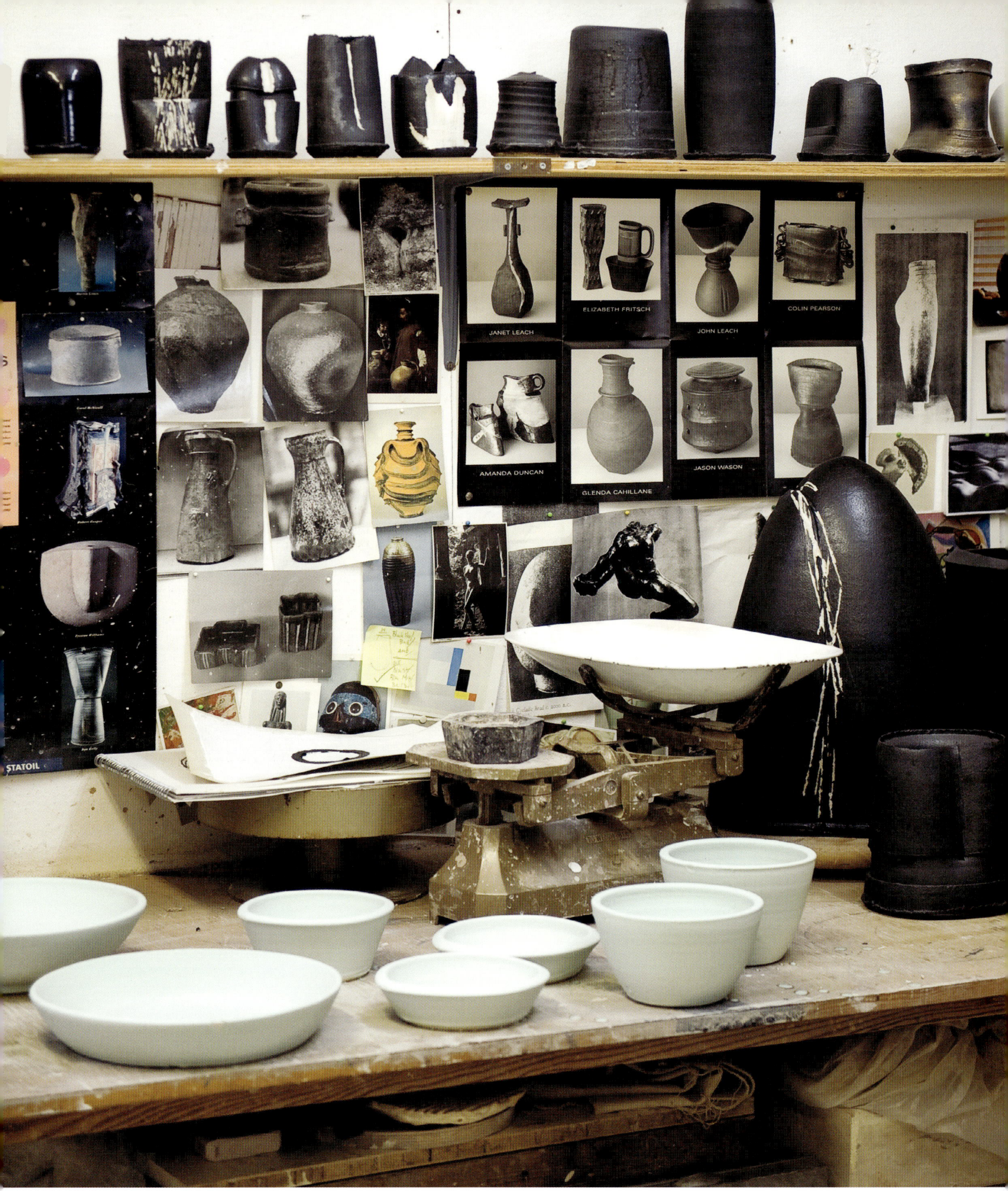
JANET LEACH
ELIZABETH FRITSCH
JOHN LEACH
COLIN PEARSON
AMANDA DUNCAN
GLENDA CAHILLANE
JASON WASON
STATOIL

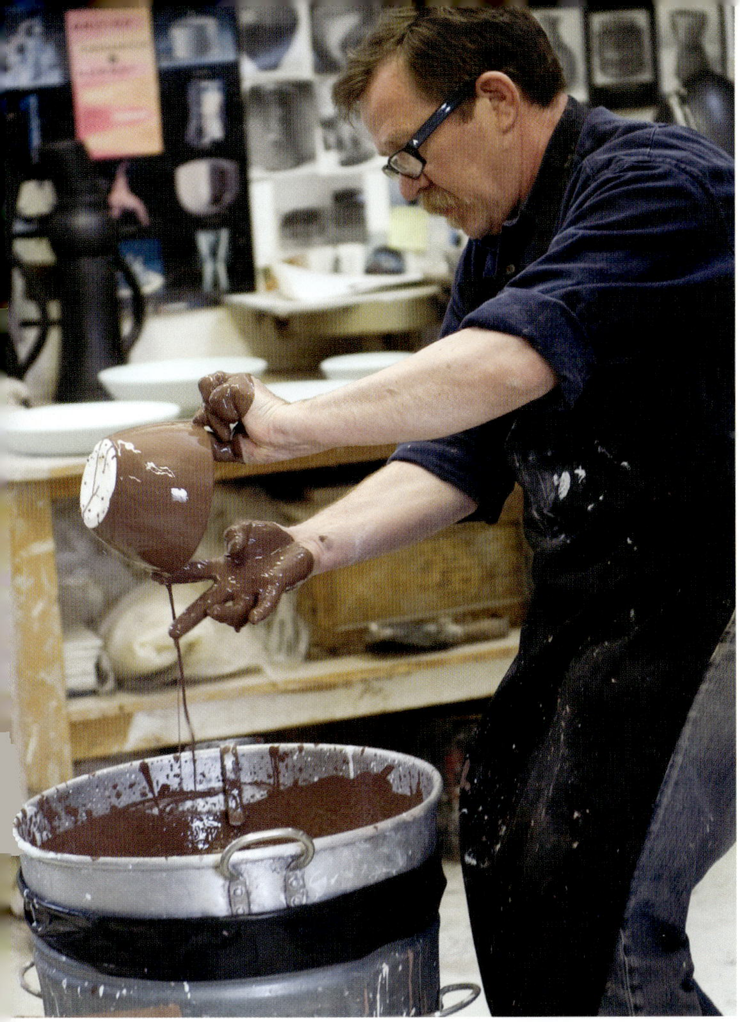

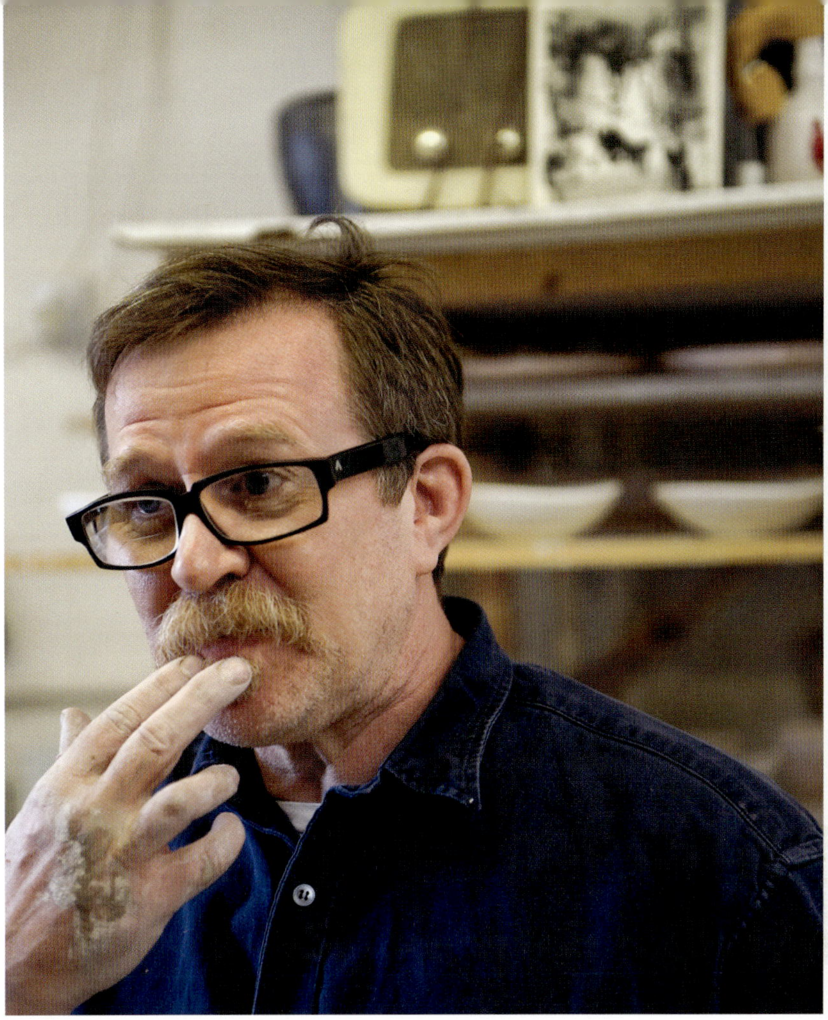

rich painterly experiments of the New York School of the 1950s and 60s and a modern, consciously more sculptural reinterpretation of Far Eastern ceramic traditions. While at the Royal College of Art he discovered the sculpture of Willem de Kooning, then showing at the Serpentine Gallery, a short walk from the RCA. Kelly was amazed at the soft, liquid quality of the clay-modelled bronzes he saw, and excited by how de Kooning's figures revelled in the soggy juicy mass of the material. Far more than a medium, it was, like the oil paint in a Kline abstract, a means of release.

Using a coarser clay, or crank, for its generous consistency, he has preferred to apply layers of oxide and a thin coat of glaze to the face of the material, allowing the clay to speak for itself, to let the movement of throwing remain very clear. While he has occasionally made small squashed pots, perhaps dribbling with wood ash, and groups of pieces in thickly thrown white porcelain – Kelly tends to make in series, working through a batch until some sort of conclusion is reached – it is with black that he has found so much to say. In this respect he is like Hans Coper, but Kelly's dynamic, both in execution and result, is far more spontaneous and loose. Yet there is nothing impulsive about Kelly's precision of craftsmanship. If he takes liberties with the material, it is because he understands it.

In the nineties Kelly began to throw open sections without bases, which allowed him a new structural freedom, conceiving new forms and only adding a base when a new shape had emerged. Some of these have resembled industrial components, and it is clear that Kelly's interest in vernacular structures (such as mass-produced clay chimney pots) has influenced his approach. Black has helped to concentrate attention on the new deviations of form that emerge – on the facial texture, the inner motion, the rising energy achieved in throwing. Against the smooth sheen of a body

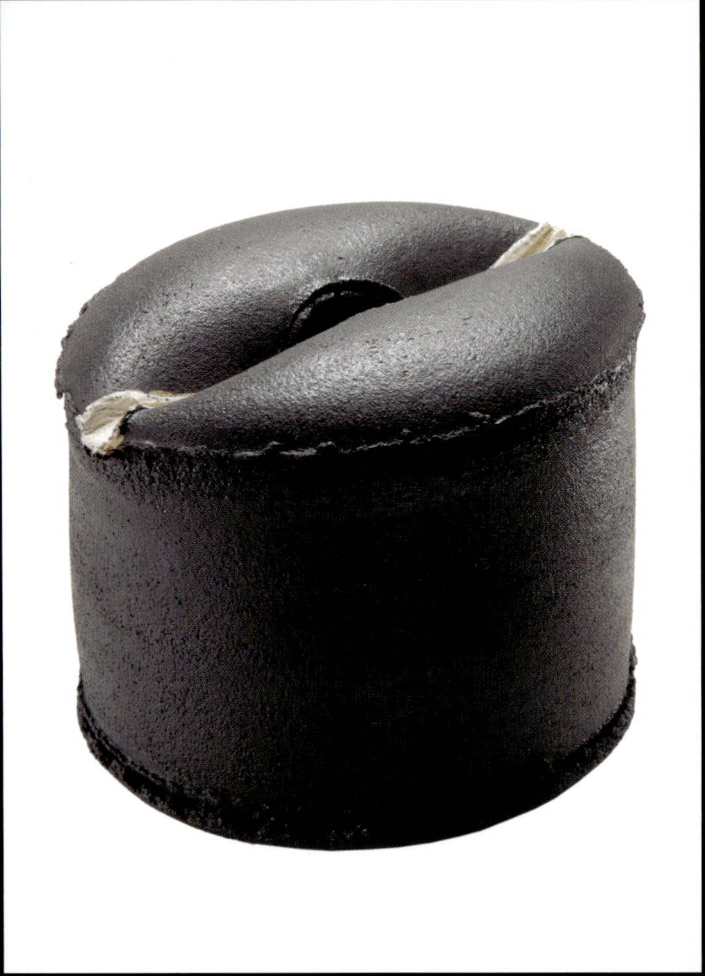

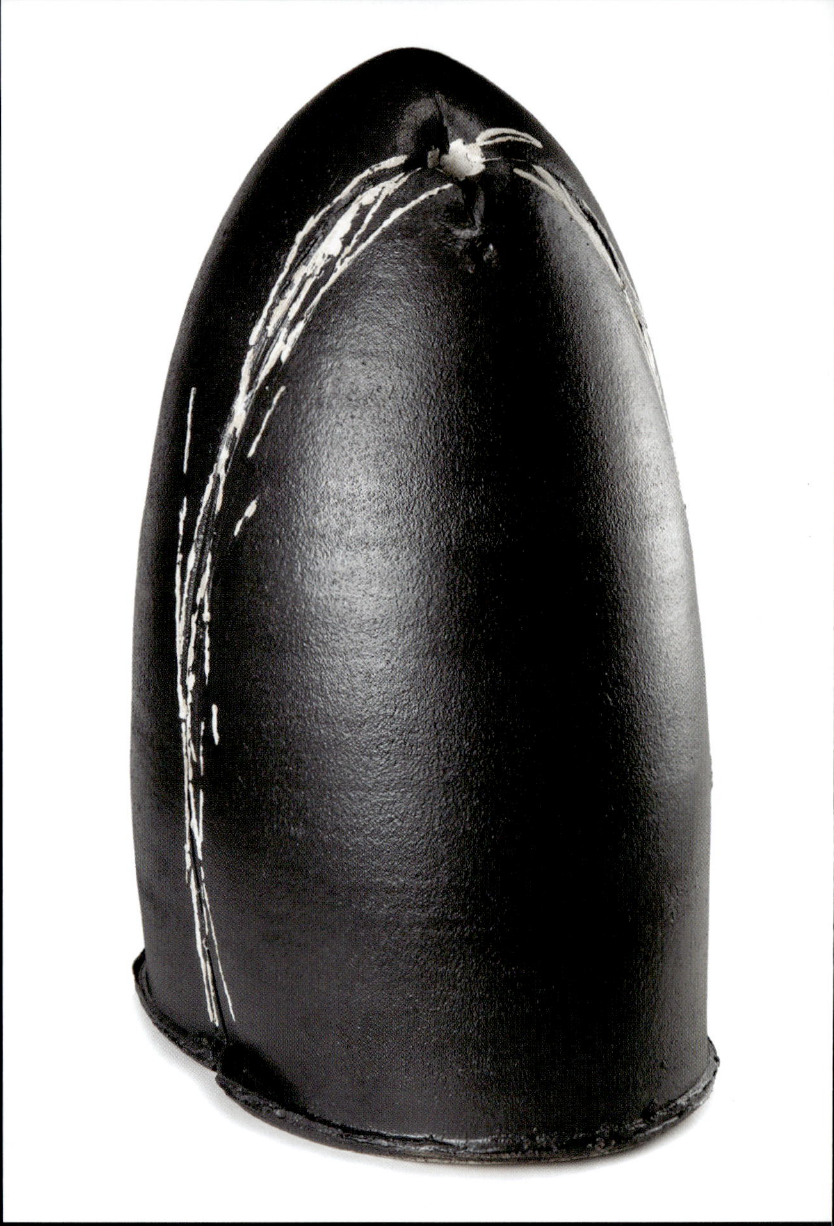

above: Vessel, *2006, stoneware.*
Height: 19cm (7½in).
right: Vessel, *2007, stoneware.*
Height 46cm (18in).
Photos: Courtesy of the artist

that swells and contracts to a concluding lip or base, the clay of the foot or rim is often left rough with flecks and shavings of clay, expressive of the speed and energy involved in executing them (and reminiscent of the cast metal from industrial lathes). Fontana-like slashes or softer, more sensual openings, often accentuated by white porcelain slip, exemplify Kelly's delight in contrasting sensations of sight and touch. The mouths into his pots are often as smooth as bone, with Kelly emphasising the potential intimacies of ceramics. Clay's innate plasticity has also been gauged in his occasionally more baroque pieces: a group of jugs made for a show at Galerie Besson in 2007 demonstrated his love of the material's sculptural spring, his enjoyment of free, curving drawing in space.

Kelly's calligraphic markings of slip, reminiscent of the gestural abstraction of Robert Motherwell and Antoni Tàpies (as well as Japanese potters like Shoji Hamada), are rarer these days: since he has pared down his language in search of a fluid simplicity and economy, some of the articulations have gone. The mysteries of containment are a constant preoccupation, that of the relationship between inside and outside, the fact

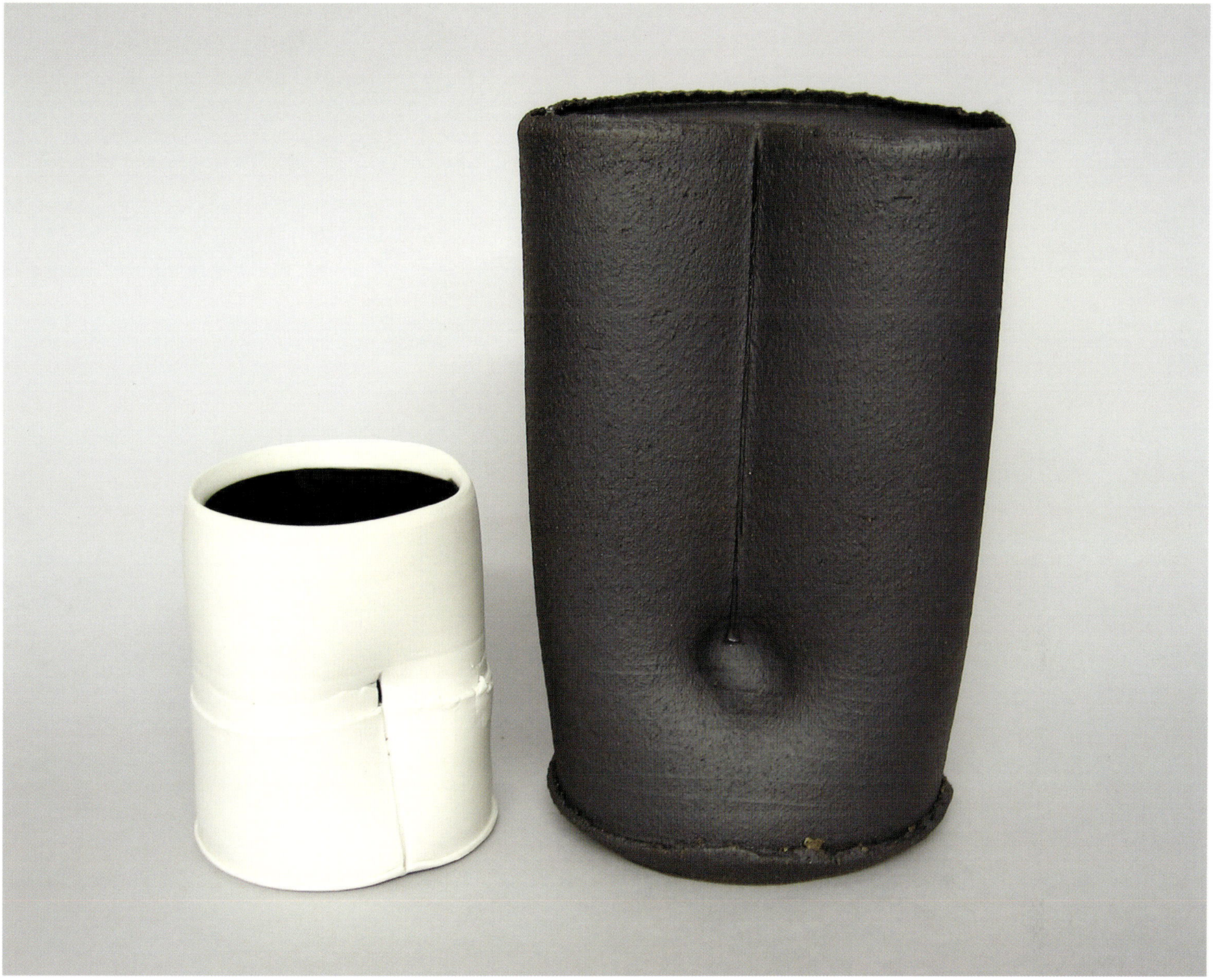

Vessels, *2006, porcelain and stoneware.*
Height: 10cm (4in); Height: 20cm (8in). Photo: Courtesy of the artist

that an interior, however hidden, is still of equal symbolic and spatial significance. In this respect his work parallels the hand-building of Gordon Baldwin: both make objects that are partly preoccupied by seductively concealed volumes. Kelly has work by Baldwin at home, along with functional pieces by, for example, Clive Bowen, Geoffrey Whiting and Isaac Button. His interest in Button and other, largely anonymous country potters shows his respect for craft techniques that deepen and evolve over years of practice.

Kelly remains an elusive potter, exhibiting infrequently and uninterested in self-promotion. Yet he remains ambitious for the art of throwing, believing the possibilities are infinite. Being creatively subsumed in its rhythms, in stream-of-consciousness making, has always been a fertile mechanism for what Colin Pearson called the 'controlled accident'. Anything can happen, any new direction can occur. In this regard he is uninterested in overly conceptual and academicised college courses; too much theory is anathema to Kelly. He simply wants the work to stand by itself – powerful objects imprinted with the dramas of their making.

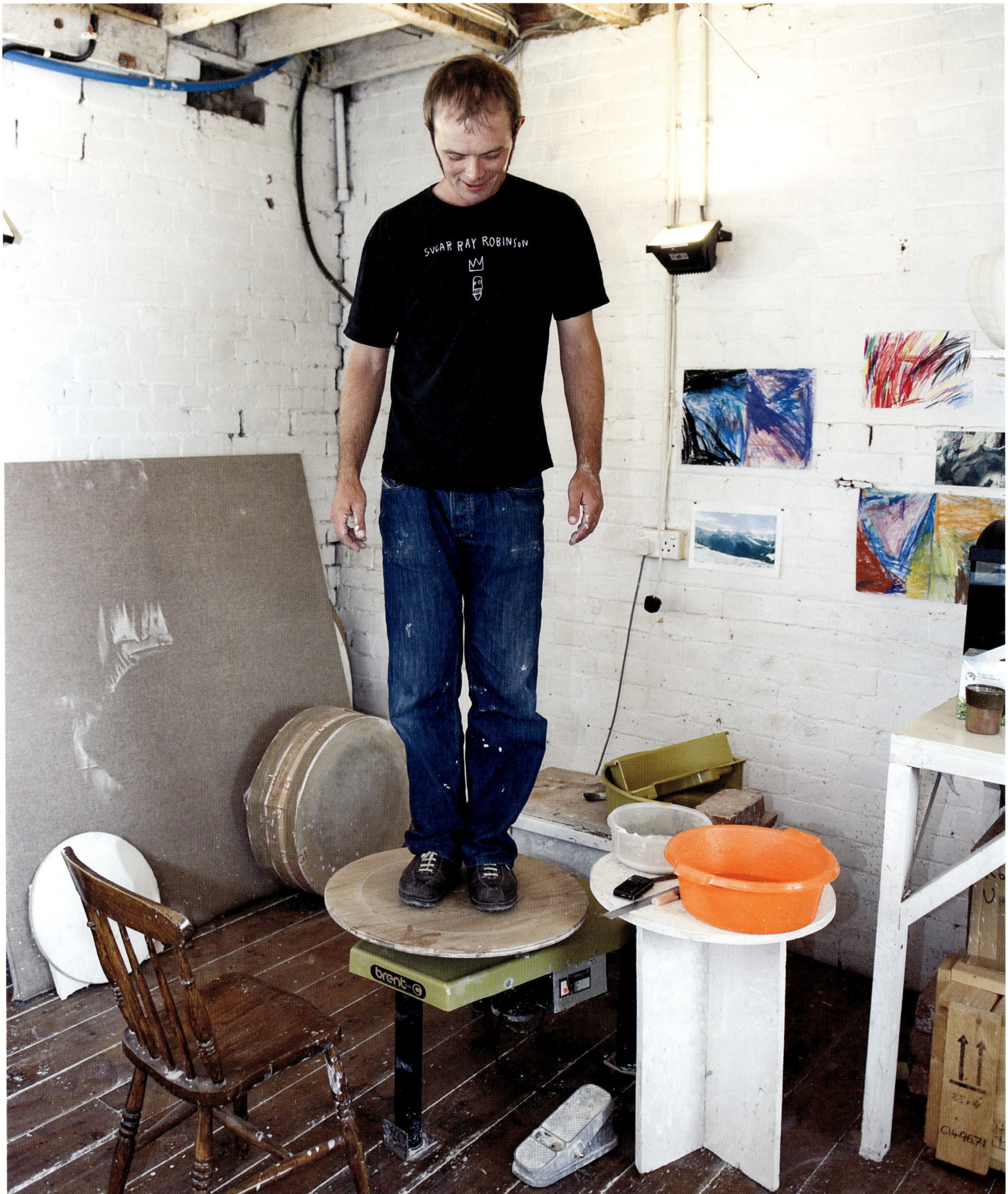
SUGAR RAY ROBINSON
brent

Daniel Fisher

DANIEL FISHER'S delicate and ethereal work, combining throwing with constructive manipulation, has established him as one of the most interesting potters to have emerged in the late 1990s. In the decade since, his vessels, which possess an often luminous and papery beauty, have quietly and imaginatively developed into objects which gauge both the fragility and the tensile strength of porcelain and stoneware, the ability of clay to be stretched and manipulated through the hands into the most fluid structures. They can make the material seem wet and unfixed, sometimes drier and bonier, the ripples and striations opening out the form into a very different kind of pot. Some pieces are softer and calmer in conception, others more rented and frenetic, full of the life of their making. Yet Fisher is essentially a 'non-scene' potter, an artist who has kept his distance from the mainstream, preferring to combine making with other work commitments, giving him the financial freedom to make what he wants, when he wants.

He shows his ceramics internationally, but not with any regularity in Britain. This makes his pots difficult to find, but always worth the journey. Living and working in secluded Gloucestershire for many years now, Fisher has always been keen to avoid the creative treadmill that comes with success, which he found at an early age. He doesn't want to churn out work that will quickly bore him – to become, in effect, a production line. It is also true that, with their dependence on the intricate and intuitive action of the fingers, his pots would soon reveal any tendency towards routine or slickness of method. His ceramics have a certain tension, a tautness as well as a structural relaxation, that gives them vigour and energy. Fisher knows he needs to retain these qualities if the work is to keep its strength and presence.

Fisher was born in 1973 and brought up in Norfolk, and his parents were both academics. The impact of the East Anglian light, the sky and the flatness of the landscape has left a lasting impression on his aesthetic. He discovered ceramics on his foundation course in Norwich and went on to study at Bath and then Camberwell School of Art. Here Lawson Oyekan and Takeshi Yasuda, visiting tutors, encouraged him to experiment and improvise with clay beyond the conventions of production ware and traditional throwing. He began to make wheel-based sculptural pieces. Altered and modified, they combined his new interest in the varied nature and consistency of clay with performance aspects, the 'action' of the making process. At the Royal College of Art his interest in the basic physical qualities of clay deepened, and he now used glaze as a lubricant to achieve new qualities of plasticity in throwing. When forms folded or collapsed he improvised by hanging them from a turntable to stretch them back into shape, thus reversing the gravitational pull of the initial form. These vessels were then completed by his innovative method of pulling, stretching and squeezing the clay into the membranous structures he has been extending and refining to this day.

Fisher's studio is in Stroud. After leaving the RCA, he converted an old Co-op bakery into a spacious workshop. Living amongst the old wool mills, he likes the anonymity of this valley, the land of Laurie Lee. The workroom is a long one. There are lengthy workbenches and, at one end, a low wheel for the initial throwing of his pots. On the window sills there is an accumulation of natural and man-made objects – including a Ewen Henderson teabowl – that suggest material for inspiration. There is also a TV, a stack of

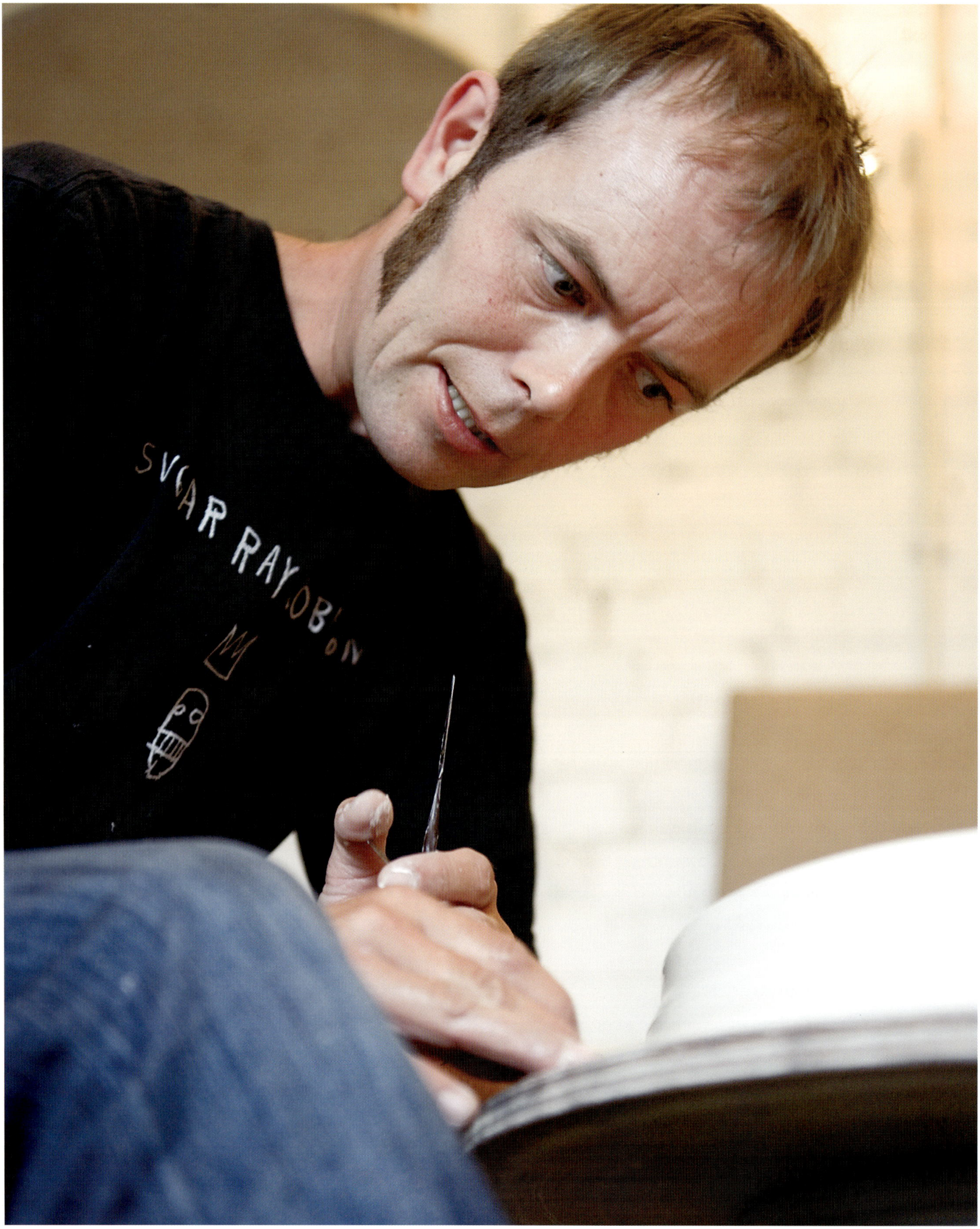
SVGAR RAY

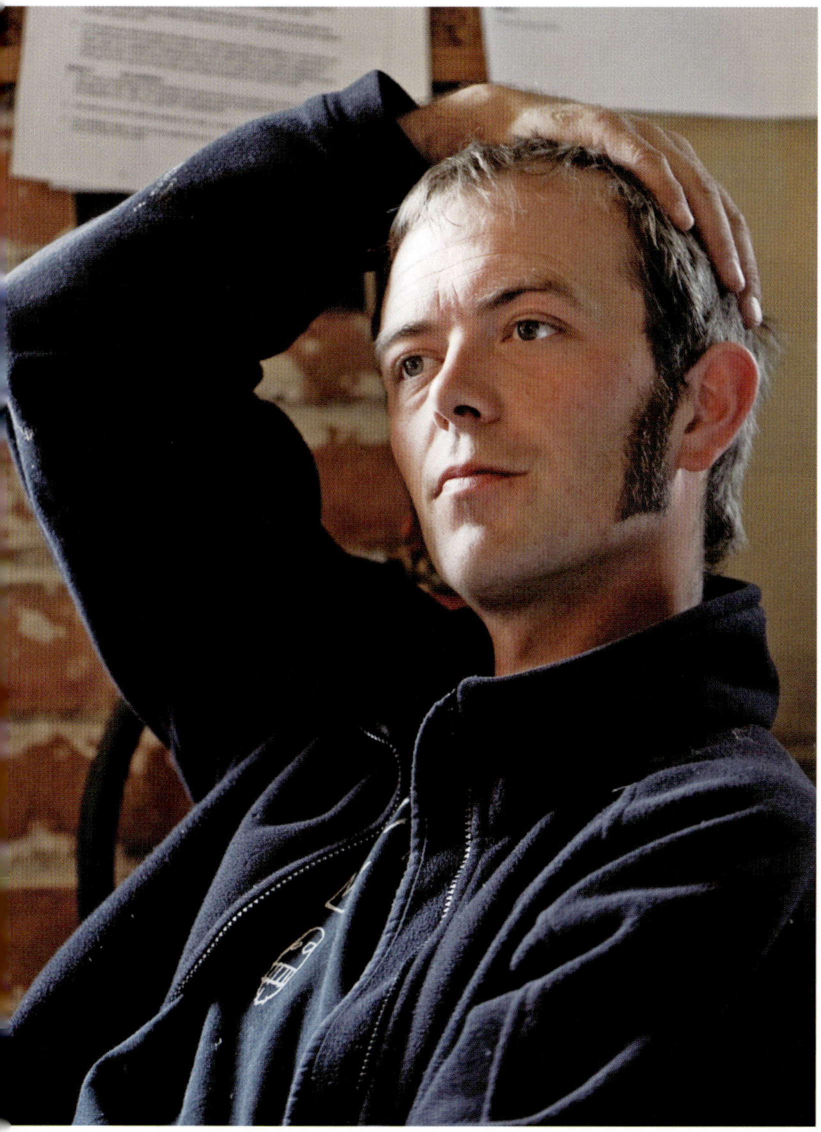

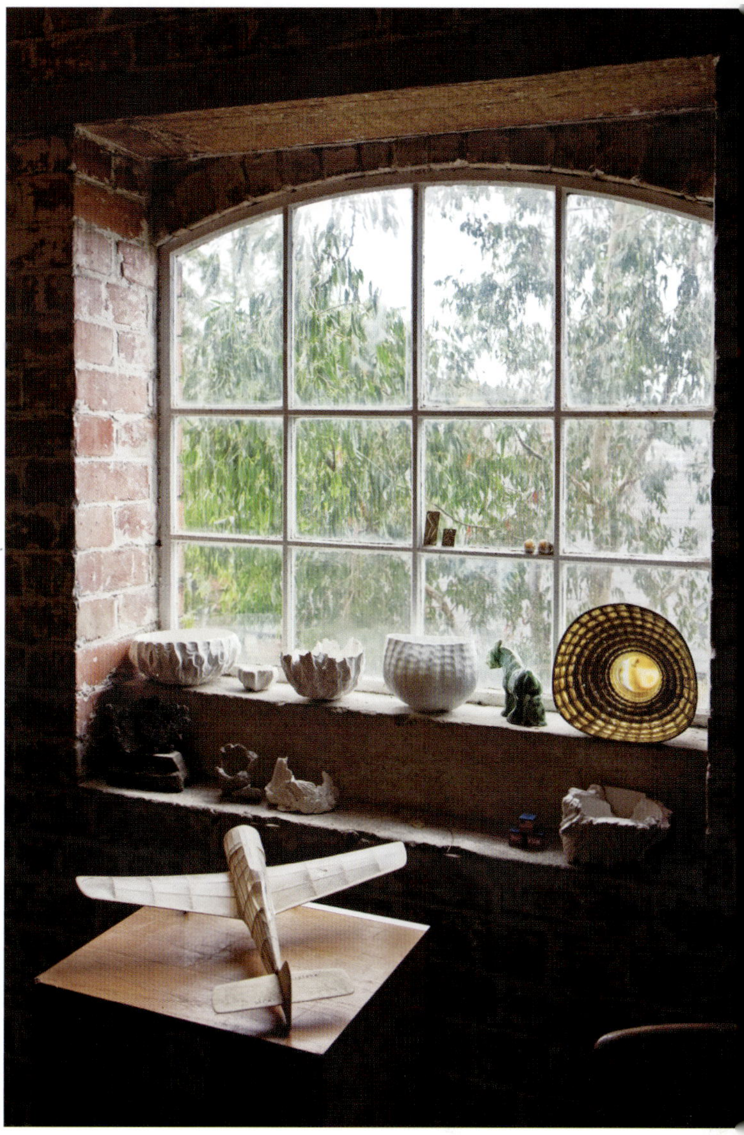

assorted videos and some comfy seats; this is a personal den as well as a place of creativity. Here you can see some of his recent work – pieces in raw glazed stoneware as well as the large lantern-like porcelain vessels that explore, so poetically, his interest in translucency and the passage of light. His stoneware, with its corrugated vertebrae and undulating tiers of glaze decoration, is now wood-fired, giving the scorched surfaces a warmer, more integrated quality. Some of Fisher's forms are reminiscent of the structures of pods or seeds, or more metallic shapes, seen and studied. Whether darkly opaque or transmitting light, the shapes have the quality of organic growth, the sense of lift powerfully directed in the pleats and rhythms of their walls, and the often flame-like serrations of their rims. The porcelain has a brittle wintry quality, shifting the material from its traditional thrown smoothness into another kind of sensuality. Fisher may knead or crease the surfaces to the point of penetration, creating tears and rents that take the clay into a more raw and elemental state, one that can remind people, variously, of coral, glass, ice, snow and other natural phenomena.

The failure rate of his high-risk approach is inevitably considerable, with frequent warping or even collapses during firing. So, more recently, he has made smaller, pinched pots, their surfaces lined with a needle; these can be made in a day, allowing him 'more control' and enabling him to

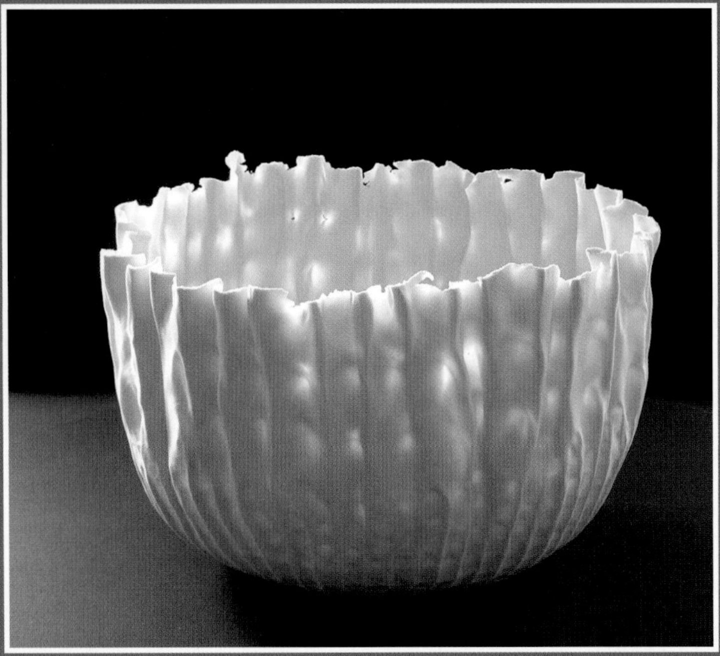

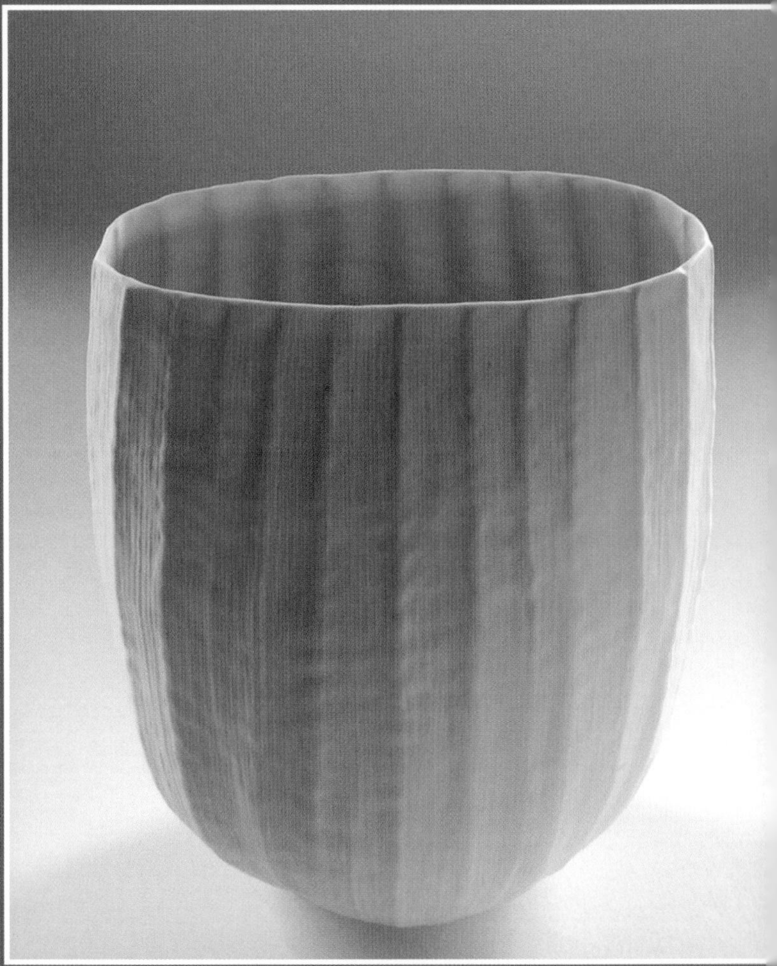

above: Flame, *2007, porcelain. Height: 25.5cm (10in.).*
right: Gourd, *2006, porcelain. Height: 23cm (9in.).*
Photos: Courtesy of the artist

enjoy the intimacy and tactility that is characteristic of their scale. The ellipses that occur in firing, once irksome, Fisher now accepts as part of the spirit of a piece. He is also more tolerant of people using his pots for flowers or some other function. Youthful purism has been supplanted by a more relaxed pragmatism.

In a bid to find more spontaneity in his working method and to produce more clearly functional work, he has also been making big porcelain platters – born out of a student project – which he throws and then inverts, so furthering his interest in the way gravity can be used to pull and manipulate the clay into shapes with a natural elasticity. These objects – which may slump further in the kiln – have a strong sense of settled motion, the subtle undulations and tensions of surface completed by creamy matt celadons. Fisher talks about the way they stand and the points of contact between base and surface. He has always had a strong concern for the formal relationships between foot and rim, and between interior and exterior, and with the different kinds of poise and balance he can achieve. The way he addresses these tensions is what gives his work its floating, levitational quality.

Like Takeshi Yasuda, Fisher has made the most of the processes that take place slightly outside his direct control. He enjoys giving the clay a certain amount of freedom, reminding us that it is an expanding, contracting and flexing

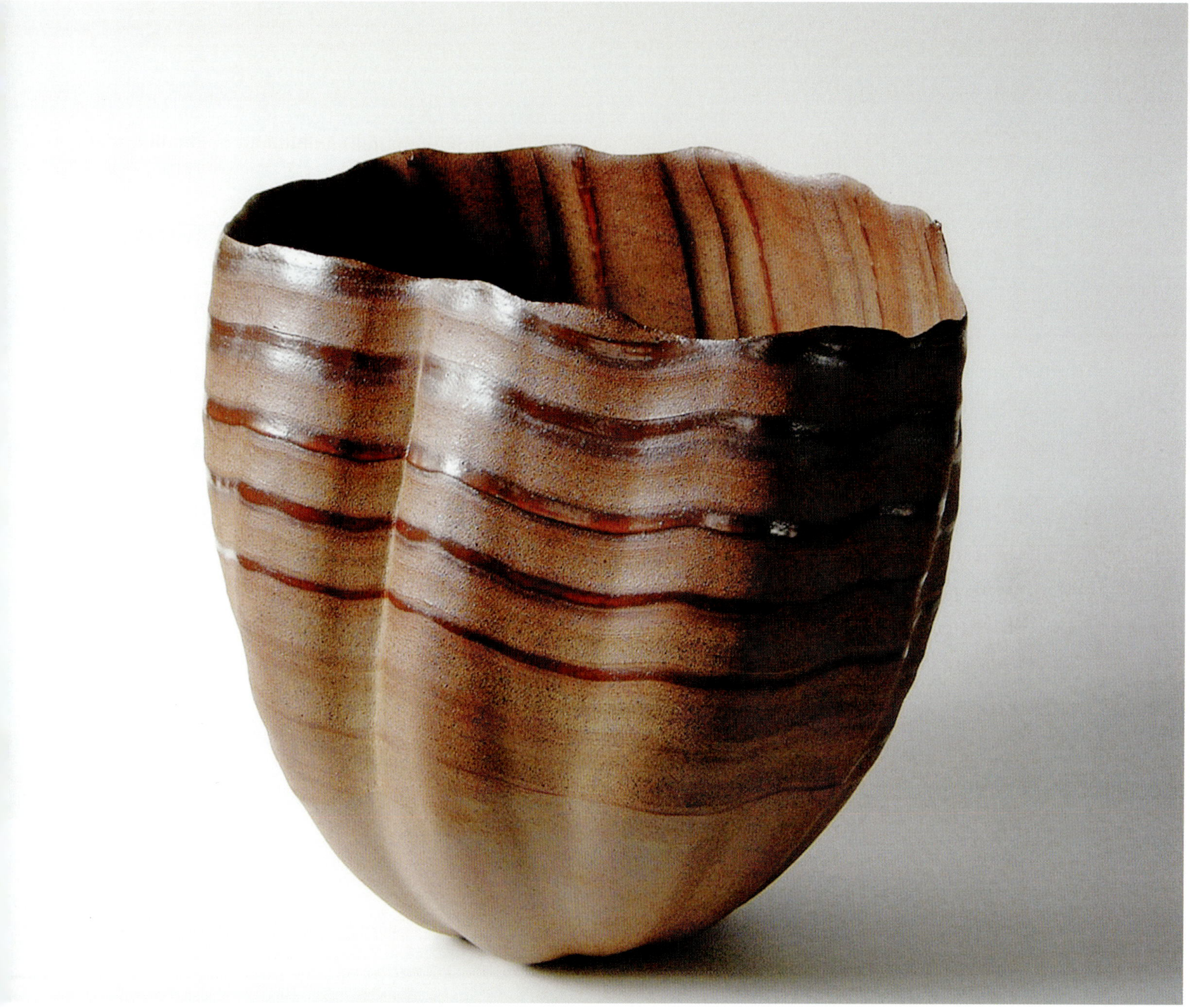

Large Vessel, *2008, stoneware.*
Height: 30.5cm (12in.). Photo: Courtesy of the artist

substance with a mind of its own. Its unpredictably may be unnerving, but it can also result in objects of great freshness and power. Fisher is not a potter of specific historical reference, but he still draws on the ceramic past in the broadest symbolic and sculptural sense. His work connects strongly with the ceremonial ritual objects used in various cultures over thousands of years. The ancient and innate relationship between the vessel, the landscape from which it derives, and our own bodies, our physical selves, is an important underlying aspect of his art. It is this mysterious sense of connection that continues to fascinate Daniel Fisher, giving his ceramics a significance beyond the decorative, beyond ornamentation, important though these qualities are.

Tina Vlassopulos

HANDBUILDING IN BRITAIN has enjoyed a particularly fertile history since the late 1950s, when potters like Dan Arbeid, Gordon Baldwin, Ruth Duckworth, Alan Wallwork and Gillian Lowndes were developing a largely vessel-based language that was essentially organic in nature. With their rugged forms and textures, these objects reintroduced us to the most immediate qualities of clay, suggesting a range of surfaces and structures in the landscape, of various natural forms seen and felt. Many of these shapes related to abstract and figurative concerns in contemporary painting and sculpture, but also, way back, to prehistory, to ancient cultures and other sources.

By the late 1970s handbuilt work was becoming more elemental, exploring simple bowl and more closed forms, still with ritualistic overtones. One thinks of the ceramics of Betty Blandino, Magdalene Odundo, Jennifer Lee, John Ward and the early work of Ewen Henderson and Sara Radstone. However, another potter who has taken the notion of the vessel and manipulated it into different types of construction is Tina Vlassopulos. In her hands the clay, in both warm terracotta and coloured stoneware, achieves a distinctive sense of movement – curling, rippling and twisting over its surfaces. Her pots have a marked energy and a sense of upward and outward expansion. In some ways a consolidation of the vocabulary of ceramics – there is now no decoration or marking – each piece still provides a new departure in investigating contour, surface and volume.

Tina Vlassopulos's studio is as understated as the work. Situated in a north London street near the Finchley Road, it is an ordered, almost laboratory-like space that reflects the clean precision of her pots. There are photographs of source material and shelves of finished pots, some dating back several years – giving a condensed idea of her artistic development. This is very much an urban workspace, but Vlassopulos's aesthetic is firmly rooted in other landscapes: her shapes suggest junctures where the land meets the sea, or perhaps hollows and undulations in the earth. On a smaller scale her forms can evoke the spreading of leaves, organisms in ground and water, or the structure of shells. The temperature is that of a southern climate, Vlassopulos's work suggests warmer Mediterranean places. So it comes as no surprise to know that although Vlassopulos was born in London in 1954, and subsequently brought up there, her origins are Greek. It is a country to which she often returns and where much of her aesthetic seems rooted. Not that she is usually specific about sources; her work seems more an abstracted meditation on both exterior and interior worlds, built up and pared down by her concentrating mind and by the physical processes of handbuilding and burnishing.

Vlassopulos trained in ceramics in the famous department at Bristol Polytechnic. Since she graduated in 1977, her work has been a long conversation with the vessel: from tall narrow containers to shapes flaring out into bowls, to spoon and cuplike forms, some extending into far more unusual structures. The approach has changed over time, of course. At one stage she enjoyed working with slips and stains, giving an added sense of colour and movement, the decoration often applied in rhythmic patterns, like the surface of a seabed or the motion of light on water. But Vlassopulos often left interiors or exteriors clear of marking, increasingly drawn as she was to the form itself, to its sags, undulations and crisp, clarifying rims. Just as she finds many of her ideas from 'within herself', she is equally

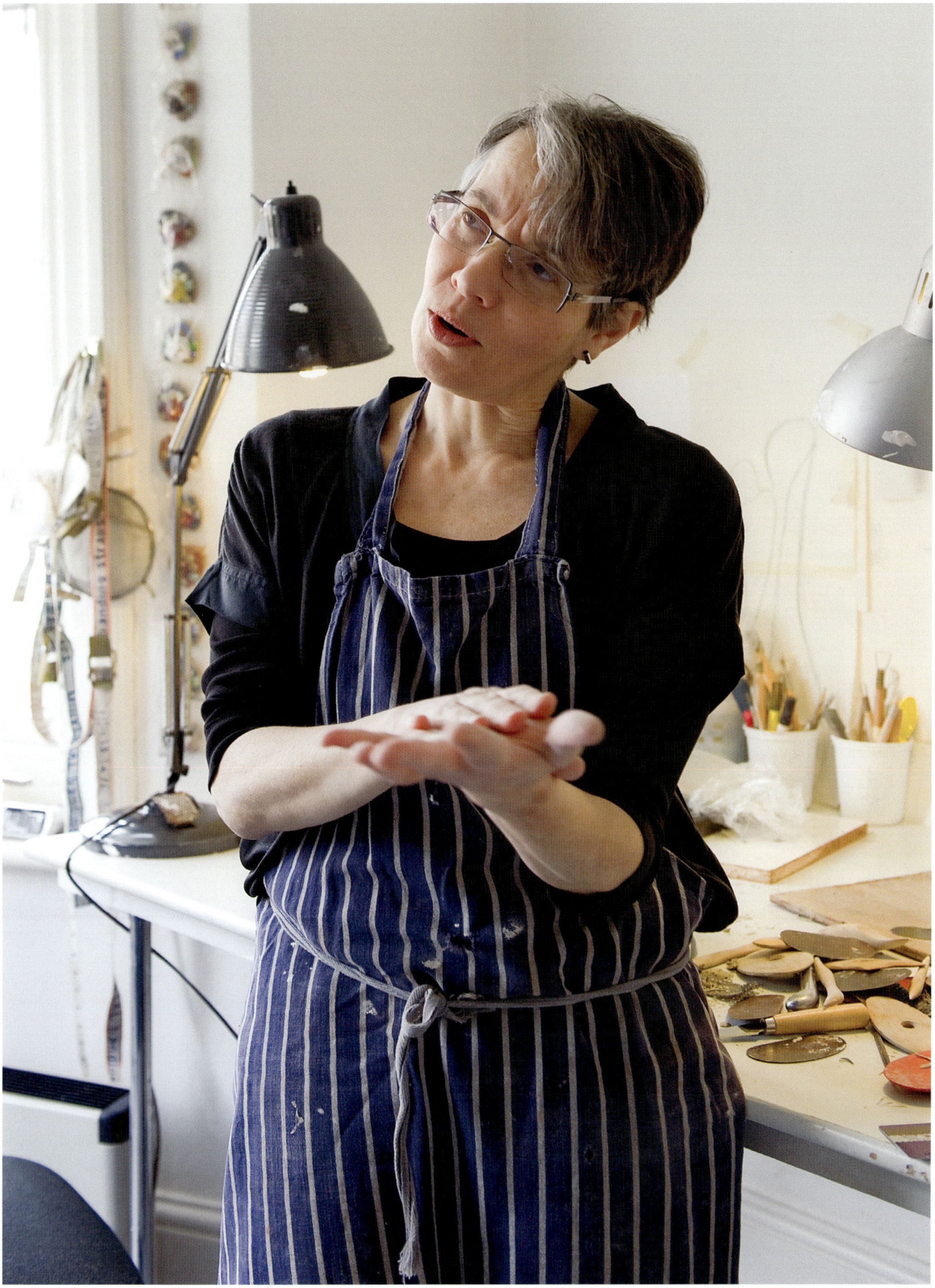

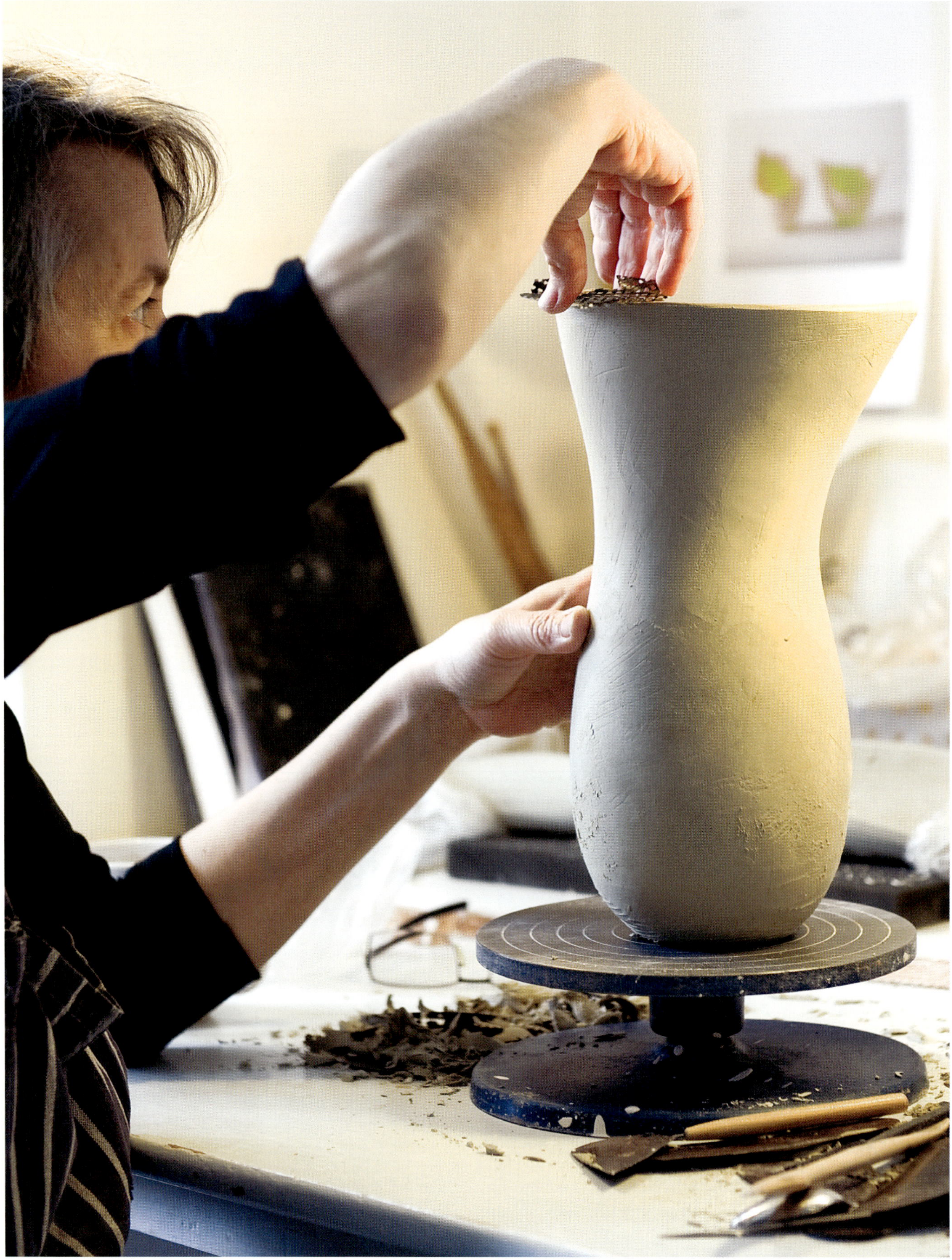

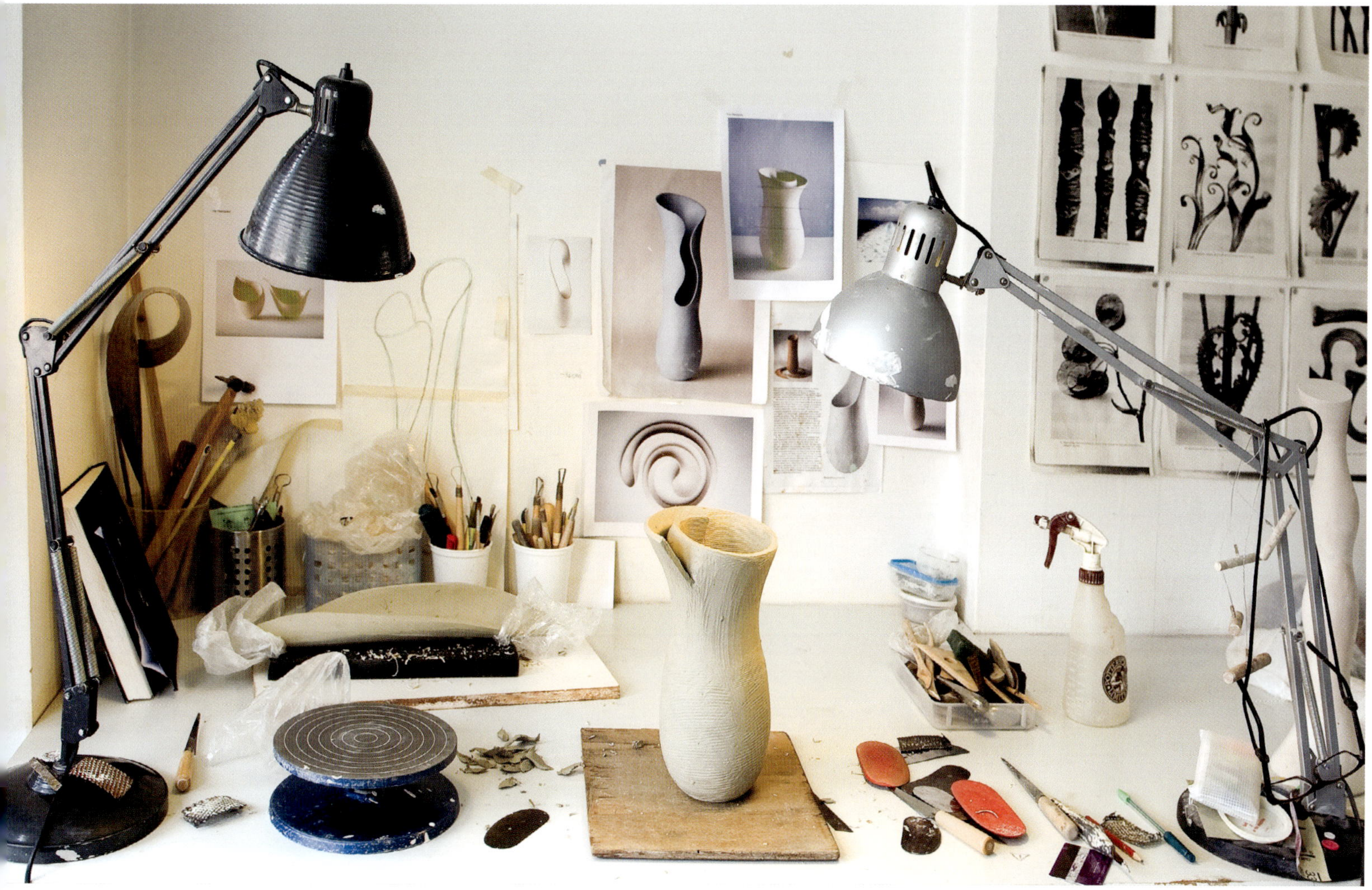

keen to get to the 'centre' of a form, to the bone of an idea. A series of pieces relating to seeds and pods was an exception to her general rule about conscious sourcing, but even these were refined into very different kinds of object. This earlier work was, like all Vlassopulos's output, intentionally decorative, offering a form of visual and tactile release for both potter and user. Her wish to provide visual enrichment has been developed in her ceramic jewellery, too.

By the mid-1990s her interest in the fundamentals of handbuilding had led to a more direct technique that dispensed with painted embellishment. She became increasingly involved in the structure of her pots, enjoying the natural warmth of red earthenware. Some of these pieces were relatively straightforward in conception, while others were more teased out, stretched and pulled into long curves, some curling like fern fronds or moving diagonally upwards like the assertive spouts on Cycladic jugs. The shapes became increasingly biomorphic and fluid as they spread out from their balancing bases, changing into other structures suggestive of ritualistic ladles or primitive life forms. Vlassopulos was evolving an increasingly elemental language, creating primordial shapes with a very primordial substance.

The process of making is a painstaking and lengthy one, often lasting several days, which involves building up and then scraping down and smoothing, followed by burnishing and polishing. Vlassopulos will work on a number of related forms – variations on a particular idea – before moving on, a method of making that instils a sense of connection and unity. Some pieces are made in pairs or in larger still-life

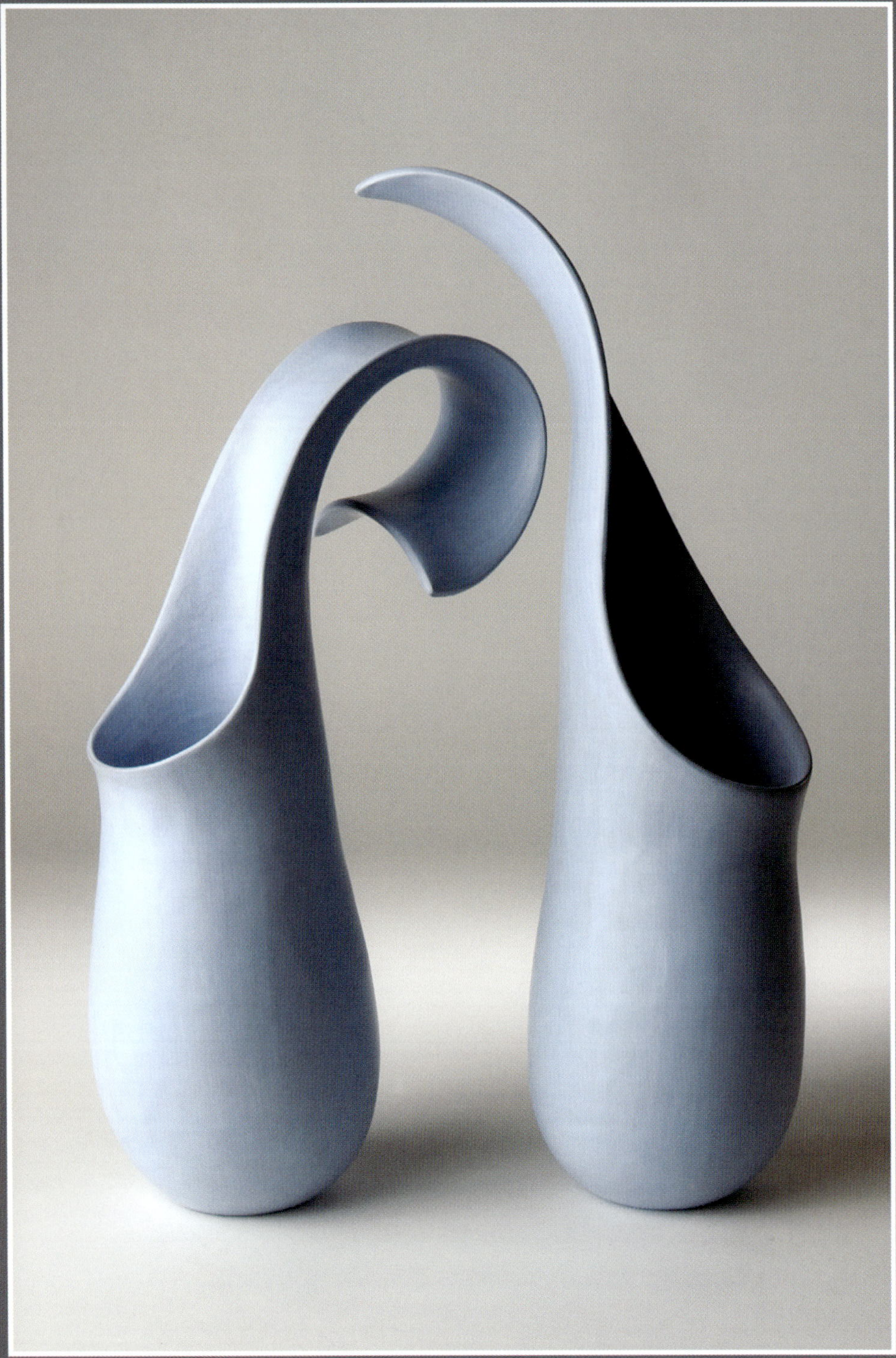

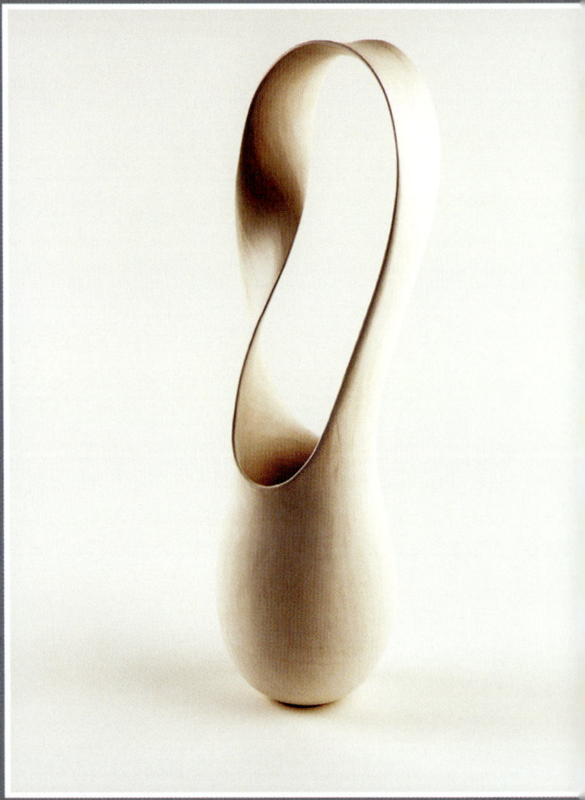

left: Affinity, *2006. Stoneware. Height: 35cm (13¾in.); Height: 41cm (16in.).*
above: Mœbius, *2002. Stoneware. Height: 44cm (17¼in.).*
Photos: Mike Abrahams

groupings, extending the rhythms of positive and negative space in Vlassopulos's work. They are objects with independent personalities, but they also create interesting interactions when arranged together. They have obliquely figurative connotations, too. The more recent pieces, mostly made in stoneware, have grown in ambition and expressive complexity – vessels with broad, ribbon-like handles looping into the air, others with Ionic-type scrolls. Some shapes

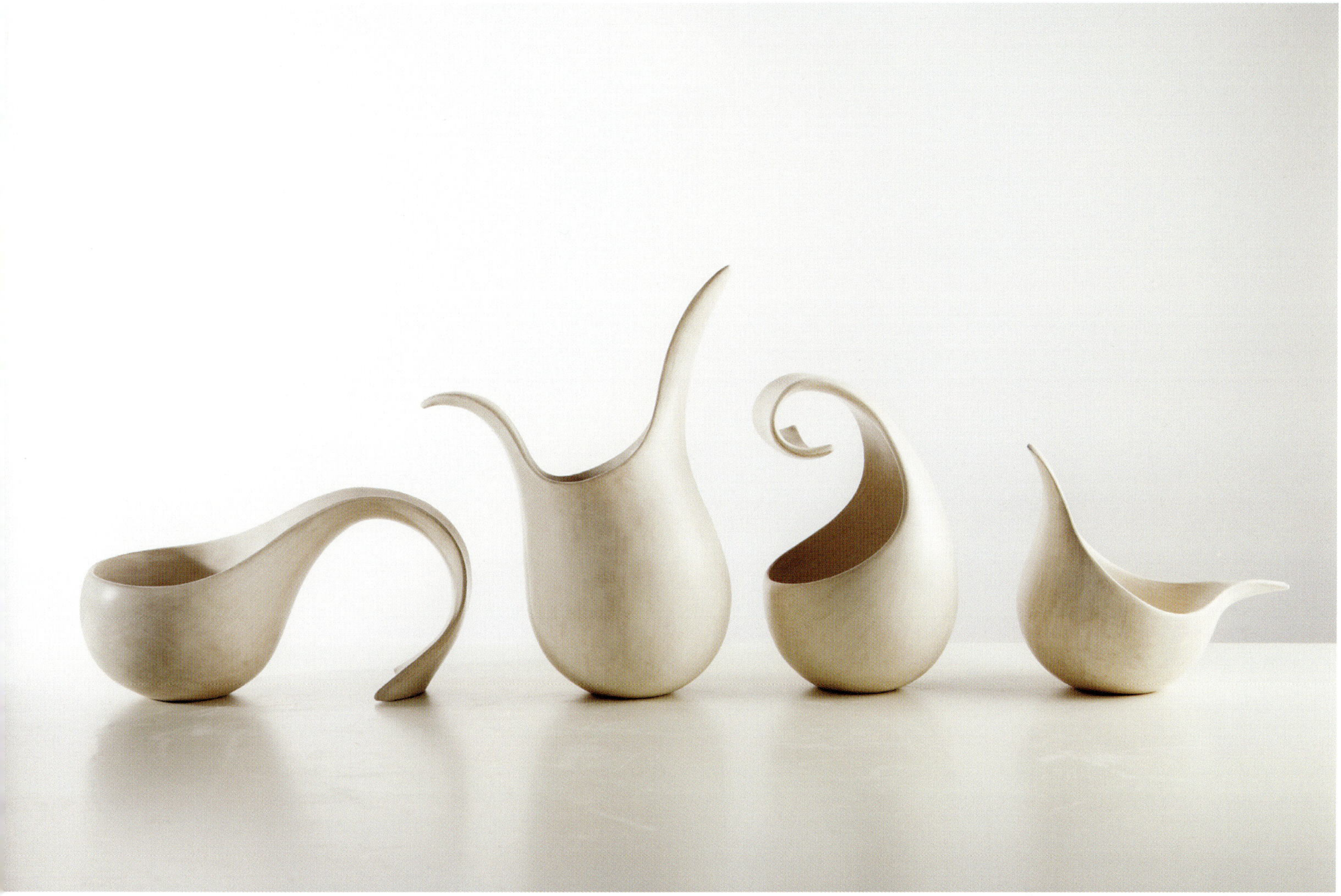

Wave, *2007, stoneware.*
Height: 24, 26, 19 and 16cm (9½, 10¼, 7½, and 6¼ in.).
Photo: Mike Abrahams

are suggestive of the curving passage of a riverbed. Like the comparable vessels of Annie Turner, Vlassopulos explores both the literal and the broader metaphorical implications of containment. One of her spiral forms, made in 2006, is a long vessel that coils like a snake. Some pieces appear to travel across their surfaces while others climb into space – a strange combination of stillness and motion.

These pots – from bold terracottas to intense, ethereal blues – reflect a serious commitment to the craft and spirit of clay. They are also full of playful celebration, objects which are refreshingly free of baggage and do not require an ounce of theory to appreciate. Vlassopulos doesn't like to intellectualise about her ceramics, preferring to let the clay speak for itself. It is this directness, this lack of pretension, which so appeals to her. It is also, of course, a richly fertile substance, one that has found fresh expression in, to borrow a phrase of Paul Valéry's, the 'abstract fecundity' of Tina's vessels.

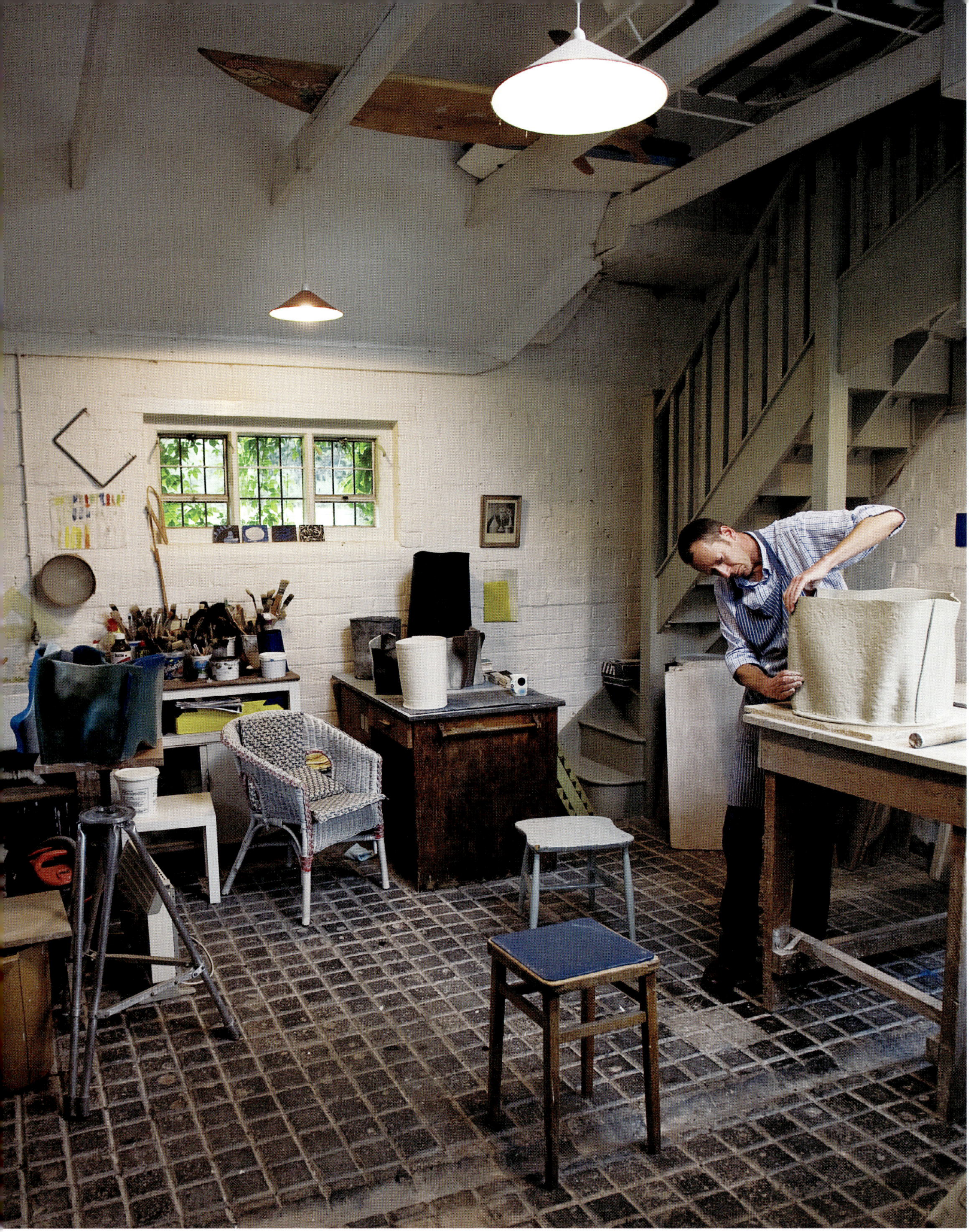

Ken Eastman

Some potters use the vessel as a means of interpreting the evolving, ever-shifting nature of form. The pot is usually an expression of permanence, but it can also – in modern studio work – investigate the character of our broader visual and sensual environment. It is an object for remaking and revising, in terms of its volumes, contours and internal space. The vessel can also be a concentration of wider concerns about the physical world. One artist who has explored these possibilities is Ken Eastman, who over some 20 years has achieved an international reputation for his prize-winning and widely collected work, in his case thinly rolled slab-built pots of considerable presence. Initially based in London, Eastman's present studio occupies what was the stable of his home in Herefordshire, a predominantly rural county on the border with Wales; on a clear day you can see the Black Mountains from his garden.

Eastman's workroom is lofty and light. On two levels, the clean and orderly space is full of pots, both completed and in the course of being made. Some of Eastman's small, intense painted abstracts decorate one wall, while upstairs there is plentiful room for storage. The atmosphere is more one of a city workshop than one found in a country backwater. On a long bench recent work is stored, while on another two pieces are in the process of being glazed, the colour built up in subtle layers of oxide and slip to achieve a nuanced depth. These pots illustrate developments realised in the last couple of years. For instance, a collaboration with Royal Crown Derby has led to the making of bone-china pieces which Eastman decorated with some of their floral-pattern transfers, and he has also made stoneware pots with flower motifs, a rare departure from the comparative austerity of his usual constructions. However, while this project with Crown Derby is ongoing – experimenting with pieces which can be produced commercially – Eastman's own work has, for the moment, returned to a quieter palette. On the bench when I visited were several large deep-blue pieces, with gently undulating walls.

Though Eastman has consistently slab-built, the work that emerged after he left the Royal College of Art in 1987 was very different to today's; this most spatial and subtly painterly of potters has gone through many transformations in the intervening period. Sculptural he may be, but Eastman is also an artist of surface, one who thinks long and hard about the layered mystery of colour and its potentially complex textures. He is as preoccupied by painting as by three-dimensional form, and has recently made some quiet pared-down pictures, where single, minimal shapes float in ambiguous space. Equally, Eastman is a potter of counterpoint, of interlocking contours. From the early 1990s his vessels explored structural interplay, built up from irregular bases – perhaps two or more shapes converging into one – their hard edges softened by cloudy brushed colour and, early in his career, simple painted motifs. From the outset Eastman enjoyed this disruption and contrast – perhaps a semicircle opened up and joined to a right angle or curves of different ratio meeting at a sharp point, the junction underlined by a change of colour. Yet the pieces looked resolved and certain.

Eastman can explore big ideas – about space, volume, enclosure and the infinities of surface – on a relatively intimate and domestic scale. A terrain is suggested – a sense of form related to a myriad of manmade and natural sources, from anonymous vernacular architecture to the clarities of modern abstract sculpture or the deep colours

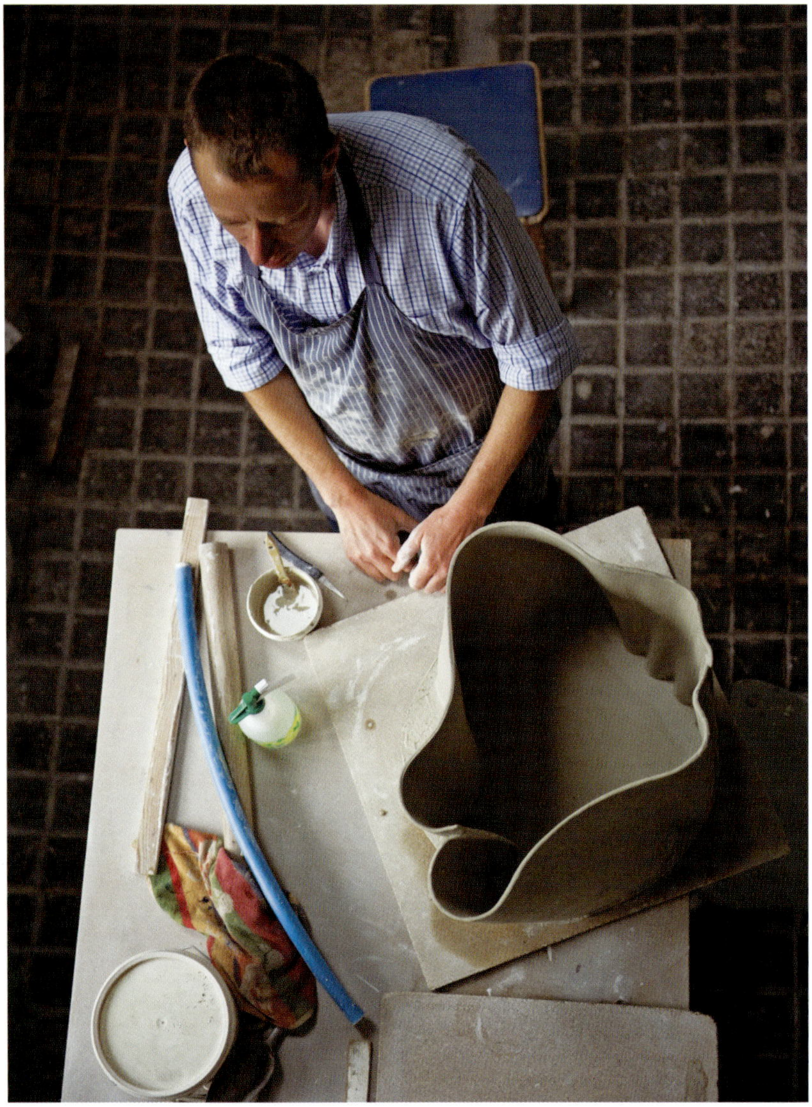

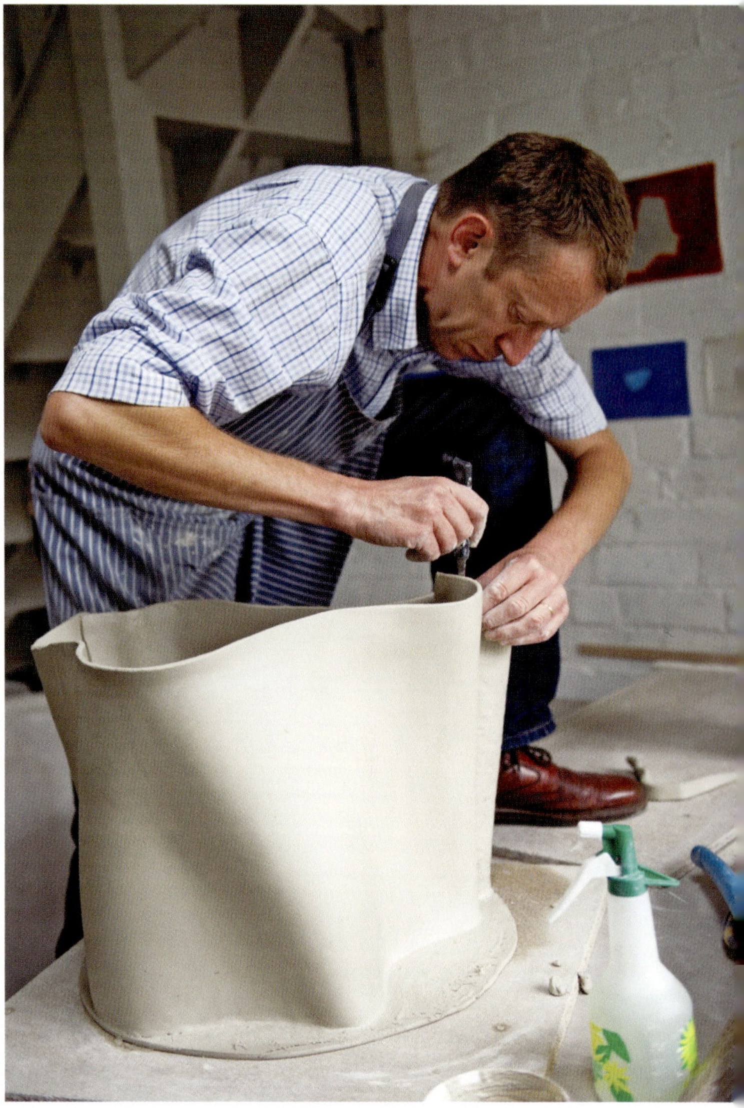

of the Herefordshire sky. Eastman's muted, often earthy colour can be evocative of a landscape, or perhaps the dry muted hues of a Renaissance fresco. While his work reflects some of the concerns of abstract painting, he makes these ideas three-dimensional. It is misleading to say that he paints 'on' his pots when glaze and colour are so integral to his sense and definition of form.

Born in Watford in 1960, Eastman trained at Edinburgh College of Art before going to the RCA. Since settling in Herefordshire in 1992, initially just down the road at Kimbolton, his work has kept moving 'somewhere between sculpture and architecture', as Jane McCabe put it (*Ken Eastman: Behind the Gates of Clay*, 2004), but always using the essential vessel – a form to which he habitually returns – as a basis for his more complex and convoluted journeys. These pots give plastic expression to his thoughts not only about the physical world, but music and poetry, what he hears and reads. At the same time they are autonomous, independent pots, with no storyline – 'about nothing', as Eastman once said – not out of nihilism or obstinacy, but because narrative readings can be reductive. A pot, after all, is complete in itself.

Yet, certain themes can soon be discerned. The vessels have always explored multiplicity. In the mid-nineties he made some complexly conjoined closed pieces – essentially compounds of architectural form. They had the structural

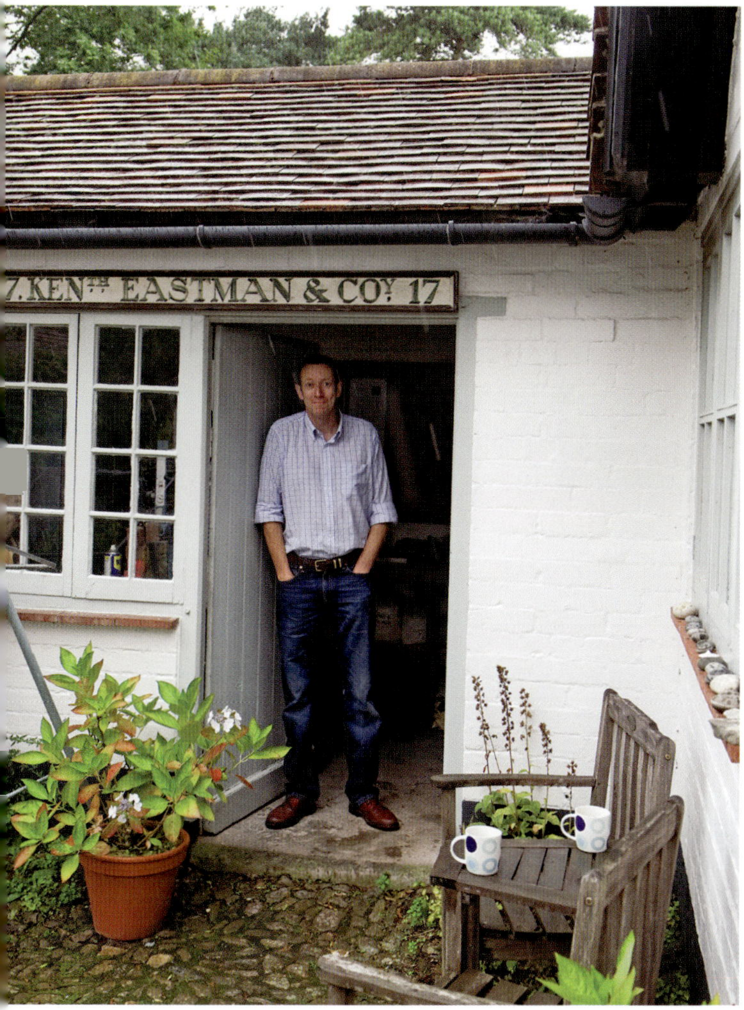

flow of Frank Gehry's architecture and the curvilinear cutting and joinery of Richard Serra's metal sculpture. Eastman is not really a minimalist potter because his language is visually too restless, his shapes always breaking out: shifting, transforming and contracting. They resist the interpretation of the photographer's flat plane. The pots need to be circumnavigated, different as they appear from every angle. Even his simplest shapes are very nuanced. In the closed forms space is still contained, but it is now mysterious and hidden. In his occasional groups of pots, kinds of still life, we can read each piece independently or as part of a sequence. In *Shelf Life,* from 1995, a line of six pieces, each is a variation on a theme – striated or smooth, open or sealed, waisted or straight-sided. The colours are like those in a Spanish still life from the 17th century: ochres, rusts and deep arid browns. These objects are both independent and collective, concerned with both unity and contrariety.

Eastman's sense of engineering, of the workbench exercise, came across strongly in the 'cut-outs' he was producing in the late 1990s – simple deliberations on form which played with identically sized tiles of clay, slicing, cutting and joining them in numerous ways. Variously shaped pieces of clay subtracted from each square were reattached in new configurations. It was another form of the Lego Eastman had as a boy, a continuation of his delight in constructive improvisation. The material here could just as easily be balsa wood or the ingredients of the pastry cook. This series may have briefly departed from his meditations on containment, but it exemplified the way he has taken a basic concept and approached it from many directions. When he made up skeletal-looking 'pots' from joined strips or slats of clay, he removed the sense of reassurance which the vessel naturally possesses. The pot was reduced to a kind of template, a blueprint dissection of what, structurally, is involved in ceramic form.

Since the late nineties the energy in Eastman's work has increased. Once established in his present studio, he was able to build up scale, abetted by more vivid, luminous colour. There was a physical liberation. In contrast to the understatement of some of the last pieces made at Kimbolton, the new work looked as if it had set sail with the wind fully behind it. It had great fluidity, billowing and rippling like Gehry's most recent designs, and was readily suggestive of metal and flowing fabric. The work had monumentality and drama, the shapes soaring and lifting as never before. This dynamic, a kind of structural flux, seemed a far cry from the relative stasis of the previous decade; yet the forms have settled down again into softer and more concentrated shapes – gently linear, like the late

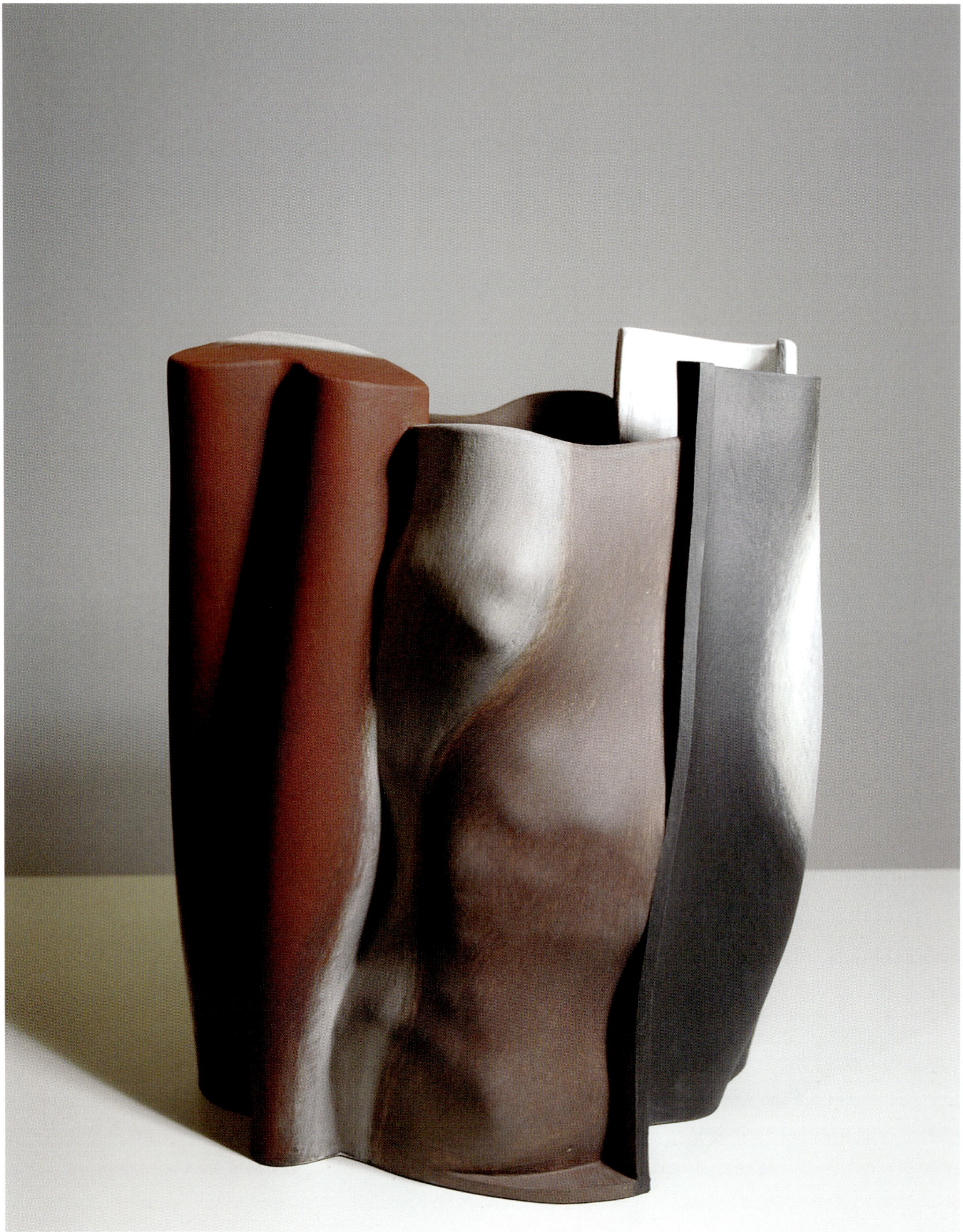

Slowburner, *2007, stoneware.*
Height: 47cm (18½in).
Photo: Barrett Marsden Gallery

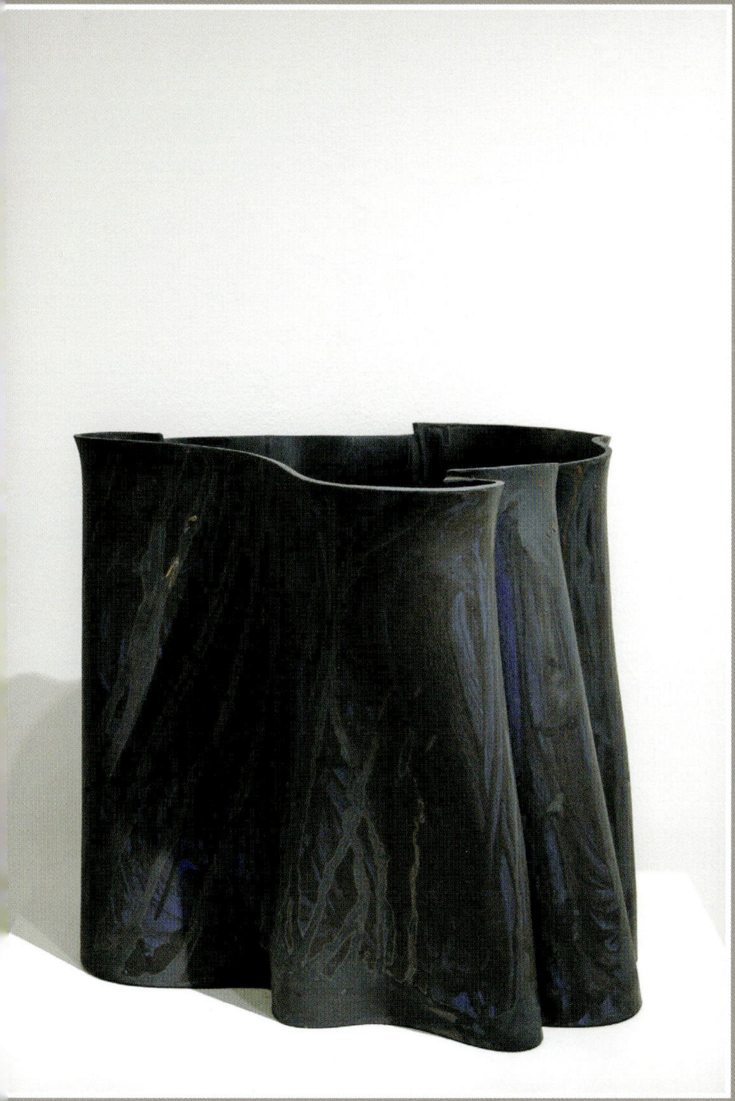

Untitled, *2008, stoneware.*
Height: 43cm (17in).
Photo: Barrett Marsden Gallery

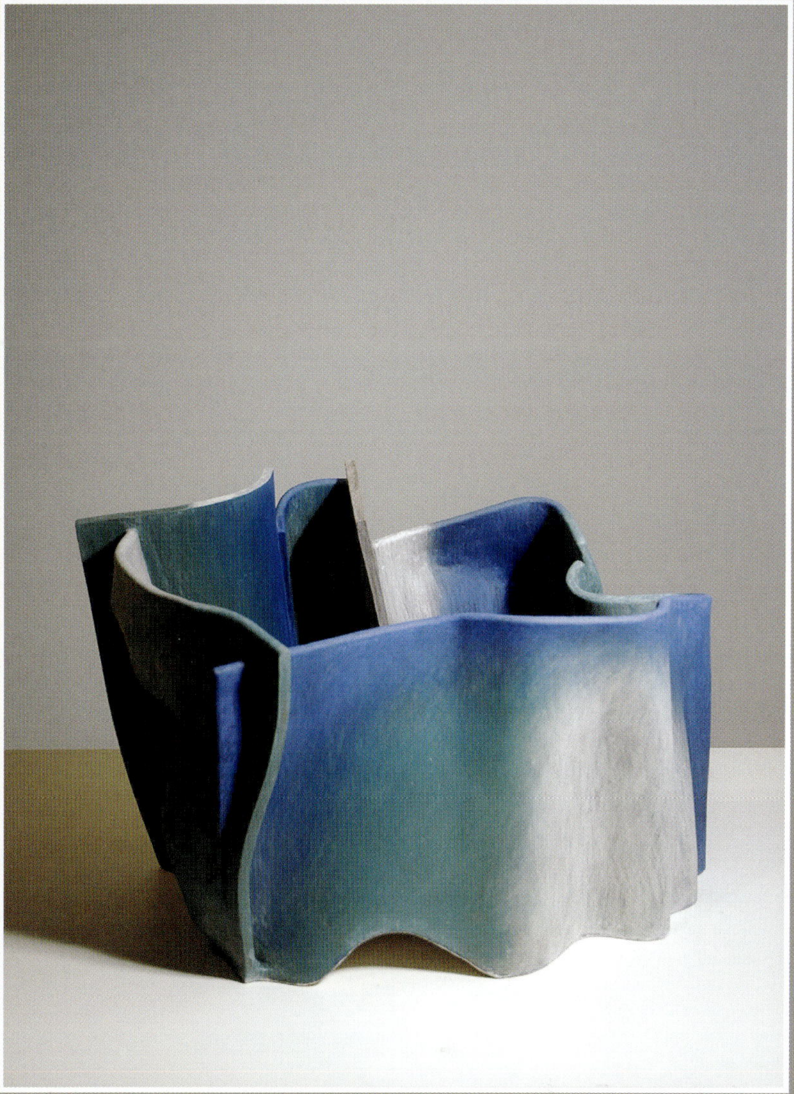

Aber Mawr, *2007, stoneware.*
Height: 34cm (13½in).
Photo: Barrett Marsden Gallery

drawings Ben Nicholson made of gothic forms. But they still have the power to disturb: the pleats and indentations that can disrupt the pot's stability, even to the point of buckling and collapse, show once again that Eastman is not afraid to undermine the traditional certainties of ceramics. His work, like Sara Radstone's, repays long study. Its subtleties are revealed over years of looking and touching. The pots seem very controlled, meticulously orchestrated, but the man who makes them is passionate and animated, with an explorer's anticipation of the next adventure. Those who really know Ken Eastman's ceramics will tell you just how sensual and responsive they are – to the colours of the seasons, to the light in the room, to the shadows crossing their surfaces.

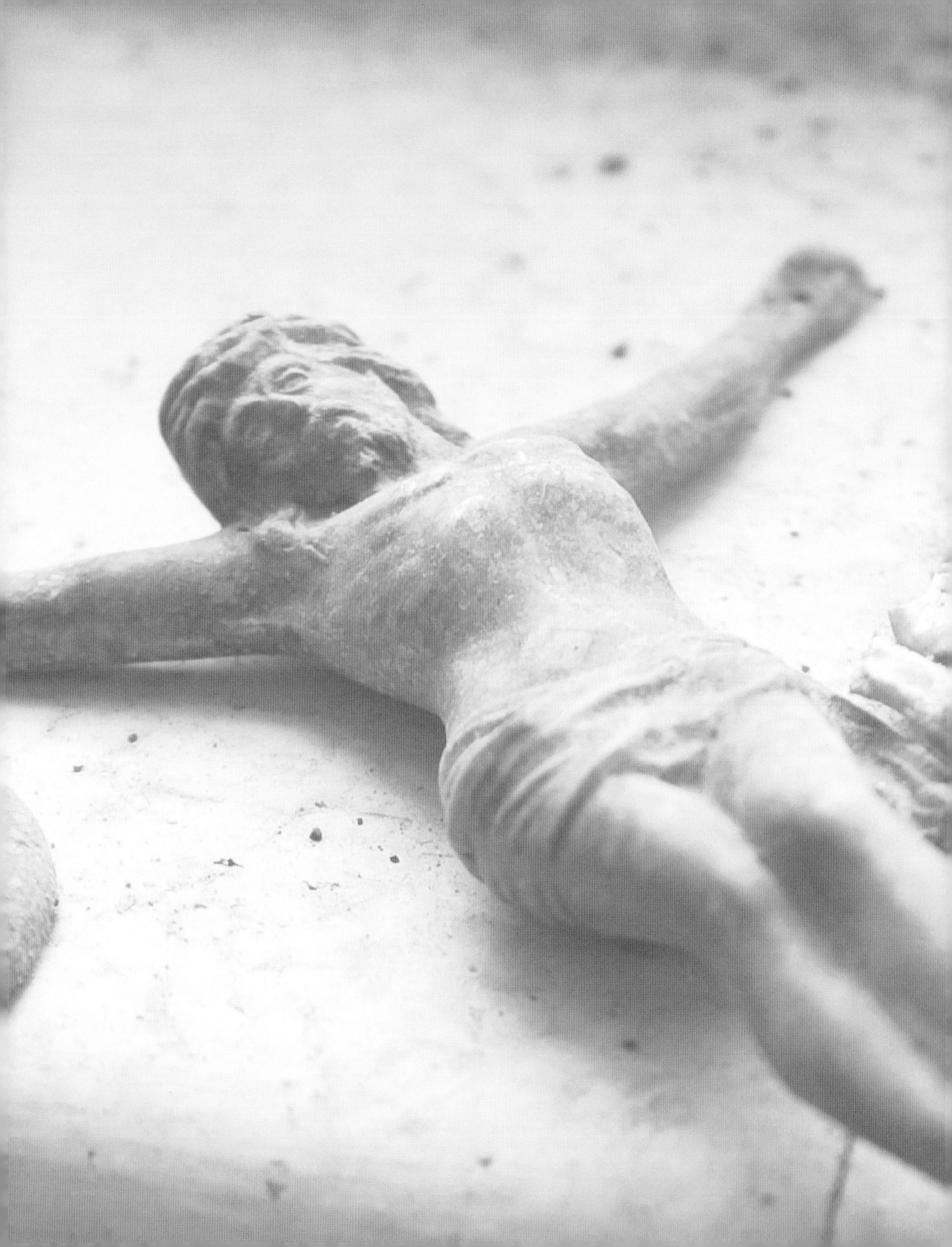

Part Three: The Figure and the Object

Clay figuration has had a long story in the history of ceramics, from Chinese T'ang dynasty tomb guardians to whimsical Staffordshire figures. Yet its development in studio practice has been spasmodic, and a stronger group of figurative artists, one generally concerned with the human condition and its complexities, as well as a celebration of the body's sensual and expressive powers, only began to emerge in the 1980s. Geoffrey Fuller and Michael Flynn invest the form with new and mystical life, exploring its relationship to myth and the landscape, in Flynn's case a probing evocation of the human drama. Philip Eglin and Claire Curneen also draw on ceramic history and broader aspects of our culture to gauge personal and collective experience, while Emma Rodgers's work is expressive of nature at its most visceral.

The ceramic 'objects' featured here are concerned with essence, both in relation to the physical qualities of the material itself and its symbolic and metaphysical value. This abstraction has grown partly out of the organic explorations of British and foreign potters in the 1960s and 70s. Sara Radstone and Annie Turner developed their language through an interest in containment and its implications, one that has led to different kinds of related structure. Neil Brownsword began his career with the figure, but his obsession with the archaeology of the pottery industry has drawn him back to the very fabric of clay and its poetic powers.

Michael Flynn

MICHAEL FLYNN IS something of an artistic nomad, dividing his time as he does between studios in Wales and Germany. There is the sense of a displaced artist, a restless spirit, perhaps due in part to his peripatetic roots. He has a strong Irish background, but he was born in Germany and spent stretches of his early life in both countries. He remains difficult to pin down (artistically as well as geographically) but may now be slowing down just a little, keen to spend more time in Cardiff where his spacious studio and flat are located very anonymously in a backstreet near the city centre. He enjoys being there, a suitably western outpost for this proud Celt who, despite his international reputation for vibrant and dynamic figurative work, still remains on the edge of the 'clubbable' ceramics world – and I know he prefers it this way. More importantly, Flynn's rather frenetic existence of studio-hopping, teaching and giving workshops all over the world seems to give the work its continued tension and frisson. His travels not only provide him with much of his source material, but, perhaps paradoxically, the kind of creative equilibrium he needs.

Flynn has an engaged, inquisitive and eclectic mind, drawing as he does on the age-old stories, myths, fairy tales and religious themes that tell us so much about ourselves. He reanimates these characters in clay, in his lively repertoire of figures – men, women and beasts – giving new currency to numerous legends through the broader relevance of the messages they offer. However, his work is not about simple storytelling. Touching as it does on personal human issues and situations, it is completed by the individual readings of the viewer. Flynn likes his work to remain ambiguous, open to interpretation, an art both of unity and confrontation, of opposing and merging energies – sculpture that provides us with questions, not answers. But we can enjoy Flynn's work simply on its own merits too, for his pure, very physical ignition of clay, colour and surface.

Flynn has stated the importance of his Irish Catholic upbringing, his early childhood in Germany and the magical experience of farm life in Ireland as major catalysts in his work. The bulls, horses, cockerels and other creatures featured in his art have their origins in Flynn's early sense of connection with the landscape, which is central to his creative outlook. The cockerel, a recurring motif, intrigues because of a complex symbolism that relates to various aspects of the human condition, from pride and strength to vigilance and fecundity, sexual energy being a strong theme in Flynn's work. But it also expresses his interest in origins and connection, reminding us that Christian motifs, for instance, have strongly pagan roots. Flynn's upbringing helped give him a powerful sense of Earth's mysteries, primeval pulses manifested in a rich variety of archetypal characters, personifying the different forces and emotions with which we contend. Flynn's travels have given him a strong sense of 'inner location', enabling him to recognise the geographical and imaginative relationships that exist among these archetypes, reinvented from one culture to another, one generation to the next, and as relevant to human identity now as they have ever been. In investigating the evolving regenerative nature of legend and folklore, he gets a little closer to the origins of human consciousness and behaviour, expressed by Flynn in humorous social and domestic observations that bring these conundrums into the present day.

Born in 1947, Flynn studied painting at Birmingham College of Art in the 1960s and after a period of teaching went to Cardiff College of Art to study ceramics, where Alan

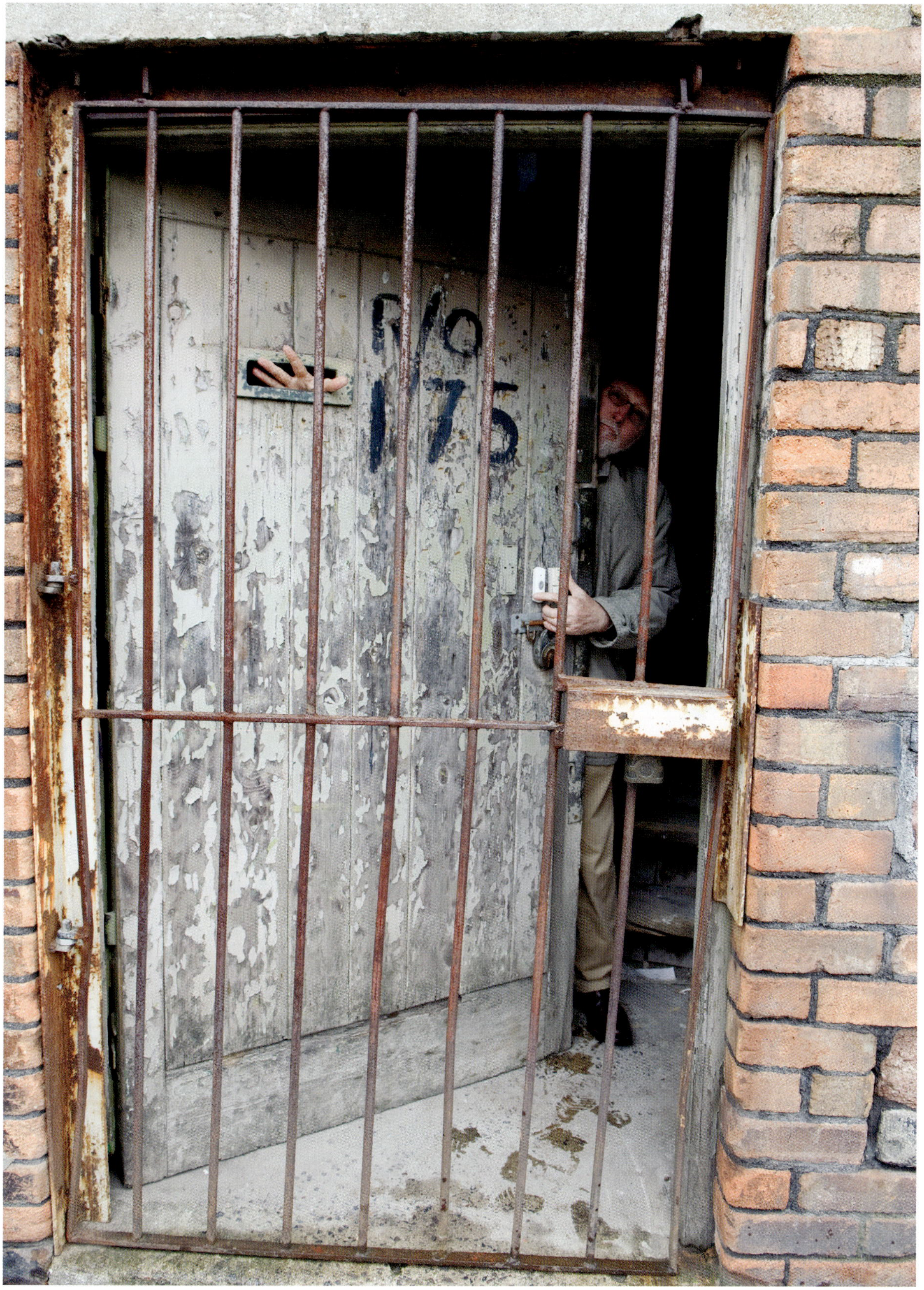
R/O
175

Barrett-Danes, the figurative potter, was a major influence. He returned there in the early 80s to pursue an MA in Fine Art, a thorough grounding that consolidated Flynn's broad visual outlook. In his studio, along with an accumulation of earlier figures, prints, drawings and wall pieces on an upper level, there was new work in progress – forms centred around his current interest in the Dionysus and Harlequin themes and their relationship to the forest. They continue Flynn's fascination with characters in nature, from Adam and Eve in the Garden of Eden to the wolf and the crow and other creatures in the law and mythology of the land. The Dionysian trail has taken him to Greece and into northern Europe, to the forests of Poland and Germany, where the Black Forest draws close to Flynn's other studio in Freiburg. It is another odyssey which has deepened his interest in the crossovers between classical and northern imagery and the Dionysian relationship between Pan, the forest wild man, and woodland deities. Connections with Harlequin also emerge.

Made in porcelain, stoneware and earthenware, and seductively glazed, the small scale of Flynn's work makes it a natural adornment of our living space, what he has called 'the domestic icon'. Stylistically, the pieces have complex origins: his porcelain belongs in part to a grand European tradition stretching from Meissen (where Flynn has worked) to Sèvres; but his figures also embody aspects of folk art, of baroque and rococo ornament, of American and Spanish religious art. His respect for sculptors like Rodin and Bourdelle is also evident. But it becomes rather superfluous to talk of 'style' when his technical approach, informed by close observation and constant drawing, is so freely his own. Subverting control by attempting to make things 'badly', conventional craft precision is of no interest to Flynn. Instead, he achieves another kind of expressive power, one that perfectly captures the drama and vigour of the scene depicted with a sense of continuously springing energy. His roughly manipulated surfaces, cracked and blistered with rich

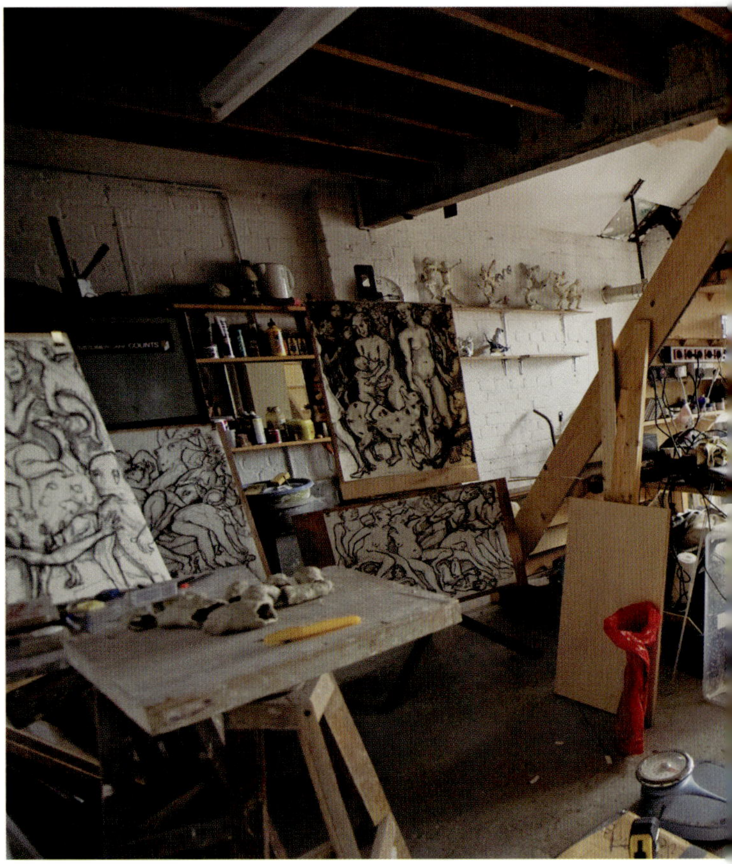

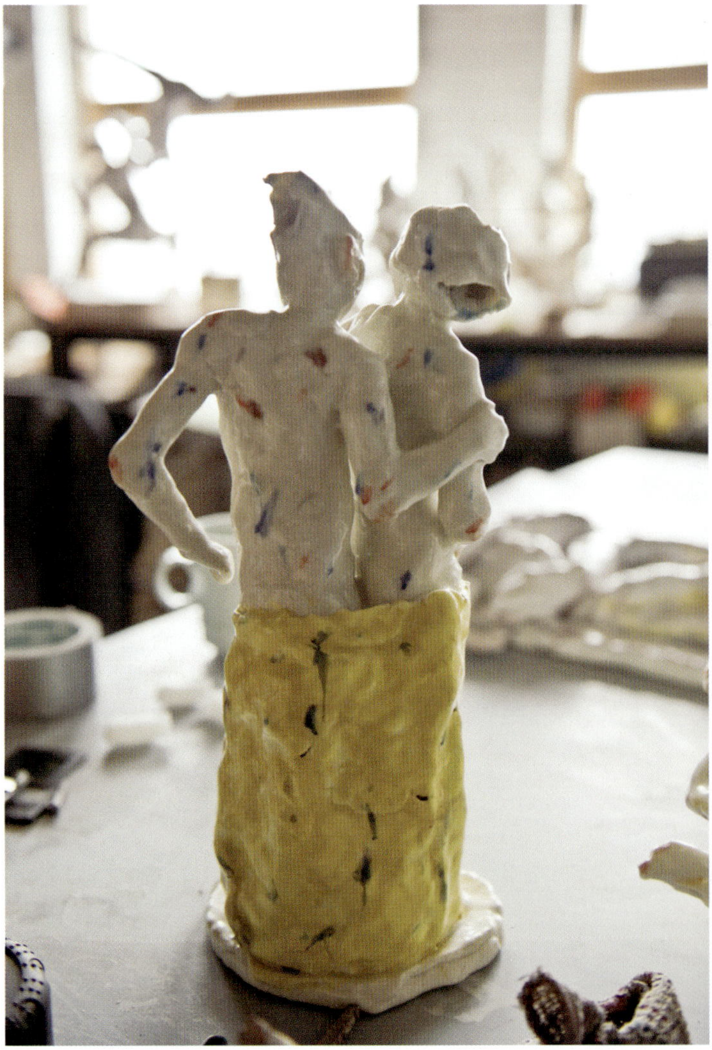

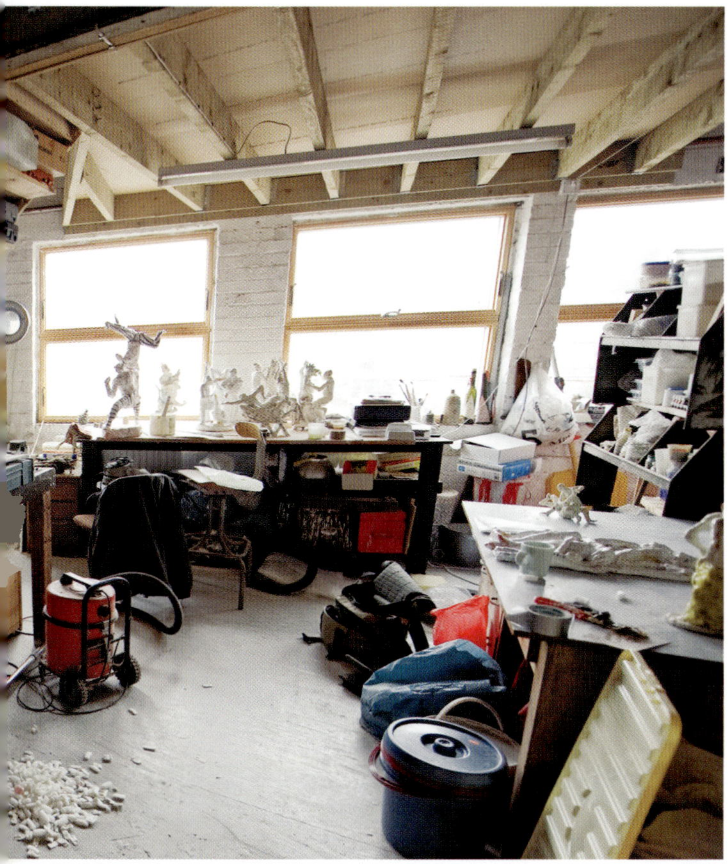

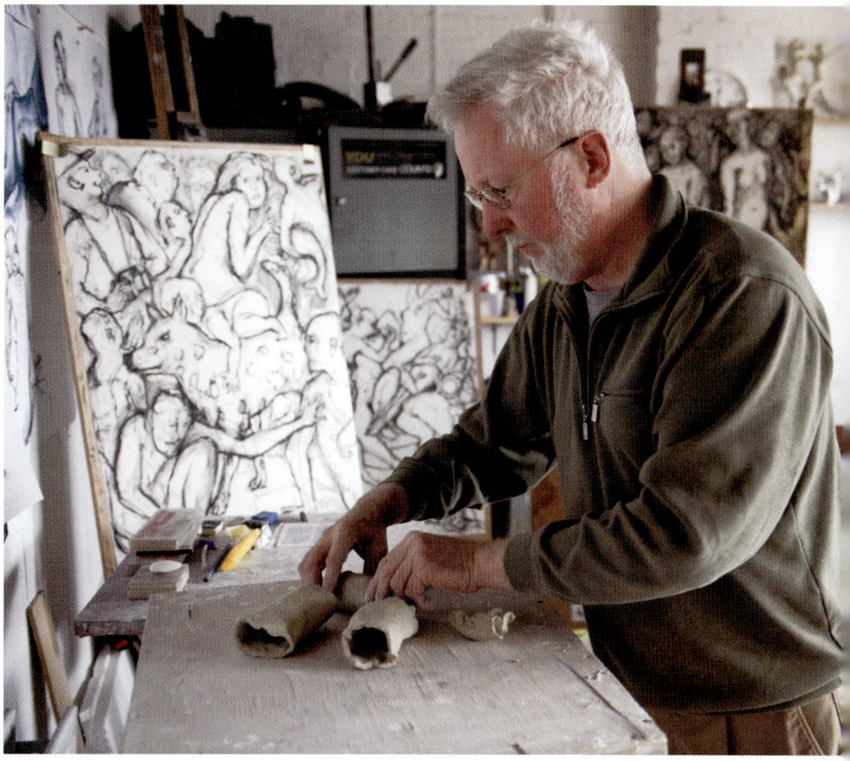

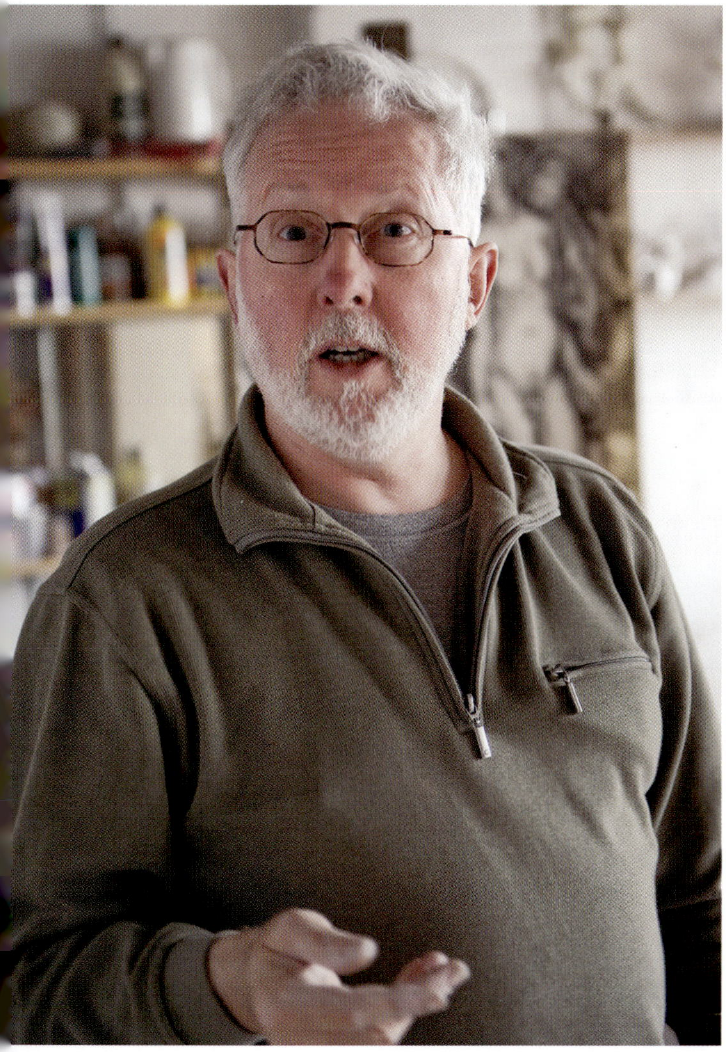

coagulations of glaze, have far more in common with the gestural modelling of artists like Peter Voulkos, Viola Frey, Giacometti and Fontana. There is nothing remotely formulaic in Flynn's highly charged depictions of beasts and beauties, runners and chasers, dancers and wrestlers involved in the battles and harmonies of human existence – all gymnastically poised in frozen movement, expressing the contrariness of our complex lives.

Flynn's work may often deal in darker issues but he always entertains. There is a very theatrical bent to his portrayals, and the theatre is what so often illustrates these situations – from circus acrobats and animal orchestras to his recurring Harlequin and Columbine pieces, which are emblematic of the eternal attractions and tensions between the sexes. His enjoyment of *commedia dell'arte* subjects moves on from the sweet melancholy of artists like Watteau to a more gutsy and visceral reading of the world. The combination of humour and pathos is sharpened into impending tragedy in subjects like his virtuoso *Ship of Fools* piece of

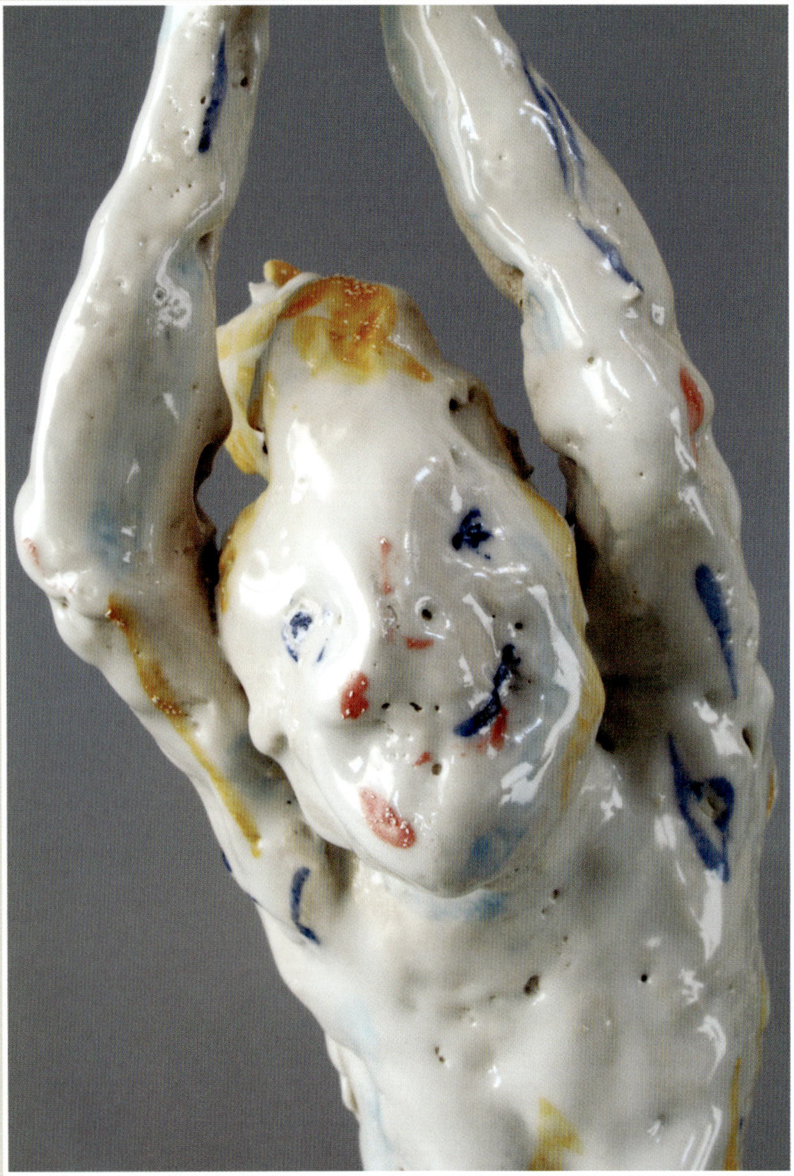

Crowded Ocean (detail), *2006, stoneware.*
Height: 47cm (18½in.). Photo: Courtesy of the artist

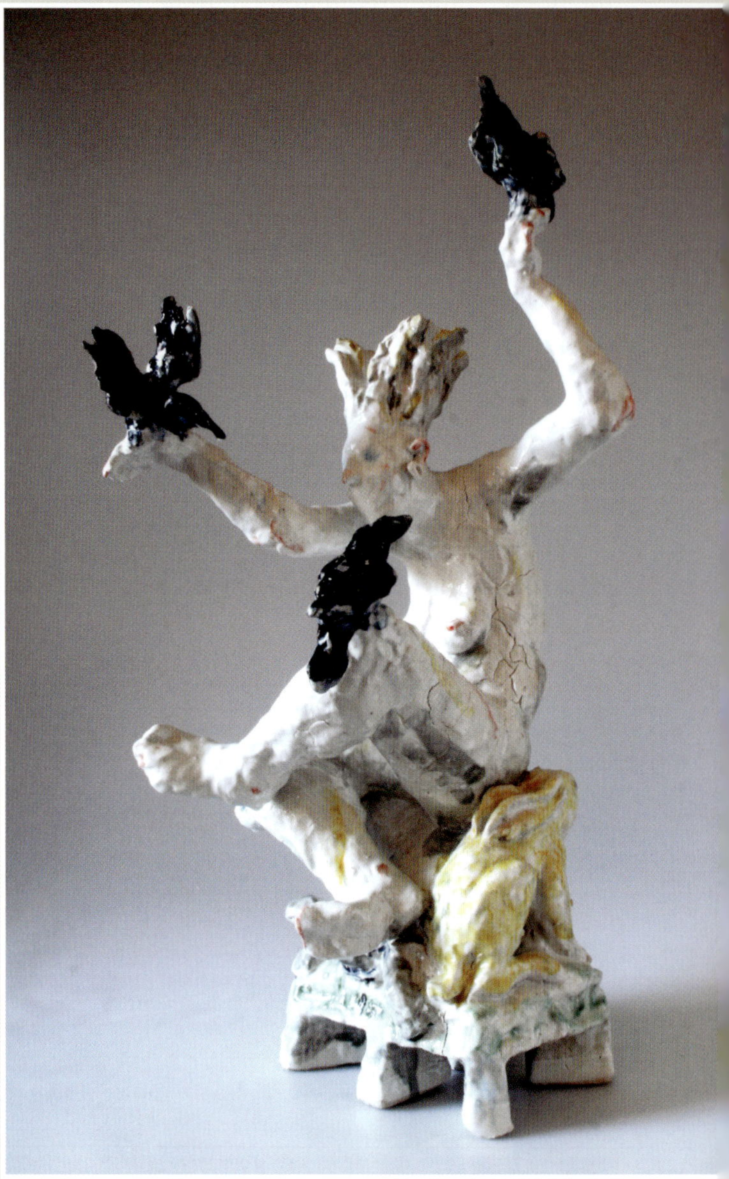

Mistress Kind, *2007, stoneware.*
Height: 51cm (20in.). Photo: Courtesy of the artist

2005, or the disquieting *Crowded Ocean*, made a year later. They were forms which, with their scenes of human panic, appear literally poised on the brink – barely balanced structures that give a strong impression of collective folly and vulnerability. Few artists have been able to deal with such emotional issues in so concentrated and intimate a way.

Flynn's work is about the vicissitudes of being alive. His exploration of physical and emotional interaction, sometimes wavering dangerously as if on a pinhead, is beautifully rendered in exuberant form, in rich glossy surfaces and painting. His sensual textures and coloration extend the essential spontaneity and flux of Flynn's theatre. He has created his own mythology, a mystical landscape in which characters act, wrestle and dance through the strange comedy and tragedy of existence. Flynn's ability to construct modern metaphors out of the allegories of legend and folklore gives his work a rare universality. It has a tension and edginess, a continued freshness, that has kept him at the forefront of clay figuration.

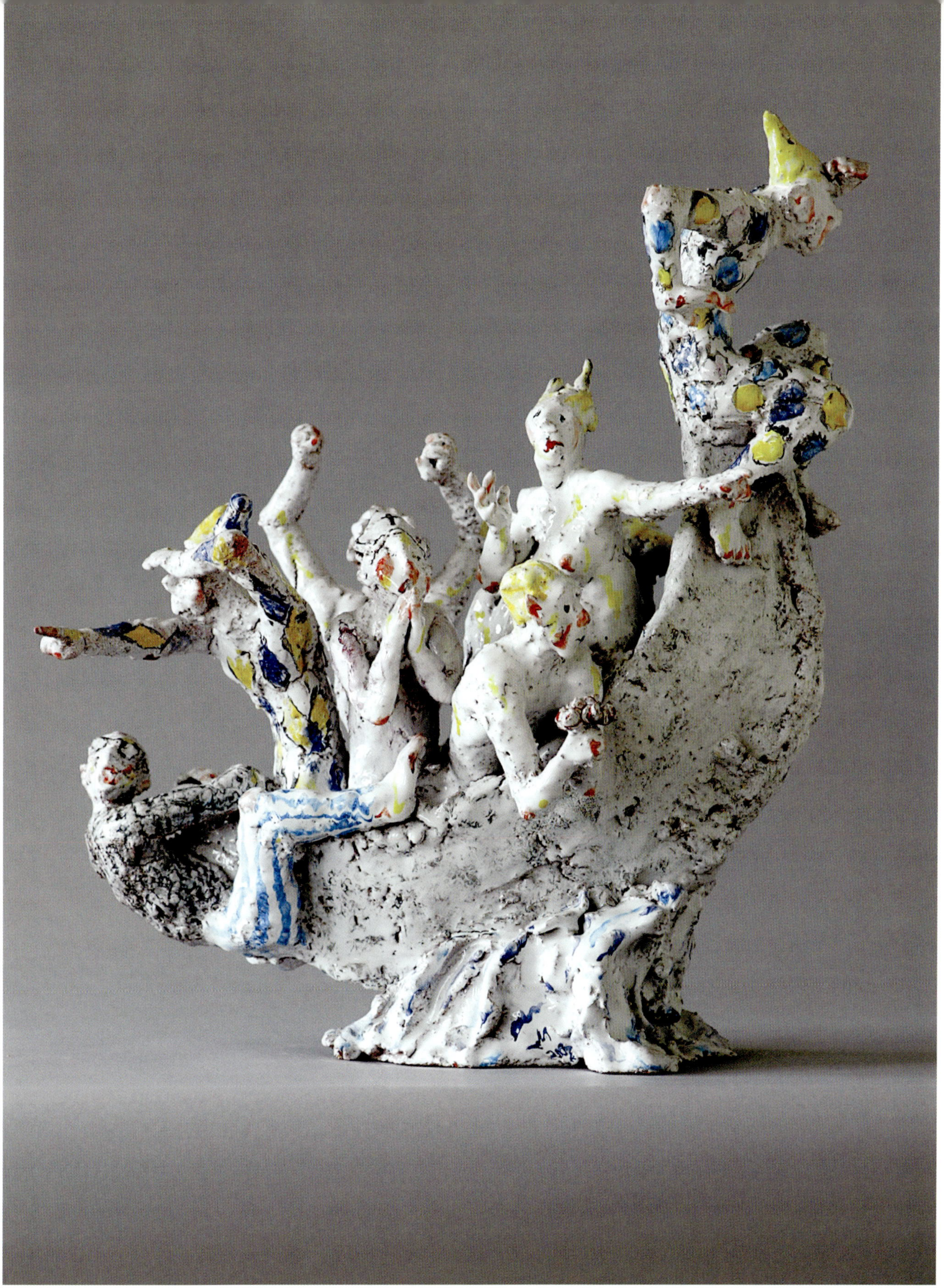

Ship of Fools, *2005, earthenware.*
Height: 52cm (20½in.). Photo: Courtesy of the artist

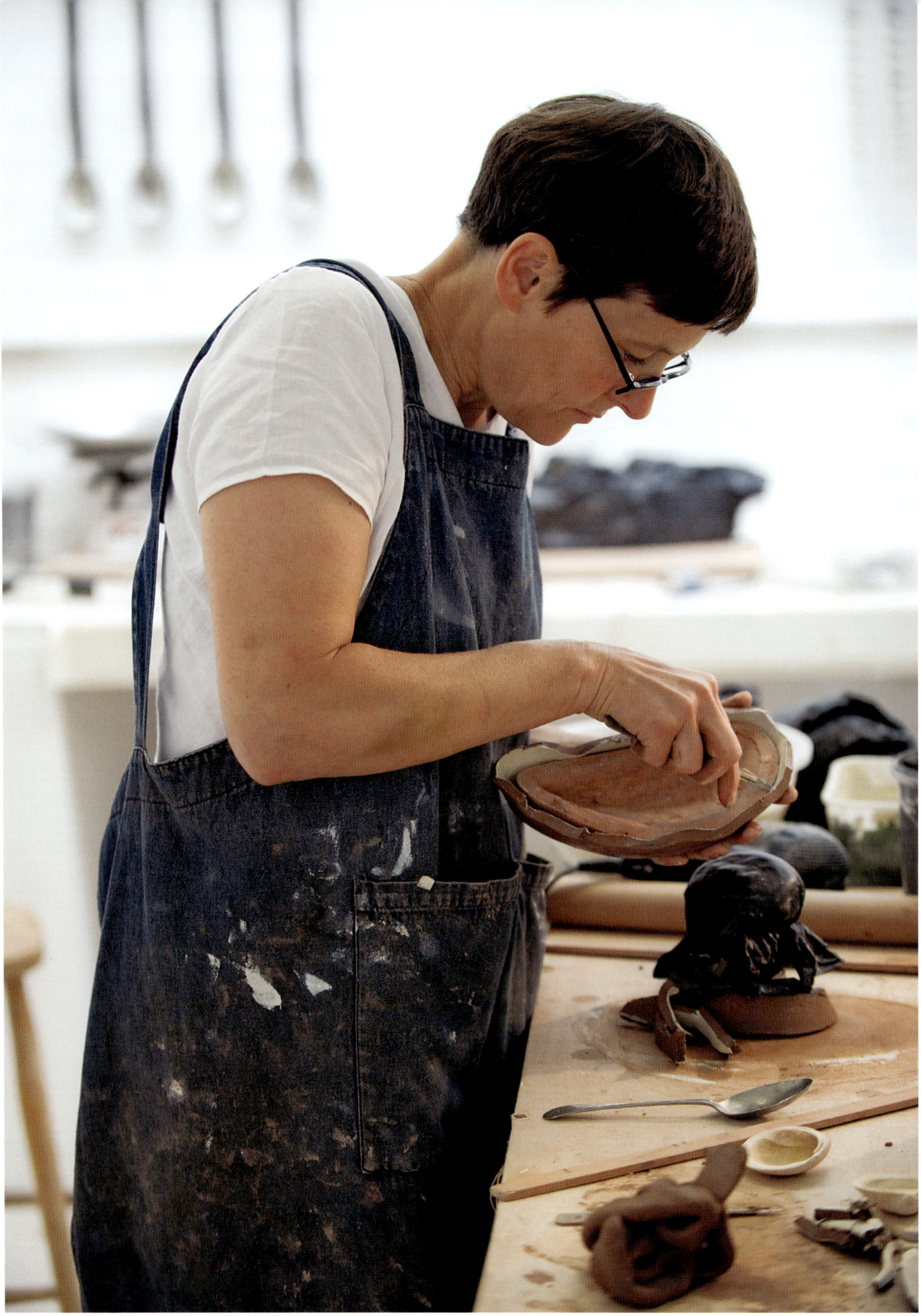

Annie Turner

ANNIE TURNER'S orderly studio is in a busy mews – Vanguard Court – just off the Peckham Road in South London. She occupies one of a number of large adjoining spaces shared with other artists. London-based potters often work cheek by jowl in this way; it makes practical and economic sense where property and space are at a premium. The comradeship that can result from this kind of collective arrangement is also important in terms of mutual support and encouragement. Delicate grid-like structures hang from the walls and intimate groups of small textured bowls rest on benches. Yet if this is the place where Annie Turner makes her work, her imagination is in a distant landscape, the area that has been the source of her ceramic sculpture for well over a decade. Turner was born into a family who have lived on the River Deben, near Woodbridge in east Suffolk, for generations. Her late father, Jim Turner, sailed on the river most of his life and passed onto his daughter his passion for boats and for this broad, richly shored stretch of the Deben in particular. Like her father, Annie has become intimately familiar with the variations and complexities of this waterscape, exploring its banks and mudflats, plumbing the depths of its waters, knowing its hidden creeks and reaches.

Turner, who was born in 1958, has been handbuilding for about 30 years now. At Bristol Polytechnic in the late seventies she made raku constructions that were as much about surface drawing and marking as overall form. At the Royal College of Art she produced work with a strong biomorphic element, reminiscent of Miró and Klee, but by the late eighties the colours were more muted and, as she put it, 'earthbound ... like the clay', with a more direct relationship to nature. She began to make pots with a strong sense of ritual, becoming increasingly absorbed by the metaphorical potency of the clay and its powers of suggestion that go beyond the physical object. With its ancient, almost primeval function of containment, the obvious connection of clay to Turner's River Deben is a potent one; she regards the river as a 'living vessel' that is constantly being transformed and reshaped. For all its tidal constancy, it is also an amorphous energy, difficult to gauge in both a literal and a broader sense.

So what has emerged after a long period of gestation is a vocabulary of sculptural forms in clay which draws on both the natural and manmade structures of the river, work that is highly autobiographical in its need to make poetic sense of a place dense with it own past (prehistoric natural remains are much in evidence, and the Sutton Hoo Saxon burial site is on the Deben's northern shore). Her art seeks to record the physical and symbolic features of a river punctuated by measures, defences and markers – objects that border, straddle or lie in the water, which are only revealed at low tide. Here, too, is the detritus that has gathered or been buried by each tidal movement.

This area is, paradoxically, a region of permanence and constant change, where the certainty of the constant stream of water is also a story of fluctuations, floods and erosion, of natural transportation and shifting deposits. After the memorable summer of floods in 2007, we realise that rivers have far more than local significance. The river is linked to the sea and beyond that to the wider world. The ill-fated whale stranded on the neighbouring River Orwell in the same year reminds us of the physical connection with distant places that rivers provide. The poet Ted Hughes saw the river in terms of the organisms within it; a

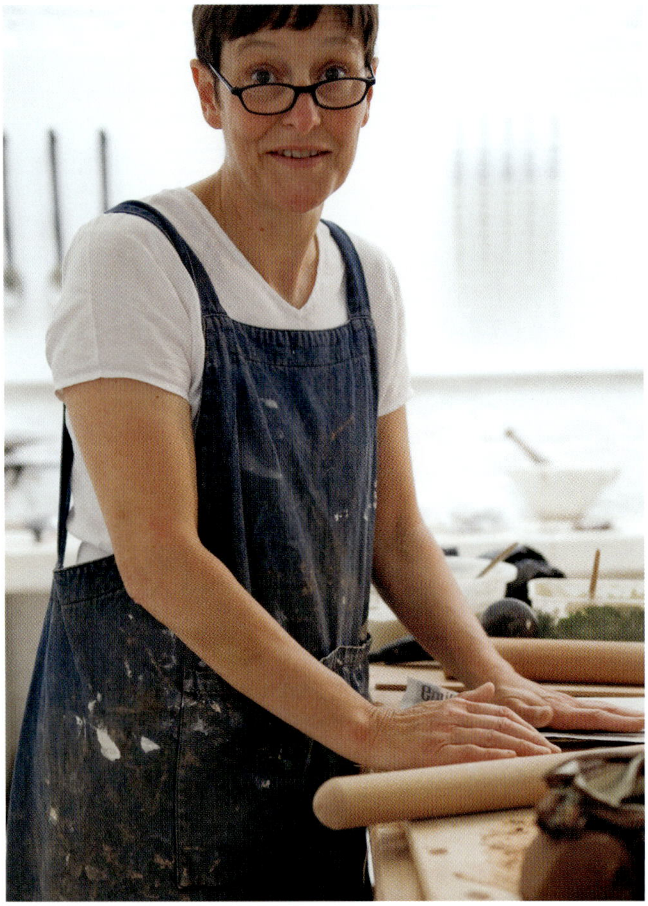

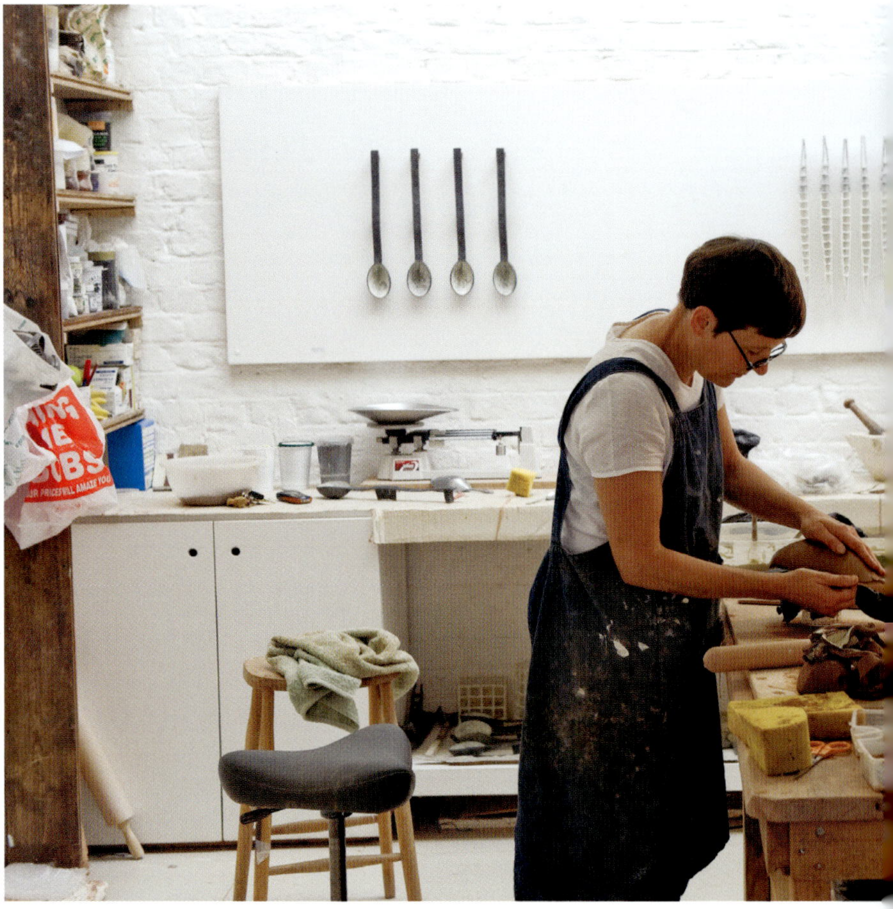

river without life is a contradiction in terms, a dead and empty thing. In this way, it provides an ecological barometer, an indicator of what is happening to the wider Earth as the climate changes. Turner's river, like Hughes's, is about much more than the water. It is a place of residue and imprints, of marks left in the mud, which find expression in the surfaces of her work – her bowls and constructions.

Where Annie was brought up, the estuary narrows at low tide to a channel, leaving a wide expanse of mudflats. It is a place of old posts and old decayed jetties, of objects that record the human efforts to mark and marshal, to impinge on, this place of flood. The sense of human and natural interaction is a subtle and delicate balance, but what emerges is a vocabulary, an archaeology, of river which Annie Turner has made her own with clay. Her 'meander bowls', individual or sometimes made in series (which may meander like a river), are usually imprinted by fossilised sharks' teeth, feathers or other objects found on her long walks – talismans that suggest the permanent as well as the more ephemeral presences on the river. These forms, like the spoons she has made, are, I think, at the core of her work – blistered and encrusted surfaces that evoke and condense the riverscape, their sense of containment a succinct summation of what the river means to her.

Her forms, treated by layers of slip and oxide, undergo a kind of attrition in the making that parallels the erosive processes of nature – the different weathers that shape and corrode the various surfaces of vegetation, wood and metal. Repeated firing deepens the patinas, so that her pieces look pitted and rust-eaten, or textured like lichen. However, if her clay can look metallic, it also has, astonishingly, the lightness of balsawood. The material is transformed. Her 'ladders', like the 'meander bowls' conceived either singly or in families, are made to hang from and

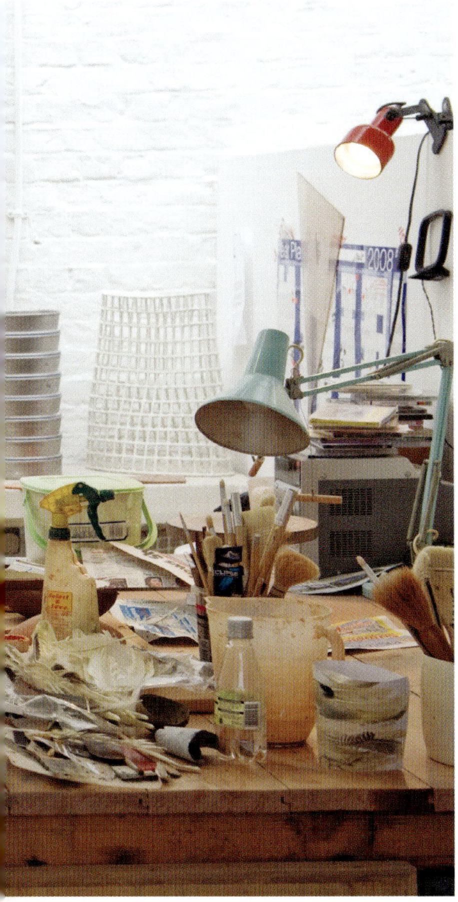

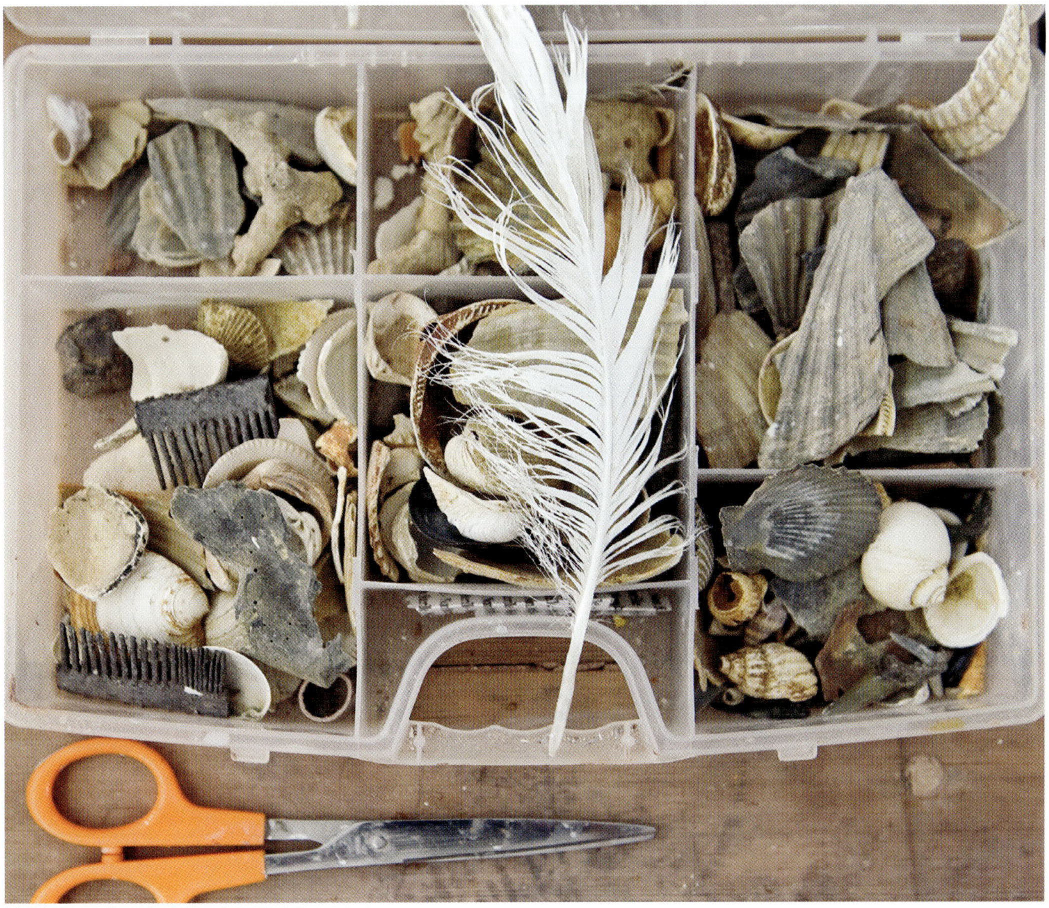

straddle walls just as they straddle boats and riverbanks. Differentiations of glaze echo the tidal marks – Turner's sculpture is a kind of measure and monitor of the river's rise and fall, a marker of passing time. The beautiful shadows cast echo the various rhythms of light and dark along its shore, but they also animate and extend her abstract forms across the space they occupy. Her bigger 'sinkers' (objects that fix moorings) and 'sluices' perhaps offer containment, an affirming sense of fixture, of belonging. The enclosed fishing nets are partly about 'recollection and collection', of association and memory gathered, stored, preserved. The way Turner collects, making precious what she finds around the river, is reminiscent of artists as diverse as Joseph Cornell and Gillian Lowndes. She is part of an intimate, highly personal tradition where objects are utilised because of their particular charge, because of the layers of meaning they can offer.

Turner's work has a rich ambiguity. Her intricate lattice works of clay (which at their most ambitious are technical feats of a high order) suggest both bony strength and fragility. Each form has a tension; some bend and warp in firing, giving a curvilinear twist. They remind us of the pressures and strong currents of the river – to borrow a phrase of R.S. Thomas's, its energy of 'furious interiors'. Turner has made sets of circulating 'eddy spoons' that follow the motion of a whirlpool, and 'funnels' in which the high-pressure action of water at the narrow mouth of the estuary is expressed in a solid structure. Some of Turner's forms are inspired by east-coast defences, like the Martello towers built to resist Napoleon. Nowadays, such structures might be a metaphor of protection against a different kind of enemy, that of our increasingly angry weather and rising river and sea levels.

More recently, Turner has broadened the scope of her

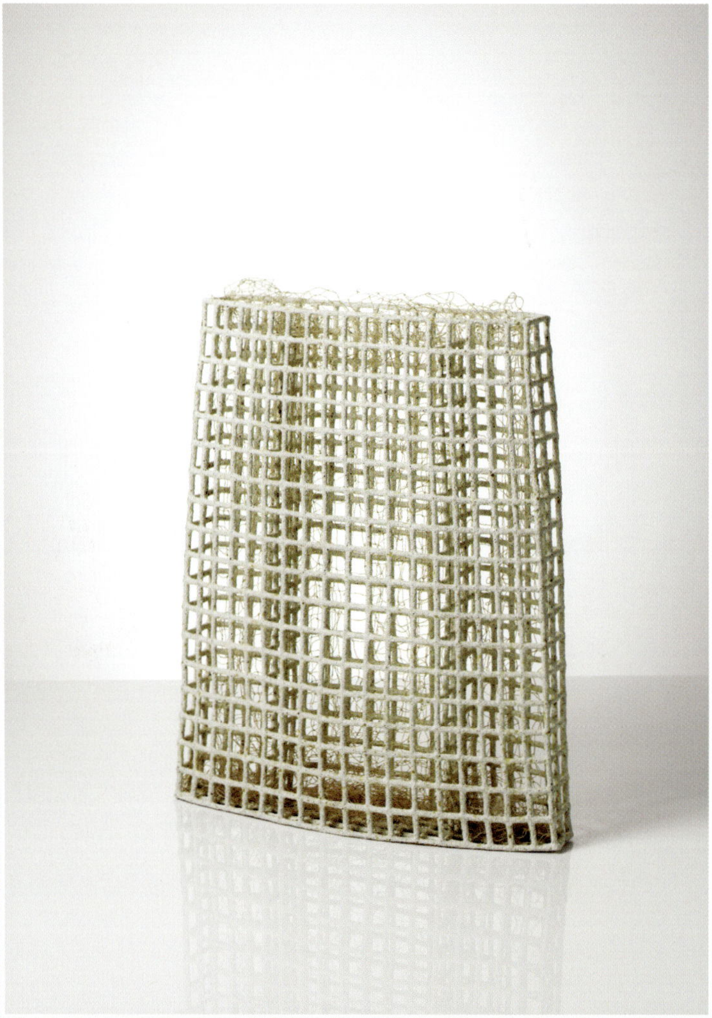

Recollection, *2007, stoneware.*
Height: 57cm (22¾in.).
Photo: Michael Harvey

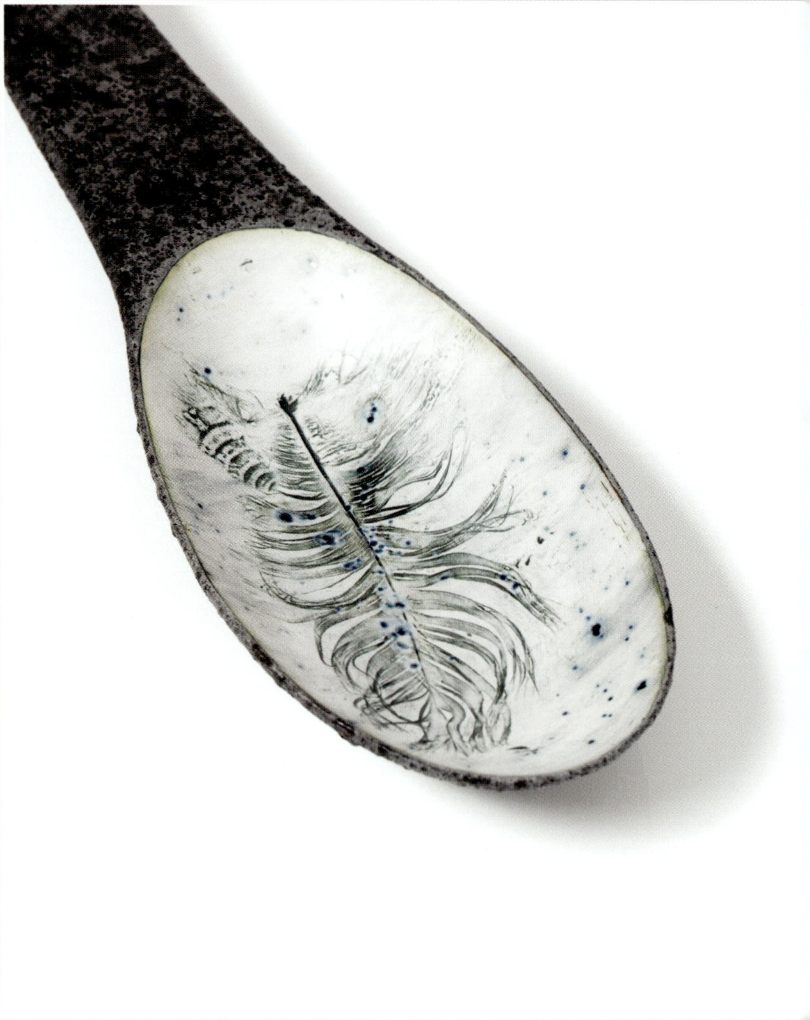

River Spoon (detail), *2007, stoneware.*
Length: 40cm (15¾in.).
Photo: Michael Harvey

work, extending her shapes into larger, more expansive forms that encapsulate the wider course and surface of the Deben. Her forms have a way of growing and transforming into other structures, a fluid, organic process and train of thought in which one theme emerges out of another. Her art is about our paradoxically stable and uncertain relationship with the river, and how it can effect us at a deeper spiritual level, a metaphor for so many aspects of our individual and collective experience. This is why her work is so embracing, why her vestigial art is so haunting. It also takes clay out of its more familiar territory into a new and eloquent structural arena.

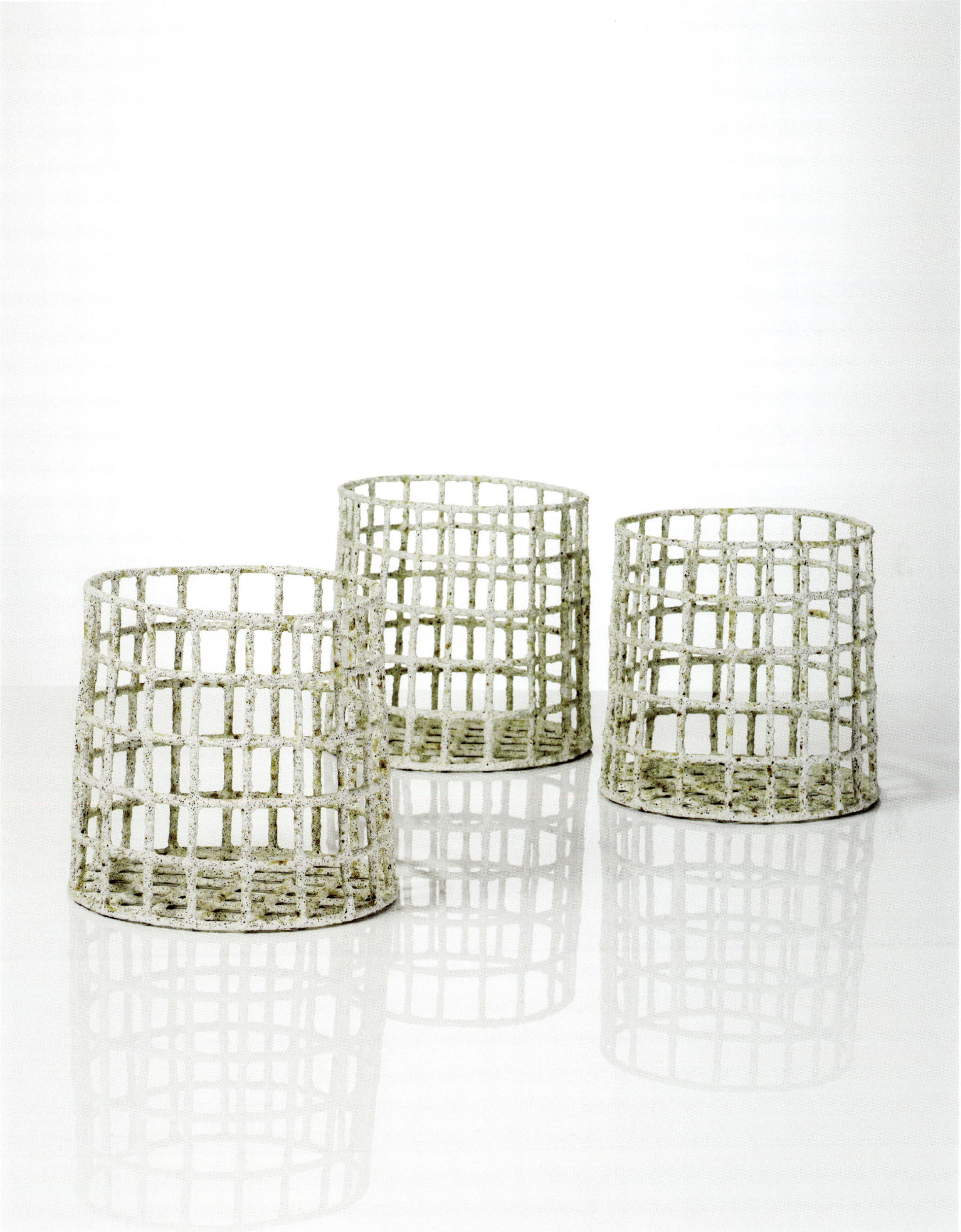

Martello Towers, *2007, stoneware.*
Height: 17cm (6¾in.).
Photo: Michael Harvey

Claire Curneen

Claire Curneen's studio is a specially built extension at the rear of her house in Cardiff. Aside from work-in-progress and completed pieces, the space seems quite bare, revealing little of Curneen's creative mind. Only a section of wall covered in various reproductions of the human form, in art, photography and film, betrays possible source material. Having only recently begun working at home, and now with a young child, it has been a period of readjustment, of finding her way back into her art – powerful figurative work of considerable pathos. Her sculpture, along with the work of Michael Flynn, her near neighbour, and Philip Eglin, has shown just how persuasive the human form can be when rendered in clay, far removed from the sentimentality or cliché with which it is often represented in ceramics. Indeed, Curneen has played a significant part in the resurgence of figuration in the 1980s and 90s, achieving an expressive depth and vulnerability through her particular manipulation of clay. These figures are much concerned with stillness, but the surfaces are freely handled and made up of strips of clay pressed into the palm. This gives the work a strong metaphorical and literal sense of imprint. Curneen explores the textural possibilities of the material to say fundamental things about the human condition.

If over the past decade she has been concentrating more on religious and mythical subjects, it is because they provide an effective vehicle for the kinds of emotional and psychological conditions in which we find ourselves, whilst also offering a sense of poetic catharsis. If this sculpture is often about forms of isolation and muted suffering, Curneen also affirms the richness and value of the human experience and the materials she uses – materials which, in her hands, become bodily landscapes of considerable beauty. Whether they be in porcelain or terracotta, hand-built or occasionally cast, her figures express a range of ideas that resonate with every aspect of our experience – cultural, emotional, spiritual and corporeal.

Curneen's recent pieces can take on an almost surreal air, with heads covered in sticks, or figures swathed in flowers and sprouting foliage, like reinventions of the medieval Green Man. A postcard of Pollaiuolo's painting *Apollo and Daphne* is pinned to her studio wall. It shows Daphne turning into a tree to escape from Apollo's desire, another clue to Curneen's current interest in the metamorphosing aspects of the body and its relationship to our shifting interior and mental states. There has been an emerging sense of the 'object', too – of fragments and relics relating to the body which express the precious, both symbolically and materially. Her recent sculpture seems more broadly to be about the whole and elements of the whole, from parts of the body to branches from a tree. A bunch of sticks bound together with red cord is full of symbolic resonance – the use of porcelain and celadon glaze adds an intrinsic worth to objects already invested with layers of meaning. In most cultures sticks are collected and used to make fires. They are life-giving. However, the stick structures enveloping some of her heads are also reminiscent of the Crown of Thorns.

Much of her new work has alluded to aspects of the Passion and to other scenes of religious suffering, but where her figures, though drawn from traditional representations, are often strangely ambivalent. Much of the potential drama is removed, a quality that attracts Curneen, whose approach is characteristically understated. Her interest in these themes is not born out of religiosity – she is not committed to a faith – but stems from a recognition that such sacrifice tells us

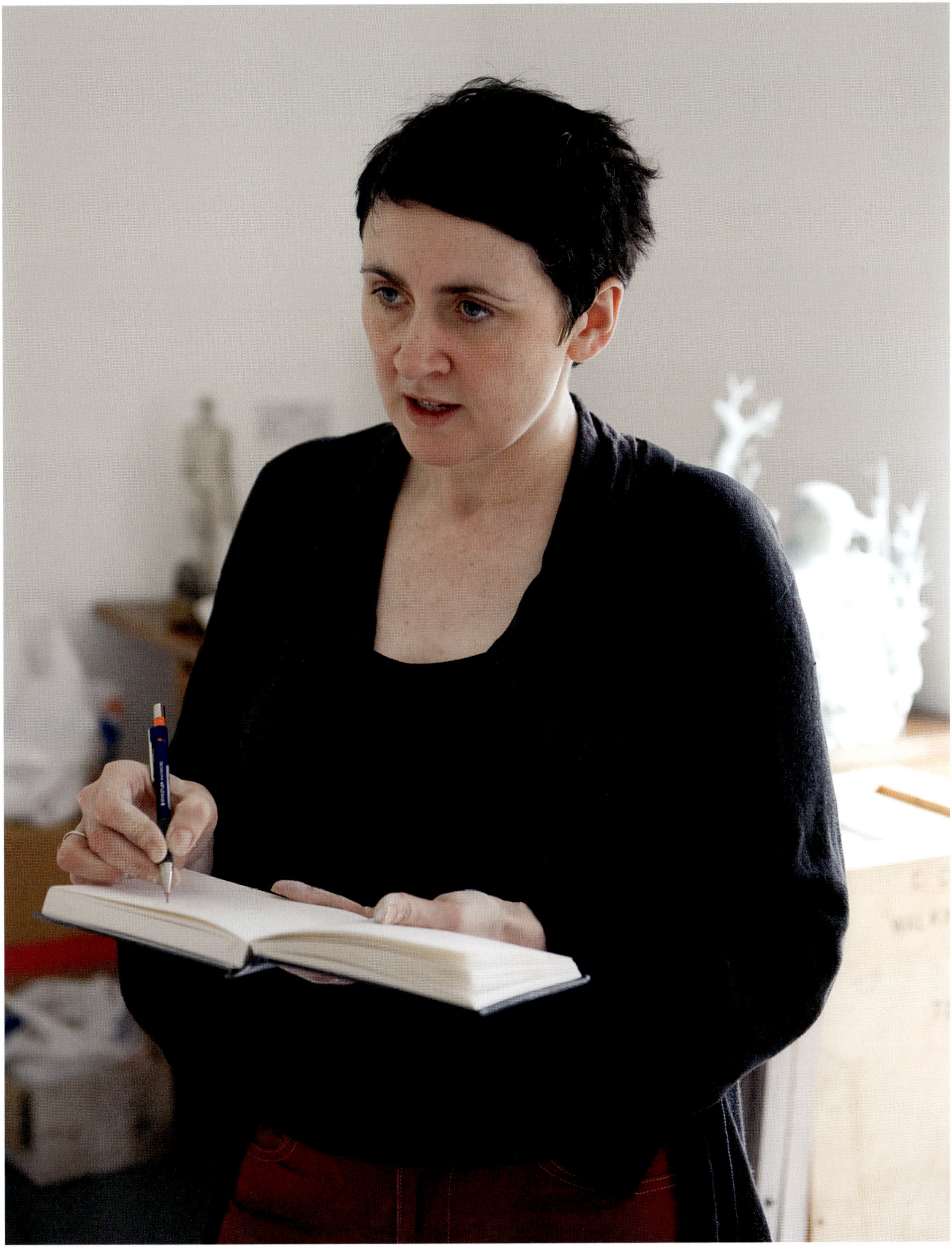

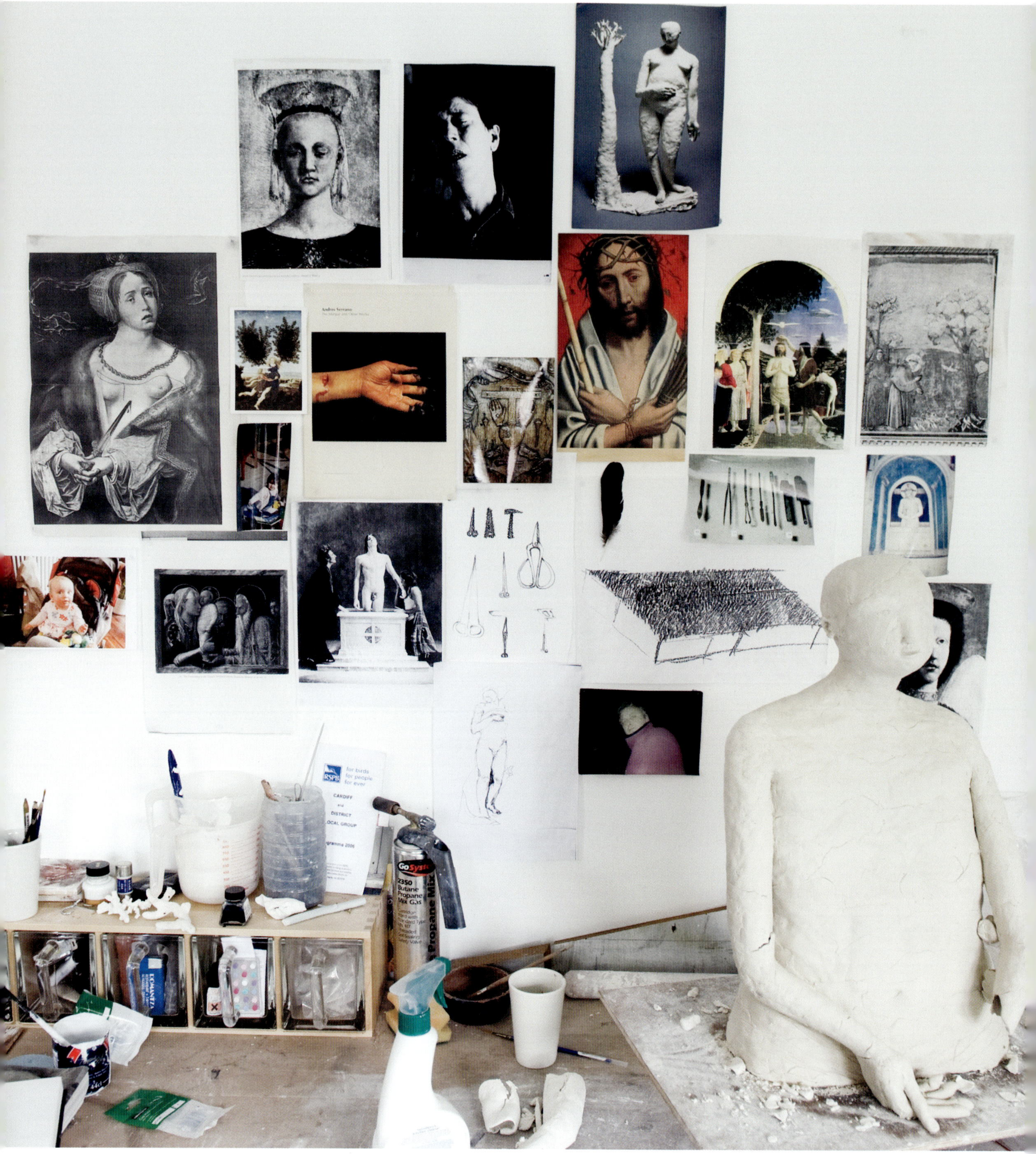
RSPB
for birds
for people
for ever
CARDIFF
and
DISTRICT
LOCAL GROUP
2350
Butane
Propane
Mix Gas
Propane Mix

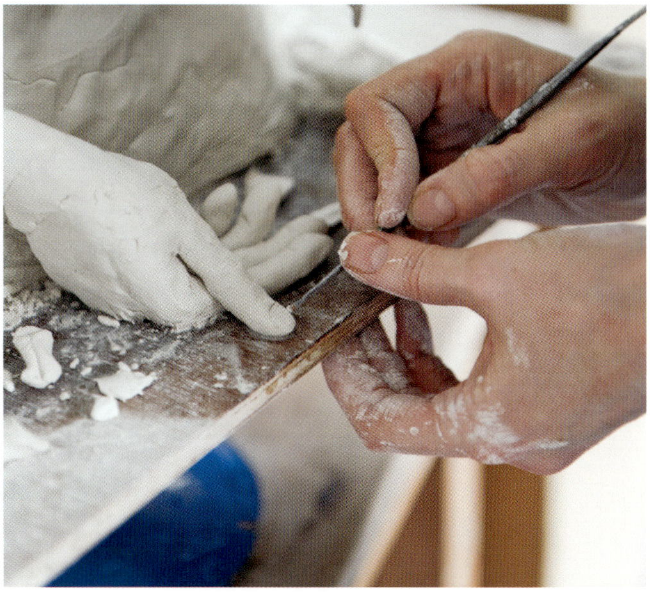

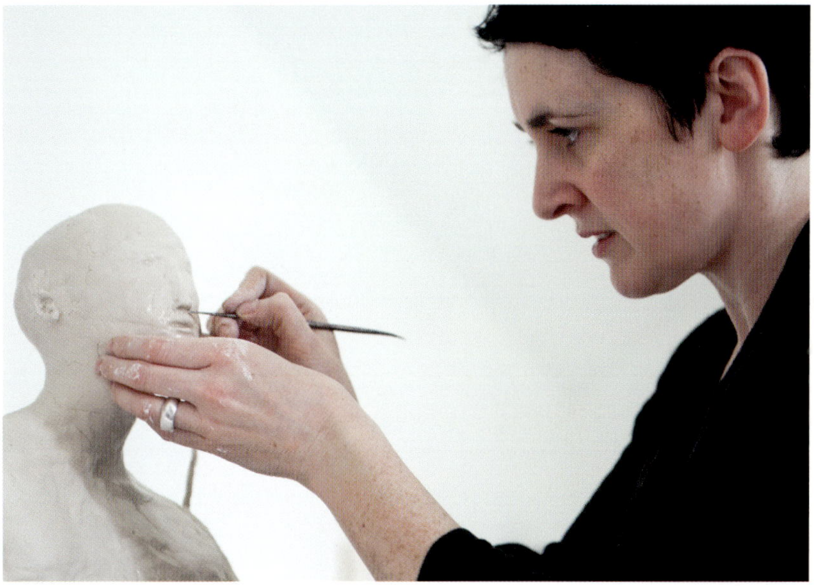

much about the human predicament. Curneen also uses these subjects to show inner human strength – a far cry from the nihilist despair of, say, Francis Bacon's use of the Crucifixion. Curneen's world is, by contrast, full of tenderness, a keen sense of the fragility of existence. Recently, she has made a series of terracotta tree forms, the material literally earth-given, of course, their gilded roots and re-growing branches a sign of regeneration. Curneen's use of gold is indicative of blood, a sign both of loss and of renewed energy and rebirth.

Curneen was born in Ireland in 1968 and brought up in a traditional Catholic household. Beginning her ceramic education in Crawford, she studied at the University of Ulster, Belfast and the University of Wales Institute in Cardiff, where she has been living ever since, combining making with teaching at her old college. As a student she made extrovert and humorous figure groups based on social observation, but changing circumstances provoked a more questioning investigation of humanity. Through the 1990s she provided a series of haunting white porcelain nudes, androgynously female figures in isolation or in lonely groups with a striking lack of conversant eye contact. Dealing with what Curneen called 'neutral humanity, the ethereal and the spiritual', they looked anonymous but their source was autobiographical. In retrospect she realises the degree to which they were about the female condition, though this was not so obvious to her at the time.

These figures were like no others: exaggerated and disproportionate, with heads shrunken, eyes and mouths diminutive, while the hands were large and pendulous, emphasising emotional gravity and weight. The clay surfaces – thin, brittle, densely worked and frequently breached – added to the psychological charge. If such work had a modern provenance it might be the figuration that emerged in Paris after the Second World War, when artists like Giacometti and Germaine Richier explored the alienation and fragmentation that followed a major conflict. Out of Curneen's sense of human melancholy grew an interest in the Christian martyrs. She also began to investigate different surfaces, covering figures and tool-like objects partially or wholly in dense clay prickles, a reference both to the stigmata and to wounding and hurt in a broader sense, to sensation that is both about touch and resistant to it.

The treatment of implements, of functional forms, rendered useless in this way is as disturbing as Meret Oppenheim's infamous fur cup and saucer. Conversely, there is again that parallel suggestion of spreading growth – seen in figures

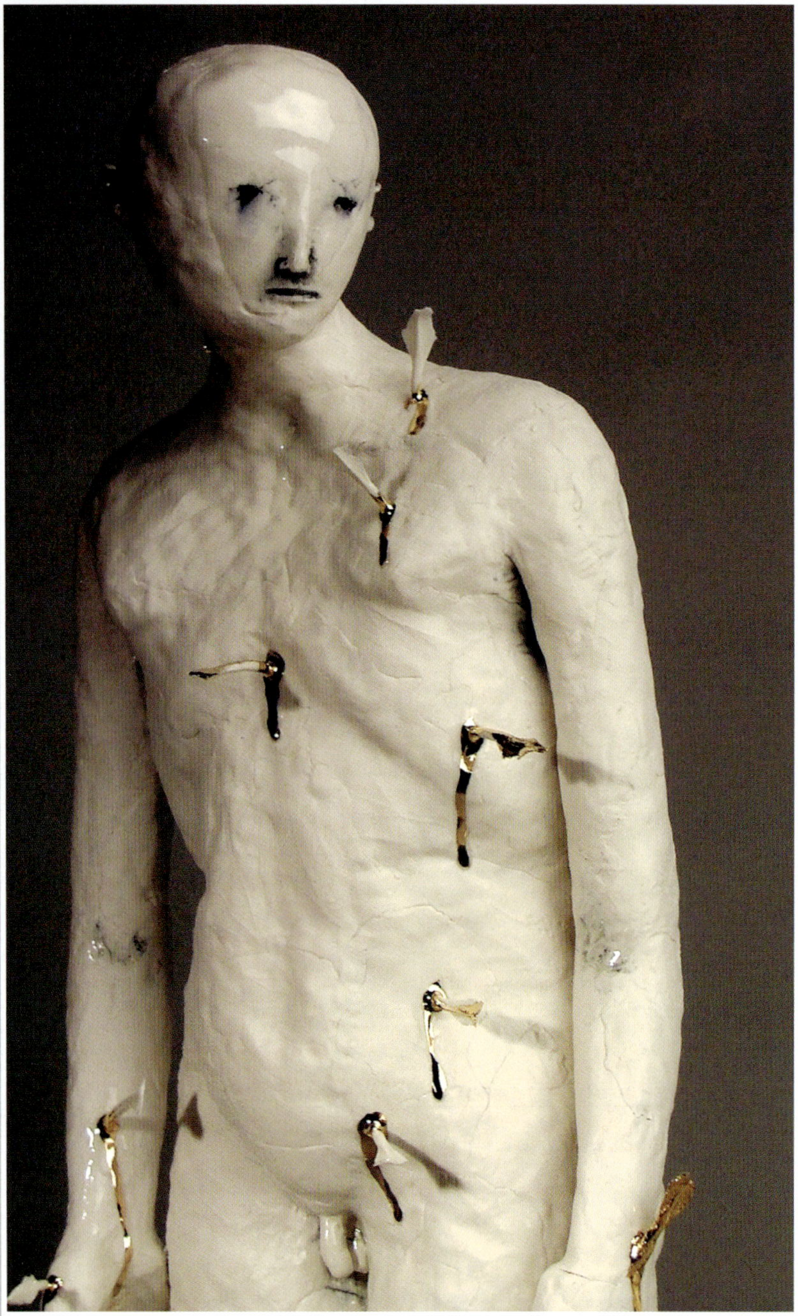

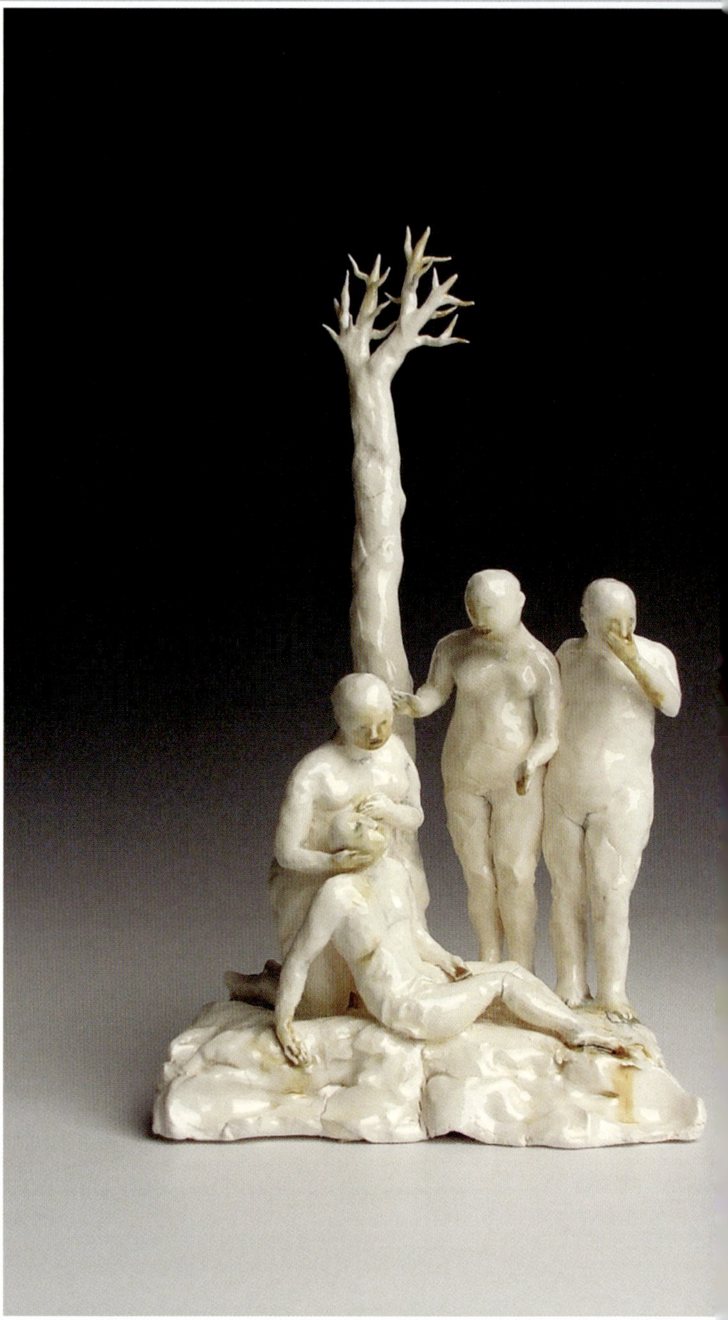

covered in blooming flowers, in trees that root and confirm the figures in their landscapes. Equally, the blood issuing from the wounds of St Sebastian and St Catherine – shown as droplets of gold – might be emblematic of retrieval and redemption. The work appears more fluid, the groups often interact; the human figure takes on a quietly heroic aspect. The flowers, in the form of floral transfers or thickly growing roses, confirm this new sense of consolation. In a similar vein, in 2003 Curneen made a porcelain heart and covered it in rosebuds, and a series of slipcast hands in prayer with gold flowing out of them; she is as much concerned with perceptions of what may be inside her forms – hers is also a sculpture of interiority. The ethereal, transfigurative aspects of the body find perfect voice in the fertile earth – such properties

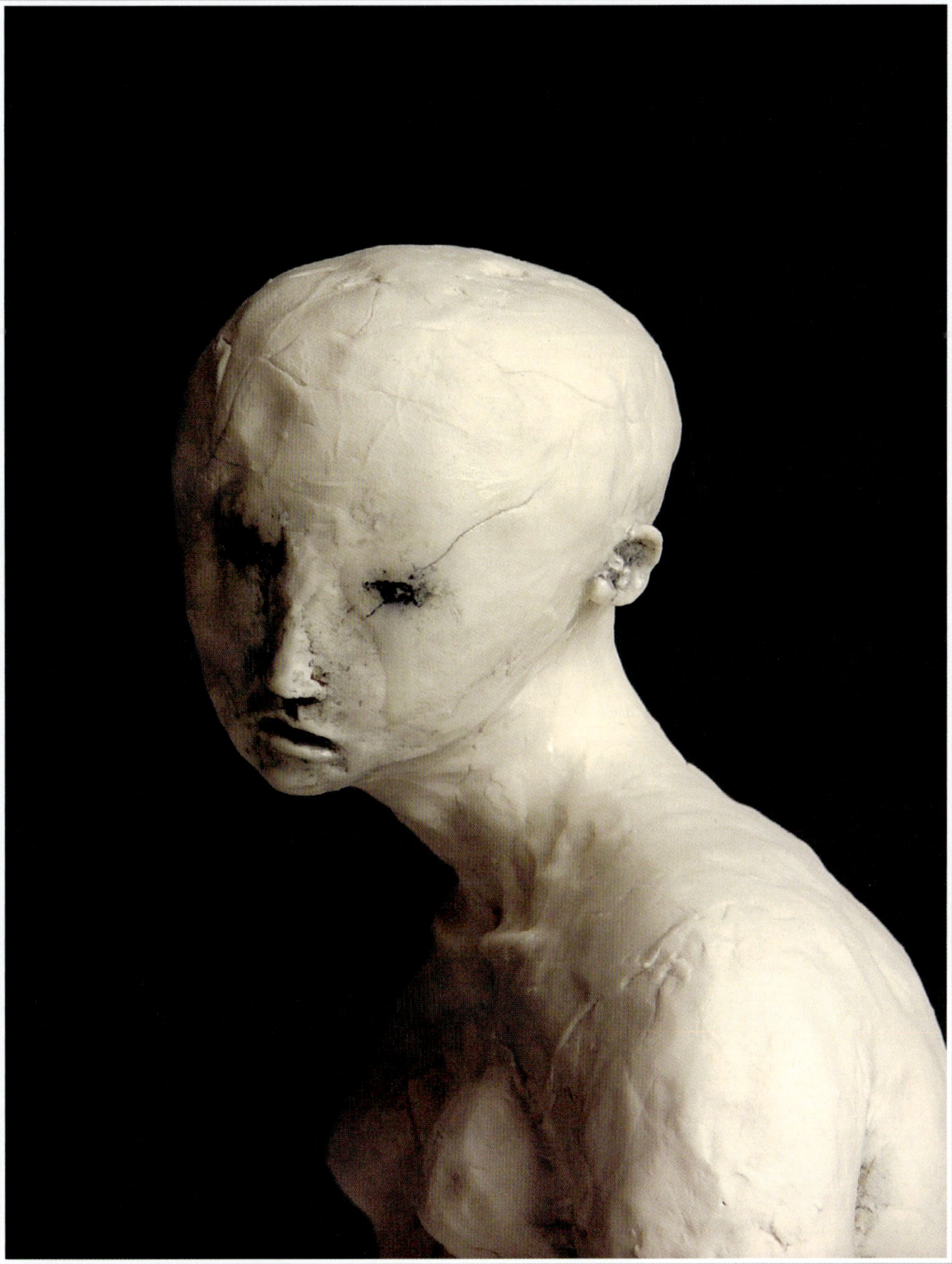

left: Standing Figure (detail), *2004, porcelain. Height: 70cm (27½in.).*
middle: Stations of the Cross, *2006, porcelain. Height: 45cm (17¾in.).*
far left: Irene tending St. Sebastian (detail), *2007, porcelain. Height: 80cm (31½in.).*
Photos: Courtesy of the artist

are inherent in clay – a sense of affirmation clearly seen in her mother-and-child pieces, notably, a major terracotta figure for St Mary's Guildhall in Boston, installed in 2007.

Curneen's work has taken many ideas from the broader history of art, but there is a strong sense of ceramic inheritance too. Clay is more than just a medium. Her use of porcelain refers back to figuration in the Chinese Song dynasty, to 18th-century Staffordshire and French Meissen. But her work is particularly sensitive and intimate; we can easily connect it with our own perception of the world and its vulnerabilities. Her use of technique and process shows how she continues to revel in the rich potential of the material, in its rewarding subtleties and malleability – in short, in its expressive potency.

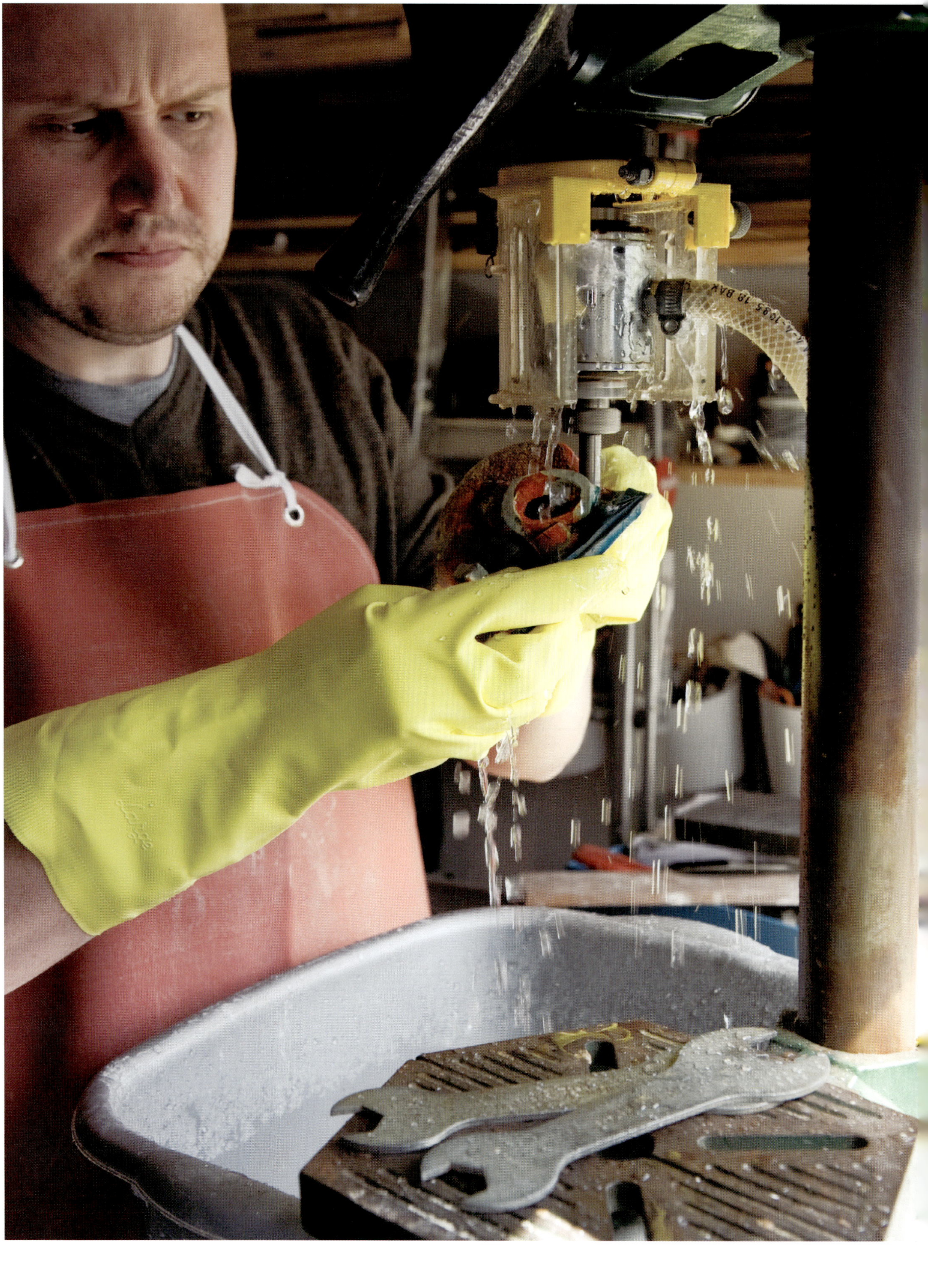

Neil Brownsword

NEIL BROWNSWORD is a ceramist who lives and works in Penkhull, a suburb of Stoke-on-Trent, near the heart of what was once a thriving pottery industry. Now in his late thirties, he makes abstract sculptural work in clay, using the detritus of local pottery manufacture to investigate the complex history and nature of factory production here, its social impact on Stoke and its slow, painful demise in modern times. In the mid-1990s Brownsword made a big impact in the world of British ceramics with strange dislocated figures made out of the shards, scrap moulds and other cast-offs and remnants of ceramic manufacture, objects that, as he puts it, 'tapped into the heritage of the industry' to make powerful statements about its present malaise. These were uncompromisingly disturbing – vulgar, colourful and funny and at the same time deeply unsettling; in fact, in the bizarre assemblage of diverse materials, they were often blatantly grotesque.

Brownsword was producing confrontational commentaries on the day-to-day experience of employment in Stoke as only someone brought up in the city and who had worked on the factory floor could do. He was struck by the futility of the lives of people stuck in the pattern of their social norms and static directionless jobs, and at a time when the pottery industry was itself in sharp decline. Factories have been steadily relocating abroad, where labour and overheads are cheaper. Brownsword cites the bald statistics: 'In 1948 approximately 79,000 people worked in the North Staffordshire industry. By 2003, it was about 11,000.'

Yet there was also a strong undercurrent of humanity and affection in this art. Brownsword, whose work for the last dozen years has been a long observational meditation on this decline, views it very much with the insight of an insider. His ceramic figures, which recall the early Staffordshire figurines he so admires, also speak of his deep feelings for this place, for its once great manufacturing history and the friendships he has made on the factory floor. Brownsword's approach has always been double-edged. There is something almost paradoxical about his ability both to celebrate and to decry what Stoke means to him, both on a personal level and as a kind of artist-anthropologist delving into this city's industrial past and present. His awareness of its changing landscape, where once vibrant areas of industry have given way to prairie-like wasteland and new incongruous luxury housing, remains acute. When the famous Spode factory recently ceased production at its original site in Stoke, the loss barely made the front page in the local newspaper, when once such closures were headline news.

Brownsword was born in the Stoke area in 1970, into a family that had worked in the ceramics industry for generations. At the age of 16 he was apprenticed at the Josiah Wedgwood factory, initially as a tableware modeller, but he managed to acquire a broader knowledge of design and making skills, resisting the accepted pattern of specialisation (something he deeply admired for the skills attained, but which he has always regarded as creatively limiting). Even as a teenager, it seems, Brownsword had a quietly rebellious streak. It was this independence of outlook, his wish to expand his artistic horizons, that took him to art college. He went on to study ceramics at Cardiff and then at the Royal College of Art in London. In 2006, he completed a practice-based doctorate at Brunel University, an experience that has allowed Brownsword to develop his skills as an articulate writer too. Now, after a period using an airy studio nearby, he's based back in Penkhull, working in a crowded upstairs

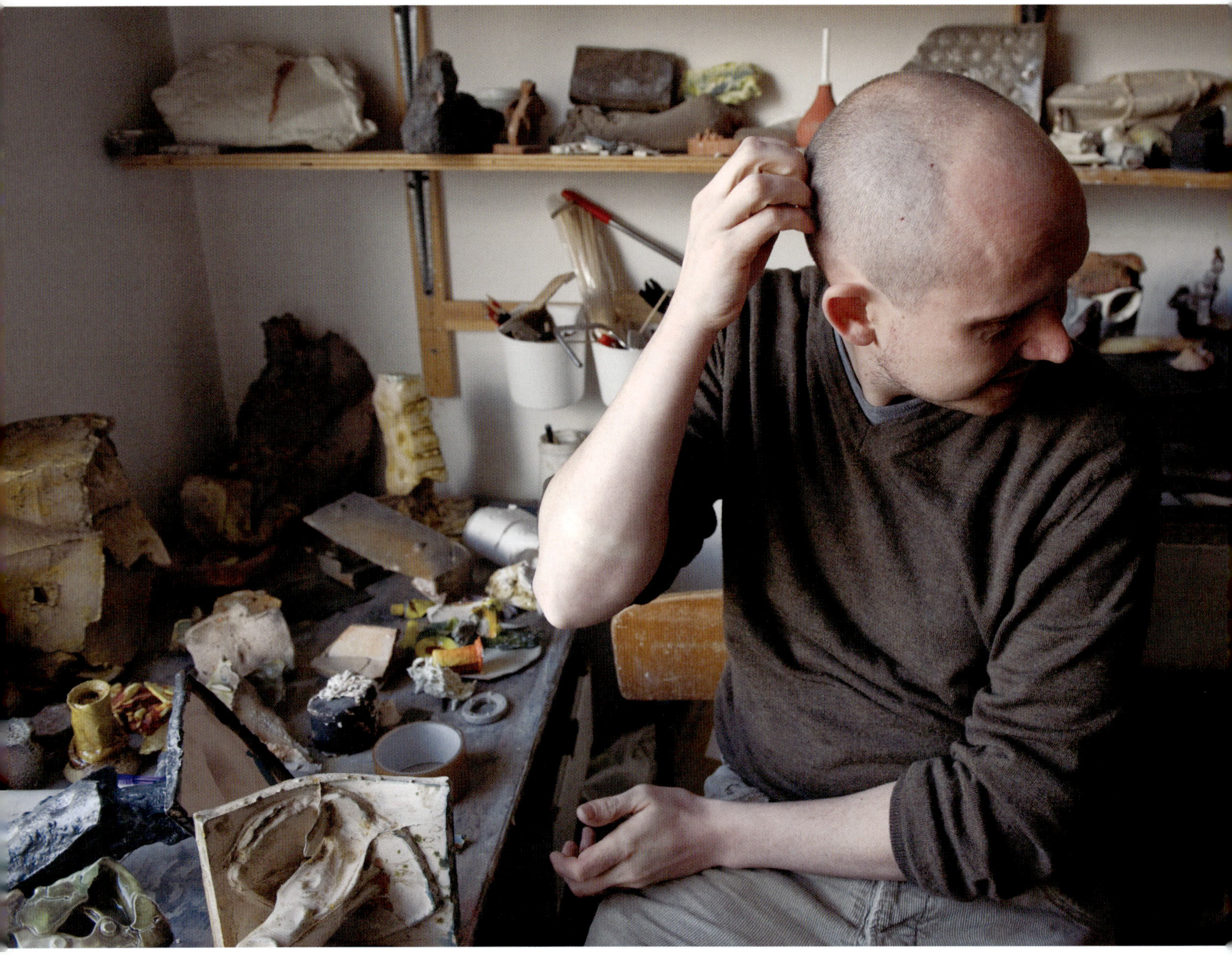

space at the rear of his terraced house. Here he is surrounded by leftover moulds, wasters and other fragments of the factory floor, as well as books that record the ceramic past and present of this place. The making process has also spilled out into a substantial shed in the back garden.

Brownsword, a very self-critical potter, recognised that his figures, while highly successful as objects, would be too easy to repeat. Not wishing to fall into a routine of slick replication, he knew a change of creative direction was necessary. A residency at the European Ceramic Work Centre at s'Hertogenbosch in Holland gave him the space and freedom to experiment and move on to a new phase, concentrating on the structure of clay itself – its wet, soft and hard qualities – and how it is affected by different processes. At this time he became more acutely aware, during a return visit to Stoke, of the stark realities of the decline in pottery manufacture, its ebbing away made more graphic as he witnessed the demolition of one particular factory during his trip. He began to take photographs of these sad events and the growing sprawl of dereliction across the Stoke

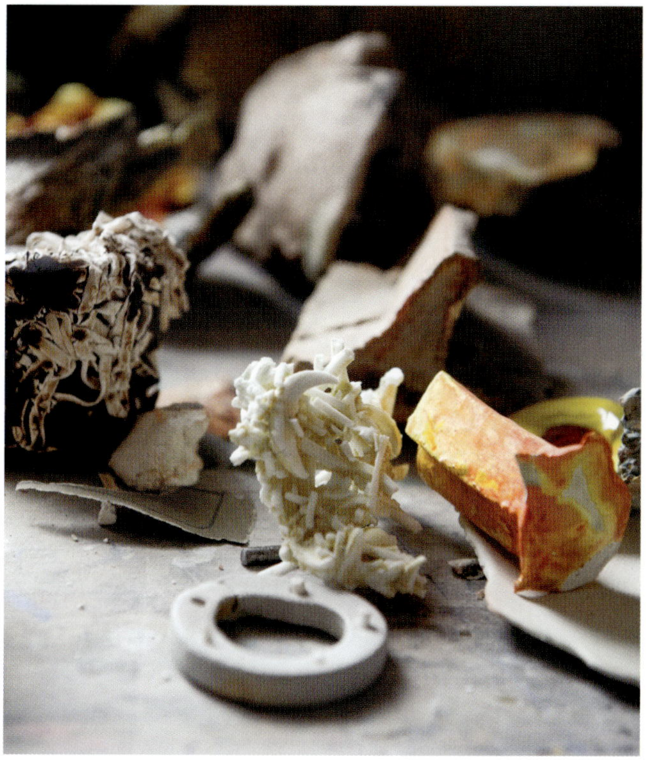

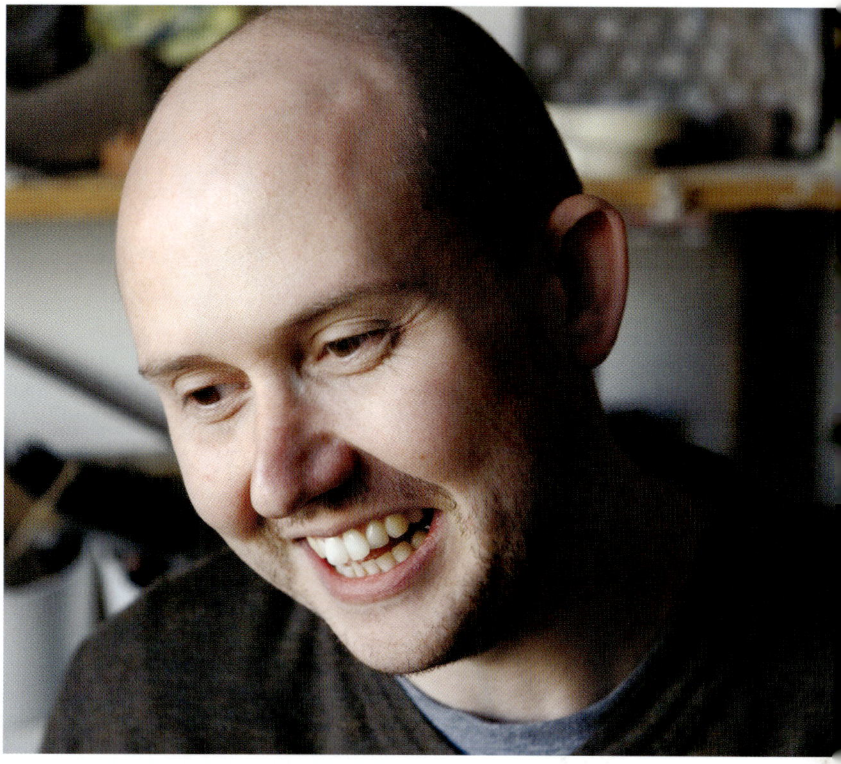

area, so indicative of the increased unemployment which has left those who have devoted their lives to this specialised industry, particularly the middle-aged, struggling to find new occupations. He began to see a powerful visual and symbolic connection between the by-products and extraneous materials of his own experimentation and the ceramic detritus of the Staffordshire industry.

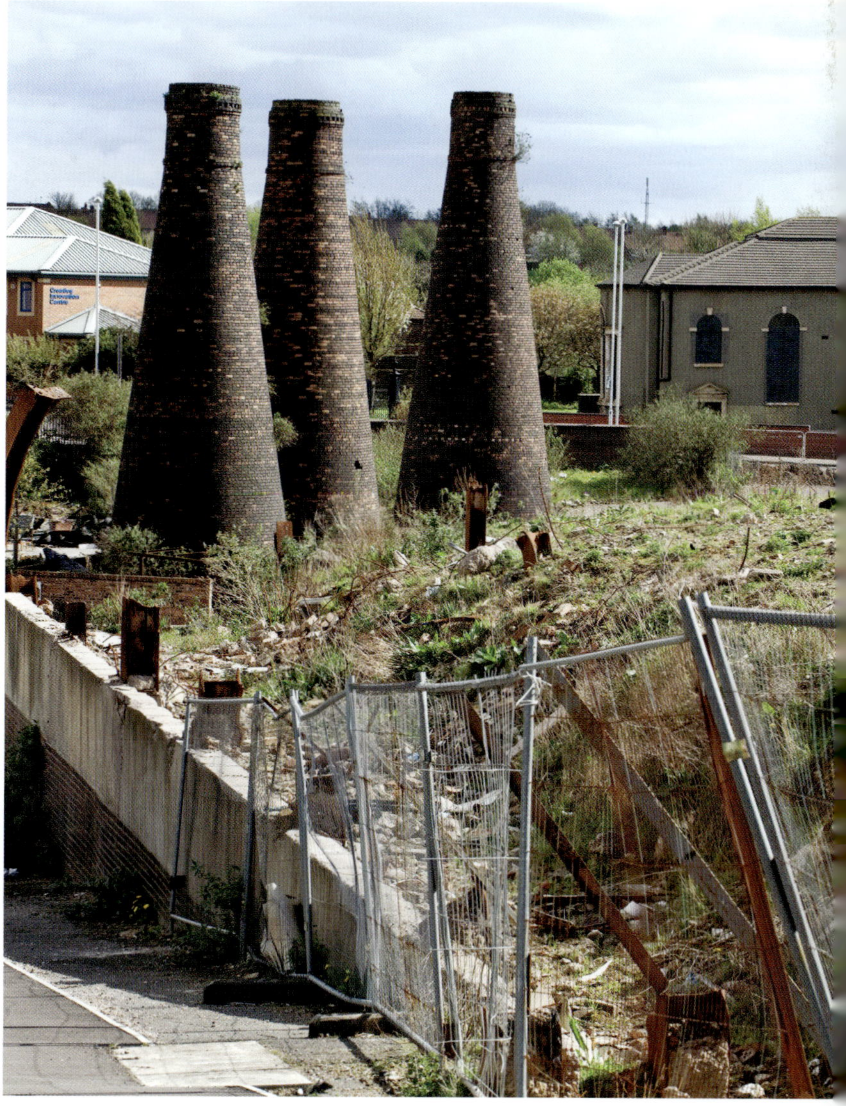

He began to look at the props, wasters (discarded pieces of defective pottery), tile presses, saggars and various bits of kiln furniture and refuse that were so strongly 'charged with the activity of everyday jobs'. In such material there was imprinted the repeated making and firing processes, the residue of production. In this archaeology of manufacture, which can be salvaged from the numerous pottery sites or viewed in the Potteries Museum's own collection, there was ample evidence of the extraordinary physical accretion of such industrial waste on the Stoke landscape. Brownsword makes the forceful point that much of the area has been built on a hardcore crust of these remnants, including the museum itself.

By collecting and reusing these various scraps – the fusings and meltings he has found – and assembling them into often

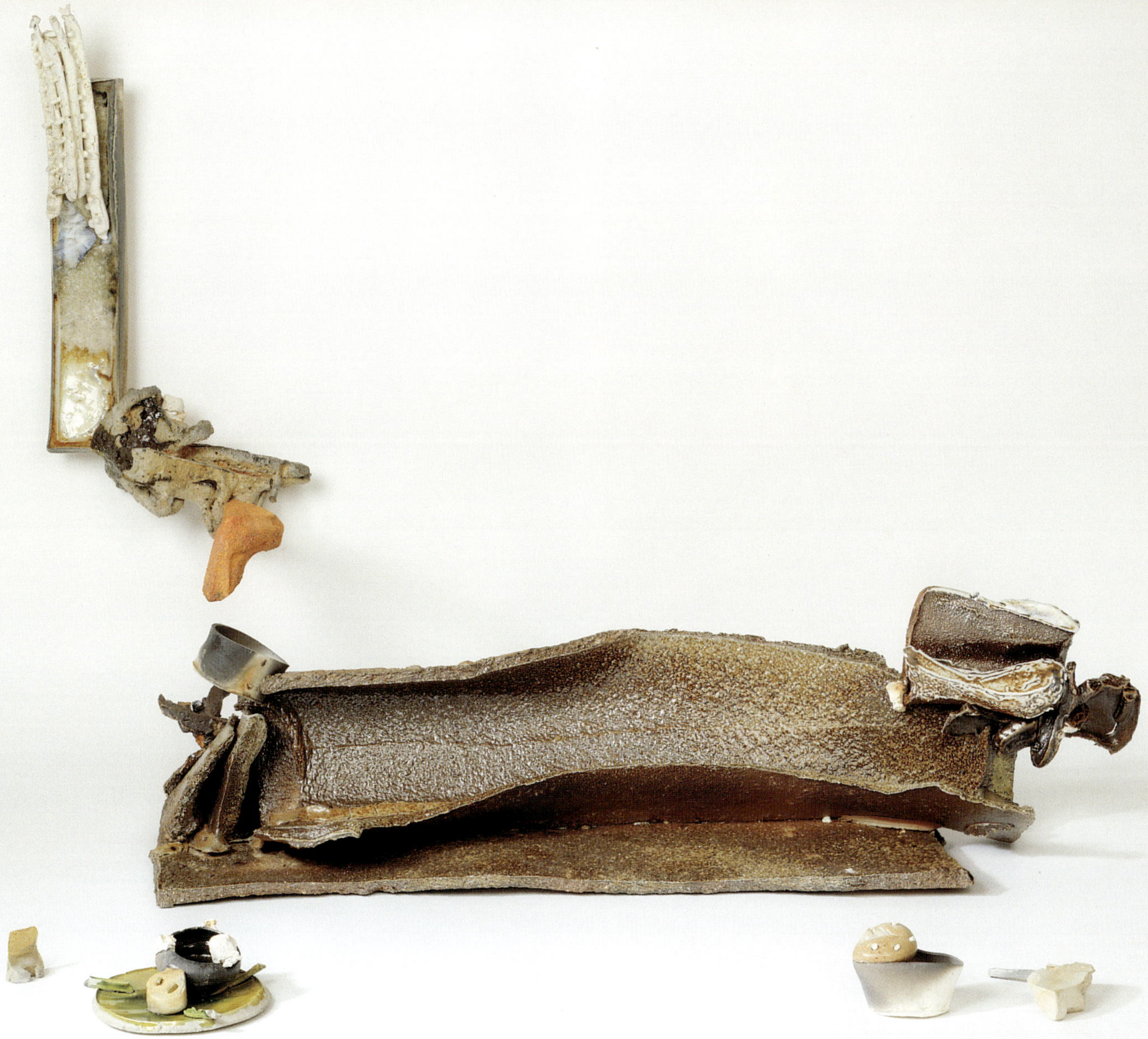

Waster No. 1, *2007, ceramic and industrial archaeology installation.*
80 x 110 x 40cm (31 x 43¼ x 15¾ in.) (6 elements).
Photo: Alan Tabor, courtesy of Galerie Besson

beautiful abstract amalgams that are often further transformed by refiring, Brownsword regenerates this material into structures and landscapes with various levels of meaning. These molten collages of clay, so memorably seen in a major show at the Potteries Museum in 2005, are resurrections of what has been discarded, memorials to industrial skill. They speak of individual and collective experience over long periods of time. Significantly, there remains a duality in Brownsword's bricolage, which laments the irrevocable loss of craft knowledge and this way of life, but is also critical of its rigidity, of the creative and social limitations in this division of labour. It touches on the psychological fallout of the production line. His constructions and assemblages become tableaux with a new kind of narrative content.

There is a provenance for this kind of work. One thinks of British ceramists like Gillian Lowndes and Gerwyn Jones,

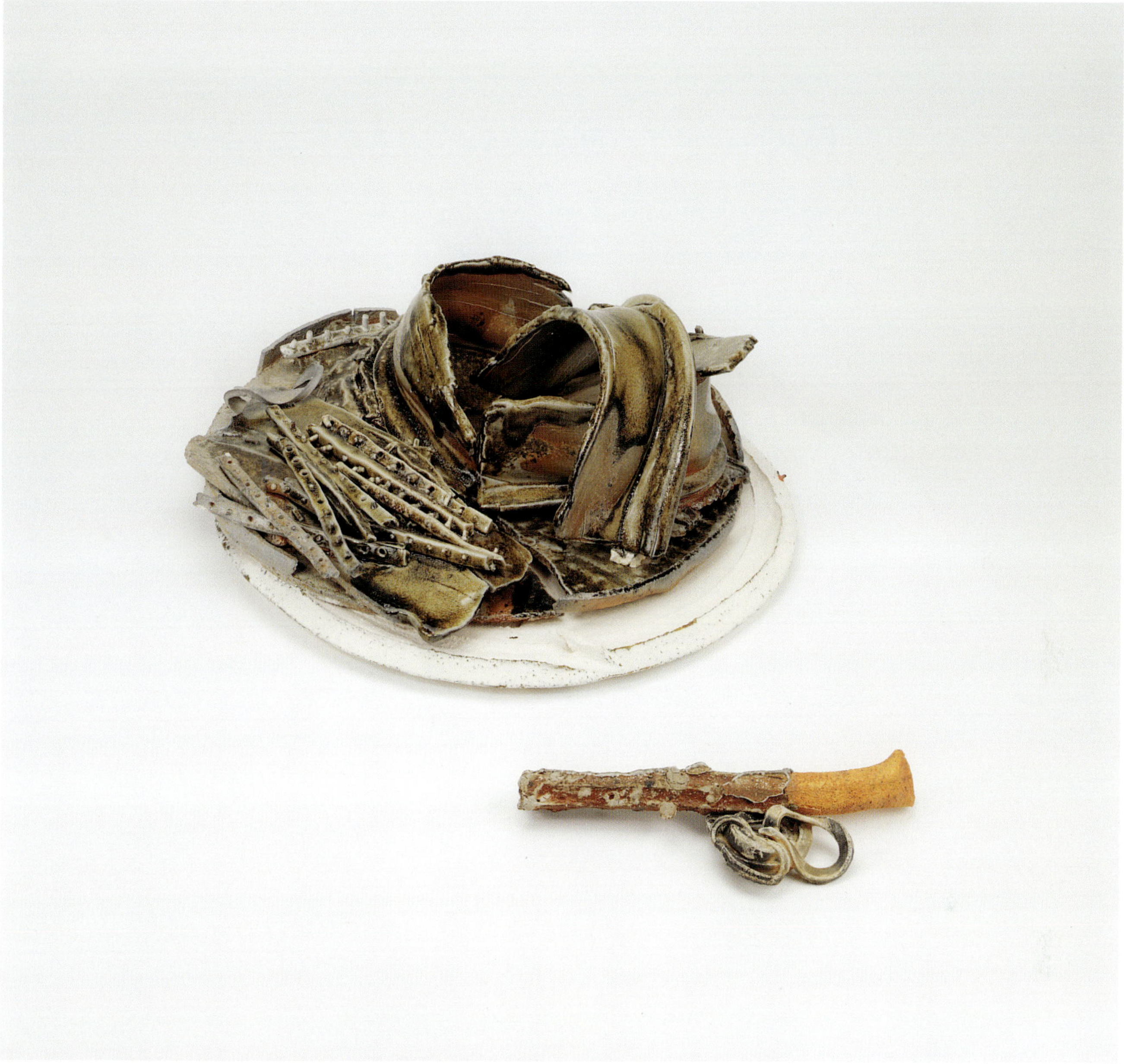

Crank, *2007, ceramic and industrial archaeology installation.*
25 x 80 x 64cm (9¾ x 31½ x 25¼in.) (2 elements).
Photo: Alan Tabor, courtesy of Galerie Besson

who have made comparable forms, objects with a similar sense of salvage, retrieval and reconstitution – imaginative montages dense with association. In this sense Brownsword goes beyond archaeology. His reuse and re-forming of the discarded contents of a mould, of the plugs that emerge from casting, of the offcuts of clay, is integrated into strangely amorphous, quietly subversive sculpture, a process in which he deliberately disables his own innate sense of craftsmanship. His art refutes the traditional decorative and functional use of clay, but while it eschews the familiar certainties of ceramics, his transmogrifications tap the richest vein of material expression. One thing is clear – that Brownsword has intelligently and sensitively evolved a language of considerable poetry, one that has much to say about the transformative fabric of clay and its potency as a way of recording human experience and historical change.

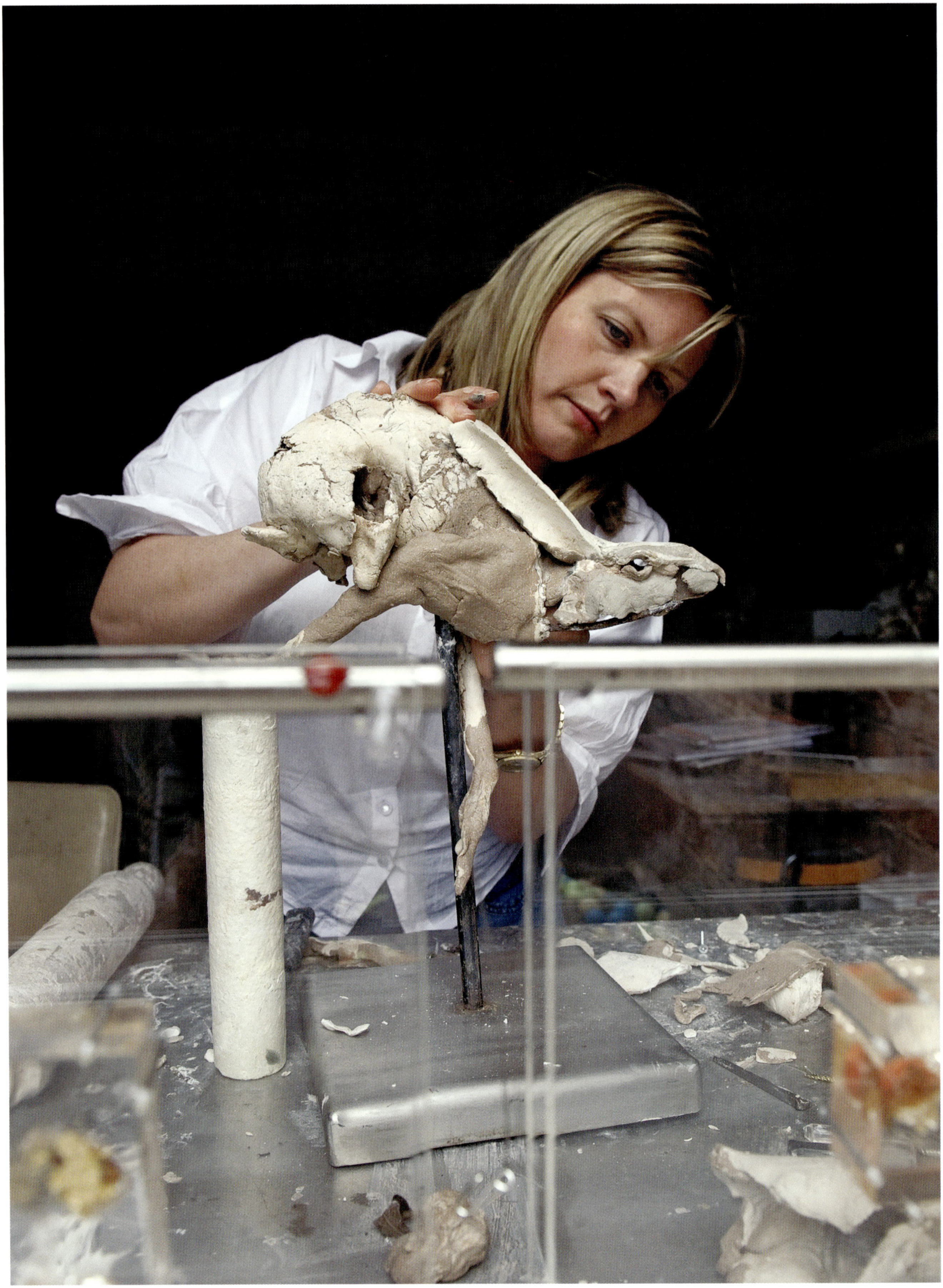

Emma Rodgers

EMMA RODGERS works at her home in Oxton, a leafy suburb on the Wirral, the fascinating peninsula that juts out into Liverpool Bay. The walls of her studio are covered in telltale images: pictures of apes, both in the wild and in captivity, dancers in movement, animal skeletons, anatomical dissections. There are also intriguing objects: desiccated frogs, items of taxidermy and perhaps on occasions a brace of pheasants. Here is an artist obviously engaged with the body and animal forms in particular, as a focus of action and both latent and released energy. Still only in her thirties, Rodgers already has an enviable reputation as one of our finest sculptors in clay. This is due not simply to her great technical skill, but also to her imaginative ability to capture something of the spirit and mystery – both the fragility and menace – of the animal world. There is nothing tame about these creatures: her territorial bulls and hares, surveying ravens and rearing horses are emphatically wild, involved in their own seasonal dramas and rituals. Others perhaps mirror some kind of human intrusion, coercion or captivity. Her richly expressive dancers, pushing into arching and twisting contortions, are just another species playing out their particular trials and struggles for life.

Rodgers was born in 1974 and from a young age had a considerable facility for drawing and modelling, a natural, intuitive grasp of flesh and bone that has, since her ceramics education at Wolverhampton University, moved from comparative literalism to a highly expressive and abstracted interpretation of her subjects. Since graduating, she has exhibited internationally, a television film has been made of her at work, and she is in numerous collections worldwide. At the time of writing, a major exhibition, surveying her art from the last decade, was being shown at Birkenhead's Williamson Art Gallery, a heady mix of the various creatures in clay, bronze and on paper that have populated Rodgers's vision since her teens.

'Red in tooth and claw' her work certainly is. It conjures up the untamed, often predatory aspect of nature evoked in the writings of Ted Hughes and the early paintings of Francis Bacon. Just as Hughes's poems recognised the visceral, often combative aspects of the landscape, so Rodgers has achieved comparable qualities of power, physicality and tenderness – a tenderness that crucially avoids sentimentality, a common trap for many artists working in this genre. It is Rodgers's ability to manipulate the material, to transfer the spontaneous sketch on the page into a three-dimensional summary of form and motion in clay, which keeps her work so vivid and penetrating. Her knowledge of anatomy is informed by film, photography and her own laboratory dissections, and by the observations of various beasts she has made on her travels, from down the road at Chester Zoo to her expeditions in the Far East. Her fascination with the intricacy and complexity of bone and tissue is continually unfolding. Some have suggested she develops her ideas through an investigation of animal myth and legend, but Rodgers is still so engaged in her analysis of animal spirit – the complexity of body and surface in stillness and flux – that a more specific narrative seems unnecessary.

She has written in an artist's statement that 'confrontation, energy, curiosity, essence of a movement and interaction are the main elements that initially draw me to a new subject, and are indicative of the very nature of the animals I have depicted'. She is fascinated by the physical weight that can be achieved through the 'masses of flesh', the 'tension, spring and strength in muscles and the creases and folds of

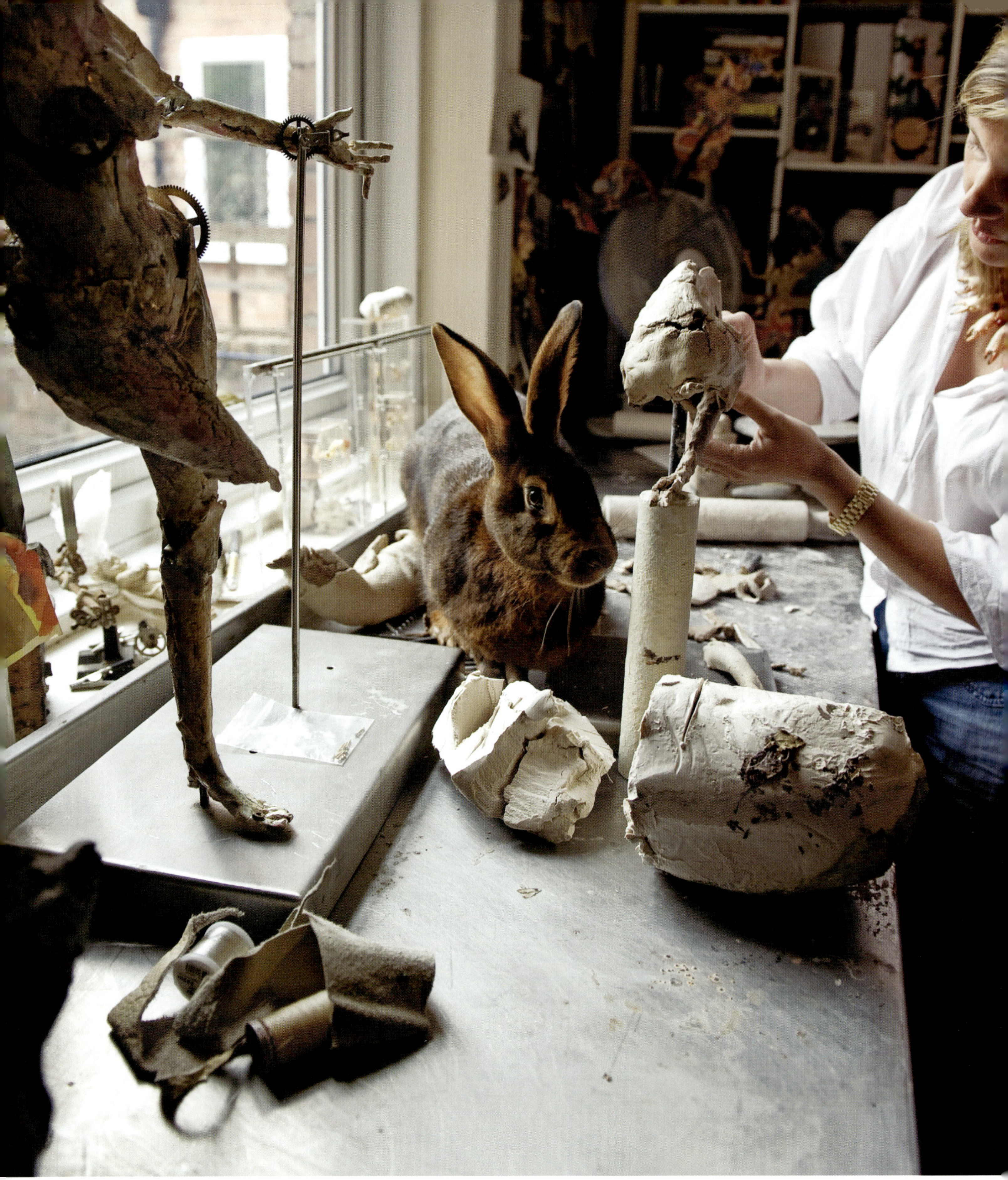

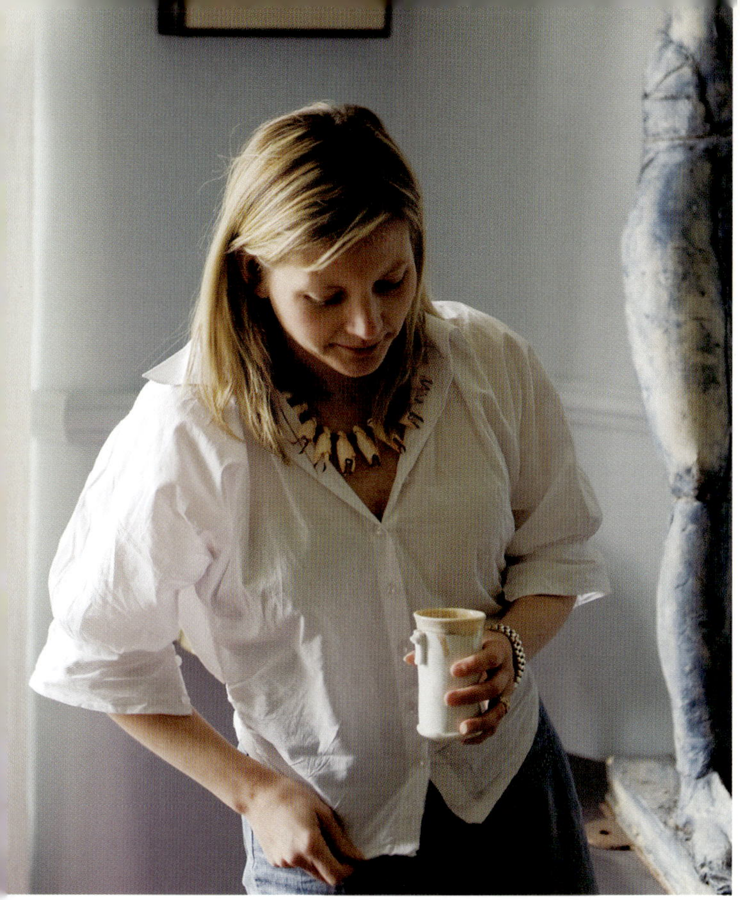

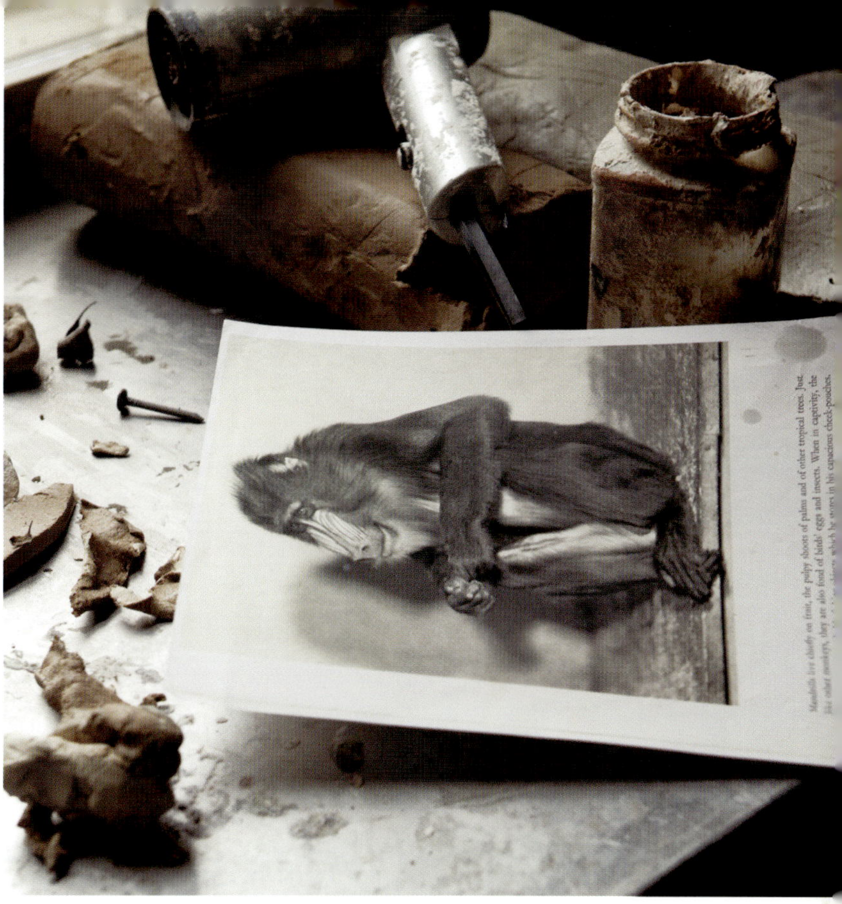

skin'. It is also about the flexing agility of limb and ligament, transforming the animated nervous lines of her sketchbook into the stretched and torn clay surfaces that have become her hallmark. The material is applied freely, to the point where it splits and ruptures, making for, as she puts it, 'a statement of omission', a powerful sense of suggestion rather than dogged detail. Her knowledge of structure enables her merely to imply a limb or a surface through a process of paring away that is as much about negative space as mass. This avoidance of conventional modelling can make more traditional and academic treatments look staid and lifeless.

Combining clays – porcelain paper clay and white stoneware, and, for smaller sculptures, earthstone and porcelain – creates fascinating bodyscapes, especially when Rodgers integrates clay with various found objects such as animal bones, nails, pieces of wire and other materials. Oxides and a variety of slips and glazes provide free painterly colour to accentuate the animated application of clay; these highlighted contours lose none of their immediacy when cast in bronze. Such an approach enables Rodgers to get beneath the skin of her subjects in both a literal and metaphorical sense. Just as her studies of the human body explore our own physical extremes, portraying stress as well as beauty – our psychological wear and tear – so some of her animals appear subjugated, mere objects for entertainment. For example, by putting a pair of monkeys on roller skates, Rodgers shows, *in extremis*, how animals can be compromised for human enjoyment.

By contrast, there are deeply poetic depictions of creatures in their own habitats: fighting hares, almost airborne in their gyrations, a baboon intimately and lovingly cradling her young, a bull about to charge. Her freezing of the moment, her capturing of the instantaneous, avoids cliché and idealisation. Each piece becomes a landscape of light and shadow, of knots and sinews, fleshy sags and tautness. There is evidence of a struggle, a making process that is distinctly hard-won. Her admiration for artists like Giacometti and Lucian Freud is revealing, given their approach to flesh,

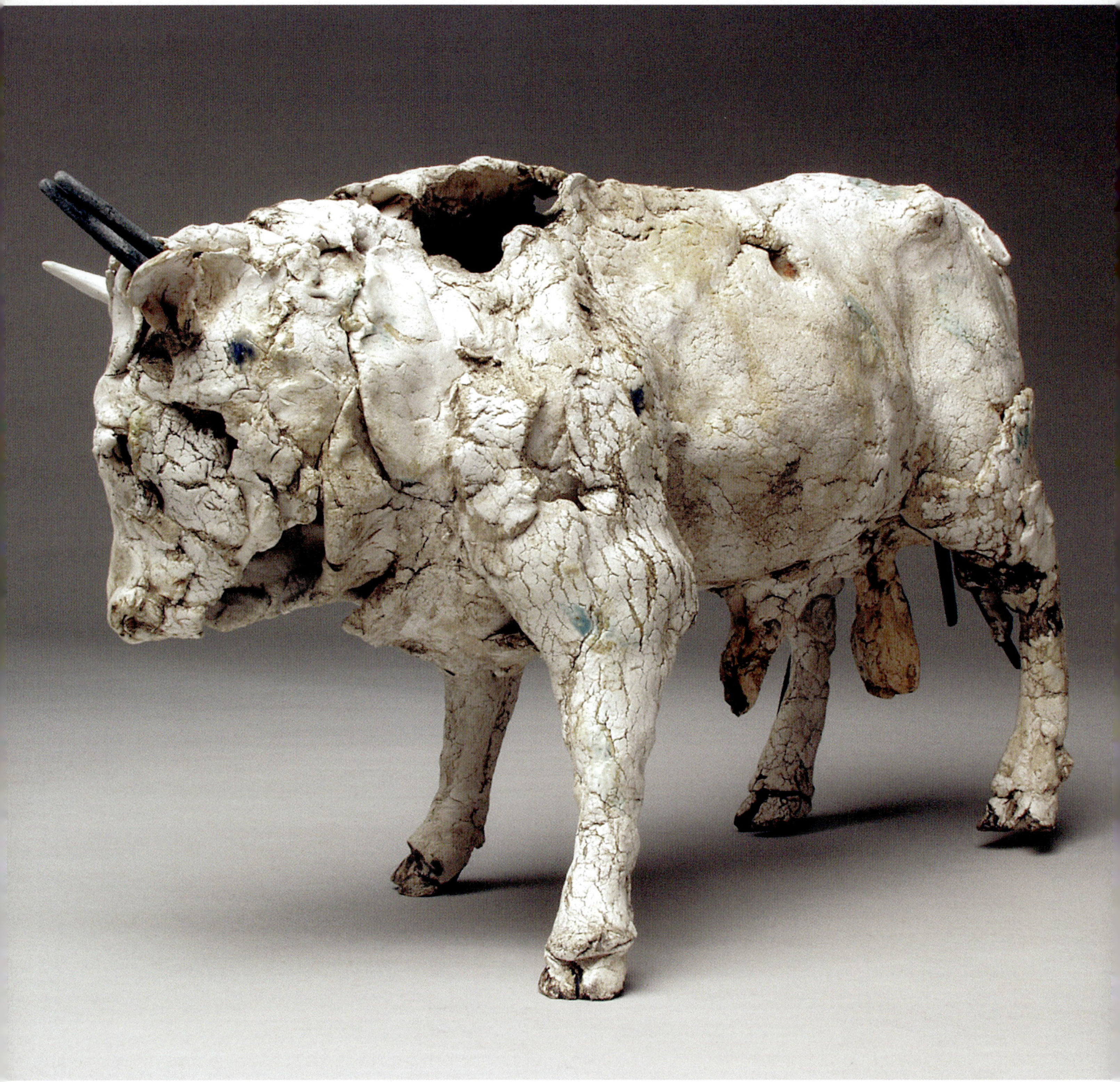

opposite: Mother and Child, *2002, mixed clays.*
Height: 56cm (19¾in).
inset: Hare, *2004, mixed clays.*
Height: 22cm (8¾in). Photos: Courtesy of the artist

above: Standing Bull, *2003, mixed clays.*
Height: 30cm (11¾in). Photo: Courtesy of the artist

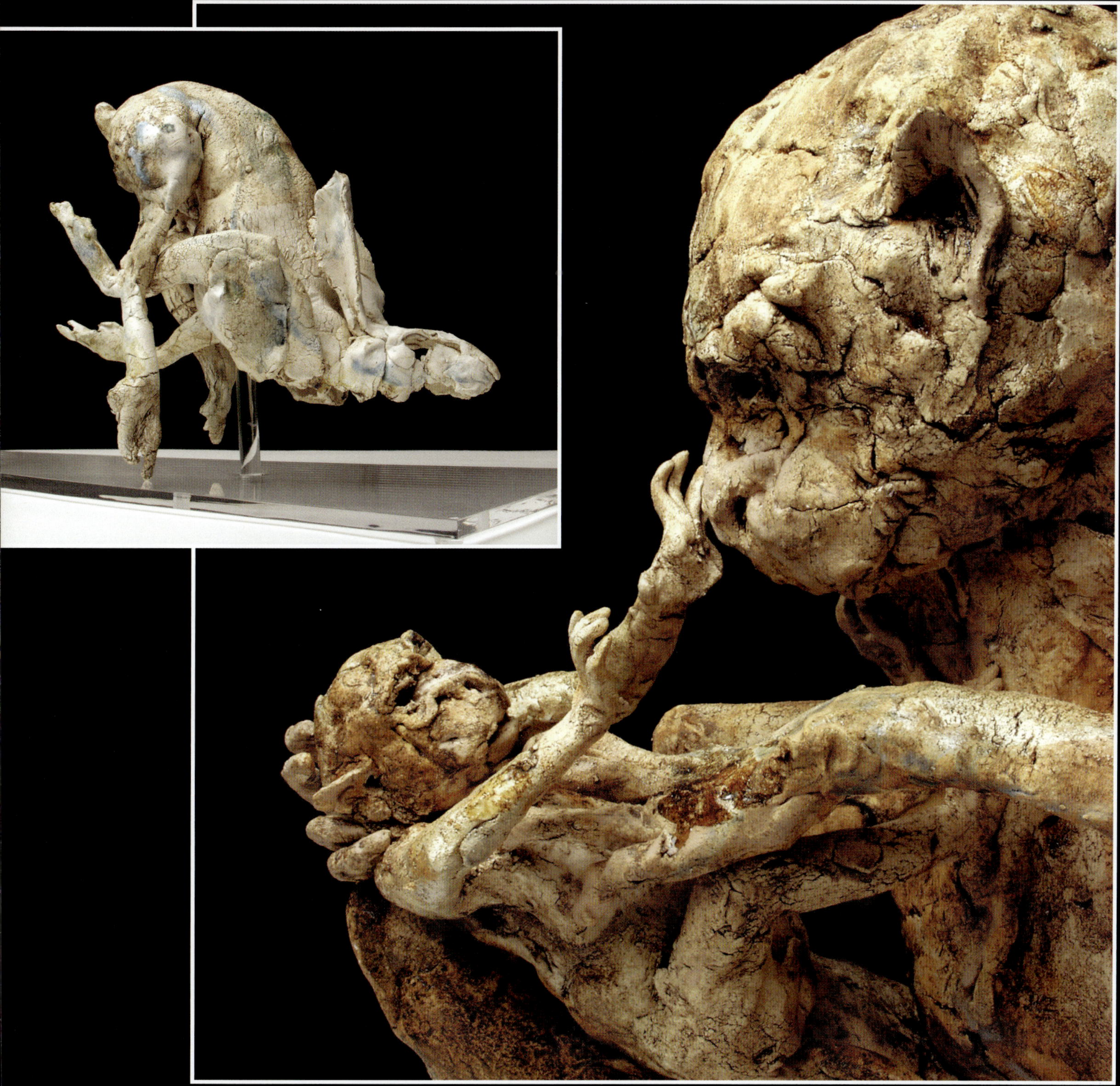

the way they dig deep, excavating the human condition. Rodgers's work is celebratory and affirming, but it also has a searing honesty. She doesn't spare us that sense of mortality as well as life force: her forms may kick, leap and twist, but you can also see through them, straight to the bone. It is a mark of the complexity of her work that it can convey both pulsing energy and exposure, with the skull and spine revealed. Life and death, after all, are inextricably linked.

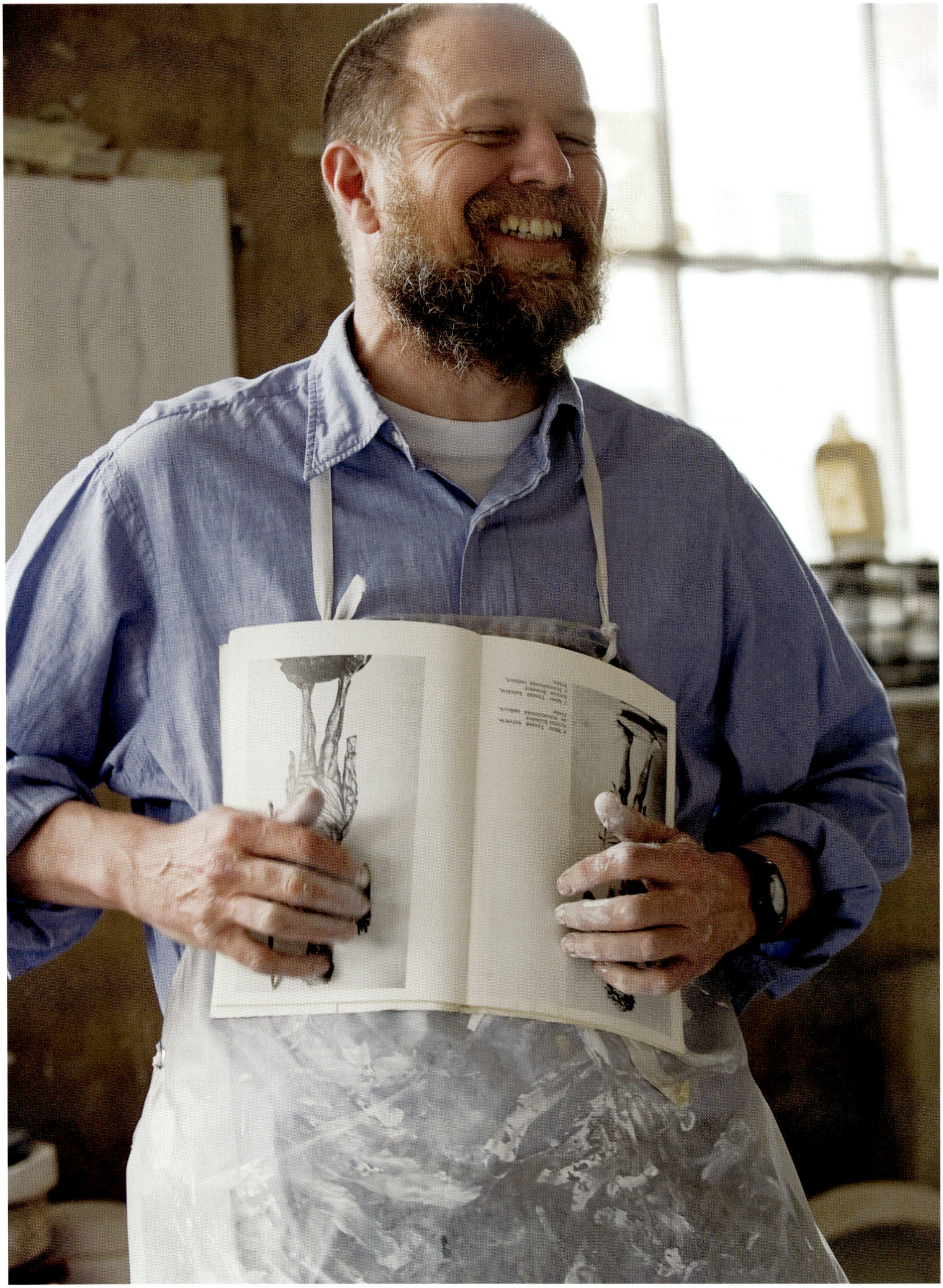

Philip Eglin

PHILIP EGLIN, born in Gibraltar in 1959, already had an international name for his figurative work when in 1986 he won the prestigious Jerwood Prize for Ceramics. His richly baroque females, relaxed, quizzical, sometimes laconic and bored, meet our gaze – bringing something of the great tradition of the western nude into a more intimate space. Eglin uses a time-honoured subject not only to praise the human form in a renewed way, but as a vehicle for his own sharp, often amused commentary on modern life. Political hypocrisy, consumerism, gender, sex, religion, sport – all these themes and more are explored by Eglin, not only in his splendidly opulent figuration, but in large rotund cylinders or 'buckets', as well as stoneware jugs and press-moulded plates and dishes.

Eglin began as a maker of pots, and this remains the basis for his more figurative odyssey. He has a particular love of English medieval wares (one of his favourite books is Bernard Rackham's Faber monograph on the subject), a period revisited in his sequences of small assembled jugs: expressive and delicate objects in brown, ochre and olive glazes that echo the patina of old pewter. But Eglin is equally a student of the 17th and 18th centuries, of pre-industrial Staffordshire figures and pots. His famous nudes and Madonnas owe as much to 18th-century salt-glaze pew groups and Whieldon wares as they do to the broader history of western art. His enthusiasm for Romanesque and Gothic carving, for the painter Lucas Cranach's 'naked charmers' as Kenneth Clark dubbed them, is far removed from the colder idealism found in Renaissance Italy or Neoclassical France. What Clark referred to as the 'anti-classical' proportions and sinuous allure of Cranach's seductive nymphs is also a major characteristic of Eglin's women – a joyful eroticism distant from the grandeur of Michelangelo or the intellectual weight of Canova. These are more like people we actually know, with warm blood flowing through their veins.

Eglin's passion, the sense of range and possibility in what he does, is very evident when you see his spacious but cluttered studio in Stoke-on-Trent. The remnants of old work and projects in progress sit side by side: a scattering of white Madonnas, a row of jugs, a group of recently finished tin-glazed dishes, a couple of bucket forms in the process of decoration. The walls are covered with numerous photographs and pictures from newspapers and magazines: Madonnas, snapshots of the Pope, some life drawings. There are plastic drinking bottles lying about (perhaps the modern disposable equivalent of the medieval jug?) and a collection of plaster and plastic New Testament characters. Eglin uses the impressions made by modern packaging and containers to delineate and decorate some of his jugs and figures, adding a contemporary vintage to traditional subjects and forms. The studio gives a strong idea of Eglin's rich eclecticism, the varied sources behind his wry take on the complexities and contradictions of 21st-century society.

Eglin actually grew up in Harlow New Town and studied ceramics at North Staffordshire Polytechnic in Stoke. He has particular memories of his student visits to the fine collections of slipware, salt glaze and other local traditions in Hanley Museum. It wasn't until he began to experiment with various ideas and processes at the Royal College of Art in the mid-eighties that a primary preoccupation with the figure began to emerge. Eglin's natural ease with the human form – its articulation and linkage of limbs, its expressive language – is due not only to his obvious observational skills, his abilities as a draughtsman, but also to his

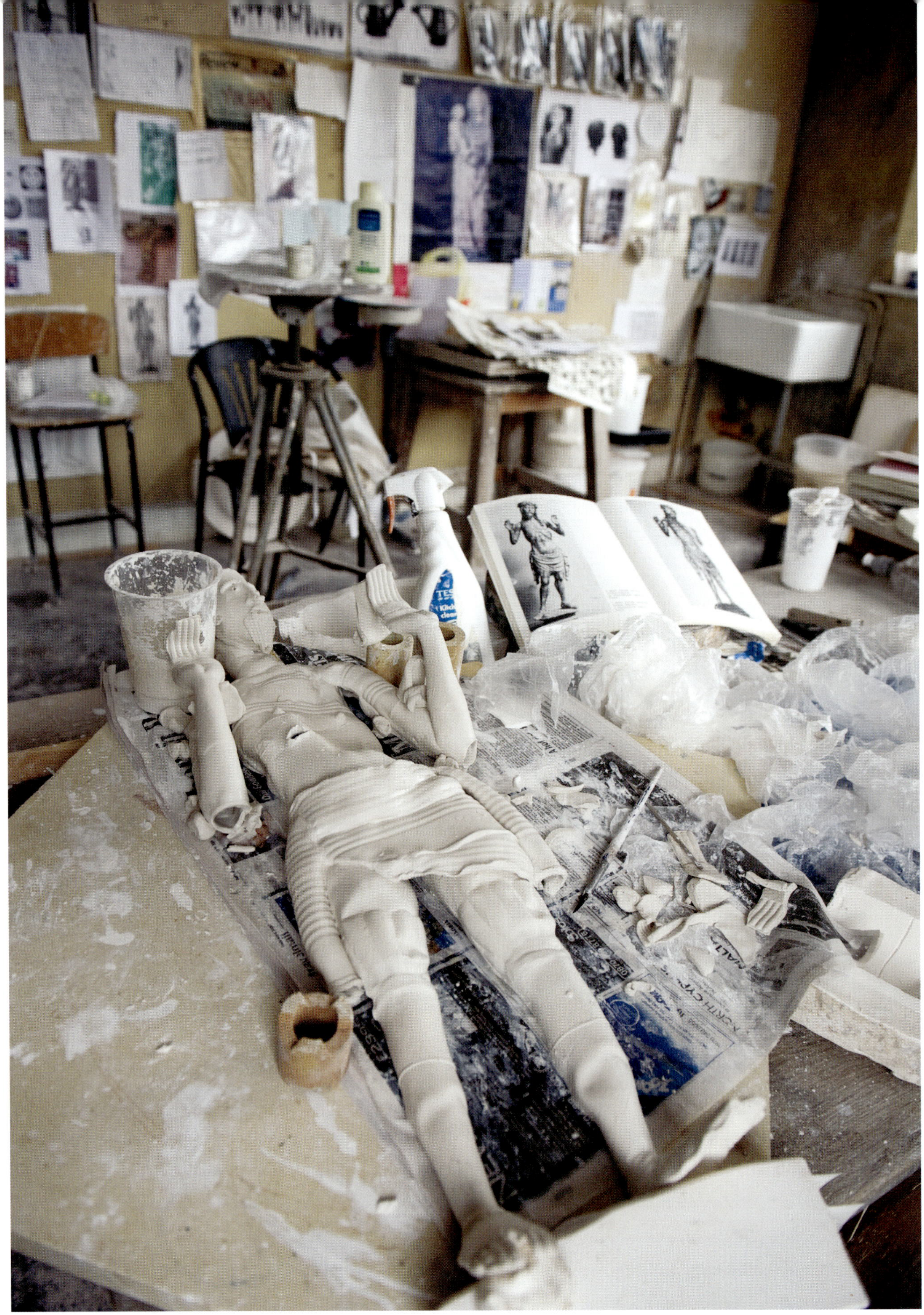

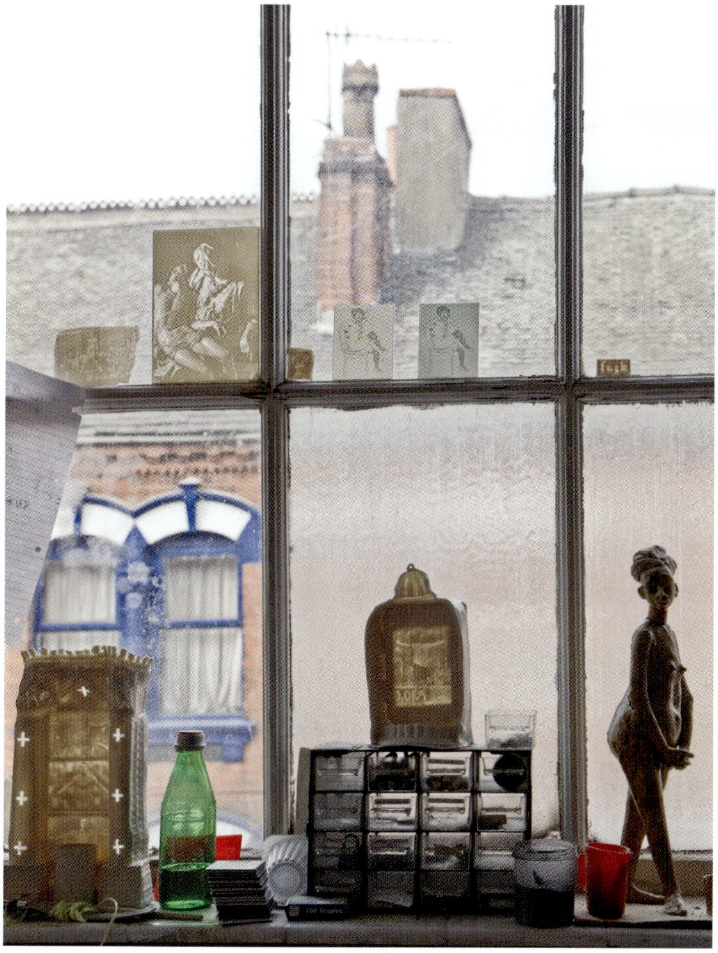

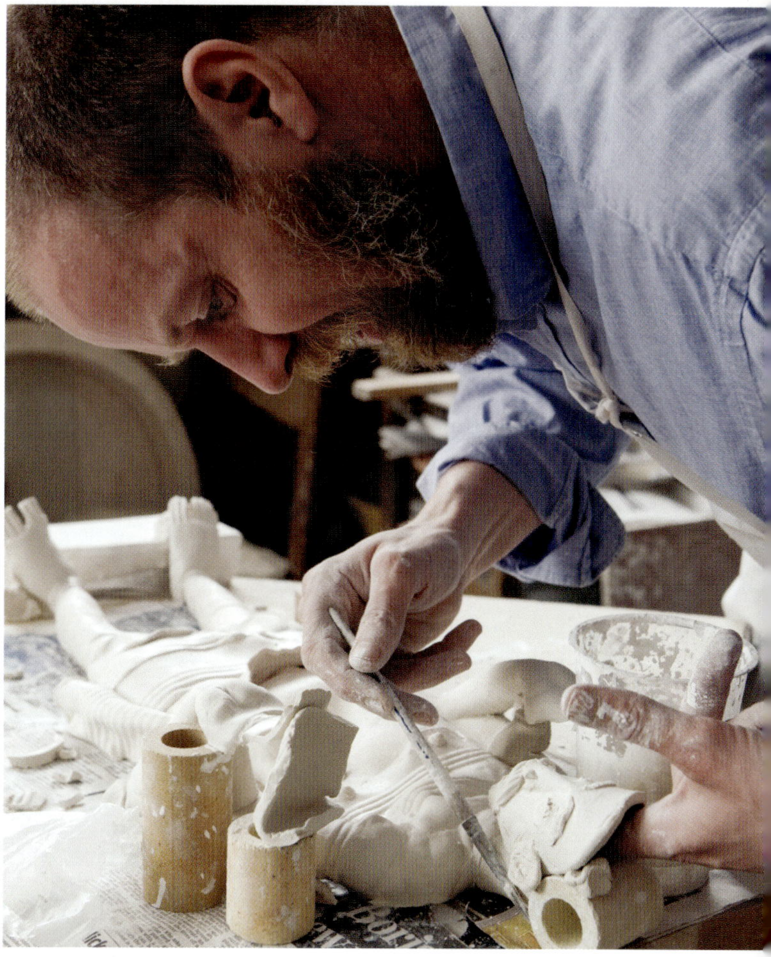

innately poetic eye, an imaginative reading not only of history but of the discarded and overlooked – disposable ephemera, news images and waste materials. His is an inventive marriage of high and more popular culture, where past and present meet.

Despite his nod to the grander themes, Eglin would baulk at his figures being thought of in purely sculptural terms. They belong to a more private and personal space; their sensuality is part of a household world, meant to be absorbed, as Eglin put it, 'into a clutter'. He is, after all, a potter, active in a decorative and vernacular tradition that goes back to those other Staffordshire craftsmen, the makers of flatbacks, figurines and posset pots. His work has something of the same innocence, idiosyncrasy and demeanour, and often uses a similar palette, with a preference for blues, ochres, browns and greens, echoing his admiration for the exuberance of early ceremonial slipware and painted delftware.

There was, from the outset, nothing tentative or hesitant about Eglin's paean to femaleness. Over the years the fluidity of form, surface and brushwork has developed into often complex bodyscapes of slips, stains, oxides and transfer imagery. Eglin's intriguing overlays, crossovers and cancellations of drawing and colour combine vibrant linearity with bold splashes, ribbons and stripes of pigment. In Eglin's layered marking, the pictograms, logos and graffiti of the urban street are incorporated into a decorative montage. His forms become complex, very personal maps of contemporary referencing, dealing in visual association and memory – though precise 'meaning' is never explicit, only suggested. There is a bravura sense of the body in every posture and attitude: sitting, reclining and standing, head on hands, legs crossed, the back straight or slumped. His nudes nonchalantly wait: some are thoughtful, others more engaged, while some are simply carefree, pushing their

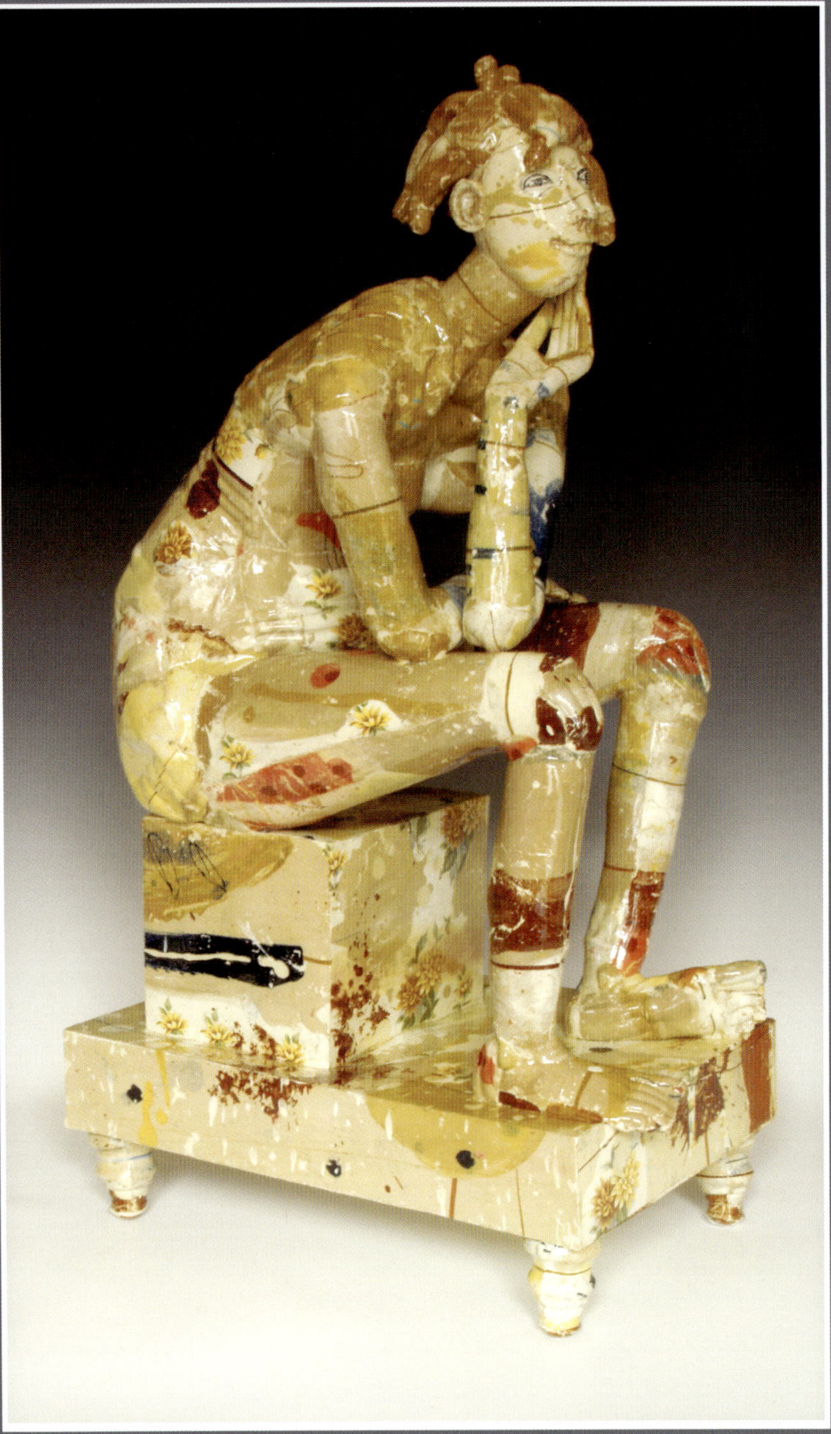

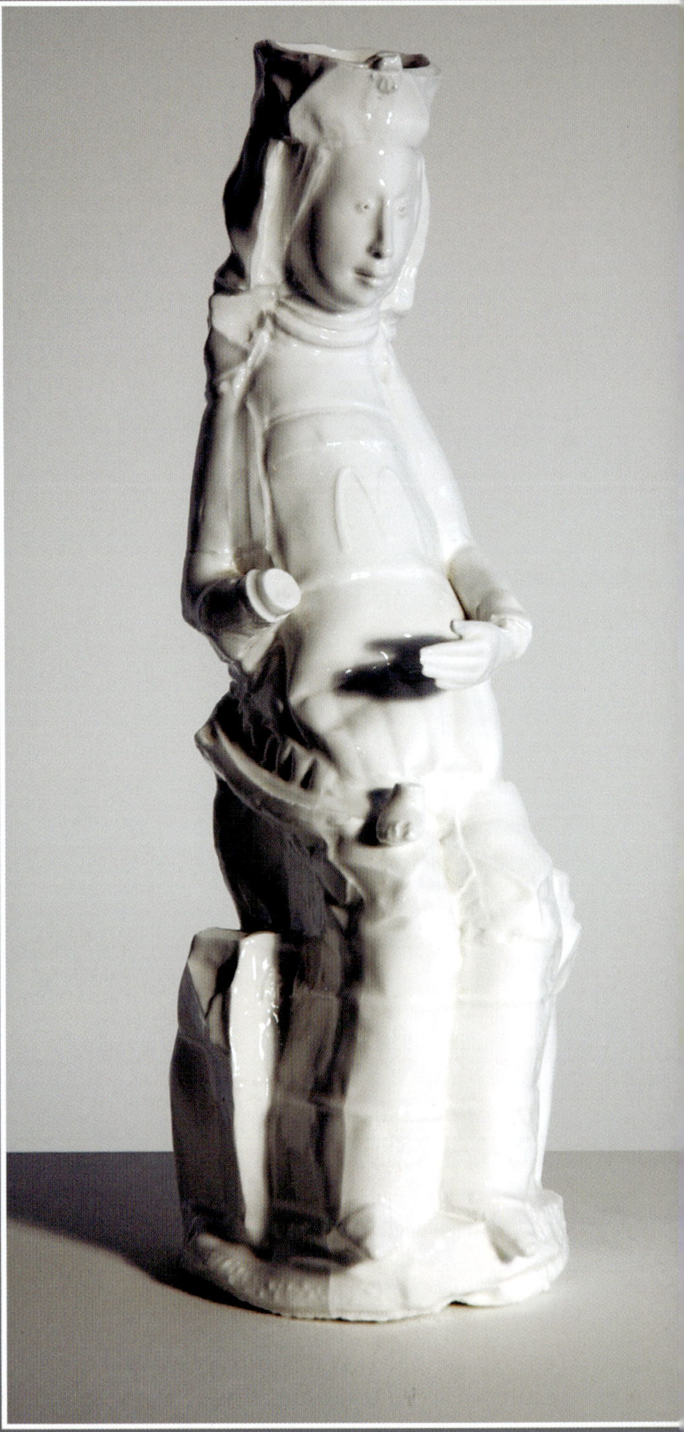

anatomies into playful distortions, kicking their legs in the air. These objects encompass the poignancy and humour, the wistfulness and enchantment, of Eglin's world.

In his white porcelain Madonnas, the cultural merging continues. These pieces combine some of the linearity of Gothic sculpture – in clay and wood as well as stone – with Qing Dynasty white Fujian Dehua figurines from China. Even the individualised heads mix eastern and western expression, while the European–oriental flow of drapery is again contrived from mouldings of discarded packaging. The

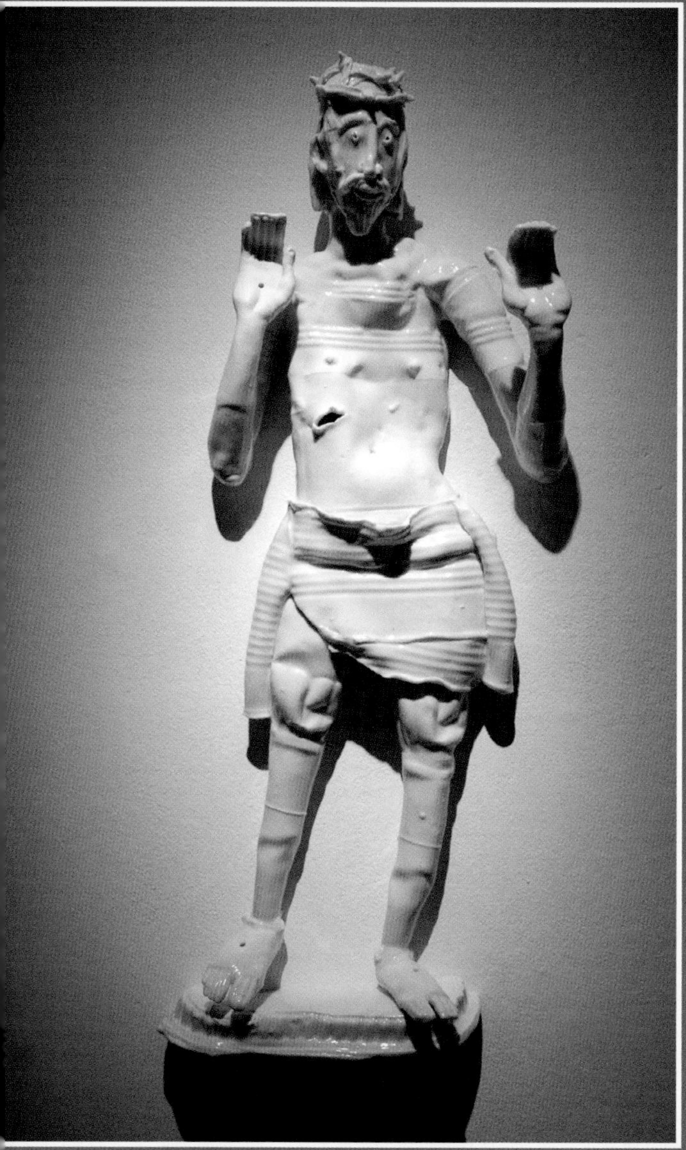

ove: Ascendant Christ, *2008, porcelain.*
eight: 62cm (24½in).
oto: Barrett Marsden Gallery
ft: White Madonna, *2002, porcelain.*
eight: 44cm (17¼in).
oto: Barrett Marsden Gallery
r left: Seated Nude I, *2006, earthenware.*
eight 60cm (23½in).
oto: Barrett Marsden Gallery

historical sources he admires are often more privately votive in nature, from a more domestic landscape, or more idiosyncratically crafted – for example, a 15th-century earthenware *Virgin and Child* he admires in the Fitzwilliam Museum. Eglin's use of plastic cartons and bottles draws from a more current type of accumulation, an emphatically 21st-century furniture. His more colourful, more densely decorated Madonnas have their religiosity subverted not only by the same press-moulded additions, but by a distinctly secular imagery including everything from commercial logos to military vignettes. The artist gives us a more complex and contradictory picture, letting us draw our own conclusions. Again, specific messages are avoided; Eglin is not judgemental.

His figurative concerns extend not only to the jugs – functional shapes with bodily connotations – but to his dishes, plates and mugs, embellished with religious figures, Venuses and characters from Eglin's other lifelong passion – football. As well as his own drawings, he often utilises the childhood images of his two sons, emulating an expressive freedom he admires in artists such as Picasso and Roger Hilton. His big buckets, covered in spontaneous layers of painting, drawing and transfers, develop his 'iconography' in the wider sense – a collage of sporting and religious heroes, of sexual, colonial and historical stereotypes and commodities. The buckets offer a broader canvas on which to explore cultural divergence and convergence. More recently he has been drawn to the parallels between religion and football, the way in which much of the symbolism of the national game has replicated that of the Christian faith and other beliefs.

If Philip Eglin is something of a dissenter in English ceramics, a modern-day Hogarth who delves deep into the complexities of our lives and makes inventive raids on art history to do it, the work is also, like Hogarth's, full of touching recognition, even affection, for the values and anomalies he finds. His work is as celebratory as his sheer enjoyment of the clay. There is something exotic and decadent about these glorious nudes in their sun baths, and the spirited, very human Madonnas. Indeed, the humanity of his work is perhaps its greatest quality; it is meant for our homes, not remote museums.

Sara Radstone

SOME CERAMISTS, as with artists in any other medium, travel out on their own, occupying a territory distant from the mainstream. They can be 'difficult', dealing with forms, themes and ideas that do not seem, on the face of it, to be readily accessible (in this section one thinks of Neil Brownsword and Annie Turner in this regard). Their particular aesthetic, far removed from conventional 'style' or 'function', is not so easy to read, but our journey of discovery is all the more worthwhile for that. In the case of Sara Radstone, her intense, concentrated art has been a pervasive presence in British ceramics for 25 years now, dealing with issues that go to the very heart of working with clay. She makes sculpture which says fundamental things about the nature and history of the material, its metaphorical significance and almost primordial power. She has taken the ancient notion of the vessel and broadened its language into various other meanings, into other unexpected forms of object and containment. Her work is about both the natural and manmade environments, evoking the textures she has found in urban and open landscapes. More recently, it has taken on a more visceral quality, with a sense that this material is not so far removed, in its corporeity, from our own physical selves.

Radstone, born in 1955, went to Camberwell School of Art in the late 1970s, a period in which the lively ceramics department included teachers such as Ewen Henderson and Gillian Lowndes. Among Radstone's student contemporaries were Henry Pim and Angus Suttie, artists who shared her sensitive and liberated attitude to ceramic form and surface, and the associations it could suggest. Having already found her own distinct voice by the time of her degree show, in 1980 Radstone was given her first exhibition by the collector and couturier Anthony Shaw, who acquired several fine pieces from that period – asymmetric, freely-formed bowls with some of the qualities of man's earliest vessels. Their organic nature related not only to the forms of Lowndes and Henderson, but to the simple elemental pots of Dan Arbeid and Ian Auld. Their textured surfaces were often inlaid with veins and patches of subtle, earthy colour. The walls and rims were pinched very thin, the contours crisp and attenuated. The work had a sense of expressive immediacy, of clay being teased, taut and stretched. Its layered symbolic value was being explored through pots that were connected to their geological origins, their ritual past; and yet, in Radstone's hands, they were also a manifestly modern response to the 20th-century environment.

The forms grew in complexity, the walls sometimes softly pitted and blistered, manipulated into intriguingly crumpled and creased structures, as if to underline their apparent fragility. Tap a Radstone pot from the 1980s – its ring is almost metallic, like tin. The colour and patina have the qualities of some kind of oxidised, recently excavated ore. There is a close interaction between interior and exterior in these open shapes, in some pieces even a sense of collapsing form and space. The distinction between the human-made and nature-made has become blurred.

By the mid-nineties Radstone had moved to a more closed concept of containment, the pots having developed into another kind of vessel, that of hollow volume; they were really objects now, alluding to boats, caskets and coffins. The inner space continued to be as important as the outer, but was now concealed. The pieces were flattened, perhaps elongated and distended. They had bodily connotations, too, a quality that pervades the work to this day –

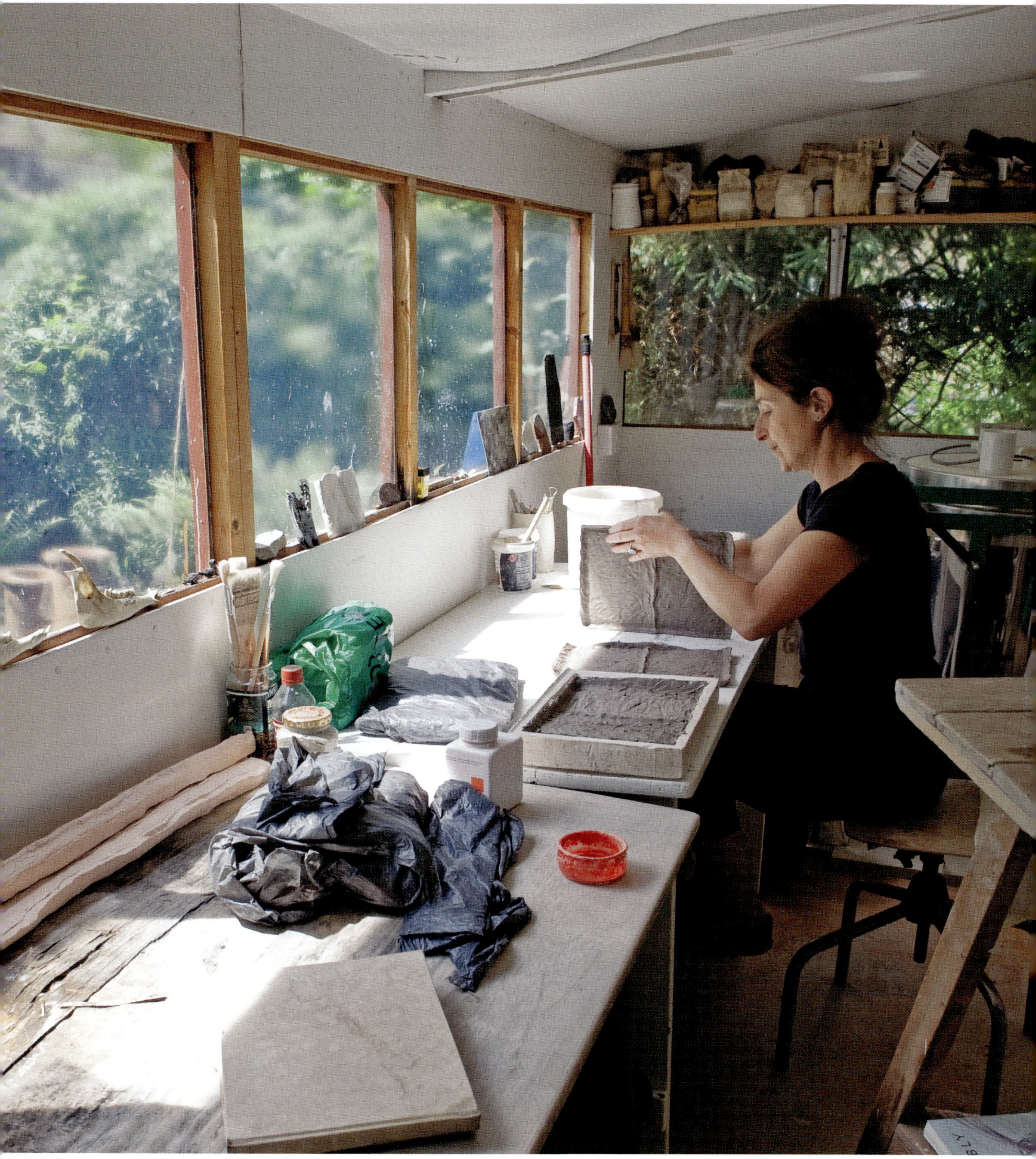

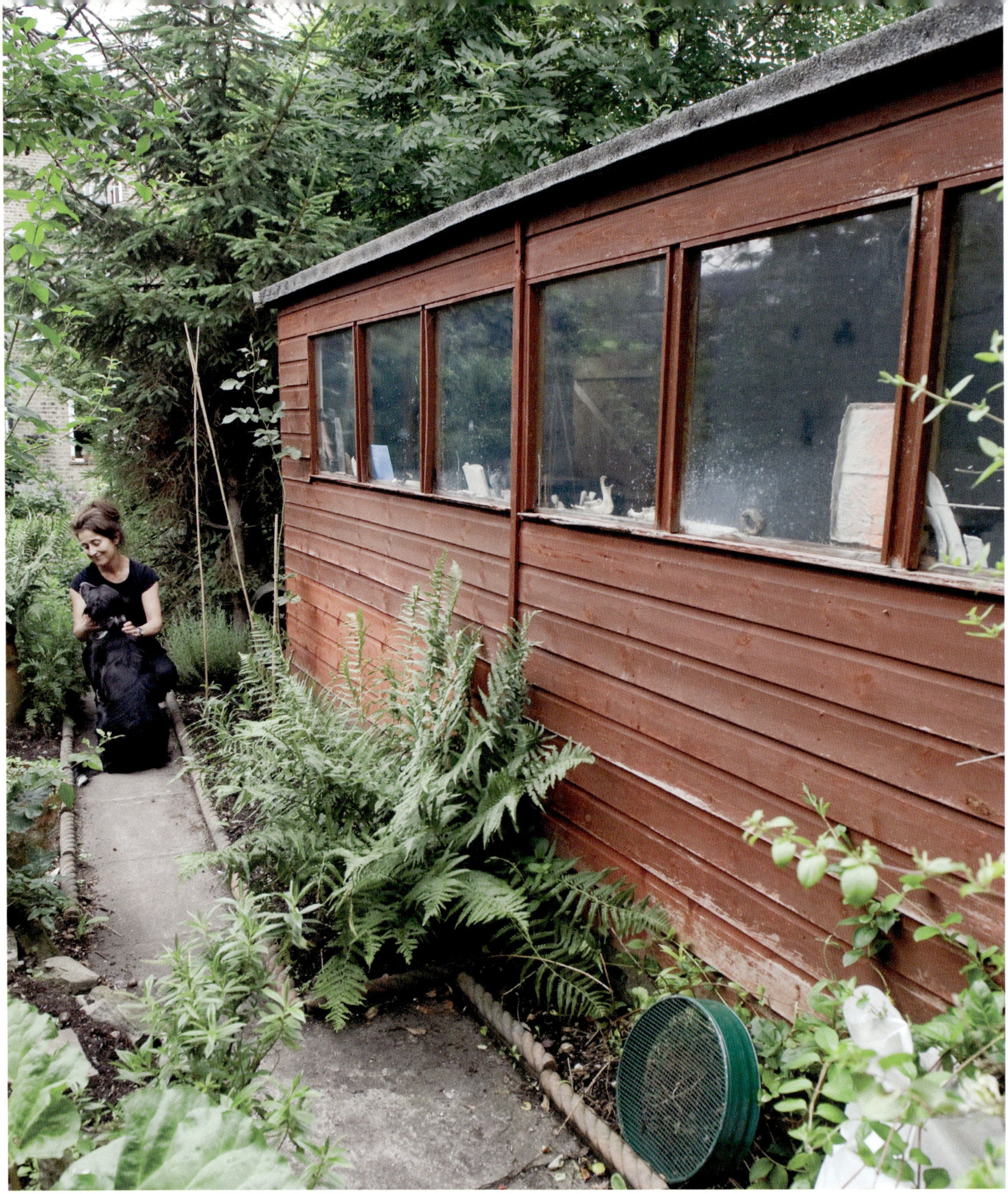

structures with echoes of the human figure, perhaps in fragmentary form. They looked as if they had gone through some process of corrosion, of attrition, worn down into a kind of bony essence, into something quite nebulous.

Abstract and figurative ideas appeared to merge, though any direct resemblance is something Radstone has always avoided: 'If it looked like something, it had failed,' she later wrote. The palette became austere, too, using a limited number of oxides and glazes to develop muted earths, rusts and greys, evoking the intricate natural surface of stone or

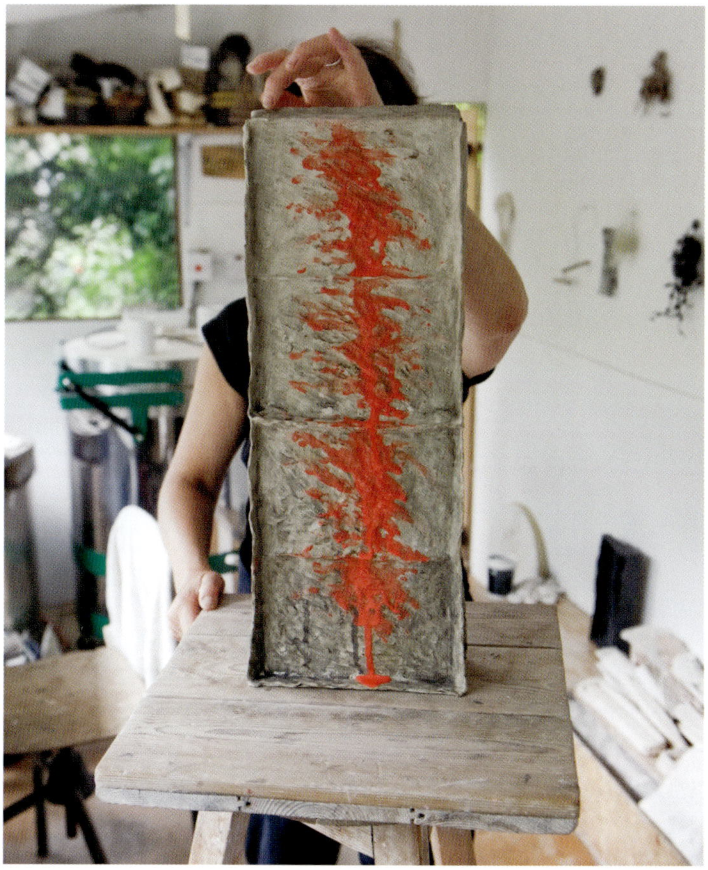

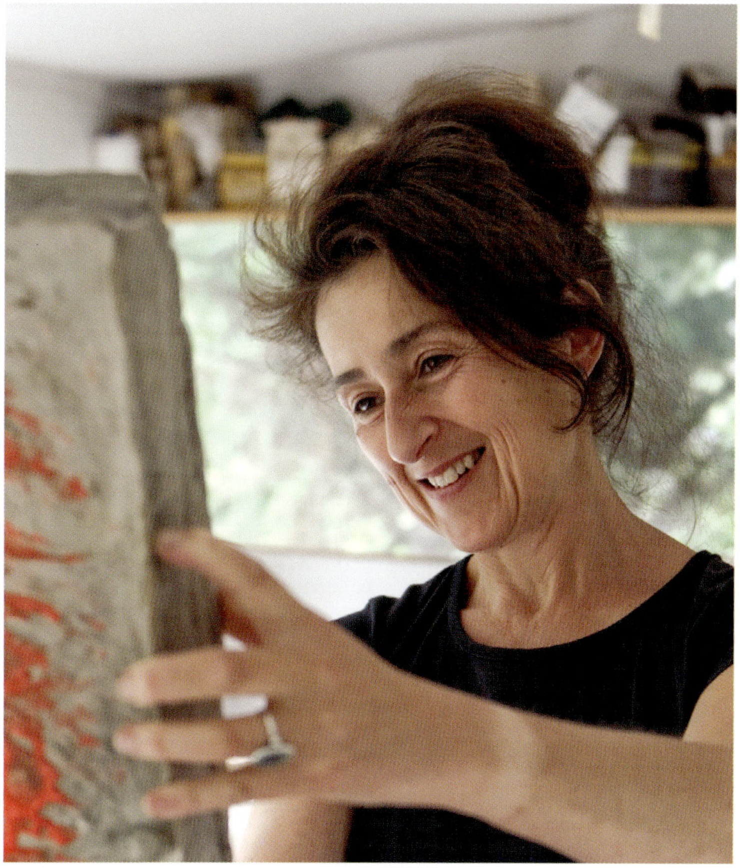

perhaps wood. The pieces were redolent of the stark physical qualities – the textures and colours – she experienced on the remote Scottish island of Lewis, where for many years she had a home. But they also explored the markings and graffiti of city places. References were intentionally oblique, subsumed into a spare purity – a sculpture as condensed as it is possible to imagine.

The language moved still further away from any conventional notion of the vessel, the pieces often long and thin, now resting or leaning against walls. The work not only expressed the passage and wear of time but also the human imprint: tracings and impressions made by many hands. Radstone's sculpture has developed into a kind of register of our experience and memory, but these objects are quiet to the point of silence and stillness. Broader forms might be marked with spinal indentations like those of the human torso or the seam in a rock. Titles, deliberately, give no specific clue. The landscape of her work is a distillation of many landscapes, offering up not only a sense of history and its accretions, but the poetic charge of particular places. The various series of open-book wall pieces (often compared in form to the lead books of the artist Anselm Kiefer) take the concept of containment a stage further, symbolic of a language or knowledge carried both within and through their surfaces. Her tendency to work in series shows how she needs to carry through an idea, an obsession, until some kind of conclusion is reached.

Radstone's work can be large in scale but is produced in her back garden in Greenwich in a surprisingly small studio which, while outwardly modest, is revealing enough inside. Fragments of her sculpture lie in groups on various surfaces, like bones or artefacts being sorted in an archaeologist's lab. Some of the bigger pieces are made in sections and then assembled, so that they may only be properly seen once in the gallery. The studio seems to work, despite Radstone's occasional irritation at its practical flaws. It is truly a chamber where her imagination can

right: Dark Red on White and Grey; Iron Brown on White, *2007, stoneware.*
Height: 53cm (21in); height: 53cm (21in).
middle: Ghost IV, *2007, stoneware.*
Height 225cm (88¾in).
far right: Still Life, *2004, stoneware.*
Height: 16cm (6¼in); Height: 36cm (14in); Height 39.5cm (15½in).
Photos: Barrett Marsden Gallery

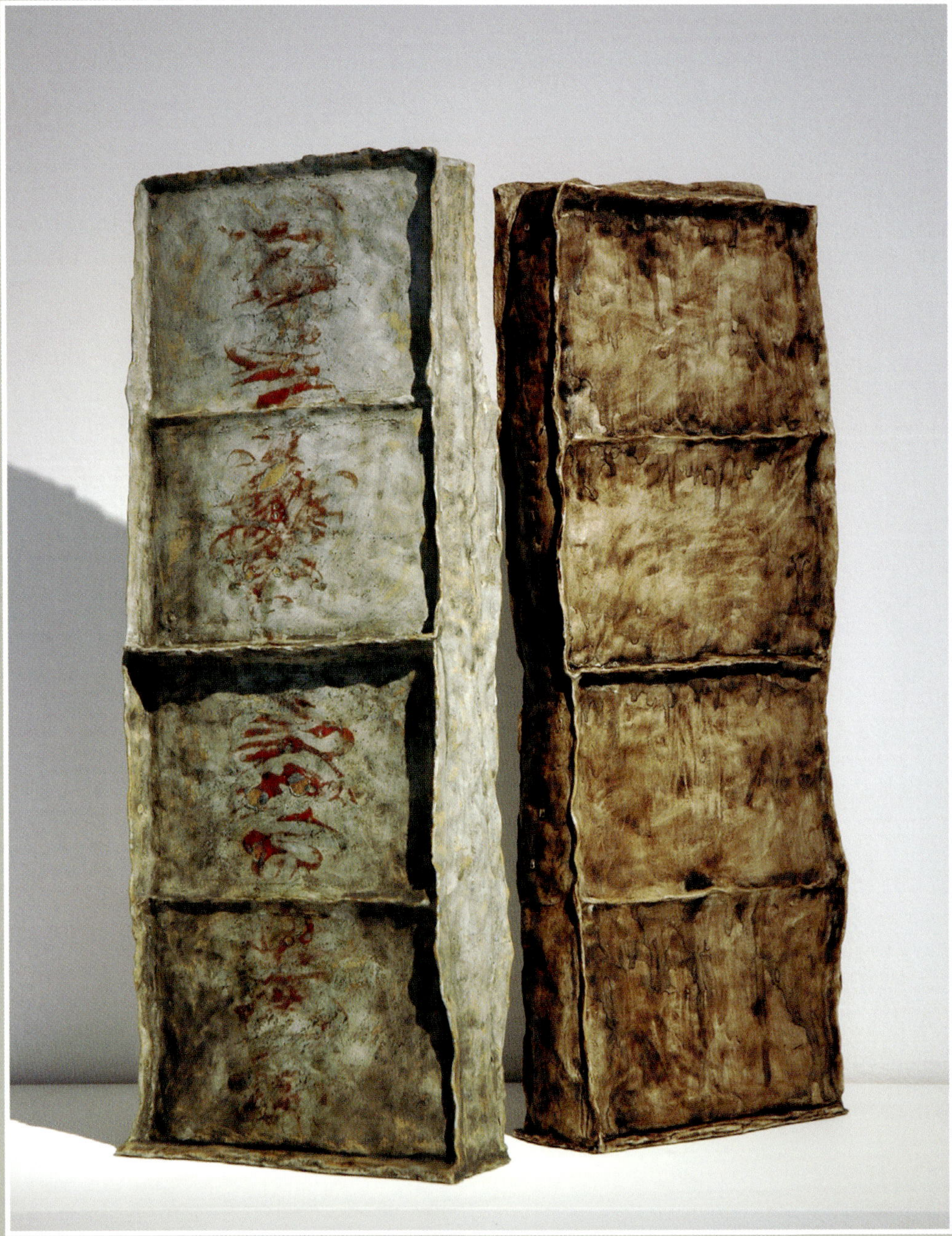

begin its process of ordering and distillation. A large map of Lewis brings the geography of one creative source into the setting of another. The linear activity of this map, its delineation of a terrain, finds a parallel in the grooves, tributaries and impressions of her ceramics. Her large, totemic pieces are architecturally memorable because of the way they harness and define the space of a gallery. Perhaps hugging a wall, these narrow strips of clay occasionally continue across the floor area, echoing the long road on Lewis – disappearing into the horizon – that led to her home there. It is work with archetypal hieratic qualities, abstracted and refined to a residuum, of Ancient Egyptian sculpture, casting long ghostly shadows.

Recently, the voice has become more ethereal, even

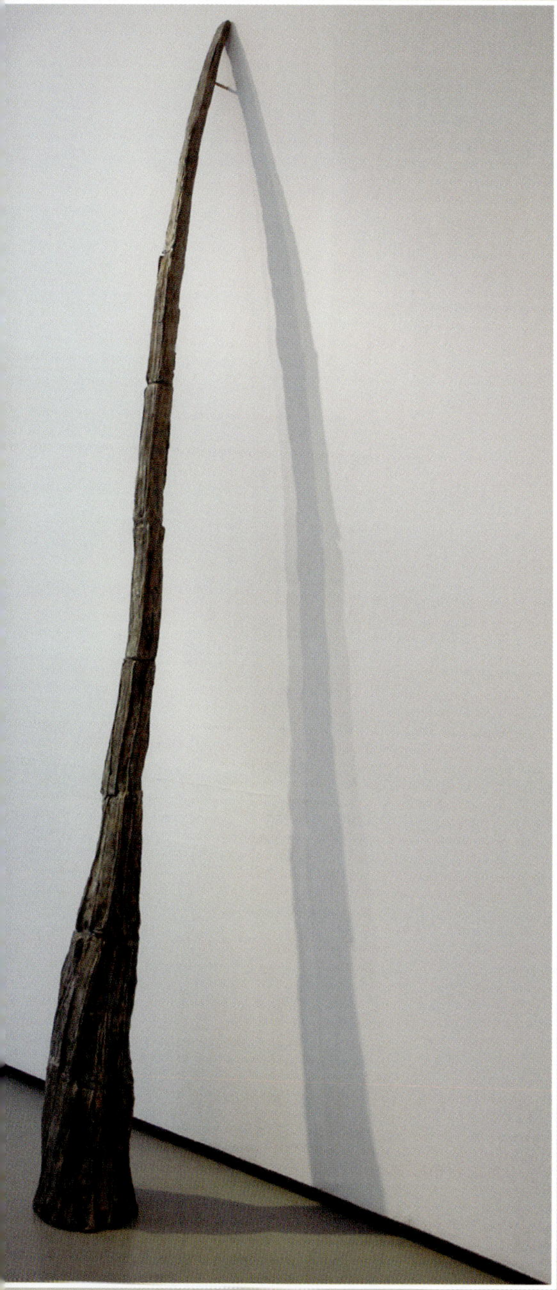

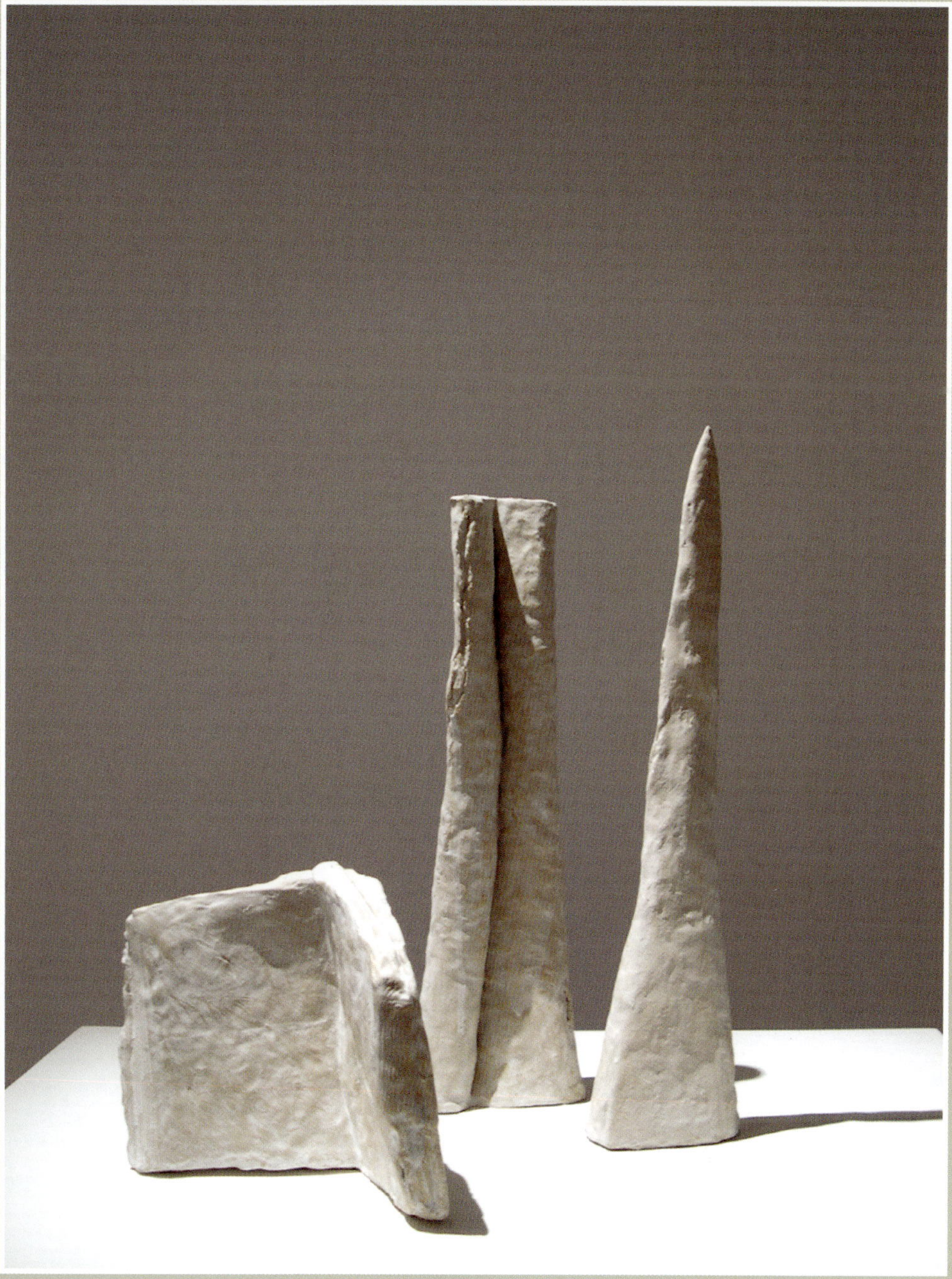

serene, as if it is working towards some emotional resolution. In the multiple-piece sculptures, hanging in vertical or horizontal groups of various sizes, or the single forms occupying floor or shelf space, there is an almost temple-like quality. A sense of obscure ceremonial function remains. Moreover, while in the past Radstone's pieces have become almost 'anti-object' in their near formlessness, the latest work has a new energy and substance. Its surfaces have acquired elements of colour once more, perhaps faint arteries of blue, or seeping red, as if the clay, filling with new life, is also bleeding. Radstone works on, to use her phrase, the 'edge of visibility'; her art has the haunting power and persistence of what we see in our peripheral vision, of what lies in the shadows.

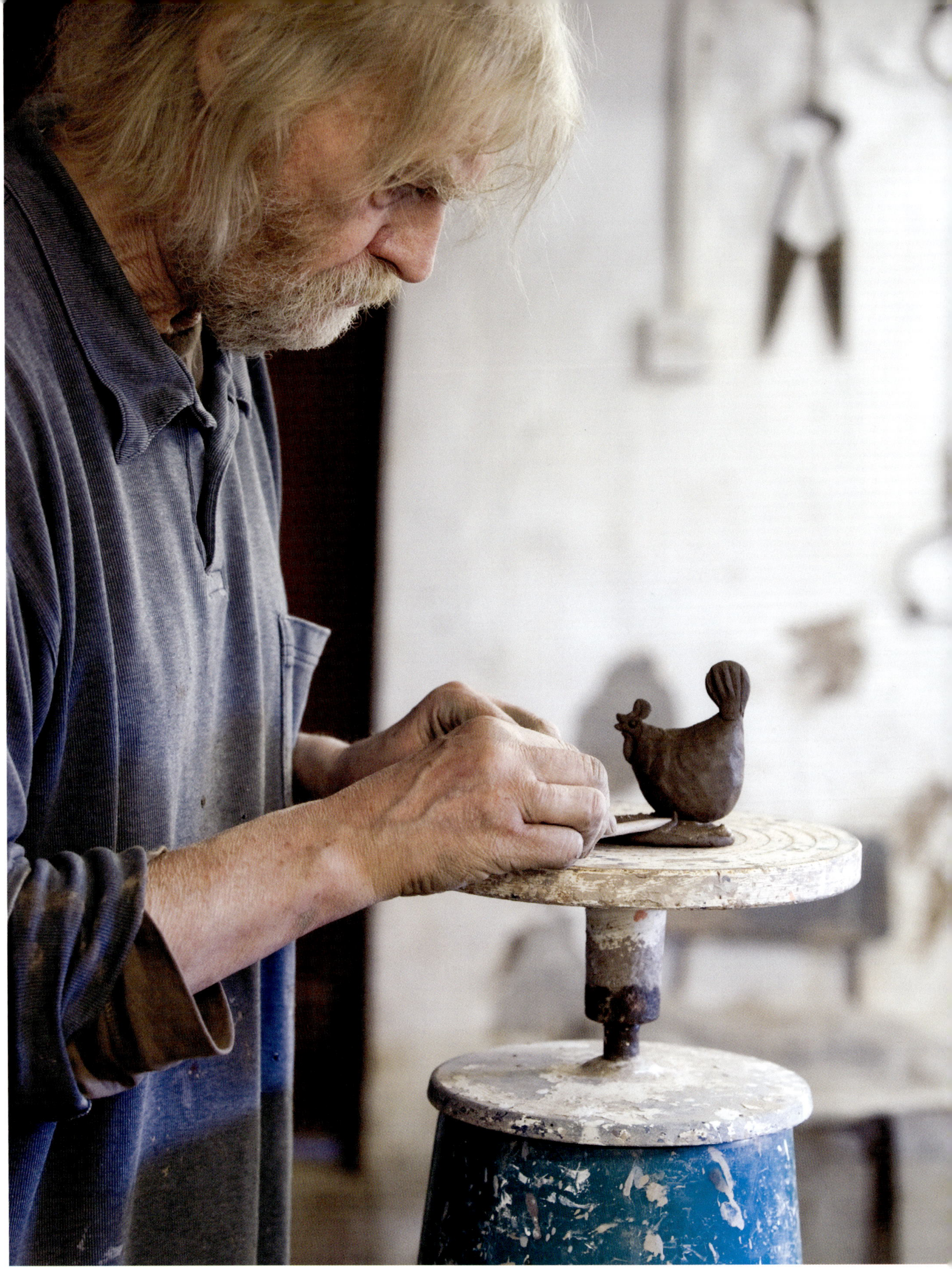

Geoffrey Fuller

GEOFFREY FULLER'S workshop, a converted cowshed, is surely unique in Britain, attached as it is to the pub that he and his wife Pat, also a potter, have run in Derbyshire for some 20 years. The Three Stags' Heads is a late 17th-century roadside establishment that has kept much of its original atmosphere, with old, simple furniture and some fine pots – not only Fuller's own work but anonymous country wares, Staffordshire figures and studio pieces by potters he admires. In some ways a pub is the most appropriate place to find such a potter: in serving hospitality, beer and good food, the historical context of the European ceramic traditions within which Fuller works is amply demonstrated. To Fuller, pottery is an enrichment of every meal and loses something if it isn't used. He has a very sensitive eye for the nuances of earthenware, bringing out its warmth and mystery in a wonderful repertoire of figures, as well as thrown and slab-built pots – objects which recapture something of the vibrant folk inheritance in English pottery. Yet his ceramics draw on many European influences, absorbed into a language that is robustly original. Fuller is one of the British ceramic world's great individualists, making forms which have earned him a high reputation not only for their inventiveness but for the empathy he has with clay.

Born in Chesterfield in 1936, Fuller did national service and spent 12 years as a librarian in Sheffield before taking up pottery at Chesterfield College of Technology in 1965. He then went to study at Farnham, where the ceramics course, run by Paul Barron and Henry Hammond, encouraged experimentation with material and process at their most direct, bringing out the unhindered qualities of clay and firing. At Farnham Fuller began salt-glazing stoneware, interested as he was in expressing the surface of the clay and not in thick, covering glazes. This concern related not only to the immediacy of pre-industrial European pots, but to Japanese traditions he discovered early on – Hagi, Shigaraki and Bizen pots – with physical qualities achieved through a particular freedom of throwing and the unpredictable course of firing. Fuller speaks with great fondness of one of his lecturers at Farnham, the charismatic Canadian potter John Reeve, someone who brought a fresh, liberal perspective to clay and helped instil in Fuller a feeling for the material in its soft and malleable state, encouraging him to explore its genuine plasticity.

After a short period at Farnham as a technician, Fuller went back to his native Derbyshire and in 1972 set up his first studio. For many years he taught on the excellent vocational ceramics course at Chesterfield, a post he held until its closure in 1987. The following year he was re-established at The Three Stags, initially attracted by its potential as a pottery space, though it brought with it the additional responsibilities of a publican; the Fullers balance these roles by making their pots in the week and opening the bar at the weekend.

His pots essentially reinterpret some of the qualities of those figures made before the Industrial Revolution and the traditions of country pottery that survived into the 20th century and avoided the conformities of mechanisation. He points out that much wheel work in studio practice has followed methods of industrial turning, thereby squeezing out much of the life of the clay. Fuller tries, by contrast, to maintain a freer, 'hands-off' approach, letting the material follow its own course. His sources are all around him: the quirks of modelling and expression in the best Staffordshire

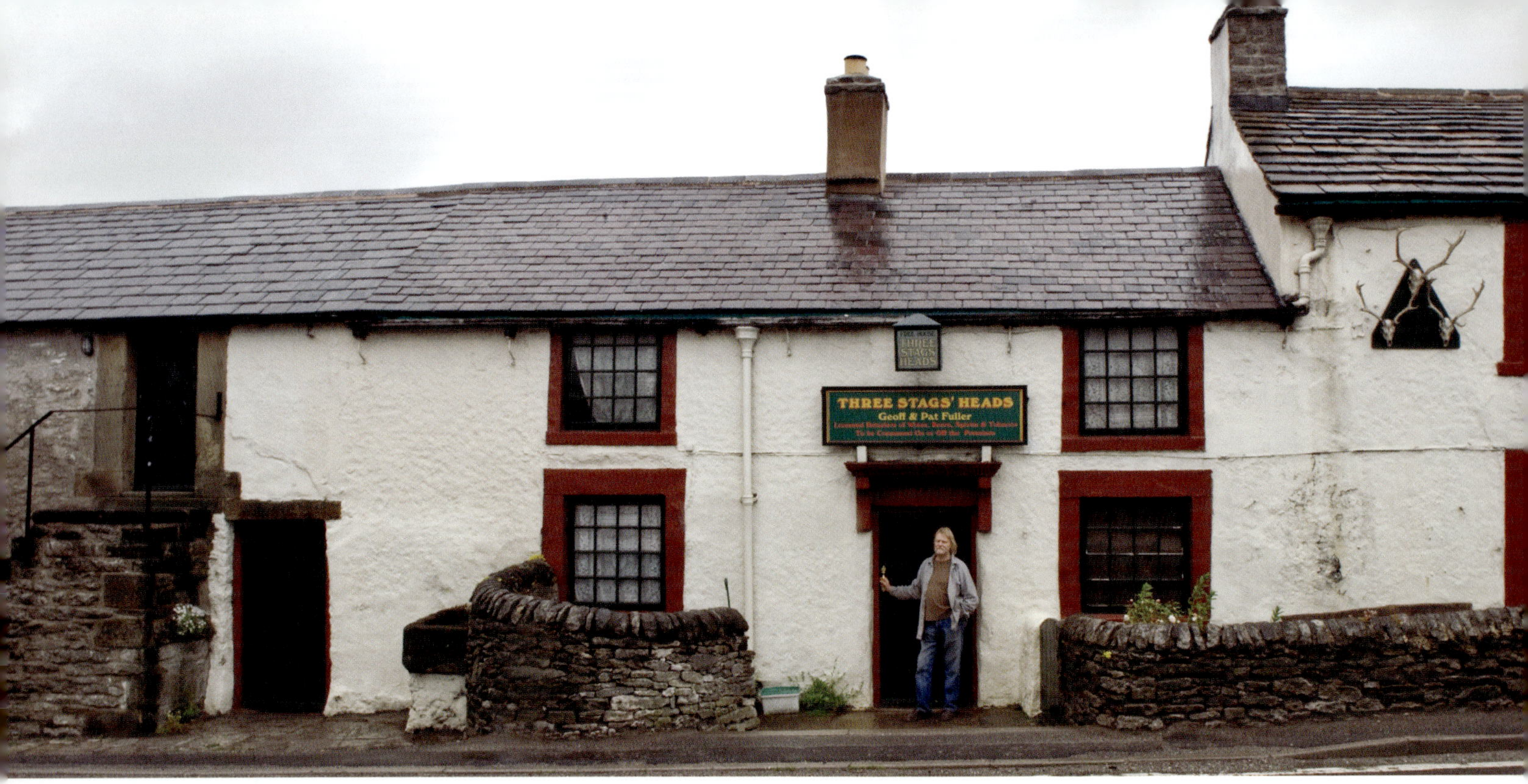
THREE STAGS' HEADS
Geoff & Pat Fuller

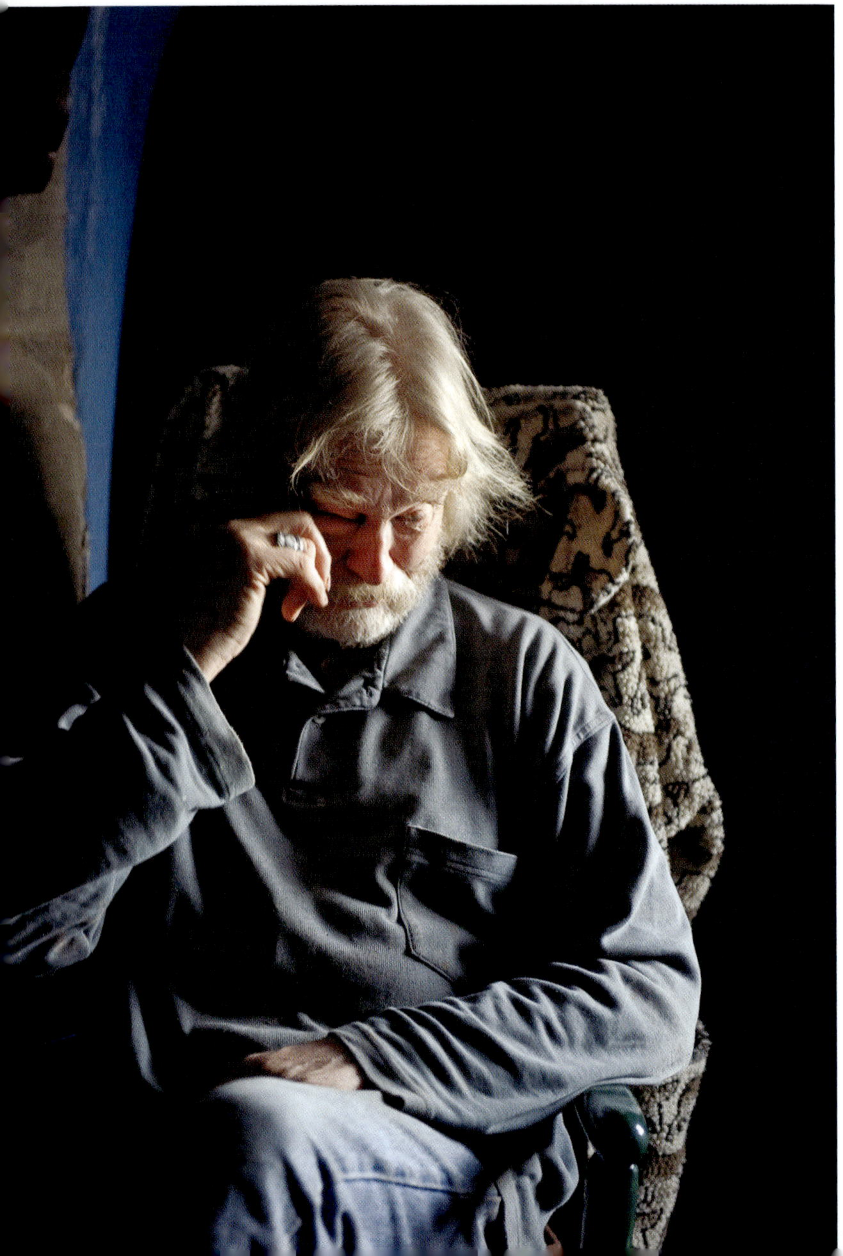

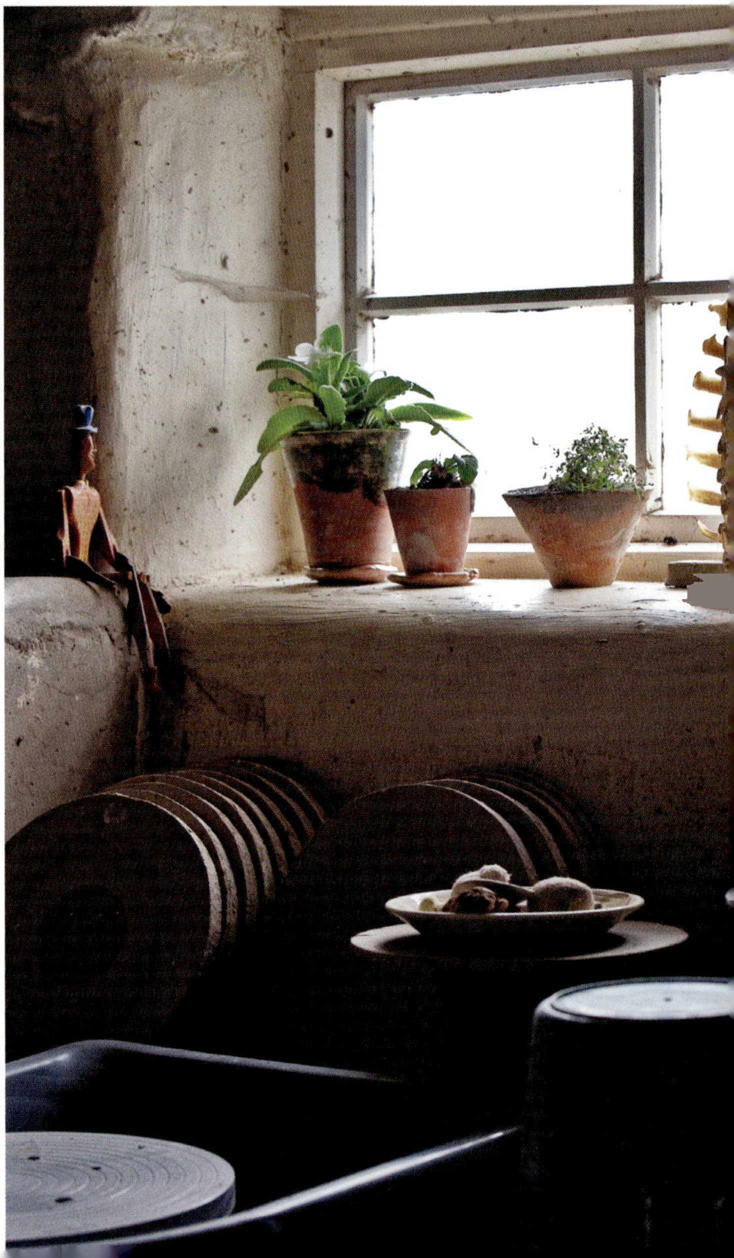

figures, as well as the thickly potted, variously textured jugs, brewing jars and crocks discovered over the years – all shapes with an unconscious, unwilled individuality, made long before our very modern notions of self-expression.

There is a special spontaneity about Fuller's pots – dishes and bowls, tankards, jugs and lidded pots – which make a virtue of their uncontrived dents and ripples, their freely applied sprigs and squeezed rims. His soft translucent greens, ochres, browns and rusts reflect the temperate coloration of his hilly landscape, a country he knows well from hours of walking its peaks and climbing its rocks. Because his slips – perhaps enlivened with swiftly applied finger decoration and additional colour – cover the pot in thin washes, the face of the clay remains very evident. Where modern earthenware can be very stark and uniform, the depth of Fuller's work is extremely satisfying. His more ornamental pots, lidded vessels and dishes with overhead handles, for example, show his intelligent and sensitive absorption of the decorative and commemorative work of various vernacular traditions: the harvest jugs, posset pots and mantle ornaments of north Devon, the wassail pots and moneyboxes of Ewenny and Buckley, the early salt-glaze pew groups and horsemen of Staffordshire.

Fuller's elaborate figurative work reinterprets – with great sensitivity – the best 18th-century pieces, reclaiming the symbolic and metaphorical role of this kind of 'cottage' sculpture for modern times. Whether we are looking at his archetypal Adam and Eve groups, surrounded by foliage and garlands, his lugubrious standing figures, his characters on horses, or the nervous attenuated energy of his greyhounds, they all show his imaginative 'untutored' modelling, an approach that belies his sophisticated understanding of form. Here again you see his refusal to work to 'academic principles', choosing instead to bring out the warmth of the clay and the poignancy, innocence and humour of his cast of players, filtered through his keen poetic eye. Fuller's sense of history is as real as his feeling for legend and folklore, for the stories of our landscape. These figures have tales to tell and events to record. Like the Green Man, so often represented in the stone bosses or wood carving of our medieval churches – sprouting leaves from his mouth – Fuller's figures are full of life and fertility, qualities literally dug out of the English earth and reanimated by the human hand.

In a market climate that currently favours the decorative and ornamental over the purely functional, these figures, which were first made for relaxation, sell particularly well. Along with the likes of Michael Flynn and Philip Eglin, Geoffrey Fuller has a reputation as one of our most imaginative figurative potters. But to distinguish between one area of his activity and another would be a mistake. His entire output is intended to embellish the household and its feasts, to add to the colour and ritual of living. To have a table with Fuller dishes, plates and tankards and, perhaps as a grand centrepiece, one of his figurative tableaux, is to properly experience not only the presentation of food at its best, but the magical allure and spirit of clay when treated with such singular vision.

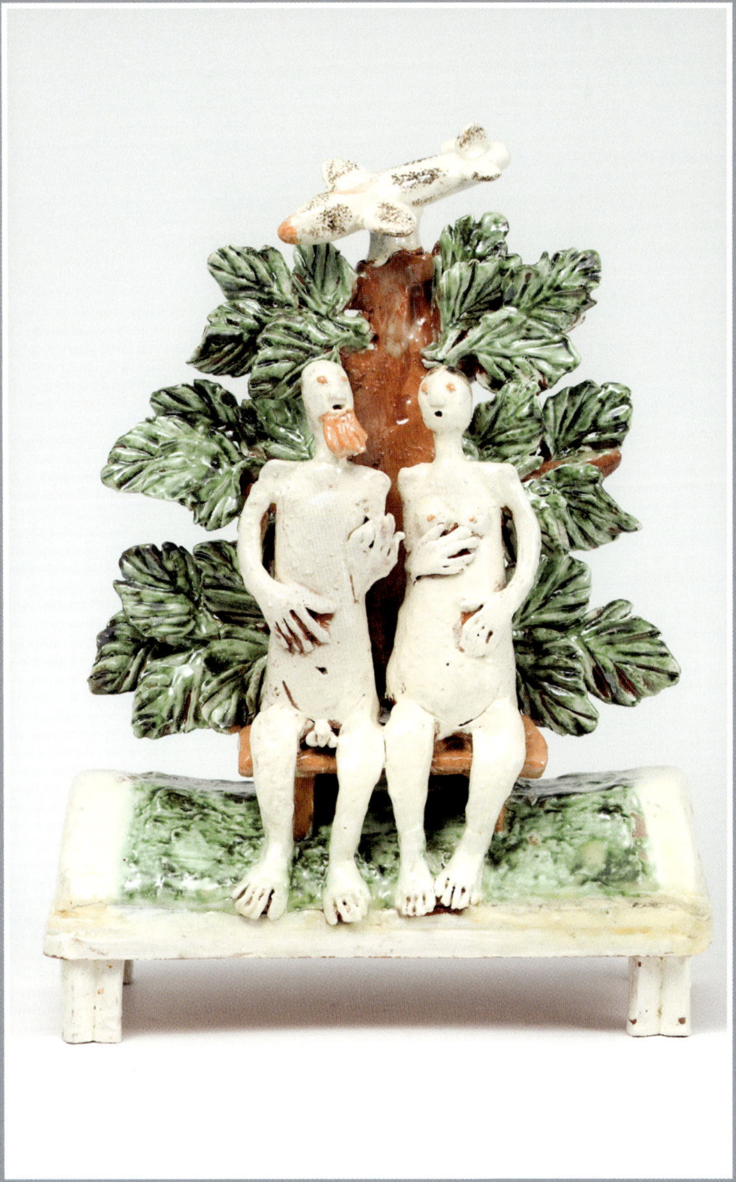

Adam and Eve Group, *2008, earthenware.*
Height: 35cm (13¾in).
Photo: Jay Goldmark, courtesy of Goldmark Gallery

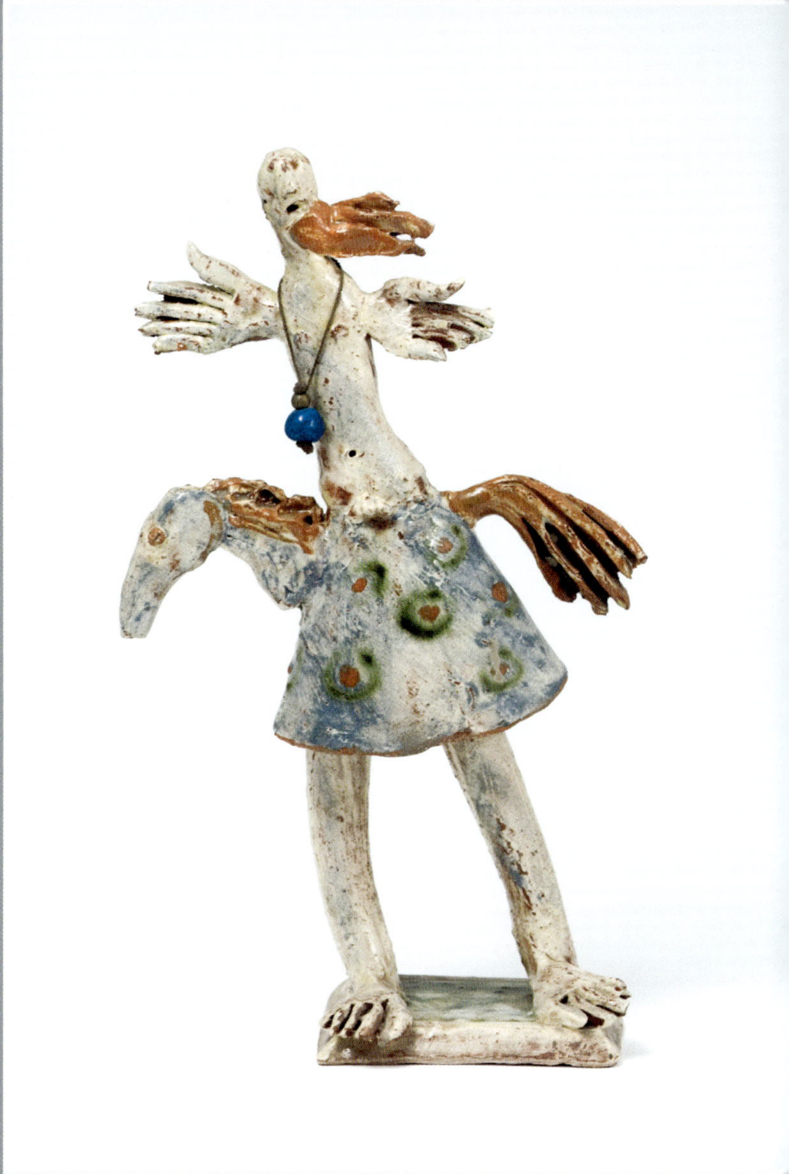

Hobby Horse, *1997, earthenware.*
Height: 33cm (13in).
Photo: Jay Goldmark, courtesy of Goldmark Gallery

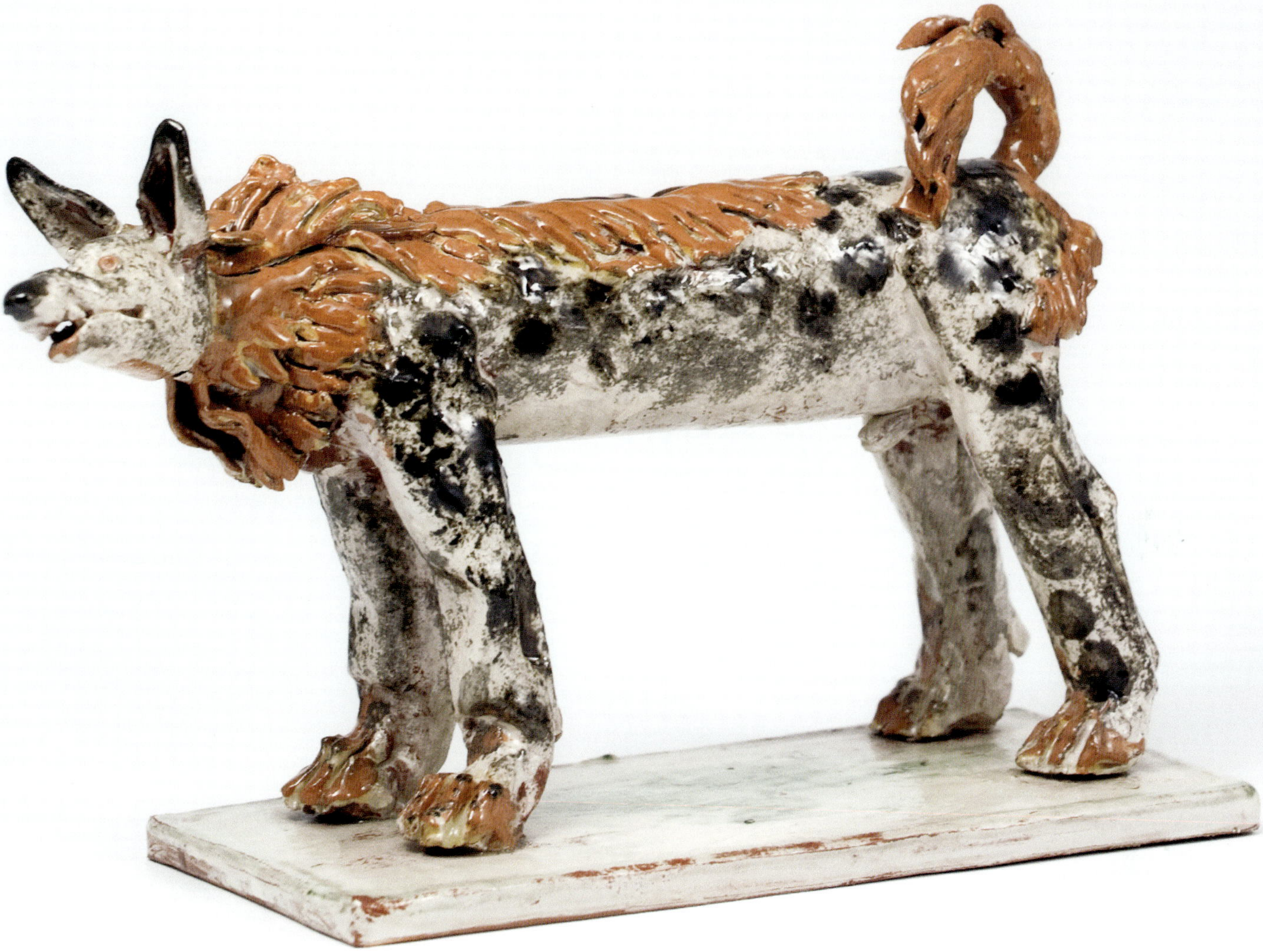

Fierce Dog, *c. 2007, earthenware.*
Height: 24cm (9½in).
Photo: Jay Goldmark, courtesy of Goldmark Gallery

Select Bibliography

General

Bellony-Rewald, Alice and Peppiatt, Michael *Imagination's Chamber: Artists and Their Studios* (London: Gordon Fraser, 1983)

Birks, Tony *The Art of the Modern Potter* (2nd edn) (London: Country Life, 1976)

Casson, Michael *Pottery in Britain Today* (London: Alec Tiranti, 1967)

Clark, Garth *The Potter's Art: A Complete History of Pottery in Britain* (London: Phaidon Press, 1995)

de Waal, Edmund *Design Sourcebook: Ceramics* (London: New Holland, 1999)

Dormer, Peter *The New Ceramics: Trends and Traditions* (London: Thames and Hudson, 1986)

Harrod, Tanya *The Crafts in Britain in the Twentieth Century* (Newhaven and London: Yale University Press, 1999)

Jones, Jeffrey *Studio Pottery in Britain 1900–2005* (London: A&C Black, 2007)

Lucie-Smith, Edward *World of the Makers: Today's Master Craftsmen and Craftswomen* (London: Paddington Press, 1975)

McGarva, Andrew *Country Pottery: Traditional Earthenware of Britain* (London: A&C Black, 2000)

Ostermann, Matthias *The Ceramic Narrative* (London: A&C Black, 2006)

Rice, Paul *British Studio Ceramics* (Ramsbury: The Crowood Press, 2002)

Rose, Muriel *Artist Potters in England* (2nd edn) (London: Faber, 1970)

Watson, Oliver *Studio Pottery: Twentieth Century British Ceramics in the Victoria & Albert Museum* (London: Phaidon Press, 1993)

Individual Potters (books and exhibition catalogues)

Birks, Tony *Lucie Rie* (London: Alpha Books/A&C Black, 1987)

Christian, John *Philip Eglin: Borrowings* (Nottingham Castle Museum and Art Gallery, 2007)

Cooper, Emmanuel *Bernard Leach: Life and Work* (Newhaven and London: Yale University Press, 2003)

Cooper, Emmanuel and Fielding, Amanda *Walter Keeler* (Ruthin Craft Centre and City Gallery, Leicester, 2004)

Dauvin, Bruno (ed.) *Emma Rodgers* (Shipston on Stour: Where I Fell in Love Gallery, 2007)

Harrod, Tanya and Goldberg, Roselee *Carol McNicoll* (London: Lund Humphries, and Leicester: The City Gallery, 2003)

Harrod, Tanya (et al.) *Neil Brownsword: Collaging History* (Stoke-on-Trent Museums, 2005)

Houston, John *Gordon Baldwin* (Middlesborough: Cleveland County Museum Service, 1983)

Hughes, Philip (ed.) *Claire Curneen: New Work* (Ruthin Craft Centre, 1997)

Hughes, Philip (ed.) *Claire Curneen: Succour* (Ruthin Craft Centre, 2003)

McCabe, Jane *Ken Eastman: Behind the Gates of Clay* (London: Barrett Marsden Gallery, 2004)

Radstone, Sara *Ceramics 1979–1997* (Aberdeen Art Gallery/An Lantair, 1997)

Watson, Oliver and Whiting, David *Jim Malone* (Bolton Art Gallery, 1996)

Watson, Oliver (et al.) *Philip Eglin* (Edinburgh: The Scottish Gallery, 1997)

Whiting, David (et al.) *The Exhilaration of Life: New Ceramics by Sandy Brown* (Rufford Craft Centre, 2000)

Whiting, David and Enright, Shane *Dan Kelly* (London: Austin Desmond Fine Art, 2002)

Whiting, David *Phil Rogers* (Uppingham: Goldmark Gallery, 2005)

Whiting, David *Clive Bowen* (Uppingham: Goldmark Gallery, 2006)

right: Clive Bowen's workshop at Shebbear.
Photo: Jay Goldmark, courtesy of Goldmark Gallery

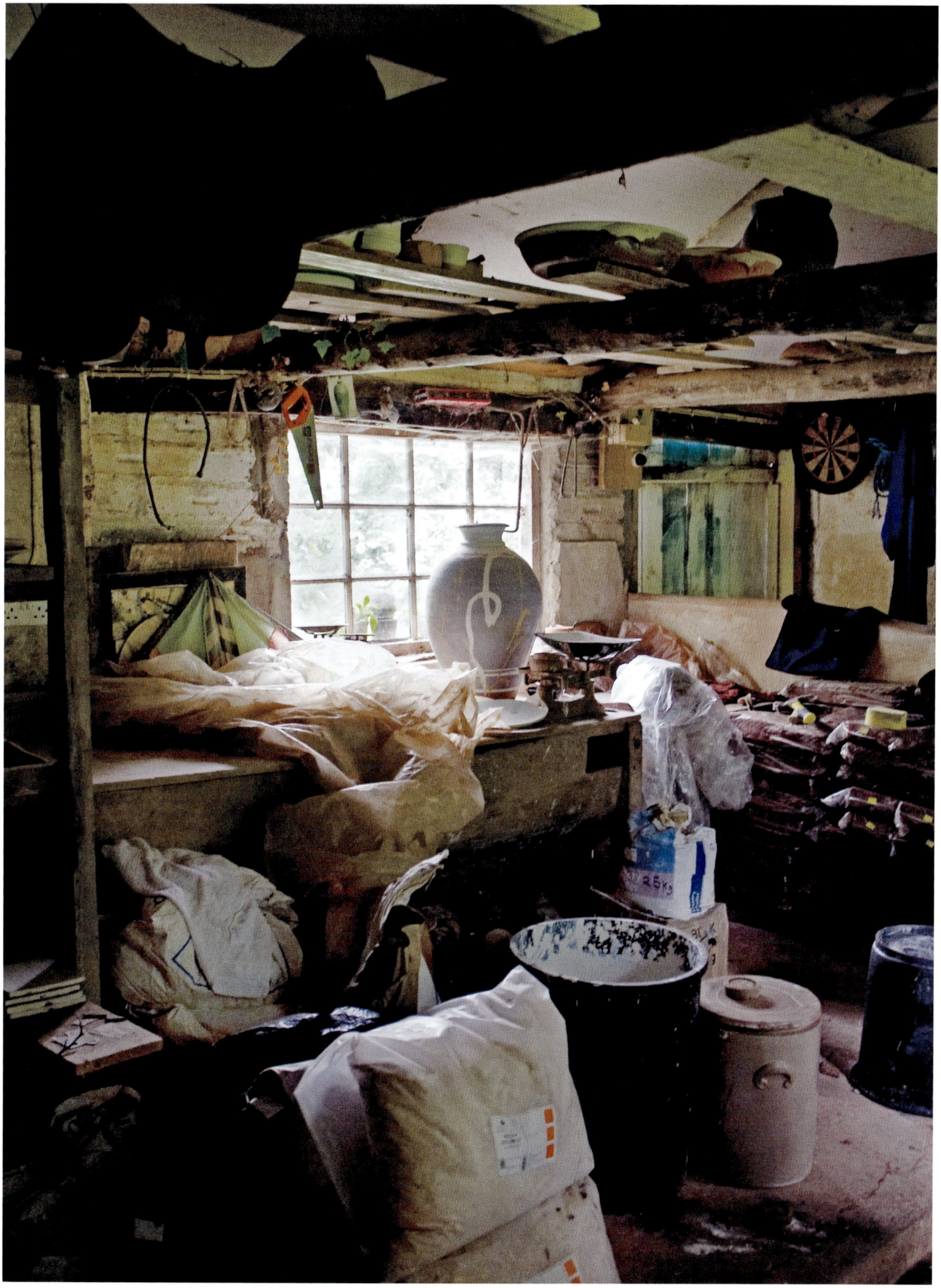